MILES

Notre Dame Studies in American Catholicism

Sponsored by the
Charles and Margaret Hall Cushwa Center
for the Study of American Catholicism

The Brownson-Hecker Correspondence
Joseph Gower and Richard Leliaert, editors

The Survival of American Innocence:
Catholicism in an Era of Disillusionment, 1920–1940
William M. Halsey

Faith and Fatherland: The Polish Church War in Wisconsin, 1896–1918
Anthony J. Kuzniewski

Chicago's Catholics: The Evolution of an American Identity
Charles Shanabruch

A Priest in Public Service: Francis J. Haas and the New Deal
Thomas E. Blantz, C.S.C.

Corporation Sole: Cardinal Mundelein and Chicago Catholicism
Edward R. Kantowicz

The Household of Faith:
Roman Catholic Devotions in Mid-Nineteenth-Century America
Ann Taves

People, Priests, and Prelates:
Ecclesiastical Democracy and the Tensions of Trusteeism
Patrick W. Carey

The Grail Movement and American Catholicism, 1940–1975
Alden V. Brown

The Diocesan Seminary in the United States:
A History from the 1780s to the Present
Joseph M. White

Church and Age Unite:
The Modernist Impulse in American Catholicism
R. Scott Appleby

Oxcart Catholicism on Fifth Avenue:
The Impact of the Puerto Rican Migration on the Archdiocese of New York
Ana María Díaz-Stevens

SEARCHING FOR CHRIST

*The Spirituality of
Dorothy Day*

BRIGID O'SHEA MERRIMAN, O.S.F.

UNIVERSITY OF NOTRE DAME PRESS
Notre Dame   London

Manufactured in the United States of America

Excerpts from THE LONG LONELINESS by Dorothy Day. Copyright 1952 by
Harper & Brothers. Reprinted by permission of HarperCollins Publishers.

Library of Congress Cataloging-in-Publication Data

Merriman, Brigid O'Shea, 1942–
    Searching for Christ : the spirituality of Dorothy Day
(1897–1980) / Brigid O'Shea Merriman.
      p.   cm. — (Notre Dame studies in American
Catholicism)
    Includes bibliographical references and index.
    ISBN 0-268-01750-6 (alk. paper)
    1. Day, Dorothy, 1897–1980.   2. Spirituality—
Catholic Church—History of doctrines—20th century.
3. Catholic Church—Doctrines—History—20th
century.   I. Title.   II. Series.
BX4705.D283M477   1994
248'.092—dc20   93-23827
                                          CIP

CONTENTS

PREFACE

As a cradle Catholic and as the daughter of an Irish mother whose strong faith is rooted deeply in the Catholic tradition, I have been engaged since childhood in asking religious questions. Whenever I found the answer unsatisfactory, I asked again, and, since I was an early reader, have long sought the answer also in the printed word. Often the answer escaped me, as it still does, bringing me before the mystery of God and of God's Love. I have also witnessed that Mystery active in the lives of others, both among my contemporaries and those who have lived before me. It matters little to me whether I have known these persons as contemporaries, through storytellers, or through my readings. They are for me the faithful witnesses of whom Emmanuel Cardinal Suhard once wrote:

> To be a witness does not consist in engaging in propaganda, nor even in stirring people up, but in being a living mystery. It means to live in such a way that one's life would not make sense if God did not exist.[1]

Dorothy Day, co-founder of the *Catholic Worker* and the movement by the same name, is for me foremost among these witnesses of the incomprehensible Goodness who is God. I am convinced that Dorothy's life may be understood only in the context of her great faith. On becoming acquainted with Dorothy several years ago, I inquired seriously about pursuing an in-depth study which would contribute to an understanding of the meaning of her spirituality for our time. Because I was then engaged in doctoral work, specializing in the area of Christian spirituality, I chose an exploration of Dorothy's lived religious experience as an exciting and challenging topic for my dissertation.

Christian Spirituality, a relatively new academic discipline, offers to the field of theology an integrative perspective on lived Christian

experience. In reality as old as Christianity itself, Christian spirituality has been variously emphasized in differing epochs of the church's
tradition. Current attempts at understanding—of which mine is an
example—strive to situate religious experience within the individual
Christian's total life. Because Dorothy desired to live the Great Commandment of love, her life was both God-directed and other directed.
Thus, whatever properly belonged to her life—prayer, work, social and
political activity—comprised the arena of her spirituality. She exemplified what her friend Virgil Michel, O.S.B., considered an expression
of contemporary sanctity: the saint as a person involved in the world
rather than apart from it. Nonetheless, because I am convinced that
Dorothy's activities flowed from the heart of her specifically religious
motivation, I have confined my examination to selected religious influences at work within her spirituality without however neglecting to
connect them with her total experience.[2]

The spiritual journey, a consistent theme in Christian spirituality, threads its way throughout Dorothy's life and writings. Her favorite passage from Pascal, "You would not seek me if you had not already
found me," aptly describes her own life's quest.[3] It is this search for
God, for God in Christ, and for Christ in those most wounded in body
and spirit which appears most strongly to have motivated Dorothy's
fidelity to her unique lay vocation in the Roman Catholic church in
the United States. For many persons today, the name of Dorothy Day
has become synonymous with a radical Christian charity for all people,
particularly for the poor. For Dorothy this love was coupled to a life
of voluntary poverty and a passionate concern for peace.

The present work examines the spirituality of Dorothy Day in
its development, in its major themes, and for its significance for the
twentieth century. The study draws upon extensive archival research
at Marquette University, at St. John's Abbey and University, at Thomas
Merton Study Center, and materials provided through the courtesy of
archivists at the Center for Eastern Christian Studies and St. Procopius
Abbey.[4] Correspondence and interviews with persons closely involved
with the Catholic Worker from its earliest period also contribute to
an understanding of Dorothy's spirituality.

Major studies of Dorothy Day have been completed in the following areas: an examination of her ecclesiology by Thomas Frary, a study
of her conversion by Roger Statnick, a biography and *All Is Grace*—
a smaller work offering an initial interpretation of her spirituality—

by William D. Miller, and a significant first chapter in Mel Piehl's *Breaking Bread.* In all of these her spirituality is either left implicit or, in the case of *All Is Grace,* presented by means of short essays which introduce samples of Dorothy's "spiritual" writings. June E. O'Connor's *The Moral Vision of Dorothy Day,* recently published, provides a first feminist study of Day. Though pursuing her work independently, the author has in some areas benefited from my own research. My contribution acknowledges all of the foregoing, and while moving within the context of this rich historiographical background, attempts to move beyond it by comprehensiveness: in chronology, in the themes treated, and in the use of critical sources. While I examine in detail only selected aspects of Dorothy's spirituality, these are brought to bear upon a greater understanding of her total life in the Spirit. Throughout the work my concern centers around the creative tension that existed between Dorothy Day's spiritual maturation and the religious and social context in which she lived.

While this study has been completed, it has in another sense only begun. My work to this present moment has been made possible by the love and encouragement of a great number of persons. An attempt to name them all would be difficult, if not impossible. I would, however, like to express my deepest gratitude to the following persons. After God, I owe the most to my mother and adoptive father, Ellen E. and Donald F. Merriman. The support of their loving concern, encouragement, and prayer has been without fail. To my father Christopher O'Shea, who has given me life and hope, I offer my thanks and love. To my brother, John, and to my sisters, Donna and Angela, my gratitude for their confidence in me and for their Merriman humor which has increased the ratio of our laugh lines over those caused by worry.

Two persons have been outstanding in their support over the past several years: Frank Houdek, S.J., who has befriended me for more than a decade, and Rosemary Bower, Ph.D., whose professional assistance and compassion are great gifts to me.

Many members of the Franciscan and Dominican families have provided support and encouragement over a lengthy period. I wish to thank first of all my primary community, the Sisters of St. Francis, Sylvania, Ohio, and in a special way Sisters Marie Andrée, Patrice Kerin and Carolyn Giera. To my sisters Allyn Ayres, O.P., Patricia N. Benson, O.P., Marianna Engels, O.P. (now deceased), and Paschal Hocum, O.S.F., I offer heartfelt thanks. They know my gratitude, but I wish to tell them once again. My Franciscan brothers of St. Barbara province have offered me hospitality, friendship, and a prayerful atmosphere for common worship during my stay in Berkeley, California. To them I am indeed grateful. Two of these friars, Joseph P. Chinnici, O.F.M., and Vincent J. Mesi, O.F.M., have given me much-treasured support by their own faith, love, and friendship. To Joe I owe the privilege of close work together in the first years of my doctoral studies. A fine scholar, he introduced me to the joys and rigors of an historical approach to theological studies, inspired the beginnings of this present work, and has encouraged its completion. To Vince I owe the example of a wonderful human being who has opened up to me new perspectives on life and offered me reason to persevere. A truly pastoral man with whom I share a great love for music, he reintroduced its sound into my life when there was literally and figuratively a great silence. I offer a special word of thanks to friends at St. Isidore's in Danville, California, and to Father Daniel E. Cardelli. One would need to travel far before finding a finer group of people or a more hospitable, kindly pastor. While all of them are dear to me, Irene and Joe Leclair, Mary Nolan Howell, and Margi Slavonia have a special place in my heart.

Archivists and librarians across the country have offered me invaluable assistance. Phillip M. Runkel, curator of the Catholic Worker collection at Marquette University, has helped me since March 1984, the time of my first visit to the archives. He has answered numerous questions and provided materials and confirmation of detail ever since. His courtesy, thoroughness, and promptness surpassed my highest expectations. My thanks also to Vincent Tegeder, O.S.B., and Ryan Perkins, O.S.B., of St. John's University and Abbey archives for their gracious hospitality as well as assistance during a summer stay in Collegeville; to Robert Daggy, Ph.D., of the Thomas Merton Study Center at Bellarmine College; to Thomas Sable, S.J., who gained access for me to available Helen Iswolsky papers; to Mary Sevilla of Stanford University Libraries, to whom I am indebted for the special arrangement which provided me with constant access to the *Catholic Worker,* 1933–1980.

Three persons have greatly aided my completion of the original work upon which this book is based. Eldon Ernst, Ph.D., faithfully "travelled" with me during a crucial two years of writing. Always gracious and available, he offered both encouragement and scholarly suggestions in a manner that consistently respected and affirmed my own research and approach to the materials. Since I first met him in spring 1984, Mel Piehl, Ph.D., has given freely of his own insight, particularly in Catholic Worker matters, and beyond them as well. The care he took in reading the typescript-in-process and the valuable suggestions he offered have been very much appreciated. Robert McAfee Brown, Ph.D., likewise followed faithfully the growth of the original manuscript. His enthusiastic interest, cogent suggestions and encouragement were received most gratefully.

This work is a better product because of all these persons. It is, however, ultimately my own and for this reason I accept full responsibility for what is written therein. It has been a labor of love, inspired by the extraordinary fidelity and love of which Dorothy Day gave and continues to give me witness. If the reader is able to take away from this work some sense of Dorothy's great integrity and holiness, then I am content.

1

A Spirituality in Context

In 1897, the publication of a French edition of the life of Paulist founder Isaac Hecker had brought to a head the debate over the Americanist vision, a liberalizing reform-oriented tendency developed in late nineteenth-century Catholicism. While discussions were confined mostly to the ecclesiastical hierarchy, the repercussions of Americanism, exacerbated by the later modernist controversy, were also felt on a wider scale in the United States. Papal condemnations of Americanism and modernism account in good measure for the narrowed social vision available to the ordinary Catholic in America during the first decades of the twentieth century.

The Americanist vision, represented by Isaac Hecker, Bishop John Keane, and others, advocated a positive image of the Catholic active in the reconstruction of society. A conservative view, represented by bishops such as Michael A. Corrigan and Bernard J. McQuaid, advocated devotional Catholicism and maintained a protective stance toward Catholic immigrants living in a predominantly Protestant environment. As the century waned, the fragile alliance between the two groups became more tenuous, evidenced by disagreements over such issues as the need for ethnically based parochial schools, the nature of Catholic higher education, the attitude toward Protestants, and membership in fraternal societies. A contemporary view, noted by Catholic historian Jay P. Dolan, encapsulated the nature of the controversy:

> there are two distinct and hostile parties in the Roman Catholic Church in America. One is led by Archbishop Ireland. It stands for Americanism and a larger independence. It is sympathetic with modern thought.

1

It believes the Roman Catholic Church should take its place in all the great moral reforms. It is small, but progressive, vigorous, and brave.

The other party is led by the overwhelming majority of the hierarchy. It is conservative, out of touch with American or modern ideas. It is the old medieval European Church, transplanted into the Nineteenth Century and this country of freedom, interesting as an antiquity and curiosity, but fast losing its power and consequently, growing in bitterness.[1]

Because of such conflicts, Paulist Father Walter Elliott's attempt to synthesize Hecker's spiritual teaching through publication of *The Life of Father Hecker* (1891), complete with laudatory preface by Archbishop John Ireland, attracted little attention. During the same period, however, a different political and spiritual climate prevailed in France. Thus, an 1897 French translation, *Le Père Hecker,* with a preface by Abbé Felix Klein, attracted international attention. It provoked not only discussions within France but also response from the United States and eventually a struggle for approval from Rome. In addition to writing the preface to the Hecker biography, Klein, a French republican professor of literature at the Catholic Institute of Paris, wrote an October 1897 article promoting his understanding of an American asceticism which responded to the needs of the times. For him, the period of passive obedience dominated by a plethora of external structures was fast departing. French monarchist Abbé Charles Maignen responded to Klein in a series of essays, later published in book form as *Le Père Hecker: Est-il un saint?* (1898). In this work Maignen argued for traditional monasticism, which embraced the evangelical vows and promoted devotionalism. French Jesuit Père A.-J. Delattre similarly rejected Hecker's intimation that a new approach to sanctity was in order, and argued that docility and obedience to authority were the primary characteristics of the Christian life. An eventual appeal to Rome resulted in Leo XIII's letter *Testem Benevolentiae* (January 1899), in which he condemned a constellation of ideas identified as Americanism. Without directing the condemnation to any one person, the pope proclaimed as an error the consideration that the church ought to adapt its doctrine to the age. He warned, moreover, that changes in discipline were to be made by the church, not by individuals.[2]

While the encyclical formally ended the Americanist question, it did not put closure on debate over a need for the expression of religious faith to adapt itself to modern culture. This was the crux of the Catholic intellectual movement known as modernism, which had worried Pius X from the inception of his pontificate in 1903. The movement was widespread throughout Europe, with France at its center. American involvement, though minimal, represented the first serious promise of Catholic intellectual endeavors in the United States. Modernists themselves comprised a broad spectrum of approaches, though all were concerned in some way with the impact of contemporary approaches to philosophy, history, and biblical criticism on traditional Catholic teaching. Afraid that the controversy was detrimental to faith, the pope acted decisively and in 1907 issued *Pascendi Dominici Gregis,* which sounded the official death toll for modernism. In addition to summarizing the perceived errors of the modernists, the encyclical prescribed practical remedies to eliminate modernism. These included the promotion of a unifying, nonhistorical Scholastic philosophy, an accent on positive theology, greater selectivity in the selection of seminary faculty, more careful censorship of clerical publications, greater vigilance on the part of bishops, and the establishment of diocesan councils whose purpose was to squelch modernist errors.[3]

Attendant upon condemnations of Americanism and modernism, conservatism had triumphed in the American Catholic church. Heightened by a recent influx of immigrants, an emphasis on devotional Catholicism fostered the ideal of *Pascendi* in that it gave support to tradition and authority within the church. With or without *Pascendi,* however, the needs of successive waves of immigrants between 1890 and 1920—predominantly from southern and eastern Europe—absorbed the attention of Catholic church leaders at all levels. The parish functioned as both worship and social center and remained a major source of cultural identity and continuity. Though meeting sacramental and devotional needs took precedence, the parish served also as the hub around which local charitable societies were organized. Rooted in an older Catholic social doctrine, the societies emphasized the corporal works of mercy toward individuals, rather than larger social reform.

A newer precedent had been set for the hierarchy's support of social justice issues by James Cardinal Gibbons' 1887 defense of the Knights of Labor and again by Leo XIII's great labor encyclical, *Rerum Novarum* (1891). Nonetheless, few members of the hierarchy dealt directly with the American labor movement, the most pressing social issue of the time. The period's greatest Catholic influence on behalf of labor was exerted by a few priests such as Peter Yorke, Peter E. Dietz, and John A. Ryan. These men realized the needs of fellow Catholics, the majority of whom belonged to the laboring classes. For the most part, however, Catholic social teaching remained little known until the 1930s. American Catholics shared generally in a passivity and lack of social vision.[4]

Dorothy Day was a notable exception to this general malaise. Both before and after her conversion to Catholicism, she reflected upon and responded actively to the social and religious sensibilities of her age. Born on 8 November 1897 in Brooklyn Heights, New York, her parents, John and Grace Satterlee Day, had been raised Congregationalist and Episcopalian respectively, but were no longer affiliated with any denomination. During Dorothy's childhood Christian influences were present but underplayed at home. Her own discovery of the Scriptures provided a lasting influence upon Dorothy's spiritual maturation and desire to make the world a better place for others.

Dorothy's first confrontation with the biblical text occurred sometime between 1904 and 1906. Having moved from New York to California in 1904, the Day family lived in a furnished house in Berkeley while waiting for their own furniture to come around the Horn. One Sunday afternoon Dorothy and her sister Della were playing in the attic. Dorothy, who had been able to read from the age of four, recalled sitting behind a table pretending that she was a teacher. As she read from a Bible she had found she was overcome by a sense of awe. Though she did not recall the precise passage, she felt as she read that a new personality was impressed upon her, that she was introduced to someone, and intuited immediately that she was discovering God. This was the first Bible she remembered having seen, and she confessed that the experience was formative:

> I knew that I had just really discovered Him because it excited me tremendously. It was as though life were fuller, richer, more exciting in every way. Here was someone that I had never really known about before and yet felt to be One whom I would never forget, that I would never get away from. The game might grow stale, it might assume new meanings, new aspects, but life would never again be the same. I had made a great discovery. . . . It was that Sunday afternoon up in the dim attic and the rich, deep feeling of having a book, which would be with me through life, that stands out in my mind now.[5]

"Having a book" was a significant symbol of the written word's instrumentality for the development of Dorothy's spirituality.

The family moved to Oakland once the furniture arrived, and because the Bible belonged in the furnished Berkeley house, Dorothy did not take it with her. In a short spurt of religious enthusiasm generated by her reading of Scripture, Dorothy participated in the churchgoing and hymn singing of her newly found Methodist friend Naomi Reed, the widowed Mrs. Reed, and the rest of the Reed children. After a falling out with the Reed family, Dorothy claimed to have ceased to bother her head with faith and churchgoing until she met her first Catholic a year later, in Chicago. Though in an isolated account Dorothy averred that some years passed before she took up Bible reading again, greater weight may be placed on her remarks that she was a faithful Bible reader since childhood, "for many passages remained with me through my earlier years to return and haunt me."[6]

A sense of belonging held a great attraction for Dorothy throughout life, and especially so after the trauma and consequent dislocation suffered because of the 1906 San Francisco earthquake. Both in Berkeley and in Oakland, Dorothy had begun to form friendships at school and enjoyed playtime in nearby open fields and at the oceanside. However, the morning of 18 April 1906 altered both her personal contentment and the family's fortune. In Dorothy's later memory, the earthquake, her mother's recent illness, and nightmares which could be assuaged only by a mother's soothing: all merged as a connected series of events. In contrast to the other three Day children, eight-year-old Dorothy had to find her own way to safety after being rolled around in bed by the earth's tremors. As if programmatic for a Catholic Worker future, just hours after the major tremblers subsided Dorothy was moved by the sight of her mother serving homeless refugees from across the bay.[7]

The now poverty-stricken Day family moved to Chicago's South Side shortly after the earthquake. Among her neighbors were Catholics such as Mrs. Barrett and Mary Harrington, whose active piety impressed upon a receptive Dorothy a sense of faith in God and in the solidarity of the Catholic Christian community. Their peaceful confidence affected Dorothy deeply and gave her a first impulse toward Catholicism. Since the industrial city served as a mecca for Catholic immigrants, it is likely that Dorothy encountered a number of other friendly Catholics in the first year or so of her 1906–1914 sojourn in Chicago.[8]

The move to Chicago also acquainted Dorothy with the Episcopal church. Dr. Wilson, rector of the local Episcopal church, visited the Day home as part of a general canvassing of the neighborhood for possible parishioners. The upshot of this pastoral call was that Dorothy began to attend the Sunday liturgy and listened to her brothers sing in the choir. Dorothy read the Bible and learned to pray and to love the psalms and anthems of the Episcopal liturgy, finding that her heart "melted within me" whenever the choir sang the *Te Deum* or the *Benedicite* [Daniel 3]. In Dorothy's memory, this occurred when she was ten years old.[9]

A series of four moves, each marking an improvement in the family's economic situation, finally situated Dorothy in a middle-class neighborhood on the north side of the city. When at age twelve she desired to join the Catholic church, both her father and an Episcopalian pastor directed her toward the Episcopal community. Baptised and confirmed an Episcopalian, as her mother had been before her, Dorothy was attracted by the sense of God's presence as she experienced it through the beauty of Episcopal worship. During this period, Dorothy evidenced a growing appreciation of the psalms through participation in worship as well as through another concerted effort to continue reading the Bible. She remained a regular churchgoer at Our Saviour's on Fullerton Avenue for at least a year, though apparently not encouraged by her parents.[10]

Impressed by and responsive to "all beauty, all joy, all music," Dorothy experienced double joy at age fourteen. The first occasion was the birth of her brother John in May 1912; the second, the experience of first love. While the second was fleeting, it became associated ever afterwards with love for her brother, who remained close to Dorothy until her death. In the first two years of his life, Dorothy greatly assisted her mother in caring for him. The daughter felt that the love she lavished on baby John and his response compensated in some way for the general lack of demonstrable affection within her family. Her responsibility in caring for the baby gave Dorothy leave to take him for long walks in the park. Pushing him in his carriage, she explored areas beyond her own neighborhood, to which she was drawn because of recent reading.[11]

The walks were symptomatic of several experiences tugging simultaneously at her consciousness: an emotional upheaval accompanying adolescence, intellectual curiosity further stimulated by her readings, the need to make sense of the reality around her in the context of faith, and the desire for experience. Regarding the reading, Dorothy noted that it "began to be socially conscious," a fact which was probably unknown to her protective father. Her older brother Donald had recently begun his journalistic career with the *Day Book,* a paper that concerned itself with labor issues, particularly those in Chicago. Dorothy read it surreptitiously, admiring the idealism of contributing poet Carl Sandburg, who inspired her brother "to look on the people as he did, with love and hope of great accomplishment." Through the paper she learned of Socialist labor leader Eugene V. Debs and of the Industrial Workers of the World (IWW), both experiencing a popularity which had peaked during Woodrow Wilson's 1912 presidential campaign. Though the novels of Dickens had previously given her insight into the problems of London's nineteenth-century poor, Dorothy's current reading struck closer to her own experience. She herself had known poverty at first hand; although now her family was personally better off, her mind and heart were more fully awakened to the plight of those in the city about her. Not only did she read the *Day Book,* however. Both Jack London's critical essays on class struggle and Upton Sinclair's *The Jungle* (1906) claimed her attention. The latter, because it related the story of poverty and struggle in Chicago, allowed Dorothy to connect it directly with her own life. It was then that she began exploratory walks in earnest, discerning in some small way her future vocation:

> I walked for miles, pushing my brother in his carriage, often with my sister at my side, she usually holding onto the carriage too. We explored until we were footsore, going up and down interminable gray streets, fascinating in their dreary sameness, past tavern after tavern, where I envisaged such scenes as that of the Polish wedding party in Sinclair's story, past houses which were sunk down a whole story below street level for block after block.
>
> . . . though my only experience of the destitute was in books, the very fact that *The Jungle* was about Chicago where I lived, whose streets I walked, made me feel that from then on my life was to be linked to theirs, their interests were to be mine; I had received a call, a vocation, a direction to my life.[12]

Though this direction was clear to Dorothy in retrospect, any such realization was inchoate at best to the sensitive adolescent. Her protestation that "all those [adolescent] years, I believed. I had faith [in God]" was a sincere utterance, yet the weight of evidence found in her recollections points to a growing argument, albeit internal, with those who professed themselves Christian. Ardent and idealistic, Dorothy was scandalized by Christians, comfortably well off, who "fawned upon" the rich. These same rich — as known to Dorothy only through reading — amassed fortunes themselves while exploiting workers in the stockyards. What Dorothy expected was that Christians truly live the gospel imperative by opening their hearts and their homes to those less fortunate than they were.[13]

While absorbed in other readings in high school, Dorothy faithfully read the New Testament, in addition to the sermons of John Wesley and the *Imitation of Christ.* She received great comfort from this triad of works and reported a particular section of the *Imitation* which struck her, revealing the perduring influence of Scripture:

> In that most popular devotional book which came out in the Middle Ages, they compared scripture to the Holy Eucharist. In the fourth book, chapter eleven, they speak of food and light as necessary for man to grow. The food was the body and blood of Christ and the light was holy scripture. They were put on an equality which is a very awesome thought. It is as though if we possessed a bible in the home, it was as though we had a private chapel with the blessed sacrament. I know that always I have been very moved by seeing people reading the Scripture.[14]

When a series of blinding headaches troubled Dorothy at about this time, her mother called in a Christian Science practitioner who lived across the street. For a while Dorothy read Christian Science literature as well as Bible passages marked out by the group for daily reading. In her autobiographical novel *The Eleventh Virgin,* Dorothy portrayed the adolescent June (a thinly disguised Dorothy) as reading the Bible with interest and translating the New Testament from Greek with diligence. In a letter written to her friend Henrietta at age fifteen, Dorothy confided that she was rereading Acts with greater care and insight: "I never went over it [Acts] so thoroughly before and now I find much more in it. Isn't it queer how the same verses will strike you at different times?"[15] The enthusiasm of this letter reflects something more than an adolescent impressionism. At the same time Dorothy

was increasingly aware of the discrepancy between the scriptural message and the many Christians who apparently failed to live its message.
She could not comprehend why Christians accepted harsh judgments
of the poor and excused indifference to their plight. Morever, certain
biblical passages themselves puzzled Dorothy, as they appeared to judge
and minimize the burden of the poor and to portray a Christ who was
indifferent to concerns of this world. Though looking for a synthesis
of the Christian message, she knew that she had not yet found it.

> I wanted, though I did not know it then, a synthesis. I wanted life and
> I wanted the abundant life. I wanted it for others too. I did not want
> just the few, the missionary-minded people like the Salvation Army, to
> be kind to the poor, as the poor. I wanted everyone to be kind. I wanted
> every home to be open to the lame, the halt and the blind, the way
> it had been after the San Francisco earthquake. Only then did people
> really live, really love their brothers. In such love was the abundant life
> and I did not have the slightest idea how to find it.[16]

Her father's protectiveness had fostered not so much innocence
as ignorance of the world about her. Obtaining this knowledge was
an essential part of Dorothy's quest for God. Her thirst for further experience, seemingly leading her away from God in the next decade,
would be slaked finally by her lived concordance between belief and
action. An undated reflection from this period attests to the struggle
which lay ahead:

> Life would be utterly unbearable if we thought we were going
> nowhere, that we had nothing to look forward to. The greatest gift life
> can offer would be faith in God and the hereafter. Why don't we have
> it? Perhaps like all gifts it must be struggled for. "God, I believe" (or
> rather, "I must believe or despair,") "Help thou my unbelief." "Take
> away my heart of stone and give me a heart of flesh."
>
> It is interesting to note that these requests are mandatory. It is
> as though God expected us to demand these things as our right, not
> to plead for them as favors.[17]

A TIME OF FERMENT (1914–1923)

In the fall of 1914 Dorothy traveled by train to Urbana, where
she would attend the University of Illinois for two years. She had won

a $300 Hearst scholarship and relished the thought of new-found independence, feeling a maturity beyond her sixteen years. Already conscious of class war through her readings, she cared little at the time about World War I, which had just begun. With respect to the international conflict, she merely reflected what was then a dominant U.S. sentiment, in accord with President Woodrow Wilson's proclamation of U.S. neutrality on 4 August 1914.

What did captivate Dorothy's attention were opportunities for broadening her horizons. As she admitted, it was experience in general that she wanted. However, as the realization of separation from home—especially from her beloved brother John—deepened, she began to feel desolate. Though overcome by a sense of having to choose the world to which she would belong, she decided that it included neither the standard values of the Epworth League nor those of the Young Women's Christian Association (YWCA). Neither were related to life as she saw it: full of injustices and ugliness in a professedly Christian world. She neglected her regular courses, finding that even history disappointed her. She perceived that it failed to teach her a method of relating past and present events, so that she could "think in terms of shaping the present to mold the future."[18] Personally in search of a way to take her place in the world and change it for the better, Dorothy continued a pattern of voracious, independent reading which she had begun in high school.

Stimulated and troubled by her reading choices—among them the New Testament, Dostoevsky, and Tolstoy—and by a respected instructor's lectures, Dorothy struggled with her religious convictions. She had already made a definitive break with the Episcopal church, due to the influence of other readings, particularly of Upton Sinclair and Jack London. She nonetheless continued to read the New Testament regularly, and found that her belief in God remained firm. The felt dichotomy between what Christianity should be and how it was practiced proved even more problematic, for what she learned of this world's problems appeared to be in conflict with a gospel which Dorothy then believed preached only passivity and otherworldliness. Writing of this period, Dorothy reminisced that she tried to push religion from her, and hardened her heart. She "had read the New Testament with fervor. But that time was past."[19] What she could not have known then was that her days of scriptural reflection were but temporarily suspended.

Dorothy felt that Christ was far removed from her, because He was "two thousand years dead and new prophets had risen up in His place."[20] For her, the contemporary prophets were representatives of radical movements, for the most part industrial in orientation: anarchist Prince Peter Kropotkin, the Haymarket martyrs of 1887, the Molly Maguires of the Pennsylvania coal fields, the Knights of Labor, Eugene Debs—not only a socialist but also a founder of the IWW—and the like. Dorothy's sense of urgency regarding the need for the great mass of workers to organize for better labor conditions would serve her in good stead in the early years of the *Catholic Worker.* In her eagerness she joined the Socialist party along with another university student, Marie Oberlander. She found the meetings dull, however, and so she attended them infrequently.

The seventeen year old supported herself, and her reading habits, with various menial jobs. Because she hoped eventually to enter the field of journalism, Dorothy submitted articles to the local paper. Those which criticized the general existing order were rejected, though some which critiqued students' working conditions were accepted for publication. She wrote also for the university paper, the *Daily Illini,* which gained her admittance into a student writing club, the Scribblers. Through the group she met Jewish student, Rayna Simons, later an ardent Communist. Dorothy's friendship with Rayna, remembered afterwards with great fondness, brought Dorothy her first contact with anti-Semitism. She was saddened that sorority membership was denied the high achieving Rayna solely because she was Jewish. Together with Rayna's Jewish fiancé, Samson Raphaelson, the two young women attended lectures, including those given by birth-control activist Rose Pastor Stokes and Socialist Scott Nearing. These rounded out Dorothy's education in dissent.[21]

The Day family's move back to New York City in the summer of 1916 brought Dorothy's formal education to an end. Not as independent as she first thought, she wanted to remain near her family and so moved to New York in search of work. The choice entailed the prospect of living on her own again, as John I. Day would not tolerate a working daughter in the house, least of all one seeking a career in journalism. Dorothy, intent on furthering a just society through journalistic endeavors, then identified with a nonreligious radicalism and made no pretensions of being a Christian. She loved the poor, however, and desired to serve them, only later admitting that she was even then in favor of the scripturally based works of mercy.

In fall 1916 she found work with the *New York Call,* a Socialist daily, and an East Side room with a poor Jewish family. Prior to persuading *Call* editor Chester Wright that he should employ her, Dorothy had used the several months of job hunting to explore the city neighborhoods. The observant and very lonely eighteen year old found the sights and sounds of the New York slums appallingly different from her remembrance of those in Chicago. Fascination as well as repulsion pulled her further beyond reading, closer to an eventual vocation among the poor:

> as I walked these streets . . . I wanted to go and live among these surroundings; in some mysterious way I felt that I would never be freed from this burden of loneliness and sorrow unless I did.[22]

Staff members of the *Call* held a variety of opinions on general labor concerns in this period when strikes were widespread. While Wright supported the American Federation of Labor, Charles Ervin, later managing editor, favored an opposing faction, the Amalgamated Clothing Workers. Joshua Wanhope, an editorial writer and a Socialist, represented the sentiments of the majority working for the paper during Dorothy's employment. Though a few favored the IWW or the Anarchist movements, Dorothy recalled that they "were more newspaper men than anything else." Young Dorothy wavered in her allegiances to Socialism, the IWW, and Anarchism. The IWW's, many of whom would become Communists after the October 1917 revolution, appealed greatly to her because of their commitment to direct action. However, as Dorothy later claimed, due to her long hours of work she never applied for formal membership in any of the New York based groups. She did attend and enjoy labor bazaars and balls sponsored by various radical groups. It was at one of these that Dorothy heard IWW speaker Elizabeth Gurley Flynn, an outstanding leader of the Mesabi iron range strikers.[23]

Dorothy's reporting assignments included coverage of strike meetings, picket lines, and peace gatherings. Many groups were theoretically opposed to the country's imminent entry into the war, notably the Emergency Peace Federation, the IWW, the Socialists, and the Anarchists, but in loyalty to the paper, Dorothy attempted to interest herself only in meetings to which she was sent. With fellow reporter and friend Irving Granich (Michael Gold), she interviewed Russian Socialist Leon Trotsky. Only one of their interview-based articles reached publication because of the Russian's disaffection with American socialism, a variety which trusted to education and legislation rather than revolt to change the social order. Impatient with gradual change herself, Dorothy sided with Trotsky. A couple of months later she joined the Madison Square Garden celebration of the March 1917 revolutionary overthrow of the czarist monarchy. Unlike the later Bolshevik revolution, the uprising was applauded generally throughout the United States as a movement toward democracy. For Dorothy and her *Call* friends the overthrow signified immediate hope for the working masses, for world peace, and for world community.

Dorothy appears to have had no direct contact with Catholics or other professed Christians at this period. She recalled no anti-religious writing in the *Call,* yet paid no attention at the time to an article by Dante Barton which featured an exposition of the church's social teachings. Her current critique of Catholics was trenchant: "Catholics then were a nation apart, a people within a people, making little impression on the tremendous non-Catholic population of the country." This perception of Catholic narrowness was confirmed for her in spring 1917, during one of her last assignments for the *Call.* With pro-war spirit then at feverish pitch, she joined with Columbia University students traveling to Washington, D.C., to protest the impending passage of the Selective Service Bill. The group held meetings at several cities along the way. At Baltimore, Catholic college students disrupted the meeting, and police attempted to break up the argument. While taken aback by the Baltimore students' behavior, the young woman had no perception of the prevailing Catholic sentiment—encouraged by the American hierarchy—which demonstrated patriotism precisely by supporting the war.[24]

In April 1917 Dorothy left the *Call* and worked for the Anti-Conscription League before joining the staff of a radical monthly entitled *Masses.* She was with the publication during the final half-year of its existence, learning skills which permitted her to function as temporary editor during the two regular editors' summer absences. The November–December 1917 issue was the magazine's last, due to enforcement of wartime postal censorship, and Dorothy found herself without employment. At the invitation of artist friend Peggy Baird, she journeyed again to Washington, D.C., this time with a group of suffragists. Though as a radical she herself never intended to vote,

Dorothy joined the women to protest the treatment of imprisoned suffragists, whom she deemed worthy of treatment as political prisoners,
and was taken into custody herself.[25]

While imprisoned at the Occoquan workhouse, Dorothy took the
Scriptures again and found a mixed comfort in the Psalms. She read
them with a sense of coming back to something which she had lost,
yet she suffered as she read. The source of her pain was threefold: first,
she felt a sense of shame for turning to God in despair; second, she
realized the need for personal conversion before any revolution could
be successful; finally, she suffered in solidarity with the entire human
family:

> All through those weary first days in jail . . . the only thoughts that
> brought comfort to my soul were those lines in the Psalms that expressed
> the terror and misery of man suddenly stricken and abandoned. Solitude
> and hunger and weariness of spirit — these sharpened my perceptions
> so that I suffered not only my own sorrow but the sorrows of those about
> me. I was no longer myself. I was man. I was no longer a young girl,
> part of a radical movement seeking justice for those oppressed, I was
> the oppressed.[26]

The question later crossed Dorothy's mind of whether her conversion process would have been accelerated had she remained in solitary
confinement. She recalled that while reading the Psalms in Occoquan
she felt a nostalgia for the devotion of her youth and wondered:

> If I had been left in solitary confinement for the thirty days to which
> I had been sentenced that nostalgia might have grown into something
> else, but the jail officials were overcome by the numbers and prominence
> of the strikers, and within a few days the hunger strike was won, and
> the women were allowed the comparative liberty of the inside of the
> jail, the right to wear their own clothes instead of the prison uniforms,
> freedom from labor, the right to receive and send out mail, order their
> own food, receive visits from their doctors or lawyers, though not their
> friends.[27]

Dorothy admitted that once the crisis had passed, Scripture ceased to
haunt her for the moment, and she was again drawn back into the
immediacy of her life as journalist. The jail experience then became
a glorious adventure.[28]

Dorothy worked at various jobs during the winter of 1917–1918, one of which was with the *Liberator,* then printing John Reed's reports from Russia. Heated discussions of revolutionary theory and the recent Bolshevik seizure of control absorbed Dorothy's days and nights. She joined the Greenwich Village scene and spent many nights at Provincetown Playhouse and in the Hell Hole, a back room of the Golden Swan saloon. Her company included an assortment of artists, writers, and radicals, among them George Granich and his brother Irving (Michael Gold), Agnes Boulton, playwright Eugene O'Neill, and anarchists Terry Karlin and Hypolite Havel. In this unlikely atmosphere of smoke and drink she first heard Catholic poet Francis Thompson's "The Hound of Heaven." Recited from memory by friend Eugene O'Neill, the pulsating story of inevitable conversion worked upon her psyche. Many mornings, after staying up all night with friends, she attended early morning Mass at St. Joseph's Church on Sixth Avenue. She knelt in the back and felt comforted by the atmosphere of worship, though she could not yet comprehend the Latin liturgy.[29]

Dorothy left Greenwich Village after witnessing the heroin-induced suicide of Louis Holladay, a Greenwich Village habitué. She began nurses' training at King's County Hospital, Brooklyn, early in 1918, after deciding that the step was not contrary to her pacifist principles. Though still interested in the labor movement, she believed nonetheless that it "went dead on me for that time." Wartime high employment rates had temporarily satisfied workers, who took little thought of continued progress in organization. While the American Federation of Labor and a number of Socialists endorsed the war, men such as Eugene Debs were still able to inspire her. She perceived that while individual groups had failed, the radical movement as a whole had not disappointed her.[30]

The discipline of hospital work stimulated the twenty year old and satisfied her desire to do something for the poor. Dorothy's almost imperceptible move toward Catholicism was furthered by contact with fellow nurse probationer, a Miss Adams. Although apparently reticent in speaking of her faith, Adams did provide Dorothy with an incentive for attending Sunday Mass on a regular basis. Another hospital companion, newspaperman Lionel Moise, exerted a far less serene influence on Dorothy. She fell in love with the former *Kansas City Star* reporter and moved in with him shortly after the 11 November 1918 armistice. World war had ceased, yet Dorothy's personal struggle had begun in earnest, narrowing her vision so that she would "only see life in the things that were immediately about me." Among the events to be included with this period is the possibility of a suicide attempt or attempts by Dorothy. If true, the attempt(s) confirm further the degree of turmoil that she experienced. Much to her sorrow, the Day-Moise affair was interrupted by Moise's departure in September 1919, after Dorothy aborted their child in hopes of retaining her hold on Moise. Shortly afterward she married Tobey Berkeley, a forty-two-year-old literary promoter, and went with him to Europe in summer of 1920. Their incompatibility was soon evident, and though they traveled together to London and Paris, Dorothy spent six months alone on the island of Capri. There she absorbed southern Italian culture and began writing her autobiographical novel, *The Eleventh Virgin*.[31]

When she returned to the United States in summer 1921, Dorothy filed for divorce and settled in Chicago, where for a time she resumed her affair with Moise. In writing of this period she alluded to a preoccupation with other matters while noting that a religious element was not entirely lacking in her life. Her discussions of Dostoevsky with an unidentified friend, who may have been Lionel Moise, led Dorothy again to Scripture. Hearing of Sonya reading the gospel to Raskolnikov in *Crime and Punishment* caused her to turn to the New Testament with love.[32]

She worked at various jobs, including a secretarial stint with the *Liberator,* then established in Chicago under the direction of Communist Robert Minor. She again took an active interest in the working class. Though the Communist party had gone underground, Dorothy sensed the radical nature of the long Sunday afternoon speeches which she attended. During this period of the so-called Palmer Red Raids, Dorothy was arrested for a second time in July 1922. She had gone to the aid of older acquaintance Mae Cramer, then rooming at a Chicago IWW hotel for men, only to be included in the general arrest of all whom the night detectives found there. Booked with prostitutes, Dorothy considered the arrest a traumatic though useful experience in terms of growth in self-knowledge and in social and moral consciousness. The young woman remained in the city until the fall of 1923, when, claiming tiredness with life in Chicago, she moved to New Orleans.[33]

HOMECOMING AND CONFLICT (1923–1932)

Dorothy looked upon her winter 1923–1924 stay in New Orleans as a temporary excursion with sister Della and Communist friend Mary Gordon. Dorothy had no difficulty in finding work on the *New Orleans Item,* for which the journalist wrote a series on taxi dancers, along with some other feature articles. Life was relatively quiet and, aside from her reporter's work, Dorothy prayed regularly in the nearby Catholic cathedral. In continuing a habit begun in New York during the war and resumed again toward the end of her Chicago stay, the New Orleans church visits marked the beginning of her "slow and sweet return to God." Spring publication of *The Eleventh Virgin* (1924) and a $2500 share in movie rights for the novel persuaded Dorothy to return to New York where, at the suggestion of Peggy Baird, she purchased a Staten Island beach cottage.[34] While living there Dorothy found the time she craved to read, reflect, and write. She rented a city apartment for the coldest winter months and continued to party for a time with radical and liberal friends both in the city and on the island. Overall it was for Dorothy a period of disengaged radicalism, "confined to conversations and week-end beach parties with Communist friends," among them Michael Gold and his brothers.[35]

Dorothy's beach neighbors of the 1920s formed an international colony of varied philosophic and religious persuasions: nominal and practicing Catholics, bohemian and literate liberals, as well as radicals. As Dorothy remembered them they were a group noted for their tolerance. It was within this conglomerate atmosphere that she found sustenance for the conversion impelled by the cumulative effect of God's grace at work within her. Foremost among the personal influences was anarchist Forster Batterham, with whom she entered a common-law marriage sometime after spring 1924. Though more philosopher than activist, Batterham kept a temporarily detached Dorothy in touch with current events through his impassioned reading aloud of the morning *Times.* Because of his own absorption in the world of nature, he opened up to Dorothy a new love for marine and plant biology. The simplicity of life with Forster, in natural surroundings, added to Dorothy's sense of peace. She began to feel that her religious search had begun in earnest: "I was happy but my very happiness made me know that there was a greater happiness to be obtained from life than any I had ever known."[36]

She read the Bible again as well as other religious literature. Not only did she read; she also reflected, weighed things, and noted that she began consciously to pray more. While pregnant with their daughter Tamar, she found herself praying the Our Father. Her scruples during these months are revealed in a 1925 diary entry which marked her reflection on why she was praying at all:

> I was thinking the other day of how inadequately we pray. Often in saying the Our Father, I find myself saying by rote the first four lines and throwing my heart into the last, asking for bread and grace and forgiveness. This selfishness humiliates me so that I go back to the beginning again in order to give thanks. "Hallowed be Thy Name. Thy kingdom come." Often I say no other prayer.
>
> I am surprised that I am beginning to pray daily. I began because I had to. I just found myself praying. I can't get down on my knees, but I can pray while I am walking. If I get down on my knees I think, "Do I really believe? Whom am I praying to?" And a terrible doubt comes over me, and a sense of shame, and I wonder if I am praying because I am lonely, because I am unhappy.
>
> But when I am walking up to the village for the mail, I find myself praying again, holding the rosary in my pocket that Mary Gordon gave me in New Orleans two years ago. . . .
>
> Then I think suddenly, scornfully, "Here you are in a stupor of content. You are biological. Like a cow. Prayer with you is like the opiate of the people." And over and over again in my mind that phrase is repeated jeeringly, "Religion is the opiate of the people."
>
> "But," I reason with myself, "I am praying because I am happy, not because I am unhappy. I did not turn to God in unhappiness, in grief, in despair,— to get consolation, to get something from Him."
>
> And encouraged that I am praying because I want to thank Him, I go on praying. No matter how dull the day, how long the walk seems, if I feel low at the beginning of the walk, the words I have been saying have insinuated themselves into my heart before I have done, so that on the trip back I neither pray nor think but am filled with exultation.[37]

There are at least two strands of her thinking in this autumnal entry. One concerns the element of thanksgiving and praise she viewed as unselfish prayer. The second relates to a certain shame at the possibility that her prayer arose also from need. It recalls a certain dread of God which had persisted since early childhood, deriving from her sense of smallness before an immense and impersonal God. The fact

of this dread comprises a recollection recorded in a manuscript fragment. In it she noted that the family's move to Oakland had brought
Dorothy joy, especially through her acquaintance with the pious Methodist family, the Reeds. But,

> it was at that time that terror entered into my life. And it came from
> a sense of God's immensity.
>
> His transcendence, not his immanence shattered me. [I would
> awake in the night to hear: crossed out] It would begin in the night,
> in my sleep perhaps, [to: crossed out] I heard a sound which began
> softly and which increased in loudness until it overpowered me and I
> would wake up crying out, frightened at the immensity of the universe,
> of the heavens, overcome by a sense of the loneliness of God, the im-
> personality of God, the frightening sense that I was small and powerless
> and about to be engulfed. I cried until my mother came to my bedside
> and held my hand until I fell asleep again.[38]

This childhood dread had been compounded by a later encounter
with a mentality represented by the remarks of an admired Urbana
professor. These had been emblazoned on her memory a decade before her journal entry on the beach. According to him, religion was
something that had brought great comfort to people during past ages
and during periods of crisis. The inference gathered by Dorothy had
been that she, as one of the strong, did not need such a prop.[39] Hence
the difficulty in accepting the comfort the Psalms afforded her while
at Occoquan, and her Staten Island struggle to ascertain that her reawakened faith was founded on a position of strength alone. For her,
this stance included the responses of joy and gratitude. Thus, she invoked the presence of joy and gratitude for beauty—both in nature
outside of herself and in the wonder that after an abortion she could
still bear a child—as counterbalance and assurance that she was not
succumbing to an opiate in any form. Rather, she believed that recent events had served to reawaken her "long submerged religious
sense."[40]

The period also marked the beginnings of an estrangement which
would eventually separate her from Batterham:

> it was impossible to talk about religion or faith to him. A wall immedi-
> ately separated us. The very love of nature, and the study of her secrets
> which was bringing me to faith, cut Forster off from religion. . . .
>   . . . the very fact that we were begetting a child made me have

a sense that we were made in the image and likeness of God, co-creators with him. . . . Because I was grateful for love, I was grateful for life, and living with Forster made me appreciate it and even reverence it still more. He had introduced me to so much that was beautiful and good that I felt I owed to him too this renewed interest in the things of the spirit.[41]

After Tamar's 4 March 1926 birth Dorothy continued her biblically based reflections, which gave her strength and comfort. However, she felt torn because of her determination to have Tamar baptized, the finalization of her own move toward Catholicism, and the perceived inevitability of the end of life with Forster because of his aversion to formal marriage. Their mutual absorption in news of the final days and 23 August 1927 execution of anarchists Nicola Sacco and Bartolomeo Vanzetti figured as an outlet for personal grief over the impending disintegration of the Day-Batterham marriage. As Dorothy considered both Forster's agony in response to the August execution and his growing delight in Tamar, the mother found it even more difficult to consider "the cruel blow I was going to strike him when I became a Catholic." In her agony—which was Forster's too—she delayed her formal conversion until December 1927.[42]

In becoming Catholic, Dorothy sought not only a profound relationship with God but also a sense of community and a means of engaging in social reform. With regard to the latter she faced a conflict which paralleled her youthful disaffection with organized Christianity. A perceived disunity between faith and its expression had drawn an adolescent Dorothy away from Episcopal affiliation toward non-Christian radicalism. In the ensuing years she had identified with various non-Christian groups who advocated better material conditions for the working classes, an endeavor which Dorothy translated as building a world in which justice prevailed. Personal dedication of individual radicals and the inspiration she derived from them remained in Dorothy's memory long after the Catholic Worker was well established:

> I can say with warmth that I loved the people I worked with and learned much from them [Socialists, IWW's, Communists.] They helped me to find God in His poor, in His abandoned ones, as I had not found Him in Christian churches.[43]

Dorothy had judged correctly that the ranks of Catholicism in the United States consisted primarily of working-class members. She envisioned that as a Catholic she would engage her native talents in serving the poor, not merely to dispense charity but also to assist in changing the present social order. However, as Dorothy's retrospectives indicate, even prior to December 1927 she was aware of a frequent dichotomy between the doctrinal ideals of Catholicism and their human implementation by church members. In one summary she noted that she "loved the Church for Christ made visible. Not for itself, because it was so often a scandal to me." Faced with the reality of affiliation with a church whose social program was generally unknown to its members, Dorothy, equipped now with greater maturity, prayed often for the grace of discernment.[44]

The next five years of Dorothy's life may be viewed as a transition and preparation for the work she would begin with Peter Maurin at the close of 1932. The interim comprised not so much a metamorphosis of Dorothy as the beginning of a personal synthesis of religious and social ideals. While searching for a greater sense of direction, she employed herself in a variety of positions and continued to care for her daughter Tamar. Dorothy terminated work with the Communist Anti-imperialist League sometime in 1928, but only after making arrangements with beach friend Freda Maruchess to assist her in caring for a dozen children that summer. During winter 1928–1929 Dorothy worked with a Christian pacifist group, the Fellowship of Reconciliation, and also wrote a play which later gave her a contract with Pathe studios in Hollywood. After a winter bout with intestinal flu left her in weakened condition and a depressing period during which she offered hospitality to a sorrowing woman known only as Lallah, Dorothy found summer 1929 employment at the Marist novitiate on Staten Island. There, Marist Father James T. McKenna, one of many priests who befriended her and encouraged her readings in Catholic literature, introduced Dorothy to Karl Adam's *The Spirit of Catholicism*, "to begin my Catholic education." While at the Marist novitiate, Dorothy wrote "The Brother and the Rooster," her first article for a Catholic publication. An unexpected 15 August 1929 phone call provided her with a three months' contract with California-based Pathe studios for the fall. The experience convinced Dorothy that the company's atmosphere was bereft of intellectual content. Nonetheless, the work provided her with financial means to spend several months in Mexico that winter and following spring. As several 1930 articles written for the Catholic journal *Commonweal* suggest, this venture provided her with an understanding of Catholic practice within peasant culture, as well as insight into the political and economic conditions of the country.[45]

On her return from Mexico with Tamar in May 1930, Dorothy encountered at first hand the economic consequences of the 29 October 1929 collapse of the New York stock market. In the United States, many companies were forced out of business, and industrial production fell within the next three years to about half of 1929 production levels. Unemployment became rampant, with at least ten million persons left without jobs by 1932. No segment of society was left untouched. While wage workers suffered intensely, persons in all walks of life — teachers, ministers, salaried executives, farmers, and others — suffered no less trauma. Numerous banks failed, heightening the sense of panic to such a degree that frightened depositors continued to withdraw and hoard their money, jeopardizing the banks still more. Herbert Hoover, elected in 1928 when a mood of optimism had prevailed, acted energetically to end the depression but to little avail.[46]

Dorothy's own perception of the situation records the impatience she remembered feeling between 1930 and 1932:

> More and more people were losing their jobs, more families were being evicted, the Unemployed Councils were being formed by the Communist groups and Workers Alliance sprang into existence. It was a time for pressure groups, for direct action, and radicalism was thriving among all groups except the Catholics. I felt out of it all. There was Catholic membership in all these groups of course, but no Catholic leadership.[47]

Catholic leadership had begun to act, though little known to Dorothy at the time. Pius XI's encyclical *Quadragesimo Anno,* had been issued on 15 May 1931. In the tradition of Leo XIII's great labor encyclical of 1891, the work addressed the contemporary economic situation. In it, Pius XI opposed the rise of totalitarianism and offered a program which, while lacking specifics, called for a general reorganization of the social order. A sense of urgency pervading the air because of the depression augured well for the popularity of the encyclical as well as for American Catholic development of social thought in general. Catholic leaders such as John A. Ryan, who had sought to awaken the Catholic conscience to social issues throughout the 1920s, found great support for his work and encouragement for greater Catholic involvement in contemporary issues.[48]

Dorothy, who had decried the lack of leaders within the church, was soon to exercise a unique role in Catholic lay leadership. A sense of contentment had come over her during the summer of 1932, which she suggested was due to the deepening of her spiritual life. In addition to a research job that occupied her days, Dorothy set aside time for early morning Mass. She began to receive Eucharist daily, attended evening Benediction, and spent a portion of her evenings reading Teresa of Avila's *Life*.

The relative quiet of summer activities gave way again in the fall to direct involvement in social issues. Informed by radical friend George Granich of a projected Hunger March on Washington, D.C., Dorothy decided to travel with the group as a reporter for the Jesuit journal *America* as well as for *Commonweal*. Overcome by a sense of the dedication of group members, many of whom were Communists, Dorothy felt anew her current lack of involvement in social issues. Before leaving Washington, she prayed earnestly at the Shrine of the Immaculate Conception, that a way be opened up to her to use her gifts in the service of others. With greater determination than ever, she wanted to "find something to do in the social order besides reporting conditions. I wanted to change them, not just report them."[49]

Her return to New York City and subsequent meeting with Peter Maurin would clarify her course for the remainder of her life. The *Catholic Worker* and the movement by the same name, which Peter and Dorothy founded, would become the locus for the development and fruition of her spirituality. Dorothy's daughter, Tamar, remained an integral part of her mother's life, much as she had in the first years after Dorothy's conversion. Dorothy herself would aspire to and achieve ultimately that synthesis which Robert Ellsberg has attributed to her, namely, that "there was absolutely no distinction between what she believed, what she wrote, and the manner in which she lived."[50] Her reading of fine literature, both as preparation for and as reflection on life experiences, contributed in large measure to this integration.

2

Literary Influences on the Spirituality of Dorothy Day

For Dorothy, literature was an instrument through which her religious sensibilities were awakened and reawakened, and her awareness of social needs strengthened. Dorothy's father had carefully monitored the children's reading and so was particular as to what books and magazines were brought into the house. She recalled specifically that volumes of Sir Walter Scott, Victor Hugo, Charles Dickens, Robert Louis Stevenson, James Fenimore Cooper, and Edgar Allan Poe comprised part of the family collection of books during their sojourn in Chicago. Dorothy herself noted that during these early years books functioned as the "only release and outlook" on things outside the home. Childhood reading set a precedent for Dorothy, who continued to find in books a refreshment, as well as a mirror, and an interpretation of reality about her.[1]

She considered books to be like so many cherished friends to whom she returned again and again to take up the conversation, as it were, wherever it left off at a prior reading. As Dorothy continued to mature, she entered each text with new perspective, so that it became a fresh conversation, with deeper insights gained. She found in reading a spiritual sustenance for everyday life. Nor was this nourishment limited to those works commonly associated with spiritual reading. Whether it be Scripture, a novel by Dostoevsky, or other fine writings, Dorothy was of the opinion that "The books will always be there. If we give up many other distractions, we can turn to them. We can browse among the millions of words written and often just what we need can nourish us, enlighten us, strengthen us—in fact, be our food just as Christ, the Word, is also our food."[2]

THE CHRISTIAN CLASSICS

Scripture

Writing in the April 1948 issue of the *Catholic Worker*, Dorothy reported that Benedictine Father Anthony [Ashcroft] reminded a group of retreatants, Dorothy among them, that both the Old and New Testaments were the story of God's love in dealing with humankind. Her own early experiences with Scripture served to confirm this judgment, for, with regard to her continual conversion, she remarked that the story of her life could be called "a love story, an encounter, a confrontation, a dialogue between the soul and God."[3]

The Bible remained Dorothy's constant companion throughout life. Scripture reading at table, in monastic fashion, marked the early days of the Catholic Worker movement in the period of residence at 115 Mott Street. Once, while preparing for the opening of a retreat, she found herself randomly opening the Bible three times in conscious imitation of Francis of Assisi, a saint whom she greatly admired and whose life of voluntary poverty and peacemaking she strove to emulate. Although a minor incident, it indicates nonetheless that Dorothy sought direction from the sacred text as much as did the medieval Francis. On another occasion, relating to her participation in a Bible study group in the 1950s, Dorothy records her puzzlement over a mentality found in pre–Vatican II Catholicism:

> I speak at length about scripture because, coming from a Protestant background, one of the anti-Catholic statements in my youth was that Catholics were not permitted to read the Bible. When I became a Catholic in my middle twenties [*sic*], I was amazed to find the tremendous freedom there was in the Church. . . . But on two occasions in the fifties I encountered young priests who were anything but understanding of our ideas. Before our Friday night meetings, a few of us used to gather together to read scripture and one young priest, coming early to the meeting, told us forcefully that we were not supposed to read scripture without a priest present. On another occasion, another priest[,] also young, chided me for having as one of our Friday night speakers a famous woman theologian who was talking to us about Karl Barth.
>
> And now what amazing changes have taken place![4]

That daily reading of the Bible was important to her is revealed in one of the several interviews in which she participated during 1972, the year of her seventy-fifth birthday. On this occasion she specifically connected Scripture with the Lacouture type retreat, which she had first experienced in the late 1930s. Dorothy's perduring love for the Bible was one of the reasons why the retreat took hold on her in the first place. In her declining years Scripture remained even more a pivotal point in Dorothy's spirituality, and its value continued to be remarked upon. She spoke authoritatively of the power of the Word, as she had found it entering the hearts of men on the soupline, of Augustine who followed the counsel to take and read, of Dostoevsky's Raskolnikov in *Crime and Punishment,* and of how that power entered into the hearts of all who took the Word to heart, no matter how faultily interpreted. For Dorothy, fidelity to Scripture was of paramount importance and was called for in periods of aridity as well as in consolation:

> The Little St. Therese used to read the Scriptures constantly (in those days she was permitted to read only part of the Old Testament, so we Catholics can rejoice in the freedom we have now, even though we recognize that freedom is dangerous, imposing terrible responsibilities on us to try to live as we believe and profess). Often this reading is like plodding through a desert, we get so little from it. And then chapters, verses, shine out with a great light and our way is made clear for us.
>
> Yes, reading is prayer—it is searching for light on the terrible problems of the day, at home and abroad, personal problems and national problems, that bring us suffering of soul and mind and body.[5]

Scriptural reflection was thus no isolated element in Dorothy's life, but was integrated with every concern of her generous heart. One of many homey incidents which found their way into the *Catholic Worker* points up Dorothy's longtime habit of Scripture reading in the early hours of the day: "This morning my Scripture reading was interrupted by Tommy Turner bringing a large jar with something fascinating to show to Joshua, the small boy who has the room next to mine, with his mother."[6] Scripture had become such a part of her that she naturally related it to her other reading, as this item reveals:

> All of Chaim Potok's books are very enlightening (*My Name is Asher Lev, The Promise, The Chosen, In the Beginning, Wanderings*). Reading Potok made me turn to Scripture more and more, to supplement my daily reading of the Psalms of David.[7]

While the Scriptures as a whole placed its claim on Dorothy, there were certain portions of both Old and New Testaments to which she found herself drawn repeatedly. Outstanding in this regard were the Psalms and the twenty-fifth chapter of Matthew. A word regarding each of these is in order.

The Psalms

Dorothy's predilection for the Psalms dates from her Episcopalian period, which given the widest margin of possibility, includes the years 1906 to 1914. She later found a certain comfort in the Psalms while at Occoquan, where she lay "reading the Psalms by the hour."[8] Dorothy considered C. S. Lewis's *Reflections on the Psalms* a sure guide to their understanding, particularly of the warlike ones. As in her first exposure to them in Chicago, the Psalms remained for Dorothy primarily a vehicle of communal worship, whether they were prayed physically alone or with others: "Always I have loved the Psalms, and my morning and evening prayers, alone and in common, are made up of them."[9] Dorothy made an explicit connection between the liturgy and the Psalms, asserting that the liturgy brought the Catholic Worker group closer to the Scriptures in general. Nor was worship isolated from social causes, from daily concerns of life, for, touched with compassion, Dorothy took the cares of others to her prayer. This is perhaps nowhere more clearly illustrated than in her "On Pilgrimage" column for September 1968. She had been journeying through the South and was appalled by the poverty and discrimination accorded blacks in the Natchez, Mississippi area:

> When I woke up this morning and began to sort out my impressions of all I had seen and heard yesterday, the tears began and I could only keep on reading the Psalms, with their cries for help to a God who does not seem to hear. Because the suffering certainly goes on, down here and up North, in Vietnam, in Nigeria, in Biafra — and everywhere.[10]

But though God may not appear to have heard, Dorothy's faith remained firm. On numerous occasions in her later life she admitted to turning to the Psalms for solace, and even for strength to endure if need be. She asserted consistently that Scripture on the one hand and the Eucharist on the other, "have in them that strength which no power on earth can withstand."[11]

Matthew 25:31–46

These Matthean verses, proclaiming the works of mercy, comprise another important scriptural key for understanding Dorothy's spirituality. It is in her writings on and her practice of these works that her Christocentrism is most clearly focused and exemplified. The Matthean passage portrays Christ at the last judgment and functions as the conclusion to the entire eschatological discourse of Matthew (24:1–25:46). Dorothy had begun to absorb the message of the concluding verses prior to her 1927 conversion, though she was unable to articulate it until later. *From Union Square to Rome* and *The Long Loneliness,* both retrospects, give the reader important clues. The former, written ostensibly to her Communist brother, John, addressed the question of whether or not one may serve Christ without knowing him. Speaking of her pre-conversion radicalism, Dorothy pondered that even in her blindness she sensed the importance of Matthew 25:40 and contended that, "feeling this as strongly as I did, is it any wonder that I was led finally to the feet of Christ?"[12] The single verse, ". . . Truly I say to you, as you did it to one of the least of my brethren, you did it to me" (Mt 25:40), had by the time of her writing become Dorothy's shorthand for the entire passage, 25:31–46. Reminiscing of the same period in *The Long Loneliness,* she remarked upon her concern for the poor, questioned the sincerity of her intention, yet asserted firmly that even then she was "in favor of the works of mercy as we know them."[13]

The genesis of her post-conversion articulation may be traced to the October 1933 issue of the *Catholic Worker,* when the movement was in its infancy. The article, "Christ in His Poor," while not written by Dorothy, could have appeared in the paper only through her approval. Internal evidence suggests that it had been selected by her as well. The article in question was a reflection on the stations of the cross, a Catholic devotion dating from the time of Francis of Assisi. Rather than focusing on the sufferings of the historical Christ alone, the article provided a meditation on the sufferings of the contemporary poor. Particular emphasis was placed on the Christian responsibility to relieve these sufferings through performance of the works of mercy.[14]

From then on, entries on the works of mercy occurred in the pages of the *Catholic Worker* with increasing frequency. The work of artist Ade Bethune began to appear with the March 1934 issue, and her print "Harbor the Harborless" initiated a significant series of illustrations of the corporal works of mercy. While the Houses of Hospitality had been listed as part of the Catholic Worker program from its first year, by September 1935 the individual practice of the works of mercy was included in the movement's platform as the first of three ways to offer immediate relief to the needy.[15]

The Christocentric orientation of this endeavor permeated an article written by Dorothy at Christmas 1937, entitled: "Look on the Face of Thy Christ." After reminding the reader that the Mott Street coffee and bread line had been of service for a full year as of that month, Dorothy appealed for material assistance in order to keep this good work going. The impetus for Dorothy was that each of these seven hundred or so men in the line represented Christ to her. The dignity they still possessed was theirs because Christ had dignified and ennobled human nature by sharing in it. The example of Christ, who himself nourished and comforted his disciples, was remarked upon through use of the pericope regarding the fish breakfast on the shores of Galilee (cf. Jn 21). Dorothy queried: "How often is Our Lord's love shown in these little ways?"[16] The corollary for Dorothy was that all are to do likewise: to show love for Christ through love for others.

The works of mercy were but a part of the overall Catholic Worker program, though an important one. While trying to change the social order, to build a new civilization "within the shell of the old," Catholic Workers were simultaneously to "perform the Works of Mercy and take care of our brothers in need." Dorothy considered that there was always more study to be done, a long-range view to take, in order to understand how far-reaching the works of mercy could be. As late as February 1979 she regretted that more could not be done: "we are so busy with the corporal works of mercy that we often neglect the spiritual ones."[17] A spirit of personal responsibility, of personal sacrifice, was concomitant with such outreach. Thus, from the outset, Dorothy associated the practice of the works of mercy with a life of voluntary poverty. This was to serve both as witness to and an identification with the poor as brothers and sisters. Over the years Dorothy viewed the Catholic Worker's dependence on the good will of others for donations as an important part of this witness. Once, when considering the possibility that they would not be able to continue their work because of lack of funds or goods, she saw themselves as participants in the defenseless portion of the poor. Should there be no more bread, she argued, there would be no bread riot, for the men see our own poverty. They know we eat the same breakfast they do. So if we had to stop, they would come, that sad morning, and receiving the tragic message, would go their way, dejected, cold and empty of body and soul. . . . But patient, with the unbearably pathetic patience of the poor.[18]

By extension, the works of mercy were seen to be the opposite of the works of war. A pacifist prior to the foundation of the Catholic Worker, Dorothy found herself almost immediately in anti-war work, some of which later took Dorothy and other Catholic Workers to jail. Given their situation, Dorothy related it to the works of mercy: "Going to jail is a spiritual work of mercy—visiting the prisoner on a grass roots level." Moreover, her opposition of the work of love to the works of violence can be traced from the early days of the movement. In 1937 for instance, she stated: "We do not believe that love can be expressed by tear gas or police clubs, by airplane bombardments and wholesale slaughter." By the 1960s she had come to juxtapose firmly the works of mercy over against the works of war, and in 1976 still asserted strongly: "The works of mercy, which Our Lord told us in the Gospels were the criteria by which we will be judged, are the opposite of the works of war." The publication of the paper itself was viewed as part of the Catholic Worker platform which hinged on Matthew 25, seen as trying to bring Christ into all areas of life:

> we have picketed ever since we started, in 1933, trying to bring the message of the church into the marketplace, as St. Paul did. Since the rule we try to follow in our active life is doing the works of mercy, which means not only feeding the hungry, but sheltering the harborless, clothing the naked, visiting the sick, the prisoner, burying the dead, but also enlightening the ignorant, we put the publication of the paper, our going out into the street and carrying picket signs, and posters, giving out leaflets, and even on occasion going to jail as part of the works of mercy.[19]

Importance of the *Imitation of Christ*

As Dorothy admitted, the *Imitation of Christ* was a book that "followed me through my days." Over and again she came across copies of the *Imitation*. The reading of it never failed to give her comfort, while it simultaneously created in her a hunger for God and for a certainty of faith. It was, she asserted, one of the books on the spiritual life which had been instrumental in her conversion. She first came across this popular devotional work when reading *The Mill on the Floss* as a requirement for a high school course. George Eliot's fictional character, Maggie Tulliver, found solace in the *Imitation* during an adolescent religious crisis, which was reason enough for Dorothy to begin reading it too. There is sufficient evidence from her writings to warrant the conclusion that she identified with the female protagonist of Eliot's work, and quite possibly, for a time, with Eliot herself, who had rejected formal religion.[20]

Dorothy's next known contact with the *Imitation* was in her late twenties, during the sojourn with her sister Della in New Orleans. Whenever Dorothy had no evening writing assignment for the *New Orleans Item,* she would slip across the street to attend evening devotions and benediction at St. Louis Cathedral. In recollections of this period, Dorothy questioned whether or not she felt the eucharistic Presence, but did recall some lines of the *Imitation.* This argues for her having either committed passages to memory as an adolescent or, what is more plausible, a then current rereading of the spiritual classic. The lines she recalled at that time were from Book IV of the work:

> Who, humbly approaching to the fountain of sweetness,
>   doth not carry thence some little sweetness?
> Who, standing by a copious fire, doth not derive therefrom
>   some little heat?[21]

These lines may be placed in the larger context of that chapter, which is a meditation on the advantages of sacramental reception of the Eucharist. As may be confirmed for a number of instances, Dorothy felt and spoke of a continuous hunger and thirst for God and for God in Christ throughout her life. Unaffiliated with either the Episcopalian or Catholic communion at this time, Dorothy was unable to receive the Eucharist sacramentally. Hence the poignancy of the lines which immediately follow the above passage:

> You, Lord, are the Fountain of all sweetness,
>   the Fire always burning and never failing.
> Therefore, though I may not draw from the fullness
>   of that fountain or drink from it to the full,
> I will refresh my thirst,
>   so that I shall not be all dried up.[22]

Throughout her pregnancy with Tamar (summer 1925 through early March 1926) and the first months of her daughter's life Dorothy turned to the *Imitation* a great deal and prayed for the gift of faith. However, while affirming faith as a gift, she asserted that "one had to want it, had to pray for it, and hunger for it, as I had been doing ever since I read the *Confessions* of St. Augustine and the *Imitation of Christ.*"[23] During the interim between Tamar's July 1926 baptism and Dorothy's own in December 1927, the mother derived strength and comfort primarily from the *Imitation* and St. Augustine's *Confessions.*

The certainty that Dorothy never abandoned her interest in the *Imitation* may be garnered from incidental remarks of her later years. Excerpts from the *Imitation* occurred frequently in the *Catholic Worker* during the 1940s, at which time Dorothy had become involved in a retreat movement based on the Ignatian Exercises. In retreat notes dated 20 July 1943 she remarked on the joy and comfort that the *Imitation* had brought to thousands and counted it among the books recommended by the leaders of the retreat. It is evident from this same manuscript that the work had recently been used at the New York Catholic Worker house as table reading, by then an established custom. Throughout the years a number of selected passages appeared in the *Catholic Worker* pages, with several references being made to Book III, chapter 5: "Of the Marvelous Effect of the Love of God." In a published response to the editors of the *Christian Century* in 1963, Dorothy listed the *Imitation* as being among nine of the works which did most to shape her vocational attitude and her philosophy of life. In later years it continued to make its way into her "On Pilgrimage" column. In the July–August 1976 edition of the *Catholic Worker* she referred to it as "that old classic scorned by some eminent theologians today." As late as January and May 1979 she recalled persons (one of whom was her brother John) who had recently brought her a copy of that "lovely little book, long a favorite with me."[24]

What appeal could this work have held for Dorothy over so long a period? True, literary characters well known to Dorothy had read it: Maggie Tulliver, who was consoled by it, and Pierre in Tolstoy's *War and Peace,* who turned to it after fighting a nearly fatal duel. Beyond this, however, the answer lay within the pages of the *Imitation* itself. The work is replete with Scripture, having as it does some eight hundred fifty scriptural passages either quoted or alluded to in the four books. It was written as a series of meditations whose purpose was to deepen one's interior or spiritual life. While insisting on compunction for sins and a filial fear of God, it recalls as well that the fruit of such sorrow is confidence and joy. This confidence rests in God's grace, through which all growth in Christian life is possible. Devotion to Christ in the Eucharist receives a great deal of emphasis, comprising the entire fourth book. All of these elements would have been important to Dorothy.

As a devotional work the *Imitation* offered a type of map for the spiritual life and in traditional fashion included sorrow for sin and gratitude for God's forgiveness and unconditional love. In the darkness and uncertainty of adolescence and young adulthood, such assurance offered solace to an ardent seeker after life such as Dorothy was. Although Book IV offers a limited perspective on the Eucharist and may be read as a privatized spirituality, the quality which Dorothy brought to her reading of it was an initial sense of communal worship during her Episcopal years, a sense which was later informed by her contact with the Catholic liturgical renewal from 1934 onwards. While she was unable to find a complete spiritual synthesis in the *Imitation,* nonetheless she discovered many nuggets of Christian wisdom therein, not the least of which was the reminder that "On the day of judgment we will not be asked what we have read, but what we have done; not how well we have discoursed, but how religiously we have lived."[25]

St. Augustine's *Confessions*

The *Confessions* of St. Augustine was the third of that trilogy of Christian literature which encouraged and supported Dorothy's conversion to Catholicism and which informed and enriched her spirituality for the rest of her life. As with the *Imitation,* she began reading the *Confessions* in her teen years. This was at age fifteen, when experiencing pubescent mood swings and an awakening of sexual desire. She confided to a school friend, Henrietta, both her restlessness and a "continual strife" over what she perceived as a dichotomy between human love and love of God. She was troubled that it was

> wrong to think so much about human love. All those feelings and cravings that come to us are sexual desires. . . . It is sensual and God is spiritual. We must harden ourselves to these feelings, for God is love and God is all, so the only love is of God and is spiritual without taint of earthliness. I am afraid that I have never really experienced this love

or I would never crave the sensual love or the thrill that comes with the meeting of lips.[26]

"This love" which Dorothy felt she had never experienced did not at that time include the consciousness of a possible reconciliation and ordering of all loves in God. Dorothy recognized in hindsight that her family members were physically undemonstrative, and she believed that made them [her] more intense, more sensual, and more conscious of the body that they [she] denied. She contrasted this with other families and friends, such as Henrietta, who were fresh and spontaneous in their affection. As a result, she felt that "this conflict [over the meaning and expression of love] was to go on for years."[27]

Dorothy took this conflict to her reading of Augustine. While she did not express herself in the same terms as he did, she struggled with the very concerns which had tormented Augustine more than fifteen hundred years before her: God's love for each of us, our love for God, rightly ordered human love, and the problem of good and evil. As with Augustine, Dorothy had been responsive from her youth to the gamut of human emotions as well as to beauty in all of its forms, particularly in nature, in music, and in human beings.

A fragment from an unpublished manuscript sheds greater light on her reading of Augustine during her search for God in New Orleans in early 1924 and during her stay at the Staten Island cottage from 1925–1929. She claimed to have externally put aside interest in religion since age sixteen, but by age twenty-six she no longer rejected religion as contrary to the struggle to advance the cause of the poor and suffering. She felt by then that the world needed more profound forces to perfect it, more saving grace to heal it, and in her own heart turned again to religion for happiness. This included a rereading of the New Testament, the *Imitation,* and the *Confessions,* and an acceptance of instruction and baptism.[28]

While living at the Staten Island beach Dorothy discovered that joy and beauty brought her to a sense of faith. Only later did she admit that her conversion began many years ago, at a time when, like Augustine, the material world around her began to speak in her heart of the love and goodness of God. She reflected at length on a lyrical passage from the *Confessions* (X.6) in which the saint noted how every created being spoke to him of the Creator.[29] Augustine both consoled and challenged her torpidity of heart:

I was living the life of a hermit [in the relative quiet of her Staten Island beach house] for a few months and had had time to read, and at that time, the book was St. Augustine. The story of his past life and his turning from that life, had struck me and I knew that I had reached a turning point in my own life. (It took me two years to get on the right road. I continued the free life I was leading then, living with a man I loved dearly, and expecting a child, joyfully. It was a naturally good life, but I had no right to it and I knew it.)

St. Augustine spoke to my condition, but I did not for some years change it.[30]

In addition to what became her favorite passage from the *Confessions* (X.6), Dorothy treasured the conversation of Augustine and Monica at Ostia (X.11). These lines, in which Augustine recalled their fleeting glimpse of the joys of heaven, were never forgotten by Dorothy, nor the promise that the joy of full union with God is beyond all present comprehension. She admitted that

I did not know then [while at the beach], as I know now, that in a way, it does not enter into the heart to understand the love of God, that over and over again it comes, this quality of in-loveness when we see an individual as God sees him, in all his beauty, and all the earth seems transformed. . . . Suddenly all around me the world has lightened, the fog has lifted, the air has cleared and one understands what man is capable of becoming and in how many ways he is indeed an image of God.[31]

Further on in this same fragment, she explained an Augustinian insight later expressed by an unidentified priest [Father Louis Farina], with which she concurred. It was offered in response to a young woman, possibly reminiscent to Dorothy of her younger self, who found herself continually falling in love with one and the other young men of the Catholic Worker. It is an instance of how Dorothy had come by then to understand that love is God's gift, and that the experience of the young woman's falling in love "was an overflowing of her own very real love for God which kept trying to find, blindly, objects for this so strong love which was present in her heart. Her own perceptions of God's love were so keen that it overflowed into her own physical life."[32]

Up until 1933, Dorothy had read only Augustine's *Confessions*. Through the influence of the retreat movement in later decades, her choice of Augustine as a spiritual guide was confirmed and further elucidated.

NINETEENTH-CENTURY RUSSIAN LITERATURE

The Works of Fyodor Dostoevsky

Russian authors had a profound effect on Dorothy. Of these, Dostoevsky's works took first place in her attention, both in her published and unpublished writings, and appeared to have had the greatest influence upon her life and way of thinking. This Russian author's fiction spoke to her of commonalities in human experience, and bringing a certain vicarious quality to all that she read, she suffered and rejoiced with the complex figures that peopled his novels. Like Kirilov in *The Possessed,* she felt that she had been haunted by God all of her life. Raskolnikov's turning to the gospels while in Siberia in *Crime and Punishment* forever endeared this character to her heart. However, it was Father Zossima's counsels and his reminiscences to Aloysha in *The Brothers Karamazov* which were emblazoned most deeply on her memory.[33]

Such selective choices of text came after a lengthy introduction to Dostoevsky's fiction as a whole. Though she read everything of Dostoevsky she could obtain while in high school and college, this reading was rather mechanical by Dorothy's later standards. During her 1921–1923 sojourn in Chicago, she was again reading her favorite Russian, at the encouragement of an unnamed friend. A clue to the state of her mind and heart at this period may be found in a work ostensibly written for her youngest brother John: "I was moved to the depths of my being by the reading of these books [Dostoevsky's novels] during my early twenties when I, too, was tasting the bitterness and the dregs of life and shuddered at its harshness and cruelty."[34] Another cryptic remark, that she entered into this rereading "with an understanding of men and suffering"[35] barely hints at what she had experienced since leaving college in the spring of 1916. In the interim there had been five years or more of life experiences which had left an indelible mark on her personality.

An indefatigable novel reader, Dorothy claimed to have spent the first few winters on the beach with the works of Dostoevsky, Tolstoy, and Dickens. This would have included the winter of 1925–1926 without question. During the period of her immediate preparation for acceptance into the Catholic church (spring 1926 through December 1927), it is uncertain that she read Dostoevsky, though she credited both him and Huysmans—"what different men!"—with having given her background.[36]

An examination of the pages of the *Catholic Worker* and other later references in Dorothy's writings attest to the fact that her interest in Dostoevsky never waned. By the May 1934 edition of the paper, she had prevailed upon Peter Maurin to arrange the sayings of the elder Zossima in the essay style which had become the hallmark of Maurin's writing. In her last "On Pilgrimage" column, she remarked simply that a dramatization of *Crime and Punishment* was scheduled to begin on TV the very evening of her writing.[37] Between these two references lay some forty-six years of reflection on the ethical and spiritual themes which were central to Dostoevsky's works. The selection of favored texts which she made over the years addressed issues of repentance, forgiveness of sins, the supreme dignity of the human person made in the image of Christ, and love for God shown in love for others, especially toward the poor. Though she did not imitate Dostoevsky in his extreme idealization of the poor, exemplified by the Russian peasant, his writings served her as a forceful reminder of the basic goodness of the human person. Political problematics and other biases of Dostoevsky's works, as for example his anti-Roman Catholic and anti-American cast of thought, had little if any bearing on what Dorothy brought to or garnered from these texts. Her reading was colored by her own perspective. Interested primarily in people rather than ideologies, she looked for a personal message, a relational one. She consistently regarded Dostoevsky as spiritual reading and turned to his works as she turned to other key texts for enlightenment and encouragement: "I do not think I could have carried on with a loving heart all these years without Dostoyevsky's understanding of poverty, suffering and drunkenness."[38] While at no point did Dorothy offer a systematic or sustained commentary on Dostoevsky's works, her attraction to various portions of his writing, and what she extracted from them, reveal much about her spirituality.

In addition to the four great novels, she alluded regularly to the whole range of Dostoevsky's writings, including his *Journal of an Author, The Friend of the Family, The Honest Thief, The Insulted and the Injured,* and *The House of the Dead.* Incidental comments about

two of these lesser-known works are illustrative of her thinking. The
first gives a clue to the motivating force behind all of her writing:

> It [*The Insulted and the Injured*] is the story of a young author—it
> might be Dostoevski himself—of the success of his first book, and of
> how he read it aloud to his foster father. The father said, "It's simply
> a little story, but it wrings your heart. What's happening all around
> you grows easier to understand and to remember, and you learn that
> the most down-trodden, humblest man is a man, too, and a brother."
> I thought as I read those words, "That is why *I* write."[39]

Not only did writing afford Dorothy a vehicle for communication,
but it was a means of expressing that active love for others, of which
Dostoevsky spoke, particularly in *The Brothers Karamazov*. In recognizing her vocation as a writer, Dorothy continued to exercise a suasive
influence on the minds and hearts of her readers and to remind or
lead them to the realization that all persons are brothers and sisters
in Christ.

A second passage centers around the question of meaningful work.
It is helpful to recall that the *Catholic Worker* itself had been initiated
in the depths of the economic depression, as a way of reaching the
worker. Both Dorothy and Peter Maurin shared the Benedictine approach to work, which confirmed its necessity and which respected the
dignity and creativity of the person. Dostoevsky addressed the same
issue in *The House of the Dead,* his thinly disguised memoir, and the
message was not lost on Dorothy. In one of her columns, she spoke
of her granddaughter, then employed on an assembly line of a small
factory. Dorothy unhesitatingly rejected this labor as debilitating and
useless. Such a situation remined her of Dostoevsky's memoir, which
she had first read as a young woman: "In *The House of the Dead,*
Dostoevsky called attention to the torture of useless works. He had
suffered it himself during his imprisonment in Siberia."[40] Here is an
instance where Dorothy exercised her gift of bringing previously written material—in this case a nineteenth-century reminiscence—to bear
upon a contemporary situation, in terms of an existent person. Her
comment is to be placed in the context of her understanding of the
memoir as a whole. Long a part of her library, Dorothy credited this
work as having provided her with information on life in prison.[41] Biographical as it is, *The House of the Dead* gives an intimate portrayal
of Dostoevsky's imprisonment in Siberia from 1850 to 1854. It tells

of the cruelty of the prison system, of unexpected kindnesses, and of
the suffering and solidarity of the oppressed. Despite the terror, these
memoirs show Dostoevsky's faith in human nature, even under the most
degraded circumstances. They provided Dorothy with a supplemen-
tary, nonscriptural reminder that Christ was to be found in every single
person she met.

The Four Great Novels

Of all the works of Dostoevsky, excerpts from and references to
characters in the four great novels appeared as a type of refrain in much
of Dorothy's writings. One such character was Kirilov, of *The Possessed,*
who commanded Dorothy's attention because of his death by suicide.
She expressed no direct association with her own supposed earlier suicide attempt(s), yet she drew another parallel between his life and her
own: both were haunted by God. Without giving autobiographical
detail, she reflected on Kirilov whenever a current situation warranted
it. One such occasion was the Vietnam protest suicide of Roger LaPorte
on 9 November 1965. Though she made no connection of attitudes
between the two, LaPorte's death reminded her of Kirilov:

> I remember how Kirilov, in Dostoievsky's *The Possessed,* took his own
> life, in this case as his supreme denial of the existence of God, to dem-
> onstrate to the world his conviction that man is not *created,* that his
> life is his own and he can lay it down as he pleases. Kirilov is the su-
> preme literary example of self-will and self-deification.[42]

Her comments on LaPorte affirm that she believed with Catholic teaching that, objectively viewed, suicide is a sin. She enlarged upon this
however, asserting that "mercy and loving kindness dictated another
judgment: that anyone who took his life was temporarily unbalanced
. . . and so absolved of guilt."[43] Also recalling the death by suicide of
ten persons she knew while young in the Catholic faith, her remarks
were again nonjudgmental, regretting only that the "dear dead" she
once knew had been without the gift of a living faith. Reflecting elsewhere on the mystery of life and death, she noted that God is a God
of mercy, who knows our capabilities far more than we ourselves and
who "reads all the secrets of the heart."[44] In this same excerpt she contrasted the atheistic death of Kirilov with that of LaPorte and others,
who "took their lives, setting themselves aflame, to suffer with those

victims of war in napalm, to be themselves, victims, rather than execu-
tioners. Certainly the motive was love. And who can look into the heart
of another?"[45] Dorothy's brushes with death had taught her a great
deal about the complexity of the human psyche, and of the merciful
goodness of God.

Dorothy found a more positive exemplification of the genius of
Dostoevsky in the figure of Raskolnikov. Though not mentioned frequently in Dorothy's writings, he merits a place in terms of the impression he made upon her. For the fictional character of *Crime and
Punishment* as well as for Dorothy, the Scriptures were instrumental
in their conversions. Long after the fact Dorothy recalled how reading
this novel as a young woman drew her to reflect upon the New Testament; the scene in which Sonya read the story of the raising of Lazarus
to the condemned murderer Raskolnikov overwhelmed her with the
power of the Word of God; finally, his taking the New Testament with
him to Siberia heralded his regeneration, and provided him with solace, much as Scripture did for Dorothy.[46]

The character of Prince Myshkin of *The Idiot* captured Dorothy's
imagination as well. The prince, an epileptic, was Dostoevsky's idealization of a Christlike figure. Myshkin is portrayed as the holy fool, a
childlike character who wins all hearts by his very simplicity. Dorothy's
reflections on Myshkin center on two areas: the difficulty of portraying
the saint, and a belief in the redemptive value of beauty. Of the first,
she wrote:

> In all secular literature it has been so difficult to portray the good man,
> the saint, that a Don Quixote is a fool; the Prince Myschkin [*sic*] is an
> epileptic, in order to arouse the sympathy of the reader, appalled by
> unrelieved sanctity.[47]

Here, Dorothy considered Dostoevsky's works in the category of secular literature, though elsewhere she referred to them as spiritual reading because of the intensity and pervasive quality of their religious
themes. It did not occur to Dorothy at the time that the portrait of
the monk Zossima (*The Brothers Karamazov*) was in essence one of
"unrelieved sanctity." This points to an underlying difficulty Dorothy
faced in her own life. While the religious professional, such as the monk,
was expected to be holy, the same expectation was not extended to the
average lay person. The retreat movement later assisted her in coming

to realize that the gospel extends a universal call to holiness, rather than one limited to religious professionals.

Occurring with a frequency second only to Dorothy's references to Zossima's teaching on love in action, is the reminder of the redemptive value of beauty which Dostoevsky placed on the lips of Prince Myshkin. As she recalled in 1968, "'The world will be saved by beauty,' Dostoievsky says in *The Idiot*. And certainly beauty lifts the mind and heart to God."[48] Beauty and goodness were two values which held a lifelong attraction for Dorothy. It may well be that the key to her fidelity in living among and caring for "the lame, the halt and the blind" was that rare quality of being able to find beauty even in its most hidden guise:

> Christ is always with us, asking for room in our hearts.
> But now it is with the voice of our contemporaries that he speaks. . . .
> It would be foolish to pretend that it is easy always to remember this. If everyone were holy and handsome, with "alter Christus" shining in neon lighting from them, it would be easy to see Christ in everyone. . . . He is disguised under every type of humanity that treads the earth.[49]

Ever responsive to beauty, as an adolescent she had sought and found it on walks among the poor neighborhoods of Chicago's West Side. Like Augustine, every delight of the senses, all beauty spoke to her of God. She also associated beauty with the Catholic Worker's commitment to Maurin's Benedictine-inspired program of "Cult, Culture and Cultivation." As Dorothy understood it, the program involved a life of voluntary poverty, as well as a synthesis of prayer, intellectual productivity, and manual labor. It was in such a setting that Dorothy envisioned that beauty and joy could flourish.[50] In addition, she counted among her friends persons such as Thomas Merton, Helene Iswolsky, and William Oleksak, who shared her appreciation for the beautiful in literature and the arts.

Among the novels Dorothy found the most nourishment from the pages of *The Brothers Karamazov*. Each reading of Ivan Karamazov's struggle with the problem of evil touched upon an area to which she had been sensitized from youth. The appeal of heroic service, and of sanctity, merged with her lifelong questions regarding the presence of evil in the world:

Why was so much done in remedying the evil instead of avoiding it in the first place? There were day nurseries for children, for instance, but why didn't fathers get money enough to take care of their families so that the mothers would not have to go out to work? There were hospitals to take care of the sick and infirm, and, of course, doctors were doing much to prevent sickness, but what of occupational diseases, and the diseases which came from not enough food for the mother and children? What of the disabled workers who received no compensation but only charity for the rest of their lives?

. . . Where were the saints to try to change the social order, not just to minister to the slaves but to do away with slavery?[51]

While in the novel Ivan Karamazov argued with his brother Aloysha Karamazov on the problem of evil related to God's permissive will, and used the suffering of children as a case in point, he was less moved by the argument than determined to use it as a philosophical basis for his rejection of God. The problem of the fictional Ivan was taken seriously by Dorothy. She viewed him as having profoundly rejected the harmony Christ died to bring because he found the sufferings of children a stumbling block. Dorothy's most personal reflection on this problem was written in her sixty-ninth year:

> there were, and always will be, great gaps in my understanding of such questions as the problem of evil in the world and God's permission of it. I cringe still at Ivan Karamazov's portrayal of "a God that permits" the torture of children, such as is going on today in the burning alive of babies in Vietnam. Theologians debate situation ethics and the new morality (leaving out of account the problem of means and ends) while the screams of the flaming human torches, civilian and soldiers, rise high to heaven. The only conclusion I have ever been able to reach is that we must pray God to increase our faith, a faith without which one cannot love or hope. "Lord, I believe, help thou my unbelief."[52]

This excerpt reveals two of Dorothy's qualities: her ability to take an abstract argument and apply it, with feeling, to a contemporary situation and the faculty to live in faith with questions for which she had no final answers.

Ivan Karamazov may be taken as the foil to the deep faith of the elder Zossima, in whom, of all the figures in Dostoevsky's works, Dorothy found the greatest food for reflection. As she once remarked in a 1972 interview, "the whole section on Fr. Zossima [in *The Brothers Kara-*

mazov] made me feel the profound importance of religion."[53] Dorothy's references to Zossima clustered primarily around the mysterious visitor of his recollections, portions of Zossima's discourses and sermons and, most importantly, his teaching on love in action. A word about these is in order.

While working on the manuscript for her book, *Therese,* Dorothy took extensive notes, some of which never appeared in the published work. One such passage was a reflection on "the ruthlessness of the Little Flower in her search for God. . . . Nothing was to come between her and the love of God."[54] In order to illustrate the relationship between this intense love of God and a concomitant love of neighbor, Dorothy felt it necessary to juxtapose Thérèse's singlemindedness with Dostoevsky's reflection on the "brotherhood of man" as placed on the lips of the mysterious visitor in *The Brothers Karamazov:*

> How hard it was for me to understand the Little Flower can be understood when you put into juxtaposition St. Therese and Dostoievsky, and the ideas that had so powerfully influenced me in Dostoievsky.
>
> The greatest idea was that of the brotherhood of man. Even before I was Catholic I had read how the older St. Teresa had said that you could not show your love for God except through love for your brother.
>
> Here is something I read in Dostoievsky [.] It was right after Father Zossima, that great character in *The Brothers Karamazov* had discovered the idea that we are all responsible for the sins of all. He is talking to a friend [the mysterious visitor] and this friend tells him:
>
> "This dream (of human brotherhood) will come to pass without doubt; it will come but not now, for every process has its law. It's a spiritual, psychological process. To transform the world, to recreate it afresh, men must turn into another path psychologically. Until you have become really, in actual fact, a brother to everyone, brotherhood will not come to pass. No sort of scientific teaching, no kind of common interest, will ever teach men to share property and privileges with equal consideration for all. Everyone will think his share too small and they will be always envying, complaining and attacking one another. You ask when it will come to pass; it will come to pass, but first we have to go [th]rough the period of isolation. . . . the isolation that prevails everywhere, above all in our age — it has not fully developed, it has not reached its limit yet. For everyone strives to keep his individuality as apart as possible, wishes to secure the greatest possible fullness of life for himself; but meanwhile all his efforts result not in attaining fullness

of life but self destruction, for instead of self realization he ends by arriving at complete solitude. All mankind in our age have split up into units, they all keep apart, each in his own groove; each one holds aloof, hides himself and hides what he has from the rest, and he ends by being repelled by others and repelling them. He heaps up riches by himself and thinks, 'how strong I am now and how secure,' and in his madness he does not understand that the more he heaps up, the more he sinks into self destructive impotence. For he is accustomed to rely upon himself alone and to cut himself off from the whole; he has trained himself not to believe in the help of others, in men and in humanity, and only trembles for fear he should lose his money and the privileges he has won for himself. Everywhere in these days men have ceased to understand that the true security is to be found in social solidarity rather than in isolated individual effort. But this terrible individualism must inevitably have an end, and all will suddenly understand how unnaturally they are separated from one another. It will be the spirit of the time, and people will marvel that they have sat so long in darkness and have not seen the light. And then the sign of the Son of Man will be seen in the heavens. . . . But until then we must keep the banner flying. Sometimes even if he has to do it alone, and his conduct seems to be crazy, a man must set an example, and so draw men's souls out of their solitude, and spur them to some act of brotherly love, that the great idea may not die."[55]

While the manuscript fragment left off at the end of this passage, Dorothy's intent may be understood by focusing on the point she made just prior to the lengthy quotation from Dostoevsky. It confirmed by way of illustration that of all the concepts in Dostoevsky which had influenced her, she considered that "the greatest idea was that of the brotherhood of man."[56] According to Zossima's visitor, with whom Dorothy concurred, the realization of this ideal depends upon the personal responsibility of each individual for its achievement. True security is to be found, not in self-aggrandizement, nor in hoarding of possessions, but in social solidarity. Solitude, in the sense of individualism, is negatively compared with the dimensions of a community spirit. Seen in this light, the Catholic Worker ideal, along with Dorothy's remarks regarding community elsewhere in her writings, may be read as a movement from selfishness to a fulfillment of the two great commandments to love.

Portions from Zossima's discourses and sermons upon which Dorothy reflected develop the message of the mysterious visitor still further:

love for the sinner, though not for the sin; a mystic awareness of the divine presence; the power of good example over judgment of another human being; the redemptive value of vicarious suffering; the path to true freedom through denial of the false self; the contrast of false solitude with that of the monk who lives his vocation.[57] More than all of these, however, Dorothy found the greatest inspiration from Zossima's counsel regarding love in action. As it appeared in Dostoevsky, a certain Mrs. Khokhlakov approached the elder with a problem of faith. In response to her scruples, the monk counseled the exercise of an active love of others in which self-deception and cowardliness are overcome. He maintained that in contrast with romantic love which demanded immediate results, active love entailed hard work and perseverance. Moreover, at the very moment when one seemed furthest from the goal of genuine love, he or she would attain not only that goal but would also behold the miraculous power of the Lord, who had been loving and mysteriously guiding that person all along. Dorothy's shorthand for the entire passage was her oft quoted, "Love in practice is a harsh and dreadful thing compared to love in dreams." By such frequent usage, others began to ascribe it to her rather than to Dostoevsky, though for Dorothy it was an answer to her scripturally based query: how can we love God whom we have not seen, without love for those whom we do see?[58]

In one of her frequent reflections on the commandment to love, she recalled both scriptural passages and the aforementioned passage from Dostoevsky. The comments which followed are revelatory of the depth of her commitment to love:

> There are some people whom it is easy to love. God in his goodness has given the heart of man the capacity for human love and it is good to compare this love between a betrothed man and woman and the love we are to bear each other. Love makes all things easy. When one loves, there is at that time a correlation between the spiritual and the material. Even the flesh itself is energized, the human spirit is made strong. All sacrifice, all suffering is easy for the sake of love. A mother will endure all-night vigils by the bedside of a sick child. With every child that is born to her, born in anguish that is quickly forgotten, all too small a price to pay, her heart is enlarged to take another in. Strength and endurance and courage are granted to her with the love she bears those near and dear to her. . . .
>
> If natural love can be so great, and we must remember that grace

builds upon nature, then how great should be the supernatural love
we should bear our fellows. . . .

This is the foundation stone of The Catholic Worker movement.
It is on this that we build. Because of love we embrace voluntary poverty
and the Works of Mercy, those two means of showing our love for our
fellows.[59]

Dorothy expressed the implications inherent in Zossima's counsel to love in action with a candor that was based on reality. She believed that to be a saint is to be a lover and that the privilege entails
both devotion and sacrifice. Though as she aged, and admitted that
love in practice became harder, she nonetheless remained firm in her
commitment, still asserting that, "It is good then to remember—to
clutch to our aching hearts those sayings of Fr. Zossima—'Love in practice is a harsh and dreadful thing compared to love in dreams.'"[60]

The Works of Leo Tolstoy

While Dorothy's references to Dostoevsky overshadow those made
to other renowned authors such as Tolstoy, nonetheless the effect of
the latter's literary and moral sensibilities upon her merits some consideration as well. Her first acquaintance with Tolstoy coincided with
her introduction to Dostoevsky in high school and in college. Her reading raised questions, yet she never ceased to believe in God:

> The Russian writers appealed to me too, and I read everything of Dos-
> toevski, as well as the stories of Gorki and Tolstoi. Both Dostoevski and
> Tolstoi made me cling to a faith in God, and yet I could not endure
> feeling an alien in it. I felt that my faith had nothing in common with
> that of Christians around me.[61]

Dorothy gave no indication as to which stories of Tolstoy occupied her
during these years, but only that they disturbed her at the same time
that they offered her consolation. Tolstoy aroused in her a still unful-
filled hope of a Christianity shown in good works, the exemplification
of faith in action. While at the university she failed to find anyone
with a vital faith who was at the same time articulate, nor did she
meet anyone "whose personal morality was matched by a social morality or who tried to make life here for others a foretaste of the life to
come."[62]

The next clearly identifiable time that she turned her attention to Tolstoy was in the summer of 1917, when she and Michael Gold read and discussed their mutual regard for the author. As she wrote some twenty years later, both Gold and Tolstoy recalled to her a remembrance of spiritual things. In her own words, "We were both reading Tolstoi at the time and were thoroughly in sympathy with the Christianity he expressed, the Christianity that dispensed with a church and a priesthood."[63] This was during the period (1914–1927) when she had no formal church affiliation, having encountered what she judged to be nominal Christianity on the part of churchgoers. However, Dorothy remembered Michael Gold telling her that her "religious instinct" was very much in evidence during these years.[64]

Dorothy's recollection of a difficult jail experience in Chicago, during July of 1922, brought back another remembrance of Tolstoy:

> Before, I had merely read about prison life and had agreed with Tolstoi that such punishment of criminals was futile when we were guilty for permitting such a system as ours to exist and that we, too, should bear the penalty for the crimes committed by those unfortunate ones. We all formed part of one body, a social body, and how could any limb of that body commit a crime alone?[65]

Setting Dorothy's thoughts in context may be helpful. She had been mistakenly arrested under suspicion of prostitution, along with a companion, Mae Cramer. Dorothy had merely been trying to help Cramer when the latter was recovering from a suicide attempt. The two women had been jailed with a group of prostitutes, whom Dorothy referred to as "those unfortunate ones." Her comment on the situation is a strong argument in favor of her having already read Tolstoy's *Resurrection*. This novel contains a portrayal of the Russian prison system, and centers around the trial of a prostitute. The story line rested on the realization of the main character, Prince Dmitry Nekhlyudov, that he is personally though indirectly responsible for the crime committed by the defendant, Katerina Maslova, with whom he had fallen in love and seduced a number of years previously.

During the first few winters of her 1925–1929 beach period, Dorothy read the novels of Tolstoy in addition to those of Dostoevsky and Dickens. A comment made more than forty years later indicates that she either read or reread *Anna Karenina* at this time and identified with the character Levin's struggle for faith. She did not positively identify other novels by name, but *Resurrection* and *War and Peace* were likely choices, judging from later remarks about having read them long ago, and the fact that she often returned to *War and Peace* as winter reading.[66]

After the Catholic Worker movement was begun in 1933, Dorothy continued her interest in Tolstoy's writings. Of the novels, she most frequently alluded to *Resurrection* and *War and Peace,* and of the short stories and parables, those having to do with human need and greed. Dorothy encouraged an ongoing study of Russian *literati* and was pleased to report in 1949 that "the first week in September we had Helene Isvolsky at the farm at Newburgh, giving a course on Dostoievsky, Tolstoi and Soloviev, the three great Russians."[67] Due to Dorothy's editorial surveillance, background articles and reviews of books written on Tolstoy appeared with relative frequency in the paper.[68]

From the corpus of Tolstoy's works, Dorothy took the greatest interest in *Resurrection* and *War and Peace.* Her references to each of these novels give some indication of their meaning for her. In the April 1941 issue of the *Catholic Worker,* for instance, she contrasted the relative ease of abstract love over personal love for other human beings as she found it portrayed in the pages of *Resurrection.* The incongruity of the situation struck her forcefully: "He [Tolstoy] tells of political prisoners in a long prison train, enduring chains and persecution for their love for their brothers, ignoring those same brothers on the long trek to Siberia."[69] She had long ago concluded that love is true only if expressed in the concrete situations of everyday life. A protestation of a universal love, of love for humankind, was deemed meaningless if not accompanied by love in action. This love, if not universal in realization, was to be universal in intention, reaching in a particular manner for Dorothy to men and women of the streets. In Tolstoy, as in Dostoevsky, Dorothy read a confirmation of this insight, and an application of the gospel commandment to love.[70] Another reference, found in Dorothy's "On Pilgrimage" column for April 1960, related news of a trip to the Doukhobors in Canada. This religious group's emigration from Russia had been sponsored in part by Tolstoy's gift to them of royalties accrued to *Resurrection.*[71] While most of the article was descriptive of the Doukhobors' situation in 1960, Dorothy had been impressed by Tolstoy's assistance to a group which had been subjected to persecution for striving to live out the ideals of the early Christian community as they understood them. Such assistance was viewed positively by Dorothy as an instance of love in action, in this case, of an author going beyond the pages of a novel in an incarnation of his insights.

By June 1965, Dorothy had reread *Resurrection* again, and her remarks betray a reserve in her appraisal of Tolstoy's genius:

> On reading again Tolstoy's great novel *Resurrection* and encountering that scornful chapter on the celebration of the liturgy in the prison which so saddened me as unworthy of genius, I suddenly thought.[,] "well, if I can put up with this in Tolstoy, I can put up with and not judge Ammon Hennacy."[72]

Earlier in life, Dorothy had sympathized with Tolstoy's approach to a Christianity *sans* priesthood and other institutional structures, but this was no longer the case. Her matured approach diverged greatly from that of the Russian author. For Tolstoy the anarchist, the community of believers could be upheld by belief in Christ and an unmediated interpretation of Scripture. For Dorothy, however, ritual and sacrament were important elements in the expression of her faith. In some sense Tolstoy's was an ideational approach to religion in keeping with an anarchism that sought to do away with institutions. For Dorothy, belief was embodied in tradition, and its expression was mediated through an engagement of the senses:

> Love must be incarnate (expressed by the flesh). One of the things I have always loved about Holy Mother Church is that all the senses and their needs are recognized and used — incense, colorful imagery in ikons and statues, music, processions, with banners, and in our Italian neighborhoods, the celebration of saint intercessors with tiny facsimiles . . . cast in silver to be hung around the saint. Fiestas in the Spanish neighborhoods, festas in the Italian, with the delightful odor of food, meats and doughnuts cooked over charcoal.[73]

By contrast with those of Tolstoy, the works of Dostoevsky admitted the full expression of the Orthodox tradition of worship as well as the validity of the religious professional in the person of the monk. Dorothy was at home in what she considered the fullness of faith's expression, such as that which Dostoevsky represented. This was one factor in Dorothy's greater attraction to the writings of Dostoevsky over those of Tolstoy. Notwithstanding these reservations, *Resurrection* otherwise continued to appeal to her, as another rereading in 1978 in the company of friends attests.[74]

War and Peace, Tolstoy's great novel, was frequently the object of Dorothy's attention. Writing to artist Fritz Eichenberg in 1964, she reminded him that she was again reading *War and Peace* and that the hunting scene with its violence appalled her. In an unpublished 1964 article for *Commonweal,* she found a point of identification with Tolstoy's thought. The context is her discussion that wars are a compulsion put upon men to prove their manhood and that within that compulsion is buried an implicit denial of personal responsibility: "Tolstoi says in *War and Peace* that the reason why many men like army life was because it relieved them of responsibility—hence the phrase, soldiering on the job."[75] Later, viewing the film version in 1968 she found refreshment in the portrayal of the Russian countryside, coupled with a sense of weariness at the interminable battle scenes:

> Helen Iswolsky, our Russian scholar in residence at Tivoli[,] and I both liked those beautiful rural scenes and were exhausted by the hours of battle, Austerlitz on Sunday and Borodino on Monday, the spectacle of tens of thousands of French and Russian soldiers mowed down in that brutal invasion, an invasion duplicated in this century also, and a slaughter which brought home to us what was going on at that very moment in Vietnam.
>
> Undoubtedly the picture will make us go back to reread Tolstoi's masterpiece.[76]

In this instance, Tolstoy's pacifism spoke to her by way of negative illustration.

None of Tolstoy's characters stood out for Dorothy with the same clarity as the *dramatis personae* of Dostoevsky's works. However, she did note two from *War and Peace,* namely Princess Marya Bokonsky and Count Pierre Bezuhov. The hospitality of the Princess Marya to the "pilgrims": the poor, the despised and rejected, spoke to Dorothy much as did Peter Maurin's recognition of the hidden dignity of those whom he called "the ambassadors of God": the downtrodden poor of the Catholic Worker breadline. Dorothy saw past the general timidity of Marya into the motivation behind her service of God's poor. It served as a confirmation for her of the responsibility which was theirs as Christians:

There are too few who will consider themselves servants, who will give up their lives to serving others, who will sow the things of this world, the things of the mind, and of the soul in order to "put on Christ"—to "be Christ" to those around us. . . .

There is too much talk of raising up of *leaders,* and too little of the raising up of servants; or rather, just too much talk, and too little *being* what we are talking about.[77]

Count Pierre Bezuhov, the amiable bungler, struck Dorothy not so much for his muddling through the turmoil of Russia's involvement in the Napoleonic wars (1805–1812), nor for his absorption in Freemasonry, but for the fact that he read the *Imitation.* Dorothy remarked simply that Pierre turned to it after fighting a nearly fatal duel with his wife's lover [Dolohov].[78] For Dorothy, Pierre figured alongside Maggie Tulliver [in *The Mill on the Floss*], as well as with contemporary religious leaders Pope John XXIII, Gandhi, and Vinoba Bhave, all of whom found spiritual sustenance in its pages. In the novel, Pierre, after arriving in Petersburg, received a copy of the work from an unknown source, and spent entire days reading it. The *Imitation* was in part responsible for his conversion, leading him from atheism to belief "in the possibility of attaining perfection, and in the possibility of brotherly and active love between men. . . ."[79] The parallel between Dorothy's life and that of the fictional Pierre lay in the fact that both first came upon the *Imitation* in a period of religious crisis and found in it comfort and guidance. That their subsequent conversions moved in different directions—Pierre to Freemasonry, Dorothy eventually to Catholicism—appeared not to matter to Day. What could not have failed to strike a chord in Dorothy, however, were the possibilities which Pierre's reading of the work held out to him: the attainment of holiness and the exercise of an active love toward others. Both of these were hallmarks of Dorothy's own spirituality.

THE CHRISTIAN PERSONALISTS

It is generally acknowledged that the Christian personalist movement, centered in France and transmitted to Dorothy through Peter Maurin, provided a large portion of the Catholic Worker's intellectual patrimony.[80] The question here is to what extent Christian personalist thinking permeated Dorothy's spirituality. To answer requires an examination of the Christian personalist movement and its principal protagonists, an interpretation of this movement as it appeared within Catholic Worker literature, and most importantly, an evaluation of the impact of Christian personalism upon Dorothy herself.

Emmanuel Mounier

The principal synthesizer of Christian personalism was Emmanuel Mounier, who in 1932 founded the journal *L'Esprit,* mouthpiece of a group of European intellectuals, endeavoring to bring religious values to bear upon moral and social issues of the period. Personalist philosophy recognized the dignity of the human person both as an individual and as a participant member of human society. Though difficult to define precisely, it provided an umbrella of thought which, while conversant with Marxism and existentialism, attempted to offer a Christian alternative for the twentieth century. Christian personalists sought to provide an ideal for Western civilization, a new synthesis which would arise out of the acceptance of Christian and secular critiques of an acquisitive bourgeois spirit. From the Catholic Mounier's perspective, "Comfort is to the bourgeois world what heroism was to the Renaissance and sanctity to medieval Christianity: the final value, the reason for all action."[81]

For Mounier, human civilization was called to move from the complaisance of bourgeois avidity to heroic sanctity, a sanctity which merged the perceived ideals of the middle ages and renaissance while remaining engaged in twentieth-century reality.[82] Mounier advocated the primacy of the spiritual, which, as he understood it, affirmed that the human person is a unity of matter and spirit: "the human person is substantially incarnate, immersed in his flesh although transcending it, as intimately as wine mixes with water."[83] Such a spirituality was oriented to this world as well as to the next and encouraged an engagement of the human person in responsible action. Positive in his anthropology, Mounier valued the human person made in the image of God, and he stressed humankind's potential for growth in freedom and responsibility toward self and others. Neither the individualism of bourgeois, capitalist-oriented society nor the suppression of the human spirit in a totalitarian state respected the dignity of the human person as God intended. The alternative Mounier proposed was a personalist communitarian civilization, where both the person's autonomy and a call to unity were equally respected. For Mounier, the desire for union is implanted in the human person and is an integrating factor of his or her existence. While offering no particulars for the development of a personalist communitarian civilization, Mounier nonetheless enunciated the principle that community or union is based on love between persons rather than political or economic constraint, both of the latter being external to the person. The person rightfully attains spiritual liberty and a genuine sense of community from within, while simultaneously entering into fellowship with others. Such intrinsically based community is attainable only because there is an autonomous self to offer. For Mounier, the life of the "we" must not dispense with the "I," for only by the recognition of person qua person can one posit the existence of genuine community.[84]

By the mid-1930s the pages of the *Catholic Worker* began to offer an interpretation of Christian personalism for predominantly American readers. As early as April 1934 Dorothy reported a related address given by Peter Maurin at a recent evening discussion at the Catholic Worker house in New York. Her article presented no direct allusion to *Esprit,* though the language employed is akin to that of the movement: personal responsibility, recognition of existing disorder, and a lack of discouragement at the prospect that ideals are often unattainable. In March 1935 the French journal was acknowledged by name in the *Catholic Worker.* By the April 1935 issue Maurin devoted one of his easy essays to *Esprit,* recognizing both the international and ecumenical flavor of the publication, and the endeavor of the January issue of the journal to promote the communitarian revolution. For Maurin, the Paris group was attempting "to promote a kind of society where man will be human to man."[85] An unsigned article by Dorothy, appearing that fall, bore the unmistakable signs of her acquaintance with the personalist movement:

> There is a general reluctance among rank and file Catholics to assume the position of leaders in Catholic action. . . . It means that they have lost the sense of what the words collectivism, personalism and individualism mean. Without realizing it, they have gone collective and want to work in a body, organize, go in for mass production of members of this or the other group, and try to achieve things collectively. Or they are individualists and think they can better conditions by looking after themselves first and devil take the hindmost. We are urging our readers to be neither collectivist nor individualist, but *personalist.* This con-

sciousness of oneself as a member of the Mystical Body of Christ will lead to great things.[86]

While for Mournier personalism implied a generic community dimension, Dorothy translated Mounier's insight in terms of membership in the Mystical Body. Mounier presupposed Christian values; Dorothy's Christocentrism was explicit, both in word and in action. Personal responsibility was the keynote of the Catholic Worker's presentation of personalism, and the American movement's expression of responsibility was never far removed from the exercise of the works of mercy. Dorothy's May 1936 editorial underscored both her Christocentrism and disclosed an integration of personalist principles with the practice of the works of mercy:

> Not only is there no chance of knowing Christ without partaking of that Food that He has left us, but also we can't know each other unless we sit down to eat together. We learn to know each other in the breaking of bread. When the stranger comes to us to be fed, we know because Christ told us so, that inasmuch as we have fed one of His hungry ones we have fed Him.
>
> That is why *the most fundamental* point in the Catholic Worker program is emphasizing our personal responsibility to perform works of mercy.[87]

In the same issue, Peter Maurin focused his attention on the communal aspect of the personalist movement. Within his article he recalled that Mounier was editor of *Esprit* and author of the recently published *La Révolution personnaliste et communautaire,* which Maurin again recommended as reading material. He likewise acknowledged Raymond de Becker as leader of the personalist movement in Belgium. Maurin had already begun to translate portions of Mounier for the *Catholic Worker* staff and succeeded in engaging the interest of the Benedictine monks of St. John's Abbey, Collegeville, as well. With the support of the monks of this abbey, notably Virgil Michel, O.S.B., he helped translate Mounier's *Manifeste au service du personnalisme,* which was published as *A Personalist Manifesto* (1938).[88] In a later column, Maurin again addressed personalist communitarianism, defining a personalist as other-centered, a person who through both word and deed brings about "the common unity of a community."[89]

Meanwhile, Dorothy's own interest in the personalist movement continued. An obituary appearing in the August 1936 issue, unsigned, though written by her, says as much about her personalism as about a deceased Father [Monsignor Nelson H.] Baker. She claimed that he was a great example of personal responsibility, a man who loved the poor, truly a leader because he was foremost a servant. With a positive anthropology as genuine as Mounier's she declared: "he [Baker] knew that with the grace of God man was capable of great things." Another unsigned article, again unmistakably Dorothy's, is a clear statement of the penetration of Christian personalism into the Catholic Worker ideal. Dorothy's encouragement of a strong devotion to the personalist revolution indicates a kindred spirit with Mounier, in her positive anthropology and her respect for the person's free will:

> We are working for the Communitarian revolution to oppose both the rugged individualism of the capitalist era, and the collectivism of the Communist revolution. We are working for the Personalist revolution because we believe in the dignity of man, the temple of the Holy Ghost, so beloved by God that He sent His son to take upon Himself our sins and die an ignominious and disgraceful death for us. We are Personalists because we believe that man, a person, a creature of body and soul, is greater than the State, of which as an individual he is a part. We are Personalists because we oppose the vesting of all authority in the hands of the state instead of in the hands of Christ the King. We are Personalists because we believe in free will, and not in the economic determinism of the Communist philosophy.
>
> And it is as Communitarians and as Personalists that we live a community life offering hospitality at St. Joseph's House on Mott Street; it as Communitarians and Personalists that we are running a farming commune at Easton, Pa.[90]

With Maurin, Dorothy viewed the establishment of the farming commune as an application of the principles of the personalist and communitarian revolution. This was no easy task, because they acted without benefit of a select group of experimenters, but with the people who came to them: the blind, the halt, and the lame, in addition to those more able in mind and body.

During the war years and beyond Dorothy's devotion to the spirit of Christian personalism persisted. Aside from her incidental comments, possibly the clearest indication of her personalism may be found in her "Day After Day" column for February 1943. Here she credited Peter Maurin directly for transmitting his personalist and communitarian philosophy to the Catholic Worker. Her own understanding of personalism embraced the importance of knowledge, love, and service of God through love and service of others. She believed that such loving service necessarily led from anthropocentrism to theocentrism: "it follows, that each of us, instead of being self-centered, must try more and more to be God-centered."[91] From a personalist standpoint, she considered that it was through the exercise of responsibility in the living out of her vocation as journalist that the communitarian aspect of the Catholic Worker movement began, in the form of houses of hospitality and farming communes. Like Mounier, she considered a solitude which values the person and his or her need for continual conversion as surety for an authentic community dimension.

After Peter Maurin's death in 1949, Dorothy persisted in her concern that Christian personalism be promoted by the American movement. The 1950 death of Emmanuel Mounier was hailed as a great loss by the members of the Catholic Worker. A tribute given him in the April 1950 edition of the paper noted Mounier's affirmation of the value of the human person and of his or her will. In October of that same year Dorothy welcomed the new periodical *Cross Currents* by printing an article which noted that the first issues promised to feature authors such as Mounier and Nicholas Berdyaev. Over the next three decades she approved personalist-inspired articles such as those written by Jack English and Robert Ludlow, and remarked on personalism in her own columns. Reviews of Mounier in translation as well as later works explaining his thought found a place in the paper as well.[92] When nearly eighty years of age Dorothy still recalled Maurin's association with French radical thinking, the founding of *Esprit,* and the Catholic Worker's efforts to promote Christian personalism:

> Peter Maurin, founder of the Catholic Worker, derived his inspiration, not only from the education he received from the Christian Brothers, but from his contact with French radical thinking. . . .
> . . . [He] kept in touch with such thinkers as Jacques Maritain . . . Peguy was the great influence in the life of Emmanuel Mounier, young student at the Sorbonne who started the magazine *Esprit,* which began publication around the same time as ours, and which led Peter Maurin to translate for us Mounier's "Personalist Manifesto" which was

followed by other articles about revolution, a necessary but nonviolent revolution which Mounier called "the Personalist and Communitarian Revolution."

Peter is dead now. He died in May 1949. But his work bears fruit still.[93]

The influence of Mounier on Dorothy was primarily secondhand. She frequently recalled that it was Peter Maurin who introduced her in the 1930s to the founder of *Esprit*. As with other works that Maurin read, he had developed a certain slogan related to the basic message. In the case of Mounier it had become: "Personal responsibility, not state responsibility," a slogan which Dorothy readily adopted.[94] For Maurin, who had grown up in the farming commune of Oultet, the concept of a localized, personal responsibility was an extension of his early Catholic and communal environment. For Dorothy, biblically motivated from childhood to relieve the sufferings of others, the watchword of personal responsibility was akin to her every desire to think globally regarding issues which affected humankind as a whole, yet to direct her active love to her immediate environment. The proof of this lay in the pages of the *Catholic Worker* itself. Issues treated in its columns revolved around unemployment, just wages, racial and ethnic discrimination, war and peace, and the like. Almost from the start, the dissemination of information through the paper was accompanied by a response to the hungry and homeless all about them. The Catholic Worker program embraced the clarification of thought, the establishment of houses of hospitality, and the establishment of farming communes. The foregoing program was expressed in Maurin's theoretical terms. Dorothy's intuitive genius translated the abstraction into the practice of the works of mercy, viewed as the exercise of personal, Christian responsibility toward others, at a personal sacrifice. Maurin's abstractions, and through him Mounier's, provided a theoretical validation for Dorothy's mode of responding in love to needs as she became aware of them.

Jacques Maritain

Jacques Maritain, whose articulation of integral humanism in the 1930s is nearly identical to Mounier's personalism, had a profound influence on the latter's philosophical and historical criticisms of bourgeois civilization. Maritain encouraged the younger philosopher's decision to found *Esprit* and guided him in the early stages of the journal's history. Beyond his association with Mounier, however, both Jacques Maritain and his wife Raïssa spent extended sojourns in the United States from the mid-1930s until 1960 and were attracted to the spirit of the Catholic Worker movement. As a consequence, both were known to Dorothy by personal acquaintance as well as through their works. Each provided Dorothy with a fuller interpretation of Christian personalism. Again, as with Mounier, it had been Maurin's prerogative to introduce his compatriots to Dorothy and fellow Catholic Workers. In the case of the Maritains, he introduced them first by way of recommending Jacques's thought and second by bridging a language barrier upon the occasion of Jacques's first visit to the New York house.[95]

As early as the December 1933 and February 1934 issues, Maritain's works were recommended to the *Catholic Worker* readers. The December 1934 issue of the paper carried an excerpt from the British periodical the *Colosseum* which featured Maritain's thought on the necessity of conversion of heart as a prerequisite for true social revolution.[96] In the same issue a letter to Peter Maurin appeared in which Maritain acknowledged and expressed appreciation to Maurin, Dorothy, Ade Bethune, and a woman named Margaret for the hospitality which they all extended him on the occasion of his first visit to the New York group in November 1934. This occasion and his other visits to the Catholic Worker were remembered fondly by Dorothy in later years.[97]

Shortly after the 1934 visit Maurin began to feature translations and interpretations of Maritain's writings in his monthly columns. The first of these, beginning in January 1935, was a free translation from portions of *Du Régime temporel et de la liberté* (1933), in which Maritain considered the importance of using pure means (Christian love) to reform the social order.[98] A winter visit and discussion with Maritain at the Catholic Worker was similarly recorded in the pages of the January 1936 issue. At this time, Maritain expressed his approval of the American movement's work, giving it his highest "admiration and approbation," and discussed with its members a range of topics concerning contemporary conditions. These included the rise of totalitarian and pluralist states, the advisability of a Christian front over against these, and a portrayal of conditions in France. Maritain encouraged involvement in contemporary concerns that sought to influence others and unite with them toward making a new social order. Like Mounier, Maritain believed in the primacy of the spiritual, which was to be achieved in this life through engagement in the present world rather than through withdrawal and separation. As would be expected, Maurin continued to recommend three of Maritain's works by name over the next several years: *The Things That Are Not Caesar's, Humanisme intégral,* and most importantly, *Freedom in the Modern World.*[99]

Nor was Dorothy silent with regard to the impression Maritain had made upon her. It appears that Maurin's enthusiasm engendered the Catholic Worker staff's interest in *Freedom in the Modern World* as most fitting for the times, with which Dorothy concurred. An important concept from this work, on the necessity of pure means, was not lost on Dorothy, as the contents of her June 1940 editorial demonstrated. In a section entitled "The Pure Mean[s] of Love," she reflected the same solicitude as did Maritain for holding fast to faith in God in troubled times. She considered, like Maritain, that humankind was still in the beginnings of Christianity. With an apocalyptic train of thought, she reflected that the end was in view, but it was the demise of an era of capitalism, or, in Maritain's phrase, an end of the bourgeois spirit, the end of *a* world, not of *the* world.[100] Beyond *Freedom in the Modern World,* however, Dorothy made selections from other portions of Maritain's works. In her column for January 1936 she quoted from Maritain's *Art and Scholasticism,* demonstrating the necessity for art as a preparation for contemplation. As Maritain had argued, art is a fundamental necessity in human life, its beauty teaching persons the pleasures of the spirit and preparing them for contemplation as the end of all human activities. Dorothy, who was greatly responsive to beauty in all of its forms, in this instance simply related the quotation to an exhibit given by Constance Mary Rowe, an artist friend of the Catholic Worker. An undated conversation with Maritain reveals that Dorothy's responsiveness may be associated with her insatiable hunger for God, and, as often expressed by her, with her unfailing desire to put on Christ. The Augustinian restlessness, the long loneliness, which Dorothy felt she shared with both Maritain and Maurin, consisted of

> a spiritual hunger . . . a loneliness that was in me, no matter how happy I was and how fulfilled in my personal life. . . . I have been asking *why* all my life; when you ask why, you're alone, because you don't ask answers from other people of questions that are not answerable — by other people. If you keep asking the question, you're restless, I suppose; but

not restless in the psychological sense. You are wondering why we're here and what this time we're here means. You're restless spiritually. Lots of our visitors are struggling with the same religious and philosophical questions that Jacques Maritain put to himself, and of course, dear Peter. I guess Peter was restless, also! . . . he [Peter] was lonely only in the sense that he missed being near God all the time. But he had a vision of God, and so he wasn't really lonely at all. He was—I think it is true of many of us—lonely only because of what he *saw, saw ahead,* the moment of that meeting, that reconciliation between the human world and the divine one.[101]

That longing for union with God, shared by Dorothy, Maritain, and Maurin, also found meaning for Dorothy—always searching for an identification with Christ—through a reflection on the meaning of the transfiguration in the life of the Christian. Though but hinted at by Dorothy in her writings, it is obvious that she and Jacques shared some similar reflections in this regard. Christ, who intimately revealed himself to his disciples in the transfiguration, was yet so ordinary that the kiss of Judas was needed to mark him out to his captors. This same Christ had to overcome the fear of that death to which his mission on earth led him. Reflecting on the transfiguration, Dorothy prayed for that same strength to love in the midst of turmoil and a larger world torn by hatred:

> I can sit in the presence of the Blessed Sacrament and wrestle for that peace in the bitterness of my soul . . . and I can find many things in Scripture to console me, to change my heart from hatred to love of enemy. . . . Picking up the Scriptures at random (as St. Francis used to do) I read about Peter, James and John who went up on the Mount of Transfiguration and saw Jesus talking with Moses and Elias, transfigured before their eyes. (A hint of the life to come, Maritain said.) Jesus transfigured! . . . Reading this story of the Transfiguration, the words stood out, words foolishly babbled, about the first building project of the Church, proposed by Peter. "Lord, shall we make here three shelters, one for you, one for Moses and one for Elias?" And the account continues, "for he did not know what to say, he was so terrified."
> . . . Deliver us, Lord, from the *fear* of the enemy. That is one of the lines in the psalms, and we are not asking God to deliver us from enemies but from the fear of them. Love casts out fear, but we have to get over the fear in order to get close enough to love them.[102]

Dorothy also invoked the support of Maritain's writings in defense of her stand on the senselessness of war. In the November 1937 issue Maritain's stand against the civil war in Spain was printed, revealing his dismay at the atrocities that were cloaked under the guise of a religious war. Most telling, however, is Dorothy's 1938 printing of a summary article on Maritain. It demonstrated that he spoke out against war in general and admonished both his hearers and readers that peace is impossible as long as human hearts are unconverted.[103]

Other concerns of Maritain, notably class or racial prejudice and the loss of the masses to the church, were close to Dorothy's heart as well. The former was addressed primarily in response to encounters with a rampant anti-Semitism, which was both ideologically and personally offensive to Maritain on the one hand and to Dorothy and Maurin on the other.[104] The *Catholic Worker* printed and reprinted a short selection from Maritain in which he maintained that racial prejudice stifled the spirit of the gospel. In January 1939 the paper carried an article noting Maritain's radio address directed against anti-Semitic propaganda, and in November of that year Dorothy reviewed with great approbation his recently published reflection *A Christian Looks at the Jewish Question.*[105] A few years later she spoke with gratitude of this work and another of Maritain's books which in her mind were closely associated. Dorothy had recently gone to Longmans Green publishers to replace

> two of our most precious books, the most reread, the most passed on —
> *St. Paul* as arranged by Maritain, with comments, and *The Christian
> Looks at the Jewish Question* by Maritain. Not to have them around
> means a blank on one's shelves. They are the kinds of books you pick
> up to read aloud from, and in conversations with visitors in the office.
> They are books which need to be referred to again and again.[106]

With regards to the problem of the loss of the masses to the church, a selection from Maritain's writings had been carried by the *Catholic Worker* on a number of occasions. The concern had been addressed with clarity by Maritain, yet it was Dorothy who clearly exemplified Maritain's insight through her very life:

> The working class has left the Church because the Christian world has
> left the working class. That the masses may live with Christ, Christians

must first live with the masses. . . . The strength of Socialists and Communists comes less from their ideology than from the fact that they live with the masses. . . . And it is necessary to bind oneself to them. . . . To apply the social doctrine of the encyclicals effectively, there is one essential — to live with the masses.[107]

While Maritain advocated the Christian's involvement in the world about him or her, he maintained that it be marked by a simultaneous interior conversion.

Though Maurin introduced the Catholic Worker movement to Maritain, it was Dorothy who was instrumental in keeping Maritain's later works before the minds of the paper's readers. To this end Dorothy commissioned and approved a number of book reviews. Each of these in its own way underscored Maritain's insights revolving around the dignity of the human person, socially responsible and firmly rooted in this world's realities, who at the same time is destined for union with God, both in this life and in the next. A number of the reviews are noteworthy, the first being *Man and the State*, carried by the paper in May 1951. Michael Harrington, the reviewer, found in this work a confirmation of Maritain's belief in the freedom and dignity of the human person, which is respected in the latter's definition of and working out of the function of the state. As defined by Maritain, the state is that part of the body politic having the special function of directing the common good through political means. It followed then that the state is an instrument of the people and hence has no proper existence independently of their will. Another work, *The Range of Reason*, reviewed in April 1953, revealed Maritain's overall concern that present society be more and more permeated by the spirit of the gospel. Another work, significant from Dorothy's perspective, was reviewed by Natalie Darcy in November 1954. The reviewer quoted Maritain's thesis that the ways to God are multiple: "For a man there are as many approaches to God as there are wanderings on the earth or paths to his own heart." For Maritain, who addressed an audience of believers and nonbelievers alike, there is the ecumenical largeness of concern in which Dorothy shared, namely, that all persons be invited to reflect on ultimate questions. Admittedly, faith is a gift, as both knew, yet their apostolic hearts yearned that all persons might come to know and love God.[108]

Jacques Maritain played a larger role in the Catholic Worker than did his wife Raïssa. For Dorothy, however, her literary friendship with the latter was important as well, as a few incidents may reveal. In December 1938 Dorothy recounted a refreshing evening spent with Raïssa and her sister, Vera Oumansoff, in the company of friends. While the French-English conversation required translation throughout the evening, Dorothy's heart warmed to Raïssa, finding that they were mutually solicitous for the worker and that they shared a love for music as well. Dorothy read avidly at least two of Raïssa's works, *We Have Been Friends Together* and *Adventures in Grace*. The first she became acquainted with as travel reading on one of her frequent trips across the country and reviewed it in her own column in February 1942. At this time Dorothy expressed appreciation for the autobiographer, who, in her love for wisdom, reminded Dorothy of her Jewish college friend Rayna Prohme. Noteworthy too, were the insights Raïssa gave regarding her friend-husband Jacques and their mutual friends, Charles Péguy and Léon Bloy. Later, Dorothy credited Raïssa's *We Have Been Friends Together* with aiding her in picturing Catholic Paris, in understanding the writer Léon Bloy, and in appreciating the "Personalist Communitarian movement in France."[109] Raïssa's other work, *Adventures in Grace*, spoke to Dorothy at a time when the Lacouture retreat occupied the forefront of her mind. The retreat addressed the relationship between God's grace and human effort in personal sanctification; so too, did *Adventures in Grace*. With an Augustinian clarity, Dorothy found no opposition between emphasizing "the need for effort toward personal sanctification and at the same time the calm faith that God can do all things. 'Love God and do as you will.'" Without expanding her commentary, Dorothy valued the work also for introducing her to a greater understanding of the artist Georges Rouault, the poet Charles Péguy, and social critic Léon Bloy.[110]

Through the Maritains, Dorothy found her approach to Christian personalism affirmed and consolidated. Particularly helpful to her was Jacques's emphasis on the dignity of each person, the necessity for steadfast faith in perilous times, and for an ongoing conversion of heart coupled with an active engagement in the world. However, the Maritains spoke to her beyond a theory of Christian personalism, beyond the language of a Christian philosophy, valid though that was. Having known them personally as well, their words took on flesh for Dorothy in a quite literal sense. For both Raïssa and Jacques Maritain, converts to Catholicism as was Dorothy, a profound yearning for God marked the journey of their lives on earth. Though Dorothy lived in the hustle and bustle of the Catholic Worker rather than in the externally more peaceable milieu of the intellectual world, she would later candidly describe herself, not without humor, as "only some aging lady who is religiously obsessed."[111]

Paul Hanly Furfey

Because Father Paul Hanly Furfey considered himself a theorist of the Catholic Worker's approach to Christian personalism, the possibility that he influenced Dorothy merits some attention. Both his personal involvement in the movement and his published works provide important clues. Ordained a priest in 1922, Furfey received his doctorate in sociology from the Catholic University of America and embarked on what was to be a successful career as a sociologist at that same institution. Furfey's six years of close association with the Catholic Worker began in late summer or early fall of 1934.[112] At that time an associate professor in Catholic University's sociology department, Furfey had recently begun to question the value of a Catholic liberal approach, which posited that the ideal society could be attained through an application of the social sciences.[113]

During a 1934 trip to New York he visited the Catholic Worker House, where he discovered an astoundingly simple answer in the ideals espoused by Dorothy Day and Peter Maurin: to take the New Testament literally. It was a major breakthrough in Furfey's consciousness, as he came to realize that it was not enough to treat poor people as cases, for they were human beings with the need to love and to be loved. What struck him most forcefully about Dorothy and Peter in 1934 was that they shared their own food and living quarters with the desperate poor of the Bowery and, in fact, loved them. As a consequence, Furfey decided to direct his scholarship to furthering this understanding. Books, articles, and presentations which followed expressed his "orientation of a convert to a personalistic brand of Catholic radicalism."[114]

While Furfey was involved theoretically with the Catholic Worker as a whole, he centered his attention initially on the Campions, a subgroup within the larger movement. The Campion Propaganda Committee, purportedly an offshoot of the parent movement, had first introduced itself in the pages of the December 1934 issue of the *Catholic Worker*. By the May 1935 issue the members referred to themselves as speaker-organizers and by the June 1935 issue established space for their own "Campion Propaganda Committee" column. Albert H. (Tom) Coddington spearheaded the group, in collaboration with other young people, among them his future wife, Dorothy Weston.[115] they were intent on moving beyond the mother movement in organizational strategies and involvement in Catholic Action, the hierarchically sanctioned form of lay Catholic social involvement at that time. They looked to Day for initial validation, which she gave, though in hindsight somewhat reluctantly. For a time, a number of Catholic Workers engaged in some of the Campion activities as well: Dorothy Day herself, Tom Coddington, Dorothy Weston, William (Bill) Callahan, and Stanley Vishnewski, among others.

Campion activities, while paralleling and externally in tune with the Catholic Worker, threatened to undermine the leadership of the Worker founders, Dorothy Day and Peter Maurin. The gradual build-up of tension at the New York house, exacerbated by Coddington's biting sarcasm, was resolved only when Coddington and Weston left the New York Catholic Worker center in the spring of 1936.[116] The tension between Day and Maurin and the younger couple centered ostensibly around a question of priorities. Day, in defense of Maurin, believed that no activity should supersede the less spectacular daily living out of the works of mercy. A tribute to Dorothy Day's largeness in this matter is the fact that no statement of judgment, or even identification by name, of this opposition appeared in her published works.[117]

Furfey was very popular with the Campions, comprised mostly of college students and college-age persons, and he supported Campion propaganda centers in New York, Boston, and Washington, D.C.[118] He was called upon frequently to direct their weekend gatherings and to lead them in days of recollection. His first weekend with them was 26–28 July 1935 at the Catholic Worker farming commune on Staten Island. There he presented eight lectures on "War and Peace." Furfey also spoke with the Boston Campion group a number of times in August of that same year. His December 1935 and early 1936 Campion discussions, sometimes led in conjunction with Martin Schirber, O.S.B., Louis Achille of Howard University, John La Farge, S.J., or sociologist Elizabeth Walsh, centered on topics as wide-ranging as the Mystical Body of Christ, the priesthood of the laity, the technique of social work, "The Saints and Sociology," and the interracial question.[119]

That the spring 1936 Weston-Coddington rupture with the Catholic Worker did not include a *de facto* rupture of the latter with Furfey or with other members of the Campions is borne out in subsequent months. August 1936 found Furfey visiting the Boston Catholic Worker group, at which time he gave a talk related to his newly published *Fire on the Earth*.[120] In addition, Bill Callahan, Stanley Vishnewski, and other Campions remained on the *Catholic Worker* staff. "Il Poverello" house in Washington, D.C., a Campion foundation encouraged by Furfey's efforts, was considered by the mother movement as a Catholic Worker branch at that time. It is apparent that Furfey was a conciliatory figure during this period, since he maintained relations with the Coddingtons as well and gave a series of instructions at their new headquarters.[121]

On 29 September 1937 Furfey addressed the Campions at "Il Poverello" house on the importance of present-day imitation of the early Christians. The talk, while based on an interpretation of the Acts of the Apostles, revolved around the central thesis of *Fire on the Earth*, that is, the necessary dependence on supernatural means as a way of reforming society. On 2 November 1937 the Pittsburgh Catholic Worker group sponsored Furfey's address to some seven hundred people, considered "a fiery talk on 'The Catholic Revolution.'"[122] Dorothy's May 1939 editorial recalled a recent talk given by Furfey in New York and indicates an agreement rather than a dependence upon the speaker's insights:

> Father Furfey emphasized those three points—poverty, hard work and obscurity. That is the life we must embrace. It does not sound very attractive, but love lights up such a life, and its radiance reaches far.[123]

"Unemployment on the Land," Furfey's contribution to the October 1939 issue of the *Catholic Worker*, revealed his pro-city affinity and set off a series of responses regarding the agrarian movement. One of the pro-land respondents was Father John Hugo of Pittsburgh, who as a proponent of the Lacouture retreat would soon affect Dorothy's life to a great extent.[124] Aside from this clash of opinions, Furfey remained close to the Catholic Worker for the time being. He accepted an invitation to serve as director for the second annual Catholic Worker retreat at the Easton farm, for which a large number of participants were expected. Dorothy's assessment following this 30 August–2 September 1940 retreat weekend was positive: "We are all tremendously grateful to Father Furfey for the three wonderful days he gave us. Everyone got renewed courage and light for the coming year, a fresh impetus all around."[125] This retreat, though it marked the end of Furfey's close involvement with the Catholic Worker, was favorably received at the time and also remembered fondly by Dorothy in later years. Present at the 1940 weekend was Josephite Father Pacifique Roy, a proponent of the Lacouture retreat, who gave his own unasked-for conferences between those presented by Furfey. Aside from the Roy incident, however, Dorothy had been exploring the message of the Lacouture retreat since 1938. A number of factors urged her to move more actively toward this retreat movement, in which she hoped to find a greater synthesis of the spiritual life than Furfey and other priest advisors had provided.[126]

Furfey was never close to Day personally, even though he admired her and the Catholic Worker movement. From the beginning he was inspired by the gospel-based radicalism and the voluntary poverty of the movement but felt even then that its scope of outreach was too narrow. Thus, in working with the Campions, he may have unwittingly contributed to the Catholic Worker–Coddington conflict and jeopardized the possibility of a closer relationship to the mother movement. Contact with Peter Maurin, who imported the thought of Emmanuel Mounier and Jacques Maritain, and with Maurin's friend Virgil Michel, O.S.B., of Collegeville, Minnesota, served Furfey as he sought to express the theoretical basis for his conversion of heart in 1934. Furfey had become immediately interested in Mounier and subscribed to the personalist inspired journal, *Esprit,* by December 1935.[127]

Fire on the Earth (1936), the author's first and most popular publication of his Christian radical period, presented his most systematic statement of the Catholic Worker ideal as he understood it. Furfey dedicated the book to the Campions and set out to express the ideals of Christian social life, based on the New Testament, then being restated and applied to modern conditions by small groups of Catholic thinkers. He counted the *Catholic Worker* among the publications which represented the "new Catholic social movement." When writing to Robert Ellsberg in 1978, Furfey still recalled the intent of this early work and asked the then managing editor of the *Catholic Worker:*

> Did you ever read my *Fire on the Earth?* I wrote that way back in 1936 to justify the Worker's personalism, to show that it is really the basic Catholic viewpoint, to emphasize its thorough orthodoxy. . . .

> I didn't just write about the Catholic Worker viewpoint. I absorbed it into my own self. The Catholic Worker viewpoint became my own viewpoint. I was converted internally.[128]

In *Fire on the Earth,* Furfey noted that the Catholic church's social ideal is based on Scripture and the church's tradition. In applying this ideal to social and economic life, he proposed to deal exclusively with a maximum or heroic standard of conduct because he considered it the real mind of the church. He concluded that living the supernatural social life implied a test of faith, an acceptance of the folly of the cross rather than reliance on the worldly prudence of scientific methods, power, and wealth. For him, "the saints saw God in the poor, and that was enough."[129]

Furfey discussed the link between the supernatural life and everyday human society, explaining it in terms of the practice of the virtues, with charity as the supreme example. On earth, he pointed out, love of God is shown in love for our neighbor, in whom Christ dwells:

> it is clear that the famous eschatological passage in the twenty-fifth chapter of St. Matthew's Gospel is not a literary extravagance but a highly exact dogmatic text. When Christ shall say on the last day: "I was thirsty and you gave Me to drink; I was a stranger and you took Me in; naked and you covered Me, sick and you visited Me; I was in prison, and you came to Me" (Matt 25:35–36), He will be speaking a literal truth, since acts performed for the love of God in our neighbor are also acts of love of God Himself.[130]

Furfey posited that social action is founded on charity, so well exemplified by the intensity of the saints, who never rested in the face of human suffering. Here, his interpretation of Matthew 25 presented a partial portrait of Dorothy's own, which stressed that social action is a work of justice as well as of love. While Matthew 25 had long been one of Dorothy's favorite scriptural passages, after 1936 she sometimes alluded to Furfey's use of the gospel text to bolster her own commentaries.[131]

Fire on the Earth, as well as Furfey's other works of his Catholic radical period, posits a tension between engagement with the world and an ethos of separatism. While acknowledging good in the created world, Furfey's predominant focus was on the sphere of evil which exists in that world. Thus, bearing witness to Christ implied for Furfey an abstention from many worldly activities rather than the engagement proposed by Mounier and Maritain. Furfey described the ethos of separatism as it could exist in the establishment of lay Catholic village communities. They should be largely self-supporting, renouncing luxury and useless display. A system of distribution would be introduced, with private property limited by justice. Furfey pointed out that the Catholic Worker group in New York was "planning such a lay community founded on Catholic principles." In Dorothy's mind, however, the move was to a farming commune which promised an integrated way of life and a remedy for unemployment rather than an avoidance of the world.[132]

In August 1936 *Fire on the Earth* received a warm welcome in the book review section of the *Catholic Worker*. The reviewer agreed with Furfey's position that Christians are called to the heroism of the saints. In the September issue Maurin referred to the maximum or heroic standard of sanctity and recommended that Furfey's work be read. A lengthy excerpt from the book was printed in the following month's issue. A subsequent pamphlet by Furfey entitled "Catholic Extremism," an abridgment of the larger work, received a positive review in the November 1936 issue of the paper.[133]

Though Furfey no longer worked directly with Dorothy Day and her companions after 1940, his Christian radical works were still followed by Dorothy in later years. His *History of Social Thought* (1942) was reviewed in the *Catholic Worker* in April 1943. Dorothy read the book attentively, as a later remark of hers indicated.[134] Furfey's 1944 publication, *The Mystery of Iniquity*, was reviewed with general affirmation in the February 1945 issue. This work further developed the basic tenets of *Fire on the Earth*, called attention to the dangers of an exaggerated nationalism, and asserted that American Catholics were to question the morality of any war, particularly the present one. Twelve years after its publication the pacifist Dorothy continued to ponder "the mystery of iniquity" and was troubled by recurring threats of violence in our world.[135] Furfey's 1966 publication, *The Respectable Murderers*, received two positive reviews in quick succession. It was the final work by the distinguished sociologist to be given space in the *Catholic Worker*. The book is yet another instance of Furfey's proposed disengagement from the world as it is, of a stand against it by protest.[136]

It may be appropriate to ask: what was the essence of Furfey's role in the Catholic Worker movement? Along with other priests he provided regular guidance during the 1930s, particularly to younger members of the group, for which Dorothy was grateful. He also provided an overall supportive clerical presence to the fledgling lay movement. At the same time Furfey benefited from his association with the Catholic Worker, most notably, in the present context, for being introduced by its leaders to the Christian personalist movement. With the perennial enthusiasm characteristic of him, Furfey sought to promulgate his own insights and at the same time to encourage and interpret the Catholic worker movement through his writings. Although excerpts from these works and reviews of them appeared in the *Catholic Worker* over the years, Dorothy herself spoke of Furfey with relative infrequency. Her references to his writings and early conferences provide a confirmation of her own thinking rather than a reflection on a fresh insight. While, like Furfey, Dorothy often wrote in protest, it was primarily against concrete injustices rather than against an abstract Kingdom of Satan. Moreover, Dorothy advocated a wholistic approach to life rather than the radical separatism proposed by Furfey.

Furfey's interpretation and popularization of Christian radicalism, though enlivened by his exposure to French Christian personalist thought, remained quintessentially Furfey and differed from the French movement in a number of areas. Furfey was first and foremost a sociologist, and while attempting to move beyond the positivism of his earliest years, he nonetheless remained closely attuned to method and results, even while disclaiming them. The philosophers Mounier and Maritain, both laymen, spoke primarily of the dignity of the human person, who is in relationship with God and with the world about him or her, and secondarily of the institutions in which he or she is to be engaged rather than engulfed. The Frenchmen's anthropology was positive, envisioning humankind collectively and individually as made in God's image. It was this that formed the basis for their ecumenical spirit, one which was foreign to Furfey at the time of his involvement with the Catholic Worker. Mounier and Maritain believed that God's grace was active in a world wounded by sin and that God's activity was pervasive. Furfey's view of reality was less nuanced; for him, the world was in constant travail, engaged in warfare between the Kingdom of God and the Kingdom of Satan. He opted for Catholic separatism, a closed system, in order to protect against defilement from a worldly spirit identified with the Kingdom of Satan. This gave his thought an apocalyptic cast which has been inappropriately applied in toto to the Catholic Worker movement as well. [137]

Furfey, then, was not as attractive a figure for Dorothy as were Mounier and Maritain. She nonetheless agreed with his basic insight, which, like the French personalists, called for a spirit of heroism, identified simultaneously with sanctity and with a radical return to the gospel. All three writers applied to the laity the universal call to holiness and called them to be a leaven for good in the world. It was this to which Dorothy responded in every area of her life. Dorothy's desire for holiness accounts also for her attraction to monasticism and to its contemporary representatives, with whom she became personally acquainted in the early 1930s.

3

The Impact of Monasticism

Sometime during her stay in Chicago (1921–1923) Dorothy became acquainted with two works of Joris K. Huysmans, *En Route* and *The Cathedral*. From her remarks it is apparent that she read *The Oblate*, also by Huysmans, as soon as the English-language edition was published in 1924. Even though a depth of insight would come later, what could not have been lost on her at first reading was the author's emphasis on church music, art and architecture, on the lives of the saints, on mysticism, on monasticism, and on the oblate tradition within monasticism. Particularly in *En Route*, Huysmans had defended the monastic orders, naming the Benedictines, Carthusians, Cistercians, and the reformed group of Cistercians popularly known as the Trappists, as the true masters of the spiritual life. Dorothy's comments regarding the Huysmans trilogy record that a reflective reading facilitated her eventual conversion to Catholicism, inasmuch as the works made her feel at home in the Catholic church. Admittedly, Huysmans had given her a greater familiarity with Catholic ritual and doctrine, yet it was the sense of being at home that was of paramount importance for Dorothy. It was this very perception of feeling at home, of belonging, which later defined a good deal of her interest in monasticism and in the liturgical movement. Like many others of her era, Dorothy searched for a sense of solidarity with others and for direction in integrating various aspects of her life, both of which she found as a member of the Catholic church.[1]

Dorothy's interest in monasticism is further evidenced by a pre-conversion awareness of the Desert Fathers, whom she recognized as forerunners of the monasticism which, centuries before her own, brought order to a world surrounded by chaos. Though she came across them in a rather unlikely source, Dorothy characteristically found the author's merits: "Anatole France introduced me to the Desert Fathers in his book, *Thaïs*, and even in that satire the beauty of the saints shone through."[2]

Yet it was not until after she met Peter Maurin in December 1932 that she became more fully aware of the heritage of St. Benedict. Peter represented for Dorothy a Catholicism deeply rooted in tradition, of which monasticism in its Benedictine expression played an important part. Coming from a French peasant background, rooted in the soil and a communal way of life, Maurin was a believable witness to that tradition and, as his bulging pockets graphically portrayed — it might be an encyclical in one and Kropotkin's *Mutual Aid* in another — he depicted for her a synthesis between the spiritual and the material, which she herself sought. No less than Dorothy, Maurin was engaged in that search for integration which was common to a number of reflective persons in the first decades of the twentieth century. Among these may be cited the French personalists discussed in the foregoing chapter; the distributist-agrarians such as Hilaire Belloc, Gilbert Keith Chesterton, Eric Gill, Father Vincent McNabb, O.P., of England, and Father J. J. Tompkins of Antigonish, Nova Scotia; and to no less degree the American Benedictines. Each of these groups addressed the perceived fragmentation of society, related to rapid changes accompanying industrialization of the Western world, to the dream of great linear progress dashed by World War I, to the ensuing materialism and disillusionment during the 1920s, and to the shattering financial crises at the end of that decade and the Depression at the beginning of the next. When viewed as a whole, however, such cataclysms served to awaken in the human heart a great openness toward the possibility of reintegration and toward the primacy of the spiritual. As Erwin Iserloh has remarked of the period:

> The call of the age for the "spirit of the whole," as expressed by Julius Langbehn, the demand for the organically grown, for life as the genuinely real and creative against intellectualism and materialism, against isolation and uprooting, the turning to the original, to the sources away from the manufactured, derived, and merely imagined were united with the new self-consciousness of awakened religious forces. These were expressed especially in the liturgical movement, the Bible movement, and the lay movement supported by a new awareness of the Church. But

these were not currents moving parallel and to be separated from one
another; rather, they influenced one another and supported one another.[3]

Whether expressed in terms of feeling at home, of belonging, of community, or in terms of reintegration of the spiritual and material, or
of a restored awareness of the dignity of the human person, such yearn-
ings, while valid in any age, were a particularly poignant expression
of the desire of a whole generation to find its place in a broken world.
For Dorothy, an eventual identification with the Benedictine tradition
offered her an appropriate affiliation for the course of her own life's
journey.

BENEDICTINE ASSOCIATION (1933–1955)

Of the various groups of Benedictines to whom Dorothy was drawn,
evidence points to St. John's Abbey in Collegeville, Minnesota, as the
first monastery with which a long relationship was established. A clue
to the genesis of the Catholic Worker's association with the monks of
St. John's may be found in a record of donations made to the Catholic
Worker movement. Since both Dorothy and Peter believed it necessary
to embrace a voluntary poverty in order to serve the poor, the movement depended on donations to keep it in existence. Consequently,
from its earliest days Dorothy sent out a series of appeals printed in
the *Catholic Worker.* In addition, she requested assistance through the
more personal form of letters addressed to heads of various Catholic
institutions across the United States. A November 1933 donation made
by Abbot Alcuin Deutsch of St. John's Abbey was quite likely in response to one of these early appeals and established contact between
the Minnesota countryside and the New York house.[4] Thus began the
abbey's longtime support of the Catholic Worker's endeavors, first in
the guise of regular monetary contributions and later on through an
exchange of ideas and publications as well as spiritual and monetary
support.

Association with Virgil Michel, O.S.B.

Of all the monks of Collegeville, it was undoubtedly Virgil Michel
who had the greatest impact on Dorothy's spirituality. Though the
promise of a lengthy friendship was cut short by his untimely death

on 26 November 1938, Michel's five-year association with the Catholic
Worker movement benefited both the monks and the lay group. Renowned as a prime mover in the American liturgical movement, Michel
had been blessed with a fertile imagination and with rarely excelled
qualities of leadership which combined a gift for organization and persuasion with an ability to respect others' insights and opinions. At his
death, Dorothy offered sincere tribute to the simplicity which was part
of Michel's greatness:

> To us at the Catholic Worker, Father Virgil was a dear friend and
> adviser, bringing to us his tremendous strength and knowledge. He first
> came to visit us at our beginnings on East Fifteenth Street. He was like
> Peter Maurin in the friendly simple way he would come in and sit down,
> starting right in on the thought that was uppermost in his mind, tell-
> ing us of the work he was engaged in at that particular moment and
> what he was planning for the future. He was at home with everyone,
> anywhere. He could sit down at a table in a tenement house kitchen,
> or under an apple tree at the farm, and talk of St. Thomas and today
> with whoever [sic] was at hand. . . . He had such faith in people, faith
> in their intelligence and spiritual capacities, that he always gave the very
> best he had generously and openheartedly. . . .
>
> He was interested in everything we were trying to do, and made
> us feel, at all the Catholic Worker groups, that we were working with
> him. When he came in it was as though we had seen him just a few
> weeks before. He was at home at once, he remembered everybody, he
> listened to everybody.[5]

Judging from Dorothy's remark, Michel's first visit to the New York
house must have been sometime before April 1935, since that month
the Catholic Worker group completed the move from East Fifteenth
Street to Charles Street. Michel's earliest communication with any of
the group took place sometime between September 1933, when he
returned from the Indian missions to resume his position as dean of
St. John's College, and his 14 February 1934 letter to Dorothy. Abbot
Deutsch later told Dorothy that it was he who advised Michel of the
new lay movement. In the 14 February 1934 letter Michel fulfilled
Dorothy's request for a regular exchange of the *Catholic Worker* issues
with *Orate Fratres,* Collegeville's liturgical periodical. In addition, he
sent her a study club outline on the liturgy and the liturgical movement, and suggested that she mention his name when asking the ab-

bot to donate a copy of all the abbey's Liturgical Press publications to the New York Catholic Worker library. An intimation of the Catholic Worker's early efforts to popularize the liturgical movement is contained in Michel's assurance that "he [Deutsch] will be glad to have them [Liturgical Press publications] sent to you, both to help you and to spread the work of the liturgical movement."[6]

Beyond Michel's remark, however, it is clear that the *Catholic Worker* staff showed an interest in the liturgical movement from the paper's outset. For instance, Peter Maurin had written a short article on the centrality of the Mass for the October 1933 edition of the paper; other early notices and articles on the liturgy appeared as well. Michel's contribution was to assist in the development of this incipient interest in liturgy, already firmly rooted in love for Christ and sincere in its attempts to integrate liturgy with daily life. As expressed in a 26 February 1934 letter to Deutsch, Dorothy and her co-workers felt then that:

> We have been trying from the start of our work to link up the liturgy with the Church's social doctrine, realizing that the doctrine of the Mystical Body of Christ is at the root of both, . . . We have included in our Catholic Workers' School several course[s] on the liturgy, emphasizing its social implications, and find there is a great demand in the small library in the office of the paper for all books on the subject, . . .
>
> We hope in any case that you will remember occasionally in your prayers the work we are trying to do, for as Father Busch wrote us recently, we need a union of forces between the liturgists and the sociologists for the sake of both.[7]

Dorothy and other Catholic Workers were to join forces with Michel as popularizers of a vital liturgical movement in the United States. In the process Dorothy reflected upon numerous pleas for social and spiritual reconstruction expressed by Michel and other promoters of the liturgical movement, on several Benedictine monks' instrumentality in the movement's growth, and no less importantly, on various presentations and manifestations of the Benedictine ideal which had become available to her. Dorothy found these areas of consideration so intertwined that she drew increasingly closer to the Benedictine way of life itself. For a clearer understanding of this development, it is important to examine the particular Benedictine experience that Michel brought to his association with Dorothy and the Catholic Worker.

Michel's Liturgical Studies in Europe

In later years Abbot Alcuin Deutsch took credit for awakening Michel's early liturgical interest through presenting him with a copy of Romano Guardini's *Vom Geist der Liturgie.* In 1924 Deutsch sent Michel to study philosophy at Sant' Anselmo's, the International Benedictine College located in Rome. There is a strong likelihood that the abbot also intended to expose him to the liturgical movement then beginning to flourish in Europe. This would be in keeping with the development of Deutsch's liturgical interest, stimulated during his own stay in Rome and his extensive European travels from 1897 to 1903.[8]

Once in Europe, Michel went immediately to visit the University of Louvain and Mont César abbey, then the center of the liturgical movement in Belgium. In addition to his primary studies in philosophy, Michel found time to attend classes in liturgy taught by Dom Lambert Beauduin (1873–1960) of Mont César. The renowned Belgian Benedictine further enkindled Michel's interest in the liturgy and in the doctrine of the Mystical Body. An avid disciple, the younger monk had many private conversations with Beauduin and by 1926 had translated his *La Piété de l'Eglise* into English. Beauduin's remembrance of Michel three decades later is insightful:

> I knew him well at Rome, and when he discovered that I was concerned with the liturgical movement at Louvain, we became quite friendly, and he often came to talk to me in private; but liturgy was not for him just a matter of study; it was above all a powerful means of doing apostolic work, by increasing the faith and devotion of the faithful.[9]

Beauduin's influence upon Michel was profound, as the latter's ensuing promotion of liturgical renewal would amply demonstrate.[10]

While still in Rome, Michel sent home liturgical books, ideas, and pleas that St. John's take the initiative in developing a liturgical renewal in the United States. In the summer between his transfer of studies from Rome to Louvain for the academic year 1924–1925, Michel spent three months of planned trips through Italy, France, Spain, and Germany. A hallmark of his travel was an endeavor to remain close to people, particularly the poor. This quality broadened his understanding of the link between worship and everyday life, and later endeared him to Catholic Workers and others with whom he came in contact as catalyst of the American liturgical movement.[11]

At Louvain, Michel outlined an ambitious program for the completion of a doctorate in philosophy in one year. He was unable to carry it out, however, since the proposal was ultimately rejected in January 1925. Consequently, he made plans for using and expanding his philosophical research upon his return to the United States in September 1925.[12]

It appears that the January decision also freed Michel to return to his thoughts for a liturgical renewal in the United States. He continued to read widely, aiming toward promotion of a liturgical ministry. Michel kept his eyes open for all possibilities and urged the abbot that publication of their own books would serve better than translations alone. He suggested that a popular liturgical review be founded and prevailed upon the abbot to make a decision soon. Upon receiving the abbot's consent and support for the future periodical *Orate Fratres* (since 1952 *Worship*), Michel had frequent lengthy discussions with Beauduin at Mont César and also consulted liturgists at Maria Laach, St. André, Maredsous, and other abbeys.[13]

Development of a Liturgical Apostolate

On his return to the United States Michel engaged a number of collaborators in founding the Liturgical Press and the liturgical journal *Orate Fratres*.[14] They strove to promote increased understanding of the church's public worship and growth in participation in the Eucharist (Mass) and the Liturgy of the Hours. Michel insisted on a revival of the Pauline imagery of the Mystical Body of Christ, a doctrine little stressed in the United States at the time.[15] The attention given community, based on incorporation in Christ, entwined with a secondarily emphasized reverence for the individual person, was a thread woven through most of Michel's later articles. His criticism of both atomistic individualism and of totalitarianism was shared by personalist and like-minded Christian thinkers of this period.

After the example of Dom Lambert Beauduin, Michel and his collaborators sought to popularize the movement beyond the confines of Benedictine abbeys, where it had its origins. In addition to promoting active participation in the liturgy itself, Michel took particular care to encourage awareness of the interconnectedness between liturgy and life. Like its counterpart in Europe for the same period, the liturgical movement in the United States during its first two decades made

a number of general advances, through an emphasis on the importance of receiving Eucharist during Mass, by encouraging participation through the dialog Mass, the *missa recitata,* and education in
Gregorian chant.[16]

The issues of *Orate Fratres* provide a valuable index of the American liturgical movement as a whole, and the development of Michel's
own thought between 1926 and 1938 is reflected in the more than one
hundred twenty articles he wrote for this journal. Dorothy had the opportunity to follow this development, since back numbers of *Orate
Fratres* were also sent to the Catholic Worker consequent to the lay
movement's initial subscription in February 1934.[17]

Later Developments: Liturgy and Life

A growing clarity in Michel's thinking began to surface in the mid-
1930s. Indicators of this may be found in a 1935 article, "The Liturgy
the Basis of Social Regeneration" and in a 1936 assessment entitled,
"The Scope of the Liturgical Movement." The development in Michel's
thinking may be attributed to a number of factors, among them his
growing friendship with Dorothy, Peter Maurin, and other members
of *The Catholic Worker* and his study of Pius XI's social encyclical
Quadragesimo Anno. Michel's attention had turned from a general,
timeless concern that Catholic Christians carry worship to their daily
lives, towards an ability to make an explicit connection between worship and a broadened view of social involvement. This approach set
the program of action for the remaining three years of Michel's life and
served as a support for the efforts of the Catholic Worker movement.[18]

From 1935 onwards, Michel's contacts with the Catholic Worker
group grew more frequent. Mutually desirous of implementing the
liturgical movement in its broadened ramifications, Michel and his collaborators as well as Dorothy and her co-workers sought harmoniza-
tion and integration of every aspect of life. Hence the appeal of the
cooperative movement of the time, which proposed a means of im-
proving economic conditions of its members chiefly through mutual
self-help rather than through rampant individualism and increasing
competition, which were seen as hallmarks of capitalistic society. The
land distribution movement, which attempted to restore a way of life
in harmony with the rhythms and demands of nature as opposed to
the perceived anonymity and mechanization of industrialized city life,

was also presented as a positive alternative. Given Dorothy's contacts with Virgil Michel, with monks of other Benedictine foundations, and the perduring influence of Peter Maurin, her interpretation of these and other contributions toward Christian social reconstruction took on a decidedly Benedictine expression.[19]

Dorothy Day and the Benedictine Charism

Within the Roman Catholic tradition, members of religious orders, such as the Benedictines, seek to live out their baptismal promises in a corporate setting. The founders of these orders envisioned a way of life which would enable their members to live as witnesses to the gospel in keeping with the particular needs of their age. Benedict of Nursia (c. 480–c. 550), the founder of Western monasticism, wrote a rule for monks which is known for its moderation and the care its author took to ensure each monk's union with Christ. The norm for the Benedictine way of life is the gospel, as it is for every Christian, yet the particular grace or charism which identifies a religious order like the Benedictines derives from the presence and action of the Holy Spirit in its founder and among its members. Though not limited to this group alone, the Benedictine charism places great value upon identification with Christ, on community, on hospitality, and on a harmony between work and prayer.[20] Dorothy was drawn to these aspects of the Benedictine charism, and thus they were abundantly expressed in her own spirituality.

Christ and Community

For the Christian, the great reality of love is expressed through identification with Christ, by a unity of friendship and brotherhood or sisterhood with Him. Benedict's rule spoke of the primacy of this love: "the love of Christ must come before all else."[21] Yet, as Dorothy well knew, such intimacy with Christ could be expressed in this life only through living relationships with other human beings. In Catholic Christian terms, the Christ dwelling within her loved the Christ within another, either actually present through grace or potentially through God's desire that all be members of Christ's Mystical Body. Dorothy often reflected on the power of this unity of love in her writings. Early in 1935, for example, she shared with her readers a prayer for the new year, that "the members [of Christ's body] might be mutually careful one for another." She recognized with St. Paul that if one person suffered, all share in this suffering; if one person rejoiced, then all share in that joy.[22] Dorothy recognized that the source of this unity lay beyond boundaries of family and present religious affiliation:

> our unity . . . is a unity at the altar rail. We are all members of the Mystical Body of Christ, and so we are closer to each other, by the tie of grace, than any blood brothers are. . . . We are our brother's keeper, and all men are our brothers whether they be Catholic or not. But of course the tie that binds Catholics is closer, the tie of grace. We partake of the same food, Christ. We put off the old man and put on Christ. The same blood flows through our veins, Christ's. We are the same flesh, Christ's. But all men are members or potential members, as St. Augustine says, and there is no time with God, so who are we to know the degree of separation between us and the Communist, the unbaptized, the God-hater, who may tomorrow, like St. Paul, love Christ[?][23]

Her compassion embraced all of humankind, as many appeals to her readers firmly attest. An excerpt from one of these reveals years of reflection on the meaning of incorporation in Christ:

> We are begging now, not only for the money we need to pay up our bills to keep us going another six months. But we beg you too not to abandon each other. Hold on to each other. We are each one responsible, one for another. We are all members or potential members of the body of Christ and so are holy. We must not rend our own flesh, made holy by Christ's incarnation. Let us love one another, without measure, even to folly.[24]

Dorothy's preoccupation with community was longstanding. She identified with an age which longed for a sense of rootedness and had searched for a religious affiliation in which she could feel at home. In the Roman Catholic church she sought the security of a sense of direction, not just for herself alone, but so that she might engage with others in common effort for justice. She concurred with Peter Maurin's emphasis on the family as the basic unit of society and the fact that, religiously speaking, we are a community of brothers and sisters. For Maurin—whose thinking derived from Christian tradition, his youthful experience of communal living, his reading of history and of the Christian personalists—it followed that "we must have a sense of personal responsibility to take care of our own, and our neighbor, at a personal sacrifice."[25] Dorothy's contacts with Virgil Michel and his Benedictine confreres, and her consequent growth in understanding of the liturgical movement, the doctrine of the Mystical Body, and of the Benedictine charism all served to consolidate her thinking with regard to the meaning of community.

Dorothy felt the need for community, not only for herself but also that she might be able to provide a sense of belonging and of solidarity for others. She had been impressed by the renewed emphasis on the community dimension in worship, as one of her private reflections attests:

> in the spiritual realm the emphasis is also communitarian. There is the beginning of a liturgical movement where greater emphasis has been placed on corporate worship, the prayer of the church as a whole rather than individual prayer, private devotion. But of course one leads to another, and vice-versa — like the swinging of a pendulum.[26]

Much of Dorothy's writing insisted on community effort and on the value of the human person as an individual. Neither submersion of the human person in a system such as the totalitarian state nor the extreme independence of rugged individualism was acceptable. What was needed was a form of community that respected the uniqueness of each person. Dorothy noted this ideal when remarking on the Catholic Worker's fondness for two saints: St. Francis, the "personalist," and St. Benedict, the "communitarian."[27]

Because Dorothy recognized both the solitude of the human heart and its insatiable yearning for wholeness and union with another, the theme of loneliness formed a thread throughout her writings that is interwoven with her reflections on community. With others, she shared a transcendental loneliness, the experience of being unable to be fully united with God in this life. Loneliness was a symbol for fragmentation, for separation from the Beloved; for Dorothy, the loneliness experienced apart from God had something to do with need for meaningful human contact. As she expressed it, "The only answer in this life, to the loneliness we are all bound to feel, is community. The living together, working together, sharing together, loving God and loving our brother, and living close to him in community so we can show our love for Him."[28] Joy, companionship, love were complete only when rooted in God.

For Dorothy, community life meant both an ordinary life, one rooted in everyday existence, and one that was shared. The foundations for the Catholic Worker community were laid in the early days of the movement, the locus being first the New York house and later extended to various Catholic Worker houses of hospitality and farms. Dorothy's understanding of community became clarified in her attempt to live it, as her reflections and frequent assessments illustrate. In this formulation she relied on Peter Maurin's interpretation as much as her own. Maurin, who engaged in lengthy discussions with Virgil Michel in the 1930s, viewed a communal movement back to the land as part of a program which would restore the Benedictine heritage and introduce order into society once again.

> The Benedictines exemplify *cult, culture,* and *cultivation.* In order to preserve their religion, their literature, their books, their art, they took to the land, lived in communities and so grew.
> Today we have lost all that and must begin again. . . .
> We must do it together, helping each other, bringing light to each other. We cannot do it alone.[29]

Peter envisioned such communities growing up throughout the land as integral to the establishment of a new institution for "a rebuilding of society within the shell of the old, with a philosophy so old that it looks like new." This vision was endorsed and faithfully promulgated by Dorothy.[30]

Writing of the Catholic Worker group, Dorothy often referred to it as a family and as a community, and tended to use the terms interchangeably. In a February 1944 article she recalled Peter Maurin's mission "to bring back the communal aspects of Christianity." She argued that while the farming communes, like the houses of hospitality in the cities, were based on the Benedictine ideal, they were not monasteries but gatherings of families. Her insistence was based on the primitive Benedictine tradition in which the community of monks comprised a spiritual family rather than a juridical establishment. By way of validating her own insight, she related Maurin's comments that the *Rule* of Benedict was written for laypersons, and in the twentieth century it was also used by Benedictine oblates who were "living a Christian life in the world." She never ceased to stress the communitarian aspect of the Catholic Worker endeavor and firmly believed that it was only through the group's sharing voluntary poverty together that members could have a truly enriched life.[31]

In later years Dorothy found herself assessing the Catholic Worker's life in community. Early in 1954 she considered the possibility of failure and in 1956 admitted that their vision of community was still not clear. Various Catholic Worker attempts to form ideal communities, particularly on the farming communes, had never been a success. She regretted that those in the Catholic Worker movement had not the vision, the time, the skill, or even the spiritual foundation to work it out. The foundation, she believed, was the ideal presented in Acts: that the community hold all things in common. In the face of seeming failure, she held to her solution: "we must deepen our own interior life and pray for understanding."[32] In 1959 she reminded her readers that the *Catholic Worker* had long spoken of human freedom, of the engagement of human responsibility rather than the use of force to achieve their goals, and noted the contradictory power present in their own community situation: "we must remember the force of dire need that has brought about our own."[33]

Undaunted, she continued to seek out models of community living, from the kibbutzim described by Buber in *Paths in Utopia,* to those of religious communities such as the Protestant Bruderhof and Catholic lay communities, including a group of Benedictine oblates living in the environs of Prinknash Abbey in England.[34] Later, Dorothy accepted that the Catholic Worker reality was in fact a part of the dream, though it differed from the unrefined vision of her first enthusiasm. Many young persons had found their life vocations through the Catholic Worker, going on to enter religious life or to establish families of their own which were permeated by gospel values. She affirmed that no one who lived in one of the houses of hospitality or the farms ever forgot "this golden period of his life." At the same time, she admitted:

> It has always required an overwhelming act of faith. I believe, because I wish to believe, help Thou my unbelief. I love because I want to love, the deepest desire of my heart is for love, for union, for communion, for community.[35]

Moreover, she came not only to accept but also to embrace what was always a part of the vision, albeit the least glamorous part: to know Christ in the face of His poor. Thus, in the last two decades of her life she spoke with greater confidence of their community of need, and acknowledged that they stressed living in voluntary poverty so that they could support many more people in community. She believed finally that she had begun to understand the mind of Christ.[36]

Hospitality: The Guest Is Christ

In chapter 53 of his *Rule,* Benedict addressed the reception which was to be accorded guests. He reminded his monks that everyone was to be received as Christ, for on the last day each monk would be told: "I was a stranger and you welcomed me" (Mt 25:35). All persons, without distinction, were to be greeted with every courtesy, including a sharing in the abbot's table, and an offering of accommodation in the guest quarters. The awareness of Christ's presence ran like a refrain throughout the chapter, with special consideration being given to the lowly:

> Great care and concern are to be shown in receiving poor people and pilgrims, because in them more particularly Christ is received; our very awe of the rich guarantees them special respect.[37]

Benedict's injunction to hospitality, with its inherent exercise of the works of mercy, carried on a tradition known from the earliest days of Christianity, a tradition later encouraged by the Fathers of the church, including Basil (330–379), Jerome (342–420), and Augustine (354–430).[38]

Dorothy, like Benedict before her, was guided by a thoroughly biblical sensibility. She had long ago been drawn to the exercise of the works of mercy enjoined in Matthew 25:31–46. Though Dorothy attempted to live out the biblical injunction, incorporating all the works of mercy as part of the Catholic Worker program, nonetheless three of these stood out with particular relief. These may be viewed as the three sisters of hospitality, namely, feeding the hungry, clothing the naked, and sheltering the homeless.

Even prior to 1932, Dorothy's understanding of hospitality, as practiced by the poor, had been grounded in her years of living on the lower east side of New York. She later admitted that this experience gave her an openness to Maurin's ideas on hospitality. It is not surprising then, that by the second issue of the *Catholic Worker,* Dorothy reported Maurin's plans for the establishment of houses of hospitality as part of his three-part social reconstruction program. These plans were described in the second of three "Easy Essays" for this edition, which reminded the reader that in the Middle Ages the bishops felt it their obligation to provide hospices for the wayfarer.

In September 1933 Dorothy commented on Maurin's gentle insistence that his three-point program — roundtable discussions, houses of hospitality, and agronomic universities (farming communes) — be implemented. The October 1933 issue carried the text of Maurin's 9 September address to the unemployed, which had been printed in the paper so as to be sent to all the bishops and archbishops attending the October assembly of the National Conference of Charities in New York. In these essays Maurin recorded a generalized history of Christian hospices or houses of hospitality and a plea that the tradition be revivified. Though it was years later that she admitted that "it takes a woman to put flesh on the bare bones of an idea,"[39] Dorothy began immediately to do just that, in this instance, with respect to the question of hospitality. She ran an article in the November edition of the paper entitled "Call for Catholic Houses for Needy Women and Girls." This same issue recorded the germ of an idea that *they* would establish houses of hospitality. The program was spelled out in an idealistic fashion and carried overtones of a strictly monastic interpretation of a life of service. Prospects for a house were in view, and their purpose at that time was stated:

> The general purpose of the Houses of Hospitality is to form a center of Catholic action in all fields, to work for, teach and preach social justice, to form a powerhouse of genuine spirituality and earnest educational and vocational work, to dignify and transform manual labor, and to work for the glory and love of God and His Church.[40]

The beginning, it was admitted, would be small and difficult. Little did Dorothy and her co-workers know how arduous their task would be and how differently the particulars of the ideal would be realized.

With the cooperation of two priests of the parish in which they resided, the Catholic Worker group had been able to open a center of hospitality by 11 December 1933. While this apartment provided housing for ten homeless and unemployed women, Dorothy dreamt of obtaining an entire, donated house which would shelter other unemployed persons — both men and women — as well as provide library space, lecture rooms, and offices for the paper. She dreamt with faith, at the same time seeking advice, doing fieldwork toward this goal, and

begging for financial assistance.[41] Meanwhile, she reported with pleasure on the Teresa-Joseph cooperative, as she termed their pioneer dwelling. Dorothy considered it a success, yet was impelled to do more. She
admitted that provision of shelter was a great need; supplying a bed
for one who needed it was a corporal work of mercy, a work which Christ
had commanded His followers to do. With a final argument which was
to become a refrain in successive years, she reminded her readers that:
"Inasmuch as you have done it unto one of the least of these, you have
done it unto Me" (Mt 25:40).[42]

Providing for Christ meant more than the guarantee of shelter.
By December 1935 Dorothy noted matter of factly that men "come
for clothes, and if we have no clothes to give them, we give them coffee
and oatmeal." At the time of her writing, about a dozen men from
along the waterfront had come to expect this simple breakfast each
morning. Nine months later, "What We Are Doing in Town and Country" comprised Dorothy's first lengthy assessment of their hospitality.
She admitted that they were hindered in their performance of the works
of mercy, as they were not well equipped, the demands being greater
than their resources. These were difficulties which were to plague
Catholic Worker members over the years and which they dealt with
bravely, attempting never to violate Christian personalist principles in
their respect for persons, but choosing to sacrifice order and efficiency
instead. Following the lead of the parent house, groups of Catholic
Workers in other cities had begun to establish their own houses of hospitality by December 1936. Dorothy held up an ideal and offered them
both hope and advice:

> Houses of Hospitality will bring workers and scholars together.
> They will provide a place for industrial workers to discuss Christian
> principles of organization as set forth in the encyclicals. They will em-
> phasize personal action, personal responsibility as opposed to political
> action and state responsibility. They will care for the unemployed and
> teach principles of cooperation and mutual aid. They will be a half-way
> house towards farming communes and homesteads.[43]

In her mind, their exercise of the works of mercy was closely linked
with possibilities for indoctrination and the establishment of farming
communes, the other two planks in Maurin's platform. To conceive
that the unemployed and the later hordes of men who came to them
broken in mind, body and spirit were capable of such achievement

required great trust in the inherent goodness and restorative powers of the human person. The grinding reality Dorothy had to face in the decades to come was to temper her optimism, but it never ultimately destroyed her faith in these ambassadors of God. She realized the largeness of the task from the outset, yet emphasized the need for small beginnings.[44]

Meanwhile, in New York the breadline on Mott Street continued to grow, consisting in February 1937 of about four hundred unemployed men who came daily for the simple fare of the Catholic Worker breakfast. Since Peter's vision that each parish have its works-of-mercy center remained largely unrealized and the suggestion that every home have a Christ room met with only minor success, much of the living out of the vision became incumbent upon the Catholic Worker, slender though its resources were. The group's response to the needy had begun imperceptibly to change the ordering of its priorities. Thus, while holding fast to Maurin's three-point program, the increase of daily responsibilities in Catholic Worker houses found hospitality taking precedence over indoctrination and the farming communes.[45]

The *Catholic Worker* responded to repeated charges that the group's exercise of hospitality served only to maintain the present order. An article appearing in the May 1940 edition appealed both to Christian history and to a sense of their sincerity. The writer maintained that hospitality was deeply rooted in Christian tradition, for early monasteries founded by St. Benedict assigned monks as hospitalers and as almoners. The former welcomed guests; the latter fed, clothed and gave shelter to those in need. With respect to the Catholic Worker movement's own attempts,

> we consider the spiritual and corporal Works of Mercy and the following of Christ to be the best revolutionary technique and a means for changing the social order rather than perpetuating it. Did not the thousands of monasteries, with their hospitality, change the entire social pattern of their day? They did not wait for a paternal state to step in nor did they stand by to see destitution precipitate bloody revolt. . . . Not bound by vows and being weak in ourselves, we try, stumblingly, to do our little bit to express faith in the hospitable tradition.[46]

Dorothy, as well as Maurin and other Catholic Workers, sought and found parallels between their time and the broad range of European history between the fall of Rome in 476 A.D. and the early years of the thirteenth century. The analysis was by no means sophisticated, for the clock could not be turned back without consideration of all the hours that had intervened, nor would feudal church-state relationships be reinstated in the twentieth century. Nonetheleess, the Workers firmly believed that the impetus toward Christian involvement in social action remained valid in every age.

The 1940s saw a change in the status of the people who stood in the Catholic Worker breadline. In addition to the unemployed, its ranks were swelled with the appearance of a greater number of the unemployable. Dorothy recognized their inherent dignity. A "rum hound" was made in the image and likeness of God no less than she; and while admitting that the houses had not achieved all that they wished to in terms of beginning to change the social order, she reminded herself as well as her readers that they were a means to that end. The farming communes had also become a part of the means and offered hospitality to wayfarers, who as the years elapsed were as diversified as those who visited the New York City house. With Peter, she looked forward to the future:

> Our Houses of Hospitality are scarcely the kind of houses that Peter Maurin has envisioned in his plan for a new social order. He recognizes that himself, and thinks in terms of the future to accomplish true centers of Catholic Action and rural centers such as he speaks of in his column this month.[47]

Without losing sight of Maurin's vision, Dorothy had already come to believe that their very continuity depended on their response to need. It was not only the bond of Christian charity but also economic necessity that kept them in existence. She doubted that the movement would hold together if they were not by then confronted thrice daily with lines of hungry men, women, and children. Just as she struggled with enlarging her concept of community to recognize that the real was as valid as the ideal, so too did she find that all the aspects of hospitality drew her and her co-workers beyond themselves, beyond the desire for a self-contained, utopian community. However, the tasks to which they had set themselves required the sustenance of a deep faith:

> All our life is bound up with other people; for almost all of us happiness and unhappiness are conditioned by our relationship with other

people. What a simplification of life it would be if we forced ourselves to see that everywhere we go is Christ, wearing out socks we have to darn, eating the food we have to cook, laughing with us, walking with us, silent with us, sleeping with us. . . . He [Christ] made heaven hinge on the way we act towards Him in his disguise of commonplace, frail and ordinary human beings.[48]

Though faith-filled, Dorothy stopped at times to marvel at the origin of the hospitality which had become a hallmark of the Catholic Worker movement. With a humor that mitigated her grief at the time of Maurin's death in 1949, she claimed that it was all Peter's fault, with his talk about hospitality, and "our writing"—Maurin included—about it in the early issues of the paper. People simply took them at their word, and now, like the mother of a large family, Dorothy felt that there was always room and food enough for one more. By then a lay novice of the Benedictines, she had begun to define her vocation in terms of the running of their houses of hospitality, retreat farms, and farming communes—the latter two also being centers of hospitality. She affirmed her belief that God, through Maurin, had sent her this work.[49]

As would be expected, Dorothy grew to appreciate the work of fellow hospitaler Abbé Pierre when she became acquainted with him in the mid-1950s. This worker priest, laboring among the poor of Paris, attempted the same direct action in performing the works of mercy as did the Catholic Worker group. Like the abbé she identified with the offscouring of both farm and city. Playfully earnest, she declared:

> Yes, all of us derelicts have a rich and beautiful life, this life of voluntary poverty on the land. And as for us derelicts in the city, I assure you there is no mission [disinfectant] smell, . . . After all, we are a community, a family, and God so loved us that as the psalmist said, He considered us little less than the angels, not as derelicts.[50]

Yet, the older she grew, the more heartbreaking the tasks attendant upon hospitality became. Dorothy felt it a minor miracle that they were enabled to continue serving the poor at table. Soup and bread assuaged their guests' anguish somewhat, but not Dorothy's. Their name and number were legion; thus, both names and faces often went unremembered. Their grief, their degradation were frequently such that the Catholic Worker's gestures of hospitality appeared to be but a bandaid applied to a cancer. Dorothy's distress spanned the decades; it had its beginnings prior to Maurin's death in 1949 and remained with her until her own. On one occasion, she recalled one of many conversations with Peter Maurin:

> "Is this what you meant when you talked about Houses of Hospitality?" I asked Peter Maurin one day when our house in Baltimore was being closed by injunction, because it was overcrowded and breaking the law when it sheltered both Negro and white.
> "It serves to arouse the conscience at least," was his only reply at that time.[51]

Even when she was no longer active, Dorothy's concern for hospitality as an important part of the performance of the works of mercy remained undiminished. She rejoiced to see a younger generation of Catholic Workers taking responsibility and agreeing with her that the works of mercy were a revolutionary yet nonviolent program of action. She knew from experience that the spiritual and corporal went together and that their exercise involved suffering. Yet, as one of her final appraisals disclosed, it never ceased to worry her that they could not do more. She had been busy with her companions for many years and had been so overtaken by three of the corporal works—the sisters of hospitality—that she felt they neglected the others, particularly the spiritual ones. Yet, the publication of the paper itself, and the energy which she devoted to the retreat movement from the 1940s onwards, are proof of her efforts toward the exercise of all of them.[52] Nor had her efforts in hospitality been in vain. While living within limitations of human resources and energy, which confined the letter of her achievement in this regard, she nonetheless mastered the spirit which gave life. An article written for the May 1978 issue of the paper aptly describes the ideal which Dorothy had achieved:

> All Christians are called to be hospitable. But it is more than serving a meal or filling a bed, opening our door—it is to open ourselves, our hearts, to the needs of others. Hospitality is not just shelter, but the quality of welcome behind it.[53]

Work and Prayer

Dorothy's interpretation of the relationship between work and prayer was influenced by her understanding of the *Rule* of Benedict. In addition to her own reading, to which she brought her life experiences, she discussed the *Rule* with Maurin and Benedictines such as Virgil Michel and Chrysostom Tarasevitch.[54] In addition a short commentary on chapter 48 of the *Rule* came into her hands in 1949 and strengthened her thinking along these lines.

A study of Benedict's *Rule* demonstrates the pervasive extent to which work occupied his attention. The monk's day was defined by his occupation with the *Opus Dei* (the Work of God), with manual labor, and with a considerable period spent in *lectio divina* (spiritual reading). The Work of God (Liturgy of the Hours) was a communal praying of the Psalms with other scriptural readings and prayers at eight separate periods or hours of a twenty-four-hour day. Elements of praise and thanksgiving were important to this prayer, and the seriousness with which the *Opus Dei* was taken may be seen in the number of entire chapters Benedict devoted to it in his *Rule*.[55] Just as in their life as a whole, monks were to prefer nothing to Christ, so in their daily living of it they were to prefer nothing to the *Opus Dei*.[56]

While the *Opus Dei* received the greater portion of Benedict's treatment of prayer, the importance of *lectio divina*, private personal prayer, and the Mass were not neglected. Time for spiritual reading was designated on the horarium and consisted primarily of a prayerful study of Scripture to aid in the work of praying the office. Petitionary prayer in common as well as silent devotional prayer were encouraged and extended beyond the time of the Work of God. The Mass, though celebrated at the time of Benedict only on Sundays and festivals, was an integral part of the monk's life.[57]

With regard to that aspect of labor commonly identified as work, the *Rule* had a good deal to say. Chapter 48 placed manual labor in the context of the entire day, giving a separate horarium for summer and winter. In its tripartite division, the day revolved around the Work of God and manual labor and was punctuated by periods for *lectio divina*. Manual labor in general was presupposed and harvesting was given explicit treatment.[58] Practice of the works of mercy was considered a major portion of the monk's toil.[59]

A theology of work, as presented in Benedict's *Rule* and its primitive interpretation, attests to the integrated nature of the monk's life, for no dichotomy was seen between work and prayer. The monk moved from the explicit Work of God to other works in service of God and back again. Work carried with it a penitential aspect, given that the monk's life bore a lenten character overall.[60] His converted life (*con-*

versatio morum) was to be marked by the toil of obedience as opposed to the disobedience of sin, in imitation of and in service to Christ. Thus, Benedict and the early interpreters of his *Rule* viewed work primarily in its obediential, penitential aspects.[61]

A second formative work for Dorothy was Rembert Sorg's *Towards a Benedictine Theology of Manual Labor.* The work contextualized the *Rule* of Benedict in order to interpret a passage found in chapter 48:

> If, however, the needs of the place require them [the monks] to labor personally in gathering the harvest, let them not grieve at that; for then are they truly monks, when they live by the labor of their hands, as our Fathers and the Apostles did. But let all things be done in moderation on account of the fainthearted.[62]

As a starting point, Sorg cursorily examined the ancient monastic theology of manual labor, which Benedict drew upon in formulating his *Rule.* Sorg argued that these sources presupposed that the monks worked to support themselves as well as to help the needy. The monk's charity, in moving beyond self, showed that "manual labor is meant to be the image and likeness of God, Whose Name is Charity and Who in overflowing goodness does the *work* of creation, both the old and the new."[63] Sorg's presentation of work as participation in God's creativity and generativity, while seminal in the thought of Benedict, moves beyond the early tradition by reflecting also the development of later monastic thought. Implicit in Sorg's work is the concept of the claustral paradise, or restoration of antelapsarian innocence within the monastery.[64]

Concluding this section, Sorg devoted some attention to the apostolicity of manual labor, in which St. Paul excelled. This apostle's purpose was presented as twofold: so as not to be a burden to those converted to Christianity and, secondly, to prove that he preached *gratis,* after the example of Christ's own love. Sorg considered that the early Benedictine monks fostered this apostolic spirit, enabling them to exert powerful missionary influence in the spread of Christianity.[65]

In examining chapter 48 Sorg posited that the Benedictine community was an *ecclesiola,* or church in miniature, in which all the cultural strata of the church were represented. Thus, though manual labor remained the norm, a healthy community discovered, fostered, and supported individual members for specialization in intellectual work or other occupations that left little time for manual labor. The ideal of Benedict remained: to imitate the Apostles in being Christ-lovers who, in all simplicity, labored freely with their hands.[66]

In his concluding section Sorg argued for a spirit of integration between work and prayer. Prayer and work, he noted, share in being modes of adoration and glorification of God. Nonetheless Benedictine prayer, which is preeminently the Divine Office, is not manual labor, and vice versa. The life which the monk supported by his labor is the Divine Office; because it is an *Opus Dei*, God's work, the Spirit of God in the monk "does both the Work and all the manual labor that subserves it."[67]

Dorothy received the Sorg study with delight and reported on it in the October 1949 edition of the *Catholic Worker*. Her article alternated between reflection on the text itself and the situation in which she was immersed. She was taken with Sorg's references to the first centuries of Christendom, with the Desert Fathers, and with other representatives of Eastern monachism upon which Benedict drew. Treatment of the threefold purpose of manual labor, in particular the second—almsgiving—was not lost on Dorothy. She wondered if Sorg was too harsh in his use of a text from the Didache, which in his mind taught alsmgiving, yet discouraged mendicancy and implicitly presupposed the obligation to work. To this Dorothy countered, "For the one time that St. Paul says, 'if a man will not work, neither let him eat,' the entire New Testament, the sayings of our Lord, incline us toward kindness towards our fellows and an aversion to judging."[68] The comment arose out of sixteen years experience in offering hospitality to those in need. Overall, Dorothy spoke appreciatively of what Sorg termed a deeper theology of manual labor. It is obvious from her remarks that Sorg's theology of work, which interpreted Benedict in light of fifteen centuries of development, was a source of inspiration to her. Thus, she concluded with a positive appraisal of Sorg's presentation and readily associated it with Maurin's synthesis:

> He [Sorg] goes in also for a deeper theology of manual labor in dealing with man as co-creator with God; taking the raw materials that God has provided, making things of use and of beauty, and thus bringing about in his life that synthesis of cult, culture, and cultivation that Peter Maurin used to talk so much about.[69]

It is of some consequence that Dorothy twice appealed to Maurin in the course of this article, once in referring to his synthesis and earlier in citing his plan for the horarium of the farming commune. Both Maurin's overall synthesis as well as his horarium were based on the Benedictine model, the second-named alloting four hours a day for manual labor, with other times specified for reading (*lectio divina*), and prayer.[70]

Beyond his friendship with Virgil Michel and his independent study of church history, Maurin was heir to the Benedictine tradition in a manner which, though derivative, was nonetheless important to Dorothy. While a member of the Institute of Brothers for Christian Schools (Christian Brothers), Maurin had absorbed the teachings of its founder, John Baptist de la Salle (1651–1719). De la Salle had recommended to his followers the writings of Cardinal Bérulle, founder of the French Oratory, which was modeled after Philip Neri's original foundation in Italy. The Roman saint was a favorite with Maurin, and he patterned his discussions and easy essays after Neri. Neri had been influenced by the Benedictine spirit in his youth, and, in the Oratory which he founded, he attempted to encourage a reform among the clergy that would entail higher spiritual ideals and greater personal dedication.[71]

Dorothy considered Maurin her teacher until the end of her days. She culled insights from him, from Sorg and others, directly from Benedict's writings, and in the end formed her own distinctive synthesis. Two pregnant comments written in her last decade will serve as prelude to a brief survey of this development:

> Peter Maurin used to say the great need of the time was to study and meditate upon a philosophy of work. St. Benedict in his rule emphasized the need of a balance of spiritual, mental and manual labor. The spiritual was also physical, in that prayers were chanted, at fixed hours during the day. . . .
>
> The work of the spirit is indeed *work,* and must be done. But my column is due, and I must write it. I must earn my bed and board.[72]

Dorothy spoke with ease of the primacy of the spiritual and the relationship of the work of prayer to other work. A sense of integration was punctuated by charming practicality and humor. Surely, by her seventy-ninth year, she had earned her bread many times over. Yet, as matriarch of a large Benedictine-inspired family, she was unceasing in her efforts to give good example.

Dorothy's synthesis, still in its formative period throughout the 1930s, was based explicitly on the person of Christ, and it was her love for him that shone through her later expression of the Benedictine spirit. She had taken seriously the words of her early advisor, Paulist Father Joseph McSorley. With him, she believed firmly that prayer was the first duty of all those working for social justice, and only that which was done for Christ and with Christ was of value.[73]

A letter written by Virgil Michel to one of his collaborators early in 1936 stands as clear testimony that Dorothy and her co-workers were by then striving to emulate the Benedictine idea encapsulated in the motto "to work and to pray." From the larger context of the letter it is evident that Michel affirmed their efforts and sought to allay the fears of some professional religious that the Catholic Worker imitation would detract from a religious order's guardianship of the ideal:

> Some aspects of their life they [the Catholic Workers] consider as fol-
> lowing the Benedictine ideal of *ora et labora* [work and prayer]. It seems
> to me that they are perfectly at liberty to do this if they wish and that
> doing so in no way implies that their life is *the* ideal living out of the
> Benedictine motto.[74]

Dorothy apparently agreed with a then popular inversion of the Bene-dictine motto, which stated that to work is to pray (*laborare est orare*). This agreement is not to be taken at face value, however. Employed by the artist Eric Gill, whose essays were rephrased by Maurin and printed in the *Catholic Worker,* users of the slogan often recognized work as the overflow of worship and not as its substitute. This was the case with Dorothy, who in addressing a group of would-be Catholic Workers in the early 1940s, admonished them that "the Mass is the Work!" All their activities were first to be offered and united frequently with the sacrifice of Christ on the cross and on the altar. Because Dorothy felt that all life flowed from worship, only thus would their work be a suc-cess, irrespective of its external attainment. By 1940 the daily pattern of life at the Catholic Worker had settled into a monklike pattern of alternation between work and prayer, sans the quiet orderliness of a traditional monastery. Dorothy observed that their days were all the same, with Mass and communion, breakfast, involvement with people

who came to them in need and with those who came to help. The
latter joined forces with her in their attempts to know God, and to
love and serve God in their fellows. To live in love: "that is all that
life is. The writing, the traveling and speaking flow out of it."[75]

The centrality of the Mass was crucial to Dorothy, and she never
ceased to consider it as the greatest work of the day. All her life was
a meeting with Christ. In performing the works of mercy, the unifying
task of the Catholic Worker's labor, she met Christ in human guise.
In the Eucharist, which she believed was the heart of her life, she met
Christ disguised in word and human symbol, received him sacramentally, and was intimately transformed by him:

> [The Mass brings] us into the closest of all contacts with our Lord Jesus
> Christ, enabling us literally to "put on Christ," as St. Paul said, and
> to begin to say with Him, "Now, not I live, but Jesus Christ in me."
> With a strong consciousness of this, we remember too those lines,
> "without Me, ye can do nothing," and "with Me you can do all things."
> . . . Only by nourishing ourselves as we have been bidden to do by Christ,
> by eating His body and drinking His blood, can we become Christ and
> put on the new man. . . . Our need to worship, to praise, to give thanks-
> giving, makes us return to the Mass daily, as the only fitting worship
> which we can offer God. . . .
>
> But the Mass begins our day, it is our food and drink, our delight,
> our refreshment, our courage, our light.[76]

In one of her frequent reminiscences, Dorothy observed that the
liturgical movement meant everything to the Catholic Worker from
the beginning. She was convinced that the Catholic Worker movement
had come about because she had been going to daily Mass, receiving
communion daily, and crying out like Samuel for direction. Moreover,
once a group formed around Peter Maurin and herself, interest in the
prayer of the Work of God developed, due to the enthusiasm of an
unnamed former Franciscan seminarian and the encouragement of Virgil Michel. Within the first few months they began the recitation of
some of the Liturgy of the Hours: sometimes vespers and always com-
pline. Current editions of the tools of good works—in this case, the
missal and variants of the breviary—and a commitment to the prayer
within, were part of Dorothy's life from then on.[77]

Encouraged by the *Rule* of Benedict, Dorothy sought closeness to
Christ in every aspect of her life. Having identified Christ as a worker,

she exerted herself in support of the labor union movement in the
1930s and the 1940s, and, as her advocacy of César Chávez and the
United Farm Workers in the 1960s and 1970s illustrates, never abandoned her efforts to work for a world in which justice dwelt. As she
had written at the time of the Bethlehem Steel strike in 1941:

> Christ was a worker, born by choice into their class, used to hardship
> and poverty. Because His feet walked where theirs have trod, because
> His hands were also broadened and soiled by tools and sweat, because
> we want to be close to Him, as close to Him in this life as we can pos-
> sibly get, because through love of Him we love our brothers, we were
> at Bethlehem (so strangely named) this past week.[78]

Dorothy believed that manual labor was one of the foundations of
the Catholic Worker movement. She viewed manual labor, voluntary
poverty, and the works of mercy as a means of reaching workers, teaching them by example and being taught by them in turn. Her understanding of the necessity of work encompassed both the explicit theology of Benedict's *Rule* and its later development. Work that was
worthy of respect was necessary for the health of body and soul; necessary as penance for sins and penance laid on humankind by God;
necessary as an exercise of creation, in which the worker became co-
creator with God, taking God's raw materials and constructing, building, sewing, cooking, sheltering, warming, and recreating self and
others.[79]

Commentary on the relationship between work and prayer
abounds in Dorothy's writings. Not only did she write a number of
lengthy articles on work, but she sponsored other persons' reflections
on the topic as well. Prayer was no less important to her, though she
preferred to make comments in passing rather than to write a lengthy
exposition. She frequently alluded to her use of the breviary and Little
Office, to attendance at daily Mass, and to her use of the missal. She
was no stranger to traditional spiritual reading, but, with the wide selection of materials in which she found food for reflection, she moved
beyond constraints which a strictly monastic interpretation of *lectio
divina* would have placed upon her. Dorothy's was a rich, personal
piety, firmly rooted in the community prayer of ecclesial worship. The
witness of her life demonstrates that she moved in Benedictine fashion,
from the Work of God in its broad sense to the works of God and

back again to prayer. She had well divined the intentions of Benedict, who endeavored with his followers to

> See how the Lord in his love shows us the way of life. Clothed then with faith and the performance of good works, let us set out on this way, with the Gospel for our guide, that we may deserve to see him *who has called* us *to his kingdom* (1 Thess 2:12).[80]

Her pursuit of this path led Dorothy to an even closer identification with the Benedictine charism, which she effected through her affiliation as a secular Benedictine oblate.

Dorothy Day, Benedictine Oblate

The secular oblates of St. Benedict belong to an ancient tradition within the Benedictine order. Persons of all walks of life have become oblates — priests, bishops, and laypersons, including some members of royalty. A person who wished to become an oblate made application to be admitted into affiliation with the monks of a particular monastery, requested their prayers and a share in their good works, and adopted a manner of life identified with the monks' *conversatio morum,* or conversion of manner of life. In the early medieval period the secular oblates were known as *confratres* (England) or *inscripti* or *donati* (continental Europe). The term *oblati* had first been used to designate young boys who were brought to the monastery by their parents to be reared and educated by the monks. By the thirteenth century, however, the term was extended to include adults who freely made an offering of themselves to the monastery of their choice. The adults ordinarily transferred a part of their material goods to the monastery in return for the privilege of association with the monks and at death were often interred within the monastic enclosure. After a waning of both monasticism and the oblate tradition in the wake of the sixteenth-century Reformation, both were revived in the middle of the nineteenth century. American Benedictine abbots' attempts to foster the institution of lay oblates may be traced to the end of the nineteenth century. By this time the affiliation had become spiritualized and was chiefly understood as a means of sharing in the prayer and good works of the monks. It was this latter conception to which Dorothy was heir.[81]

The vehicle of Dorothy's earliest known acquaintance with monasticism was her reading of a trilogy of Huysmans' novels. One of these, *The Oblate,* traced the main lines of the author's initiation as a Benedictine oblate through the novel's chief character, Durtal. Dorothy's more serious exposure to the oblate tradition began in the 1930s, chiefly through her collaboration with Virgil Michel and other Benedictines. Correspondence between Michel and other members of the Catholic Worker group served to further Dorothy's awareness of the oblate tradition.[82] She also received encouragement from her friends Raïssa and Jacques Maritain, who had become oblates shortly after their conversion to the Catholic faith.[83]

While Dorothy did not move toward affiliation with any of the oblate groups in the 1930s, she was aware of them and in at least one instance was inspired by the presence of a growing number of oblates in the United States. Since she was spiritually close to Collegeville and followed *Orate Fratres* avidly, it is probable that she knew of Abbot Deutsch's *Manual for Oblates of St. Benedict,* which was published in 1937.[84]

Her connection with another group, the English Benedictine congregation at Portsmouth, Rhode Island, had begun to surface by this time, and may be easily traced through Dorothy's friendship with Ade Bethune. This Belgian immigrant, a staff artist for the *Catholic Worker* in its early years, had established her studio at Newport, Rhode Island, by November 1936 and in a relatively short time was engaged in teaching arts and crafts at the nearby priory school at Portsmouth. In 1940 Bethune was added to the roster of oblates attached to this English Benedictine priory, setting a precedent for Dorothy, whose oblate affiliation with the group may be dated from 1942. It is obvious that Dorothy had become acquainted with the Portsmouth group herself, as well as through Bethune. An early 1937 letter from the prior, J. Hugh Diman, O.S.B., requested a renewal of their subscription to the paper, a fact which is strong evidence in support of the priory's contact with the movement early in 1936. Moreover, one of their young members, Father Joseph Woods, O.S.B., spent several summers at the Catholic Worker farm, gave a series of evening talks at the house on Mott Street, and presented days of recollection there, at Newport, and at Portsmouth during the years 1937–1943. Dorothy attended these as frequently as possible. Her notes and comments from this period and recollections made years afterwards testify to the impact which

Woods had upon her as a speaker, particularly through his references to God's love and forgiveness shown in the parable of the Hebrew prophet Hosea.[85]

Dorothy clearly associated her oblate conversion with her reading of the Fathers of the desert and alluded to her preoccupation with them on several occasions. She had been directed generally to the Fathers of the church by Peter Maurin, who insisted that such study formed the basis for the social reconstruction advocated by Pius XI. For Dorothy the term *Fathers* included both those of Western origin such as Ambrose, Augustine, and Benedict and those of the desert and semi-desert regions of the Middle East, such as Anthony of Egypt, Basil of Cappadocia, Ephraim the Syrian, Cassian, and other lesser-known figures. Those of the Middle East are important for the present consideration, since the most ancient monastic literature, on which Benedict the founder of Western monasticism depended, consisted of a collection of sayings attributed to the Desert Fathers. That Dorothy was familiar with them is evident from an incidental remark made early in 1941: "On my way to the printers this morning I thought of the monk in the desert who measured distances by decades of the rosary."[86] A slim volume of Helen Waddell's *The Desert Fathers* came into her hands shortly after its American publication in 1942 and was the single work which Dorothy felt was most responsible for her oblate conversion. By September 1943 she shared with her readers both the fact of summer talks on the *Rule* of Benedict given to oblates by Thomas Verner Moore, O.S.B., and her recent decision to take a year's sabbatical from the Catholic Worker movement. The sabbatical was viewed by her as a desert experience, a time for interior renewal. Her readings then and later included frequent rereadings of *The Desert Fathers* and a range of works on Eastern monachism.[87]

Judging from her frequent allusions to the same portion of Helen Waddell's work, it is clear that Dorothy had developed an appreciation for Ephraim the Syrian (c. 306–373). He was a quiet scholar, and without fail a man of hospitality to all who came to him. In the crisis of famine which visited his countryside, Ephraim "turned man of affairs, building a rough-and-ready hospital of three hundred beds, nursing and feeding those who had any spark of life in them, burying the dead."[88] He wore himself out in the exercise of the works of mercy, much as did Dorothy in the twentieth century. Undoubtedly, she was inspired by his example, but also by the context and ardor of the saint's prayer recorded in "The Life of St. Mary the Harlot." An excerpt from the prayer, which Dorothy frequently reprinted, consists of the following lines:

> Sorrow on me, beloved! that I unapt and reluctant in my will abide, and behold, winter hath come upon me, and the infinite tempest hath found me naked and spoiled and with no perfecting of good in me. I marvel at myself, O my beloved, how I daily default and daily do repent; I build up for an hour and an hour overthrows what I have built.
>
> At evening I say, tomorrow I will repent, but when morning comes, joyous I waste the day. Again at evening I say, I shall keep vigil all night and I shall entreat the Lord to have mercy on my sins. But when night is come, I am full of sleep.
>
> Behold, those who received their talent along with me strive by day and night to trade with it, that they may win the word of praise and rule ten cities. But I, in my sloth, hid mine in the earth and my Lord makes haste to come, and behold, my heart trembles and I weep the day of my negligence and know not what excuse to bring. Have mercy upon me, Thou, Who alone art without sin, and save me, Who alone art pitiful and kind.[89]

The prayer is Ephraim's own, and in its complete form as found in Waddell, concluded his story of the penitent Mary and her uncle, the blessed monk Abraham. It follows upon Ephraim's assessment of the loving forgiveness Mary received from God, of the inspiration which her converted life offered to all who knew her, of the sanctity of both uncle and niece, and concluded with Ephraim's realization of his own need for repentence. Upon a narrow reading of Waddell's selection from Ephraim's works one might associate the forgiveness which Mary received with Dorothy's compunction for the bohemian years of her preconverted life. Dorothy's affection for the prayer would include that certainly but also embraced the sense of gratitude for God's mercy expressed by Ephraim himself. Dorothy's compunction extended beyond the sexual sphere, for attuned to God's working within her, she was sensitive to her failings in all areas. The sure confidence in God's mercy which found its way into her spirituality was based upon a positive anthropology which runs through the Psalms, through the Christian personalists Mounier and Maritain, and upon the image of mercy presented by the Desert Fathers.[90]

It is clear that Dorothy remained affiliated with the Portsmouth priory at least until 1946.[91] However, she eventually moved the locus of her oblate affiliation to the monks of St. Procopius Abbey in Lisle, Illinois, with whom she made her full profession in April of 1955. The broad strokes of this movement may be traced from data presented in Dorothy's writings, in her friend Helene Iswolsky's references, and in recent testimonies of Vitus Buresh, O.S.B., and Christian Ceplecha, O.S.B., both monks of St. Procopius Abbey. The earliest pertinent reference to St. Procopius may be found in the June 1935 issue of the *Catholic Worker* and consists simply of a notice of a vocation pamphlet written by Augustine Studeny, O.S.B., a monk of St. Procopius. By mid-November 1940 Dorothy had stopped off at the Lisle abbey in the course of one of her speaking tours. From her description in the December issue of the paper, it is probable that this was her first visit to St. Procopius. Helene Iswolsky, a Russian émigrée who arrived in the United States in June 1941, had occasion to meet Father Chrysostom Tarasevitch, O.S.B., monk and instructor at St. Procopius College, while she was engaged in a lecture circuit of Catholic colleges in 1943. Iswolsky's memoir vividly recalled the event, giving her perspective on the monk's importance:

> In Chicago, I also met Father Chrysostom Tarasevich [*sic*], a Benedictine monk of the Byzantine rite. He came from Belorussia, one of the Soviet republics whose language and culture are very similar to those of Russia and the Ukraine. This meeting was the beginning of a friendship of many years with this outstanding priest so deeply imbued with Eastern spirituality and the love of the Russian people, in war and in peace. . . . Later, I met him in New York, where he often came to preach at retreats for the *Catholic Worker*. He did much to promote my own ecumenical work.[92]

Helene's reminiscence of that first meeting is important, since there are a number of points of convergence which relate to Dorothy. First, a friendship had already begun to develop between Dorothy and Helene, following upon their first meeting sometime before December 1941; second, by that time each knew of the other's love for Russian spirituality and culture; third, St. Procopius was by 1943 well established as an ecumenical center whose special mission was to labor for the reunion of the Eastern (Orthodox) churches with Rome.

Dorothy's early appreciation of the mission of St. Procopius may be gathered from a reprint found in the September 1943 edition of

the *Catholic Worker.* Entitled "Slavonic Mission," it presented the Benedictine center, with its high school, college, and seminary and its work
among Slavonic immigrants in the Midwest, as well equipped to foster
an understanding of Russian culture. The essay projected the abbey's
hope of sending Benedictines of the Eastern rite as missioners to Russia as soon as this became feasible. Another link with the abbey arrived
in the person of Michael Kovalak, who after several years as a seminarian at St. Procopius joined the Catholic Worker group, remaining
affiliated with the latter until his death in 1977. Since Kovalak is known
to have lovingly cared for Maurin toward the end of his terminal illness, obviously the former monk had joined the Catholic Worker
movement sometime prior to Maurin's death on 15 May 1949. Lisle
Benedictines Buresh and Ceplecha recalled hearing Dorothy speak at
the college on at least one occasion, placing the event in the late 1940s.
In November 1951 Dorothy recorded a then recent talk of hers at St.
Procopius Abbey, a fact which argues for her established association
with the abbey by this time.[93] The pages of the *Catholic Worker* witness further contact with the monks of St. Procopius, particularly with
Rembert Sorg, O.S.B., and Chrysostom Tarasevitch, O.S.B.

Dorothy was greatly impressed by Rembert Sorg's presentation
and living out of a Benedictine theology of work. A short quotation
from Sorg, entitled "Manual Labor as Mortification," appeared in the
March 1948 issue of the paper. It was printed without comment or further identification but illustrates that Dorothy was aware of him prior
to the publication of his work, *Towards a Benedictine Theology of
Manual Labor.* Dorothy's spoke with appreciation of the last named
work in her October 1949 essay "Work." At the time of writing the
column, she was well acquainted with Sorg, the articles he had written
for *Orate Fratres,* and the fact that he was "living his philosophy of
labor" at Holy Cross Mission in Wisconsin. Sorg visited the Catholic
Worker farm on Staten Island on at least one occasion, on 21 April
1951, when he led a roundtable discussion of a theology of manual
labor. It is quite possible that he was among the monks of the Lisle
abbey who periodically conducted days of recollection for a New York
group of oblates affiliated with St. Procopius. Dorothy's interest in
Sorg's mission in Fifield, Wisconsin, with its community of oblate families living around the monastery, is illustrated by her printing of "Benedictines and the Catholic Worker Movement" in the March 1953 issue

of the paper. That she followed his later literary efforts is evident from a May 1958 review of his study of the newly instituted liturgy of St. Joseph the Workman.[94]

Chrysostom Tarasevitch, O.S.B., known for his efforts toward rapprochement between the Roman Catholic and Russian Orthodox churches, was a closer friend. Three of his letters to the Catholic Worker group appeared in the paper as a prelude to his two-part article "The Church in Russia," which appeared in the May and June 1949 issues of the *Catholic Worker*. One of the monks who conducted days of recollection for the New York group of St. Procopius oblates, Tarasevitch also gave retreats and talks at New York Catholic Worker locations. Given Dorothy's interest in Russian spirituality and her ecumenical spirit, it is plausible that she followed his articles in *Orates Fratres* as well. She later spoke of him as a beloved friend and frequently got in touch with him when her speaking trips took her to Chicago.[95]

Imperceptibly, Dorothy found herself drawing closer to St. Procopius Abbey. Sometime before the end of 1954, she was in communication with Father Claude [Viktora, O.S.B.], then director of oblates. She recalled speaking to him during her mid-November stay there, her official purpose being to present a lecture at the college. Six months later she reported joyfully to her readers of her recent profession as a full oblate:

> How Peter [Maurin] loved St. Benedict whose motto was "Work and Pray." He is happy, no doubt, that I, his co-worker, was professed last month as a full oblate of St. Benedict, attached to St. Procopius Abbey, the mission of which is to work for unity between east and west, and which aims to set up a shrine to the eastern saints, at the monastery at Lisle, Illinois.[96]

Her profession was made on 26 April 1955 and was ratified by two monks of St. Procopius, Abbot Ambrose L. Ondrak, O.S.B., and Brendan Mc-Grath, O.S.B. Two years later, Dorothy again commented on the significance of her oblate profession and her predilection for St. Procopius Abbey:

> Now I am a professed oblate of the St. Procopius family, and have been for the last two years, which means that I am a part of the Benedictine family all over the world, and a member of the Benedictine community at Lisle and every month a news letter comes from St. Procopius, from the pen of Fr. Richard [Sonka, O.S.B.], oblate master. My special

love for St. Procopius is because its special function is to pray for the reunion of Rome and the Eastern Church. Their monks can offer Mass in the Eastern or Roman rite and when Fr. Chrysostom [Tarasevitch] came to give us retreats at Maryfarm, we sang the liturgy of St. John Chrysostom. St. Procopius is also to be the shrine of the Eastern saints in this country.[97]

EXPANSION OF MONASTIC INTERESTS (1955–1980)

The esteem in which Dorothy held the Benedictine tradition was uneclipsed in the period following upon her profession as a lay Benedictine oblate. While her interests expanded, the Benedictine influence remained a constant and included her fidelity to prayer, her valuing of manual labor, her concern for hospitality to the end of her days, and her unfailing desire to provide a familial community setting for both guests and staff of the Catholic Worker. Witnesses to this fidelity include Stanley Vishnewski, one of her co-workers, who in the late 1960s recalled the lasting influence of the Benedictine charism upon the movement:

> The Benedictine Tradition has had a great influence on the Catholic Worker. Peter Maurin used to tell us in his conferences how the Benedictine Monks swept over Europe after the fall of the Roman Empire and established "Farming Communes" which helped keep learning alive during the so-called Dark Ages.
> I am sure that without the influence of the Benedictines that there would be very little in the Catholic Worker Movement—For from the Benedictines we got the ideal of Hospitality—Guest Houses—Farming Communes—Liturgical Prayer. Take these away and there is very little left in the Catholic Worker Program.[98]

Two letters written within the last sixteen years of her life attest to the high priority Dorothy gave her status as a Benedictine oblate. In the first, addressed in 1966 to Colman Barry, O.S.B., of Collegeville, she graciously declined an honorary degree from St. John's University and then reminded President Barry of her Benedictine affiliation:

> Let me say first of all, that I love Saint John's and have loved the Benedictines ever since the days of Fr. Virgil Michel who was so great a friend of Peter Maurin. From the beginning of the Catholic Worker I have always been made welcome there. I am myself an oblate of Saint Benedict

of Saint Procopius Abbey and many of our former Catholic Workers are oblates. This letter would be too long [if I were] to tell all we have learned from Saint Benedict.[99]

A decade later, she received an invitation from Charles Finnegan, O.F.M., then minister provincial, to become affiliated with the Franciscans of Holy Name province. Her answer was a simple, "I'm a Benedictine oblate,"[100] which in her mind precluded a simultaneous formal affiliation with a second major religious order.

These responses are illustrative of her allegiance to the commitment, and she enriched it by other Benedictine-inspired contacts. Among her Benedictine friends she counted Mother Benedict Duss, O.S.B., of Regina Laudis Abbey and Brother David Steindl-Rast, O.S.B., of Mount Saviour Monastery.[101] Most telling among such contacts, however, was her friendship with Thomas (Father M. Louis) Merton, O.C.S.O. (1915–1968), of Gethsemani Abbey and her later interest in the Trappist-inspired fraternities of Charles de Foucauld (1858–1916).

Thomas Merton: A Kindred Spirit

Dorothy's link with the monks of Gethsemani in Kentucky had been established even before Merton entered the monastery in 1941. The Order of Cistercians of Strict Observance (Trappists) was heir to a number of reforms within the Benedictine tradition, the first of them dating back to the end of the eleventh century. Successive waves of reform sought to reestablish the primitive observance of the *Rule* of Benedict. Emphasis was placed on utmost simplicity and austerity of life, on communal recitation of the Divine Office, and upon restoring manual labor to the life of the monk.[102] Dorothy had become acquainted with the Trappists of Gethsemani through Abbot Frederic M. Dunne's response to one of her appeals. The Trappist's earliest extant letter, dated 15 April 1936, was addressed generically to "the editors," implying that Dorothy's friendship with Dunne was not yet established. Correspondence over the next decade, addressed directly to Dorothy, reveals that he and his monks actively supported her and the movement through prayer and monetary donations, and that the abbot—if not the monks in general—read her writings. Dorothy confided both Catholic Worker and family concerns to Abbot Dunne and later remarked to Merton what a good friend the old abbot had been.[103]

In 1948 American readers welcomed the publication of Merton's autobiography, *The Seven Storey Mountain,* and the same year his first contributions appeared in the *Catholic Worker.* Reviews of Merton's larger works, quotations from them, articles by him on a range of subjects, and an occasional poem were published regularly in the paper over the next twenty years, and then occasionally after his death in 1968. While a survey of Merton's contributions to the *Catholic Worker* provides insights, the heart of the Day-Merton friendship and reciprocal influence may best be grasped through looking at their correspondence. Their letters to one another are filled with pathos and humor, and above all with sensitivity to the things of the Spirit. It is obvious that by 1959, the eleventh year of Merton's appearance in the *Catholic Worker* and the year of their first extant letters, a solid and mutually respectful friendship had developed between them.

An understanding of the evolution of their friendship up until 1959 can be gleaned from examining early Merton contributions to the paper. The first of these, a poem entitled, "Clairvaux Prison," was printed in the January 1948 edition of the *Catholic Worker,* and it was followed in April by a short review of *Figures for an Apocalypse,* a collection of Merton's poetry. These made little impact, but the printing of a lengthy excerpt from his *Seeds of Contemplation* in April 1949 augured well for future contributions. This selection spoke of the necessity of an ordinary routine of work and poverty, lived out of love, in order to find God and to give God to others. Merton's recognition of the namelessness and other indignities suffered by the poor showed a depth of awareness unexpected in a cloistered, contemplative monk and could not have failed to alert Dorothy.[104] That she and her co-workers followed his works avidly is evident from positive book reviews of ten of Merton's books which appeared in the *Catholic Worker* throughout the 1950s. Given that lengthy selections from *The Sign of Jonas* and *Thoughts in Solitude* were printed in the paper, it is likely that the themes of these works struck deep chords within Dorothy.[105]

In her June 1959 letter to Merton, the first of those which survive, Dorothy expressed gratitude for his recent letter and gifts that he had sent on to the Catholic Worker crowd, and remembered again the impact that his gift copies of *The Seven Storey Mountain,* sent some years ago, had on them. Several members of the Catholic Worker group were entrusted to his prayer, and the letter includes incidental remarks about the de Foucauld association and her recent imprisonment for disregarding air raid shelter warnings. In Merton's 9 July 1959 reply, he acknowledged:

> I am touched deeply by your witness for peace. You are very right in going at it along the lines of Satyagraha. I see no other way, though of course the angles of the problem are not all clear. I am certainly with you on taking some kind of stand and acting accordingly. . . . Don't worry about whether or not in every point you are perfectly right according to everybody's books: you are right before God as far as you can go and you are fighting for a truth that is clear enough and important enough. What more can anybody do?[106]

It was Dorothy's witness for peace which influenced Merton's own thinking. The importance of peace, their mutual interest in the monastic tradition, the need for perseverance and concern for others marked their correspondence until its abrupt termination by Merton's death on 10 December 1968.

Writing at Christmas of 1959, she offered him an extra volume of Cassian. The book was later received by Merton with gratitude, and the exchange bespoke their interest in the very sources that had nourished their patron, Benedict. Dorothy confided to Merton her constant prayer for perseverance, as well as her disposition of trust in God's providence. This revelation was both for her encouragement and for his consolation. The mention of perseverance evoked a response in Merton's next letter:

> Perseverance—yes, more and more one sees that it is the great thing. But there is a thing that must not be overlooked. Perseverance is not hanging on to some course which we have set our minds to, and refusing to let go. It is not even a matter of getting a bulldog grip on the faith and not letting the devil pry us loose from it—though many of the saints made it look that way. Really, there is something lacking in such a hope as that. Hope is a greater scandal than we think. I am coming to think that God (may He be praised in His great mystery) loves and helps best those who are so beat and have so much nothing when they come to die that it is almost as if they had persevered in nothing but had gradually lost everything, piece by piece, until there was nothing left but God. Hence perseverance is not hanging on but letting go. That of course is terrible. But as you say so rightly, it is a question of His hanging on to us, by the hair of the head, that is from on top and beyond, where we cannot see or reach.[107]

In her 4 June 1960 letter to Merton, Dorothy declared "of course we want the Prometheus," a chapter for his forthcoming *The New Man.* Shortly afterwards Merton sent the essay in draft form, as he did with much of his work, for her preview and comment. Inviting a friendly exchange, Dorothy later inquired whether Merton had received the Cassian, spoke of her use of Dostoevsky as spiritual reading, and wondered whether Merton also read him. She mentioned that it was a stressful time for her, as she was concerned over Tamar's latest pregnancy and her son-in-law David Hennessy's chronic illness. As she begged for Merton's prayers, she assured him of her own. Merton's response of 17 August 1960 remarked on the Cassian *Conferences* as a welcome addition to the novitiate library and as helpful to him in presenting Cassian to the novices. He regarded the *Conferences,* one of the sourcebooks for Benedict, as their "only real manual of ascetic theology. I love Cassian, though I cannot always be as tough as he is." As in the *Seeds of Contemplation,* previously quoted by her in the *Catholic Worker,* he contrasted the self-satisfied poverty of his state of life with the stark reality of the poverty of the destitute whom he had met the previous day at the Little Sisters of the Poor in Louisville. Because he was not poor (i.e., destitute), in the monastery, he wondered if he were true to Christ. In response to Dorothy's questions he reflected on his love for Dostoevsky and concluded with a prayer for their mutual perseverance.[108]

In her 10 October missive, Dorothy acknowledged Merton's gift of *Disputed Questions.* It is apparent that at the time of writing, Dorothy had read at least two of the essays: "The Pasternak Affair" and "The Spirituality of Sinai," the latter being a study of the sixth-century Eastern monk, John Climacus (570–649). She read other essays in this collection as well and took their message to heart, for excerpts from two of them later appeared in the *Catholic Worker.* The first was selected from the essay entitled "Notes for a Philosophy of Solitude," in which Merton stressed the spiritual journey as growth from the false to the true self. The second excerpt, from "Christianity and Totalitarianism," underscored the necessity for a Christianity which respected the freedom of each person, and which entailed personal commitment rather than mindless adherence to a mass movement. In the course of this letter, Dorothy posited the value of Christian freedom, in line with the excerpt selected by the paper, but because of bitterness and criticism which had spread among staff members at the Catholic Worker, she trembled at her responsibility:

All this rebellion makes me long for obedience, hunger and thirst for it, as a woman does for a husband whom she can esteem and who will direct her. Women especially cry out against their terrible freedom. But trying to be obedient and also personally responsible, responsive to the calls made upon one, means we are overburdened.[109]

It is important to notice that at this writing, Dorothy was exhausted after a summer spent caring for Tamar's children on the occasion of the birth of her daughter's ninth child, from worry over her son-in-law's physical and mental health, in addition to the onus of regular life at the Catholic Worker during a difficult period. Yet, despite her own sense of futility, she was mindful of the encouragement that her friend needed. She assured an uncertain Merton that his writing was the work God wanted him to do, no matter how much he tried to run away from it.

Merton's searching letter of 23 July 1961 indicated to Dorothy the personal helplessness he felt in the face of world conditions in general and the implied situation of Vietnam in particular. He contrasted the frustration of the Catholic Worker staff in the face of reality with his own removed awareness. The courage to recognize and to deal with the face of reality to overcome one's own delusions of grandeur or self-sufficiency, to do all that one can to better conditions, yet to realize that success depends ultimately on God: all these are themes from which Merton seldom strayed. Yet, he worried that his own writings contributed to a general sense of delusion, in that they would be used in the service of falsity. The label, a "Catholic position," attached to them was easily associated with a system that desired to defend itself, and God's glory, with bombs. His enclosure of a gruesome poem on Auschwitz underscored the monk's preoccupation with a horror of all wars.[110]

Dorothy's precipitous publication of this poem, "Chant to Be Used in Processions around a Site with Furnaces," caused Merton some consternation because it had not first passed the Trappist censors. This is evident from the apology of Dorothy's 15 August letter to him, censorship by his superiors being a factor which had not entered her mind. At the date of writing she was still in the midst of a personally difficult period because of her son-in-law's chronic illness and the strain which this placed on her daughter and their large family. In spite of this, Dorothy was able to look at the worldwide threat of nuclear warfare and take courage from the words of a saint who was also a favorite of Merton's: "Juliana of Norwich said that the worst has already happened and been repaired. Nothing worse can ever befall us."[111]

The censorship of his writings on current issues was problematic for Merton, and he confided as much to Dorothy. He knew that it was not due to a question of faith and morals, but because his superiors thought that Trappists should not write about controversial topics. Merton felt obligated to take world conditions seriously and to say what his conscience dictated, provided that it was not contrary to faith and the church's teaching authority. The problem was one of being in a situation where obedience to his superiors threatened to silence him interminably on important moral issues. Crucial for him was the fact that in the nuclear war issue, others—troubled by cowardice rather than censorship by superiors—were likewise silent. An agonized faith sears this letter:

> somehow God always makes it possible for me to say what seems to be necessary, and hence there is no question that I am completely in His hands where I am and that I should therefore continue as I am doing. But why this awful silence and apathy on the part of Catholics, clergy, hierarchy, lay people on this terrible issue on which the very continued existence of the human race depends?[112]

By 22 September 1961, Merton had an already censored article "The Root of War," ready for inclusion in the pages of the *Catholic Worker.* Printed in October, it soon appeared as a chapter in his *New Seeds of Contemplation.* In the quick note attached to the article sent for the paper, Merton affirmed Dorothy as a collaborator in the work for peace, and pledged to be united with her in prayer and trust in working for the abolition of war in any way he could, even though there be slight hope of success. Addressing her, he judged that in this issue "you have been one of the few that have really responded to God."[113]

Shortly afterwards the paper carried Merton's article on "The Shelter Ethic," in the course of which he defended the right of a man to ward off intruders from his family air raid shelter by force of arms, should such necessity arise. Dorothy disagreed with Merton's approach, and without naming him, said as much in her column for December. She believed that the gospel message supported her stand as a pacifist and concluded that "the theologians who justify a man's right to defend himself, are preaching *casuistry*, dealing with *cases* which should be dealt with in the confessional, not in the pulpit or the press." Merton addressed this criticism in his 20 December 1961 letter to her, consciously moving from casuistry to her own ground of argument, namely, the dignity of each person. In accord with the thinking of the Greek Fathers—with whom he felt more at ease than with the Scholastics—Merton spoke of the restoration of the fullness of human nature in each person through the grace of God. He posited that a true understanding of the natural law, rather than being a reduction of the argument to cases, enabled one to view natural law—the law of our human nature—as that which inclined our inmost heart to conform to the image of God. Such a view of natural law also inclined one to respect and love our neighbor as the image of God, rather than as our enemy. Thus, the person who wished to enter the hypothetical shelter was viewed as another self rather than as an enemy who must be repulsed. An enemy embraced as another self, as brother or sister, is enemy no longer. In rethinking and clarifying his position, Merton found himself in accord with Dorothy's vision of the person as precious in the sight of God.[114]

That Merton was not ostracized from the *Catholic Worker* is evident from subsequent issues of the paper. His substantial article on ethics and war was featured in the March and April 1962 issues. In March of that year he wrote again to Dorothy, requesting that minor revisions be made on a recent paper he had contributed on peace and Christian responsibility. He also commended himself to Dorothy's prayer, as he felt badly in need of light and guidance regarding his efforts and writings on the world situation and peace. He admitted that impetuosity and good will were not enough, but that the Spirit of God would enable persons to derive light even from their own mistakes. In a later response to Dorothy's no longer extant spring letter to him, Merton commiserated with her on the smallness of the peace movement in the United States, wondered about the formation of the American Pax group, and shared his concern over the materials for a forthcoming book on peace. He agreed with her that while activity was important, honest prayer before God was their greatest recourse.[115]

Dorothy's 4 June 1962 letter to him was replete with praise for his efforts on behalf of peace. Without hesitation, she compared Merton favorably with retreat movement leader Father John J. Hugo:

I want to thank you from my heart for the articles you have written and which have been so widely reprinted all over the country. Your[s] has been the first voice among the theologians since Fr. Hugo and his companions in the second world war. Of course I understand from your "letters" which Elbert Sissom let me see on my recent visit to Washginton [*sic*] that you are not a pacifist and that you are speaking in terms of modern war. This may draw the Catholic layman further along the way of peace.[116]

She had by then accepted his position on war as a positive contribution toward peace. Merton acknowledged in his 16 June letter that theoretically he was not a pacifist and so held that there was such a thing as a just war, even today. But in reality all the present century's wars—conventional, guerrilla, or the Cold War itself—were shot through with evil, falsity, injustice, and sin to such a degree that one could only with difficulty extricate the truths and the causes for which the fighting was going on. Thus, while they differed in theory, he found himself agreeing with Dorothy in the practical order:

I am with you, except in so far, only, as a policy of totally uncompromising pacifism may tend in effect to defeat itself and yield to one of the other forms of injustice. And I think that your position has an immense importance as a symbolic statement that is irreplaceable and utterly necessary. I also think it is a scandal that most Christians are not solidly lined up with you. I certainly am.[117]

Merton remarked with apparent equanimity on the fact that his latest book, "Peace in a Post-Christian Era," was not to be published. He observed that his superiors feared that he had gone too far, that he was moving away from the contemplative vocation into "dangerous ground." He determined to go back to the Fathers—Cassiodorus, Cyprian, Tertullian, and the like—and expected to do a book on Cassian some time. Remembering with gratitude the translation of Cassian she had sent some time ago, he concluded with a note on the necessity for personal conversion and a commendation that Dorothy's presence and example were especially precious to him.

Midsummer letters crossed between them commenting on Dorothy's forthcoming trip to Cuba and recording her gratitude for his prayers and for the essays on spiritual direction and on the English mystics which he had recently sent. The evidence of his August 1962 letter to her points to a Merton who cannot *not* write about war and peace issues. He had just sent a letter to Hiroshima in which he felt he made at least a gesture toward peace. He sorrowed with Dorothy that Pax, the American peace movement, was not getting off to a good start. He felt that Catholics were both frustrated and passive, and sought recourse in Dorothy's prayer for him. He gave the lie to the equanimity of his letter of two months past, stating, "I see clearly the futility and misdirection of my own life. But God can accept waste, I suppose, if it is well intended. My gift of zero."[118] Dorothy's 23 August response was both newsy and encouraging. She shared her plans for her September trip to Cuba and a peace pilgrimage with Hildegarde Goss Mayr and her husband, Kasper Mayr, projected for the following April. Comments about the Pax group reveal that the youthful leaders appeared full of enthusiasm but lacked the ability to follow through with action. To a despondent Merton she expressed her delight with the general reaction to his previous articles, which were being picked up and published "all over," and assured him that the *Catholic Worker* could reprint them as well.[119]

Alongside the paper's January 1963 review of a book on peace which Merton had edited may be found a review article of Ignace Lepp's *The Christian Failure.* The reviewer was Merton himself, writing under a pseudonym. The book was based on Lepp's diary, written during the Nazi occupation of France. It illustrated the passivity of the French clergy and the well-to-do laity who collaborated with the Vichy regime in accepting the totalitarian power of Hitler. While purportedly a review of Lepp, the article provided Merton an opportunity to decry the passivity of religious people and clergy in addressing social problems, the most notable being the threat of nuclear warfare. A second pseudonymously published article from this period dealt with the courage of the Danish nonviolent resistance to Hitler. Other excerpts from Merton included a portion of the Pasternak essay, an unidentified selection on the value of writing, and a selection from *New Seeds of Contemplation.* There was a review of *The Prison Meditations of Father Delp,* highlighting Merton's introduction, and one of Merton's study of Clement of Alexandria.[120] Dorothy's extant letters during this period are full of encouragement and gratitude. In March 1963, for instance, she reminded him of the joy his selections from the Desert Fathers had given her, assured him of her confidence that he would persevere, and commended his gift as a writer: "I am sure it [your writing] is a gift of God and you are just as likely to dry up and not be able to write anything later on, so you might as well do all you can now."[121]

While there is a lacuna in extant Day-Merton correspondence from December 1963 through June 1965, Merton was represented in the *Catholic Worker* by favorable reviews of his *A Thomas Merton Reader, Emblems of a Season of Fury,* and *Seeds of Destruction.* Dorothy's June 1965 letter to him evidences no actual break in their communication. She had been reading *The Prison Meditations of Father Delp,* with Merton's introduction, and thanked and praised him once again for his writings: "You will never know the people you have reached, the good you have done." She begged for prayers for their mutual friend Karl Stern, as well as for her daughter, Tamar. In response Merton sent an article on Maximus the Confessor for the *Catholic Worker,* along with an observation that the church was going through difficult yet hopeful times. Both had watched the question of the bomb getting back into schema 13 at the Second Vatican Council, which Merton described as disturbing.[122]

A crisis in Merton's relationship to the peace movement occurred at the end of that year. The suicide of Roger LaPorte, a recent affiliate of the Catholic Worker movement, was the precipitating factor. While not holding the Catholic Worker responsible for what he believed was the encroachment of an ominous spirit of irrationality in peace efforts, Merton felt obliged to end his public identification with peace groups such as Pax and Catholic Peace Fellowship. On 11 November 1965 Merton recorded his distress in a telegram to Dorothy and was promptly answered in her 15 November letter to him. She apprised him of the situation, neither magnifying nor underplaying recent events among draft card burners and other protestors for peace. She admitted that her friend's reaction in holding the Catholic Worker responsible for the LaPorte tragedy might well have been general. She accepted this responsibility, not because she encouraged the drastic measure, but because "as members of one Body [Christ] we are all responsible for each other." She wondered if he had been reading recent issues of the *Catholic Worker* and alerted him to the speech on war, racism, and the media delivered by Cardinal Paul-Emile Léger several months ago. As if to calm the shock that she knew Merton felt, she placed the LaPorte tragedy in the larger context of the situation in Vietnam and rejoiced that others had joined the Catholic Worker in protesting the inhumanity of war — a burden which the movement had borne for thirty-three years. Again, she gave an assurance that his works—in this instance, *The Seven Storey Mountain*—continued to reach others and concluded with a simple statement: "We all love you dearly and please keep praying for us."[123]

Merton's reply offered both sincere apology and explanation for the November telegram. Obviously he was torn between his innate need to write, his superiors' prohibition against writing on controversial current events, and his vocation to solitude. Moreover, someone responding to his proposed withdrawal from public involvement in the peace movement had argued that Merton's entire life was an evasion. The dilemma was compounded by author-friend James Douglass's insistence that he write something on peace. Merton's despondence extended to an admitted inability to write anything for the *Catholic Worker* for the time being and to a soul-searching endeavor to live out his vocation as monk. Dorothy's reply shows that she took her friend seriously, appreciated his contemplative vocation, and refrained from judging either him or his superiors in his retreat from direct writing for and sponsorship of the peace movement. Employing the example of both her own 1943–1944 solitude-sabbatical from the *Catholic Worker* and the recent silencing of Father Daniel Berrigan, S.J., in the form of an assignment to South America, she confirmed that Merton's dilemma could have value in deepening his own experience and knowledge. As always, she thanked him for the inspiration of his writings and in this instance for an unnamed book of his which had just arrived.[124]

Dorothy's response gave Merton courage and enabled him to reach a solution with his sponsorship of Catholic Peace Fellowship. He would continue as a sponsor in that he heartily endorsed the members' pastoral activities, but would make it clear that he did not take responsibility for every political act of theirs. On the subject of religious obedience, the instance of Berrigan's transfer by his Jesuit superiors caused him to reflect on his own painful situation:

> I have had enough experience in twenty four years of monastic life to know that even if certain measures of Superiors may be a little unfair one never loses anything by obeying, quite the contrary, and God sometimes reserves special gifts and an extra fruitfulness for us, something we could not have gained without this sacrifice. I hope Dan [Berrigan] is taking it well and I am sure he is. As you say, his silence will say much, probably a great deal more than a lot of noise by his friends. However, Superiors will also have to learn by experience that the Decree on Re-

ligious, in the Council, meant what it said: that subjects are to be trusted more and given more latitude in important matters. Maybe some will learn the hard way. But I agree with you, the religious himself should obey and trust God. There is no better way. If there were Our Lord would have show[n] it to us. His example led to the Cross.[125]

Merton's words reveal his interior struggle and the confidence with which he spoke to his friend. Like Christ, Merton had his own Gethsemani, of which his monastery served as a nominal reminder.

Dorothy's 1965 Christmas card, with its greetings and insistence that he read the *Catholic Worker* with regularity, met with a prompt reply from Merton. It proved an occasion for him to affirm the value of the paper and to offer Dorothy sincere tribute. He said that he was hard put to express in words how great an impact the Catholic Worker movement had on him, but offered the following for her consideration:

> it stands for my own youth and for the kind of influences that shaped my own life thirty years ago. It happened that I went to Friendship House rather than CW because I was at Columbia; FH was just down the hill and so on. But CW stands for so much that has always been meaningful to me: I associate it with similar trends of thought, like that of the English Dominicans [e.g., Vincent McNabb and other authors of *Blackfriars*] and Eric Gill, who also were very important to me. And Maritain. And so on. *Catholic Worker* is part of my life, Dorothy. I am sure the world is full of people who would say the same. . . .
>
> If there were no Catholic Worker and such forms of witness, I would never have joined the Catholic Church.[126]

Dorothy and Merton were kindred spirits. They had been influenced by some of the same thinkers; both were converts who loved the church, yet struggled, in the one instance, with its social backwardness and, in the other, with rigid control identified with obedience to God's will; both employed their writing skills to raise the consciousness of others, yet felt that what they did was so little; both anguished over a world situation in which there was no peace; both relied on the monastic tradition as framework for their lives, while moving beyond a rigidly archaic interpretation of its meaning for the contemporary world.

The last-named concern is clearly represented in an essay published in the *Catholic Worker* shortly afterwards. Written as an introduction to a work by Philip Berrigan, S.S.J., Merton remarked upon the church's present work of renewal, using Berrigan's work as background for his own discussion. Holiness, whether that of the monk or of the laity, was to be concerned with the needs of the world. To be a stranger to the needs of others and to the hopes and perils of the contemporary world was to be a stranger to Christ Himself, for which no amount of interiority could supply. Neither monk nor layperson was called to escape into a false piety of withdrawal. It was crucial to Merton that the monk realize that he was neither an ethereal, unworldly being, nor a glorified canon appointed to chant the office and to teach school. Rather, he must rediscover the meaning of his vocation by moving away from institutional rigidity and drawing closer to the simplicity and labor of the laity, which had been a hallmark of the early Benedictine tradition. Merton presented no concrete plan for Christian renewal in general nor for the monk's life in particular but hoped to offer insight and a challenge to move beyond crustacean forms of observance.[127]

By September 1966 Merton had ready a study on Camus, which was written expressly for the *Catholic Worker.* In the letter which accompanied it he informed Dorothy that he had recently made a permanent commitment to live in the hermitage at Gethsemani. He asked for Dorothy's prayers and consoled her that, in spite of present exaggerated zeal for new things in the wake of the Vatican Council, the Spirit remained an instructive and guiding presence. Published in December 1966, "Albert Camus and the Church" affirms the importance of truth and deplores its current denial in the language of both persons and institutions. Merton posited that because we live in a world of lies, it is therefore a world of violence and murder. To rebuild a world of peace, then, we must recover the language and the thinking of peace. It was incumbent on church leaders no less than on others to realize the power behind the written and spoken word and to act accordingly. Of crucial importance was the publication of church pronouncements which were clear and intelligible to ordinary persons, in order that they have the needed impact on contemporary society.[128] Dorothy judged it a wonderful article, and begged Merton to send any materials he had, as she and her co-workers always welcomed them with great joy. She commented on her present reading of his *Conjectures of a Guilty Bystander,* observing that "we all feel that way," and without naming it, alerted him to her article "In Peace Is My Bitterness Most Bitter."

A reference to a prayer of St. Ephraim, which she had found many years ago in Waddell's *Desert Fathers,* prompted a reflection on the blessings and challenges of her life:

> Our life is incomparably rich in many ways, in our reading, in our liturgy. I even feel guilty about that, feeling that I am spiritually self-indulgent. However, there are deserts too to cross. Women always have the good remedy of housework, meals, people to take care of and that pulls us through. [129]

In reply, Merton commented on the article she referred to in her letter, which was her latest piece on the American responsibility for war. He judged it well done, restrained, speaking more of love than of reproof, and thanked her for speaking up in this way, for it had to be done. He implied that her voice was the conscience of the church, in that she spoke up where church leaders failed to do so. His ecclesiology, like hers, was based on a community dimension rather than on hierarchical structure:

> The moral insensitivity of those in authority, on certain points so utterly crucial for man and for the Church, has to be pointed out and if possible dispelled. It does not imply that we ourselves are perfect or infallible. But what is a Church after all but a community in which truth is shared, not a monopoly that dispenses it from the top down. Light travels on a two way street in our Church: or I hope it does. If it doesn't then there is something to be changed. [130]

By way of conclusion, he raised the question of doing a study on the native American, Ishi. It appeared in the March–April 1967 issue of the paper and was followed shortly afterwards by two other articles on native Americans. Though most evident in the first essay, all served as a vehicle of comparison between atrocities visited upon these people and present-day victims of the Vietnam conflict.

In a summer note to Merton, Dorothy reported with pleasure on recent peace groups' meetings. A request for the loan of Guardini's *The Last Things* and St. Catherine of Genoa's writing on purgatory for their mutual friend Karl Stern bespoke Dorothy's confidence in the generosity of her Trappist friend. As a subsequent letter revealed, this confidence was not disappointed. At this 18 August writing, Merton was nearly ready to send on an article on Auschwitz, and reflected on his difficult but fruitful solitude, of which Dorothy, with a depth of understanding, had once spoken. As Merton observed,

> The hermit life is no joke at all, and no picnic, but in it one gradually comes face to face with the awful need of self-emptying and even of a kind of annihilation so that God may be all, and also the apparent impossibility of it. And of course the total folly of trying to find ways of doing it oneself. The great comfort is in the goodness and sweetness and nearness of all God has made, and the created isness which makes Him first of all present in us, speaking us [*sic*]. Then that other word: "Follow."[131]

On its completion, Dorothy read Merton's review article on Auschwitz and found it an overwhelming account. She published it in the November 1967 issue of the paper, considering it appropriate to the Catholic practice of special remembrance of the dead during that month. Merton's reply noted that in working on things like the Auschwitz piece, which forced him to consider the depth and seriousness of the issue of war and its atrocities, he felt the triviality of all possible monastic efforts at penance. He was trapped by the great frustration of wanting to *do* something, which was somewhat allayed by his realization of God's greatness and immense mercy. Although he knew and had written as much, he found it difficult to remember that peace began within the heart of each person. Dorothy's response, citing the example of members of the de Foucauld group, shows her understanding of the contemplative dimension of Merton's life as well as of her own. Faith was to be nourished in the solitude of prayer before God. That Dorothy agreed with Merton's own perceptions is revealed through the annotations she made on her copy of Merton's circular letter for Advent-Christmas 1967. A portion which she underlined and held to her heart includes his cogent remarks on racial and foreign violence, his admonition to sober, Christian hope, and his call for courage and loving responsibility in a difficult age:

> The times are difficult. They call for courage and faith. Faith is in the end a lonely virtue. Lonely especially where a deeply authentic community of love is not an accomplished fact, but a job to be begun over and over: I am not referring to Gethsemani, where there is a respectable amount of love, but to all Christian communities in general. Love is not something we get from Mother Church as a child gets milk from

the breast: it also has to be *given*. We don't get any love if we don't
give any. . . . Let us pray for one another, love one another in truth,
in the sobriety of earnest, Christian hope: for hope, says Paul[,] does
not deceive.[132]

Writing to Dorothy at Christmas time, Merton commended her
on the December issue of the *Catholic Worker* and inquired about a
review article, "The Sacred City," which he had recently submitted.
Published in January 1968, it presented a study of the peaceful Zapotec
culture, now extinct, as a moment of reflection for contemporary society. The Zapotec study was contemporized two months later by the
Catholic Worker's publication of a chapter from Merton's forthcoming
Faith and Violence. In it Merton decried the canonization of violence
in general, the use of napalm, particularly on women and children,
and questioned the draft law which he felt stupidly sacrificed young
men's lives in the tragic error of the war in Vietnam.[133]

"The Wild Places," published in June 1968, was the last Merton
article to appear in the *Catholic Worker* before his death and dealt
with the American attitude to nature in the past four centuries. In
the course of the essay Merton associated an ecological sensitivity with
peacemaking, for wanton acts against nature were parallel to the destruction of war, the most fearful aspect of each being their justifica-
tion by pseudo-Christian clichés. That his efforts for peace had been
toned down, rather than extinguished, is evident from this article as
well as in his last letters. On 25 July, for instance, he expressed his desire to write for the *Catholic Worker* whenever he had a chance and
referred to a recent paper he had written for the Pax conference.[134]

Dorothy's reply the following month acknowledged this paper,
which she found fascinating, and informed him of the Peloquin con-
cert she had attended that evening in which four of his freedom songs
were performed. Stimulated and inspired by the performance, Dorothy
took time before retiring for the night to write what is her final extant
letter to Merton. One can sense her joy at another opportunity for encouraging a dear friend: "It is one a.m. and I had to write to you at
once; I have been so entranced by the music and the words. . . . You
have enriched our lives so many times."[135] Several months later, her
joy was transmuted by shock at Merton's unexpected death on 10 December 1968. Her grief was registered in that month's issue of the
Catholic Worker, in which she also addressed rumors that, discontented

with his Trappist commitment, he had intended to leave his monastery. She sought to refute the rumors by way of excerpts from Merton's letters, which underscored his sincerity and dedication to the Trappist way of life.[136]

Merton's memory was kept very much alive by friends, including Dorothy. She saw to it that his circular letter from spring 1967 was printed in the May 1969 issue of the paper, giving it the title "Technology and Hope." The letter juxtaposed the benefits of a technology wisely used and the devastation of scientific advancements used to kill. Technology, while holding out promises for great good, was nonetheless Janus-like in its actual employment, for "we rush in and save lives from tropical diseases, then we come along with napalm and burn up the people we have saved."[137]

In her 1970 article for *The Third Hour,* Dorothy relied on Merton's *Contemplative Prayer* as a starting point for her discussion. The *Catholic Worker* continued to print excerpts from his works, covering a range of topics. These included a statement on the necessary integration between sacred and secular through a proper understanding of work, thoughts on peace and nonviolence, on freedom from domination which is proper to the human person, on Christ's rejection by the powerful of the world and his place among the downtrodden, on the transforming power of hope in Christ's resurrection, and above all on the responsibility for a genuine and active love of others. This had once been described by Merton, in terms of the doctrine of the Mystical Body, as "the resetting of a Body of broken bones."[138] Dorothy continued to solicit reviews of his posthumously published writings, and she read and reread his books. In 1975 she composed an introduction to a collection of four Merton essays on native Americans, which inspired her still. As late as December 1978, she was rereading *The Sign of Jonas,* and through this parable of hope heard her friend speak once again, reminding her that "the life of every monk, every priest, every Christian is signed with the sign of Jonas, because we all live by the power of Christ's resurrection."[139]

The Fraternities of Charles de Foucauld

Recluse Charles de Foucauld, a former Trappist, and the religious fraternities inspired by him comprise another monastic influence upon Dorothy.[140] Her interest in de Foucauld dates back to the early 1930s.

Shortly after Peter Maurin met Dorothy in December 1932, he introduced her to the story of the French hermit of the Sahara and found her a copy of René Bazin's *Charles de Foucauld* to read. She studied this work again during her 1943–1944 sabbatical and associated the modern desert monk with those portrayed in Helen Waddell's *Desert Fathers,* which she was also rereading at the time. Dorothy's unpublished notes and comments made in the *Catholic Worker* during the later 1940s and early 1950s attest to her continued interest in de Foucauld and a growing awareness of the various twentieth-century religious groups known loosely as the family of de Foucauld.[141]

In April 1954 Dorothy reported favorably on the March visit of René Voillaume, virtual founder of the Little Brothers of Jesus, to the Catholic Worker headquarters on Chrystie Street. The cumulative effect of Dorothy's reading and exposure had left her positively disposed both to the Little Brothers and to the Little Sisters of Jesus, whose Rule of life—Trappist in tone—was inspired by de Foucauld. She summarized the groups' vocation as one of loving presence rather than of organizational strategy:

> They are not thinking in terms of civilization or culture, or point four programs, but simply of love and friendship. To work, to suffer, to be poor with others. They were not starting houses, clinics, schools, but were living so poor [*sic*] that there was nothing else to give, but just themselves. We envied them this Franciscan poverty and thought, "how much better this work than ours."[142]

A week-long lecture tour to Montreal in spring 1955 brought Dorothy into personal contact with the Little Sisters of Jesus. While experiencing the hospitality of Catholic Worker Marjorie Connors in the poorest section of the city, she visited with the seven Little Sisters who lived in the apartment just above them. At the time of writing from Montreal, she anticipated sharing in the sisters' evening meal on Thursday. Though she never mentioned having joined them afterwards for their nocturnal hour of adoration before Christ present in the Blessed Sacrament, it is evident that she agreed with their pious practice. At the very least the time spent with the Little Sisters was for Dorothy an opportunity to learn more of the family of de Foucauld, to which she was increasingly drawn.[143]

Dorothy's network of friends and associates shared her enthusiasm and continued to assist her in expanding her knowledge of de Foucauld-inspired groups. No later than September of 1958 she had read René Voillaume's *Seeds of the Desert* and had received privately translated chapters which had been omitted from the English edition. The first, on poverty and love, she obtained through the courtesy of a Mr. Ryan, then a seminarian studying in Washington, D.C. The second, on her-mitages, was translated and sent to her by former Catholic Worker Jack English (then Brother Charles), who had recently been ordained deacon at the Trappist monastery at Conyers, Georgia. It became communal reading at the Catholic Worker house in New York. The seminarian, Mr. Ryan, had stopped in for a visit with Dorothy on 10 September 1958 and was the occasion for her remarks on de Foucauld in the Oc-tober issue of the paper:

> . . . a young seminarian came in, on his way back to Washington, and he is much interested in the Little Brothers of Charles de Foucauld, as am I. He told me of one English speaking brother in the Fraternité El-Abiodh Sidi-Checkh in Sud Oranais, Algeria, and of a priest in Mon-treal and an interne in a Far Rockaway Hospital, all of whom are mem-bers of or prospective members of some part of this new order in the Church, which has secular institutes in formation for women and men, and a Fraternity for priests to associate themselves with them. Fr. Bren-nan, who teaches at the Seminary in Rochester is one of them too, a new friend whom I shall always see when I go to Rochester to visit our *Catholic Worker* group there.[144]

Less than a year later, she joined Catholic Workers Charles But-terworth and Beth Rogers in a 26–30 June 1959 retreat in Montreal, sponsored by the secular fraternity for persons interested in the spiri-tual family of Charles de Foucauld. Retreat conferences were presented by her friend Father Joseph P. Brennan, Scripture professor at St. Ber-nard's Seminary in Rochester, New York, and by Father Jacques Leclerc, chaplain at Maisoneuve Hospital in Montreal. Immediately following, she participated in the 1–4 July continuation of the retreat, which was sponsored by the de Foucauld lay women's branch of the Jesus Caritas fraternity. Prior to attending these sequential retreats, Dorothy had confided to Thomas Merton, early in June, that she hoped to join either the secular institute or the Charles of Jesus Association. At the time of writing to him, she expected in any event to remain very much a part of the Catholic Worker movement. Afterwards, she described the retreat to her readers, and expressed the hope that monthly meetings would be sponsored locally for persons interested in the lay fraternity of de Foucauld.[145]

By the end of 1959 Dorothy was engrossed in reading Anne Fremantle's *Desert Calling,* one of the biographies of de Foucauld recommended by the Jesus Caritas fraternity. Writing to Merton on 22 January 1960, she asked in passing, "Did I tell you I am a postulant in the Jesus Caritas Fraternity of the Charles de Foucault [*sic*] family?" Labor Day weekend 1961 found her at the Benedictine monastery of Mount Saviour, where she and six other Catholic Workers began a five-day retreat with the Charles de Foucauld Secular Fraternity.[146]

Journeying to Rome in spring 1963, as a part of a pilgrimage of Women for Peace, she visited the Little Sisters' motherhouse in Rome and later commented on its location: the grounds of the Trappist monastery at Tre Fontana. Dorothy herself did not remark on the appropriateness of the location, yet it bears some symbolic significance, as the Little Brothers and Little Sisters and their offshoots owe a good deal to de Foucauld's formative years as a Trappist.[147]

Extant material from summer 1963 indicates that some priests and laybrothers of the United States fraternity strongly advocated a radical disengagement from the world, even for secular fraternity members. Because accepting this stance would curtail Dorothy's activities, especially those for peace, she withdrew reluctantly from official affiliation with the fraternity. Father Voillaume and the secular fraternity's international coordinators, André and Cinette Ferrière, supported Dorothy's activism, though they felt it inappropriate to intervene in what they considered another country's internal matter. Afterwards, Dorothy continued her interest in de Foucauld groups, particularly in the Little Sisters of Jesus.[148]

She felt a special kinship with the Little Sisters, and having visited a number of their fraternities in the course of her travels, Dorothy was able to participate somewhat in their lives. As revealed by numerous remarks in her writings, she was inspired by their witness of humble service to the poor and their dedication to prayer. Dorothy befriended the Little Brothers and Sisters who lived in New York and followed their activities with a supportive interest. In summer 1973, when two Maryknoll Sisters, inspired by the Little Sisters, had sought to establish their house of prayer in the lower east side of New York City, Dorothy advertised their need and prayed to the Maritains for them, noting that Jacques had spent his final years as a Little Brother.[149]

Dorothy's bedtime reading frequently included René Voillaume's latest books, and her spring 1975 mention of his *Christian Vocation* as then nourishing her "mental and spiritual life" attests to this fact. Later guest speakers at the Catholic Worker house included Giorgio Gonnella, who on 14 January 1977 spoke to the group on "The Spirituality of Charles de Foucauld." She maintained contact with René Voillaume, noting in the paper for February 1978 that he was again in town and that he concelebrated an evening Mass with New York Little Brother, Father Peter. This liturgy was celebrated in the Catholic Worker chapel, followed by a friendly discussion with Voillaume afterwards. As late as September 1980 Dorothy still received with interest a new work by Voillaume, *The Truth Will Make You Free: Letters to the Little Brothers,* and hoped to read it in the near future.

Dorothy had frequently looked backwards in time during her closing years and found much for which to be grateful. On one of these occasions, when recalling Maurin's instrumentality in acquainting her with de Foucauld, she noted:

> Away back in the thirties, when Peter Maurin was my daily guest, . . . he told me the story of Charles de Foucauld and the spirituality of this "desert father," whose Little Brothers now live in slums as well as deserts, and are priests as well as brothers, and earn their own living by the sweat of their brow, in factories or at other manual labor. The Little Brothers among us now live in a slum, yet surround themselves with beauty. Taking a grimy apartment in a miserable East Side tenement, they just see that it is scrubbed and cleaned, bright and shiny, painted well so it will last, and then, so simply and barely furnished that the Crucifix and holy ikons light up the place. Peter Maurin gave me the life of Charles de Foucauld to read. He said, "This is the spirituality for our day."[150]

Dorothy credited Maurin with the assessment that de Foucauld's was a spirituality for the present day. However, it was Dorothy who tested and confirmed that insight. She came to view the poverty and simplicity of de Foucauld-inspired fraternities as signs of a new flowering of monasticism in the twentieth century. Since Dorothy's own attention to the poor was unfailing, she easily identified with Little Brothers and Little Sisters who dwelt, prayed, and worked in the midst of the poor. Particularly appealing to her was the fact that they ministered to others out of their lived experience rather than through the organized charity characteristic of most religious insitutions.

Moreover, Dorothy applied the term *Desert Father* to de Foucauld, based on her long acquaintance with the forerunners of monasticism from an early reading of Anatole France. She had supplemented this by frequent study of Waddell's *Desert Fathers* and a growing appreciation of the desert's significance for growth in holiness. An integral element in the larger Judeo-Christian tradition, the desert has been experienced both geographically and symbolically as a place of solitude, as a place where the absence of clutter and noisy distraction encourages a reprioritizing of needs and wants. It is a scene of testing, such as Christ experienced prior to his public ministry. It is a space where, removed from comforts and accustomed human companionship, the person is left to his or her own resources and voluntarily begins to strip away that which is nonessential. Unencumbered, the person encounters God and is slowly transformed into God's likeness. While the early Desert Fathers and de Foucauld embraced a literal desert existence, Dorothy shared with them its symbolic significance. The moments of solitude she savored while traveling and the 1943–1944 sabbatical she proposed for herself in conscious imitation of the desert tradition were a part of that movement. In later decades she explored with Thomas Merton their mutual interest in the Desert Fathers, appreciated and supported the Trappist's vocation to solitude, and acknowledged to him the place of the desert tradition in the development of her own spirituality. Her horizons had broadened from an early interest in the Desert Fathers to an immersion in contemporary Benedictine monachism through her own identification with the Benedictine charism as a lay oblate, through her friendship with Thomas Merton, and through the inspiration she derived from de Foucauld, monk of the Sahara. She had come full circle.

An understanding of the monastic tradition had greatly enriched Dorothy's development and was one of many components of her total religious experience. Her interest in the retreat movement, which began to surface in the late 1930s, augmented the sense of direction and synthesis which she had found within Benedictine and Benedictine-based groups.

4

Significance of the Retreat Movement

The retreat movement ranks among the great twentieth-century instruments for renewal in Catholic spirituality. While still considered mainly as the province of priests and religious in the first half of the century, retreats for the laity also began to be taken seriously. The spiritual exercises identified as a retreat were commonly understood during the pontificates of Pius XI (1922–1939) and Pius XII (1939–1958) as comprising a period of time and place removed from ordinary activity. In this period of prayerful silence and meditation a person took spiritual inventory for the purpose of finding vocational direction or revitalization in the Christian life. Whether engaged in alone or in the company of others, this activity was thought to be best guided by a priest, who gave either individual direction or general instruction in the form of conferences.[1]

Pius XI viewed his pontificate in terms of the advancement of peace among nations through submission of all to the universal reign of Christ. Having adopted as his motto "the peace of Christ in the Kingdom of Christ,"[2] not surprisingly he looked to the retreat as a means for personal growth in Christ and for attainment of both inner and outer peace. As a second benefit of the retreat, he stressed its apostolic dimension:

> we can hardly number those who, being duly exercised in a sacred re-
> treat, come forth from it "rooted and built up" in Christ; filled with
> light, heaped up with joy, and flooded with that "peace which surpasseth
> all understanding." Moreover, from this perfection of life, which is
> manifestly obtained from the Spiritual Exercises; besides that inward
> peace of the soul, there springs forth spontaneously another most choice
> fruit, which redounds to the great advantage of the social life: namely
> that desire of gaining souls to Christ which is known as the Apostolic
> Spirit.[3]

131

This pontiff wished to see these spiritual exercises, particularly those identified with Ignatius of Loyola, extended more widely not only among the clergy but also among the laity who were active in the church. They were to view the time spent in retreat as benefit to their work for Christ. For this reason, retreats for the laity were to be cultivated assiduously. In effect Pius XI affirmed the retreat as an ongoing tool of instruction for "manifold cohorts of the Catholic Action" working "in cooperation . . . with the apostolic hierarchy."[4]

The pope recommended retreats for the mass of Catholic believers as well and considered them an aid in personal orientation to and development of Christian life. He commended by name "Retreats for Workmen," which had already sprung up in some regions. Days of recollection, which flourished in religious communities and among diocesan priests, were encouraged as an extension of the spiritual exercises and were to be adopted for the laity as well. The days of recollection were considered a real benefit for those whose family responsibilities kept them from using the full retreat. The pontiff's desire to extend the experience of the retreat was based on a firm confidence that "a spiritual regeneration will follow."[5] In the next two decades, Dorothy, no less than Lacouture and his priestly disciples, fell heir to this pontifical confidence and to its ramifications.

PERIOD OF LACOUTURE ACTIVITY (1931–1939)

The retreat associated with Onesimus Lacouture, S.J. (1881–1951), was one of the most noteworthy early twentieth-century developments of the Ignatian retreat in North America.[6] A Jesuit of the province of Quebec, Lacouture had been trained in the Spiritual Exercises. While pastor of the Iroquois mission at Caughnawaga, near Montreal (1923–1927), he began giving conferences on the spiritual life to the Sisters of St. Anne and to several other religious communities. Once appointed to the Jesuit mission band by his provincial, Lacouture preached in numerous parishes and religious communities from 1927 to 1931. In April 1931, at the Jesuit Novitiate in Montreal, he directed his first retreat for priests based on the Exercises. By 1939 he had preached 132 clergy retreats, consisting of mixed groups of bishops, diocesan and religious priests, both in Canada and the United States. There were also occasional retreats to religious and lay groups. Lacouture felt that through retreat ministry he had answered God's call to promote a vigorous return to gospel teachings.[7]

The Exercises of Ignatius of Loyola, from which Lacouture derived the framework for his own preaching, are divided into four "weeks." Taken as a whole, they are intended to guide the progress of the adult Christian from conversion to spiritual maturity. While essentially faithful to the Exercises, Lacouture compressed his founder's themes into three sections, each of which Lacouture called a series. Thus, the Ignatian first week was devoted to purification of heart and spirit, and this comprised the theme of Lacouture's first series. The Ignatian second and third weeks, which developed respectively the following of Christ and union with him, were collapsed by the Canadian Jesuit into a second series. The founder's fourth week concentrated on the theme of docility to the Holy Spirit, who leads the Christian both to the summit of mystic union and to perfect charity in the exercise of the apostolate. This final week of the Exercises formed the basis for Lacouture's third series.[8]

After a slow start, Lacouture's work met with growing success from 1932 onwards. Yet, the retreat movement was simultaneously troubled by an underlying current of opposition which eventually led to a curtailment of the Jesuit's activities. This was due not to the fact that Lacouture employed the Exercises but to the manner in which he used them. A major source of difficulty lay in a nearly exclusive concentration upon the first series, which was later imitated by his disciples. Out of 132 priest retreats, Lacouture presented the second series a mere thirteen times and appears to have neglected the third series entirely.[9] This situation derived from a number of factors. Lacouture himself favored the first series over the others; second, because each of the retreats was preached to priests as a group, only some of whom had completed the first series, presentation of the first appeared more feasible; third, because of an increasing demand for the first series, it became physically impossible for Lacouture to schedule the other two. By presenting the first series almost exclusively, however, he offered at best a truncated version of the Exercises. As a consequence, emphasis remained on conversion of life without offering guidance in the next stages of Christian maturity.

In essence, then, Lacouture's preaching depended upon an interpretation of the first week of the Exercises. As did Ignatius, he stressed the principle and foundation for the Christian's life: "to praise, reverence, and serve God our Lord, and by this means to save his soul." In applying this foundation Lacouture made his central themes the love of God and love for neighbor, with stress upon total conformity

to God's will *in practice,* down to the smallest detail. It was in the practical application of these teachings that Lacouture met with opposition. The refrain, "if you truly love Christ," prefaced the presentation
of a host of heroic consequences for the priest retreatant's life and, by
extension, for all sincere Catholic Christians. Action for the love of Christ
encompassed Lacouture's teaching on prayer, detachment, imitation
of Christ's poverty, and love for those who are difficult to love. The
lover of Christ was to contemplate him, pass hours in prayer, and seek
to know Christ through constant meditation on Scripture. Detachment
was viewed as a consequence of this life of deep prayer. The priest retreatant was to refrain from use of the radio, to travel only as necessary
and useful to his ministry and apostolate, to renounce frivolous reading,
and to entrust the laity with temporal administration of church institutions such as the parish. The lover of Christ would seek to imitate
him in his poverty, in flight from the world and social events, in obedience, in crucifixion and death. Finally the heroic Christian was to
love and aid the poor and lowly, sinners, prostitutes, and addicts. The
priest was to spend hours in the confessional and to give to the poor
all that was not strictly necessary for himself.[10]

Lacouture called all persons to a life of heroic Christianity, regardless of their vocations. A particular tension in this era involved the overcoming of a mentality which considered vowed religious as a spiritual
elite, who had a certain monopoly on the attainment of sanctity. Thus,
Lacouture was reproached, not only for posing to secular priests and
to the laity the desire for the highest sanctity, but supposedly demanding of them the same detachment and absolutism required of religious.
While some priests, religious, and married persons were imprudent
in the application of Lacouture's teaching, it is evident that Lacouture
intended but to preach the evangelical call to holiness, as found in
Matthew, for instance: "You, therefore, must be perfect, as your heavenly
Father is perfect" (5:48). Anselme Longpré, Lacouture's biographer, has
noted in the latter's defense that he led people with good sense and
sought to rectify their misunderstandings whenever they were brought
to his attention.[11]

While Lacouture found support among some bishops and priests
of note, a number of others feared the consequences of his teaching.
The fact that Lacouture relied only on an outline and sketchy notes
during his active preaching period served to complicate the situation.
Thus, the retreat teaching was spread through auditory remembrances

and circulation of notes taken by priests during their retreats. These notes, the quality of which varied, provided Lacouture's critics with the only written documentation available to them at the time. For this reason, early criticisms of the Lacouture movement are to be read as an assessment of interpretations of the retreat as much as of Lacouture's actual preaching.[12]

The first traceable caution applied to the retreat appeared in an October 1933 letter written to Lacouture by Monsignor Antonio Camirand, a priest of the diocese of Nicolet. A widely respected theological writer, the monsignor had followed the Lacouture retreat and found much to commend it. However, he offered a number of criticisms concerning the Jesuit's teachings regarding purity of intention, the danger of natural motives in the spiritual life, the relationship between the natural and supernatural, some expressions of which appeared to verge on Jansenist anathemas against nature, and the call of all to sanctity. Through Anselme Longpré, a young priest friend of both men, clarifications were given to Camirand concerning what Lacouture actually intended, especially regarding the universal call to holiness. A subsequent rereading of Francis de Sales' *The Introduction to the Devout Life* on the vocation of the laity to the highest sanctity provided both Longpré and Camirand with a confirmation of the validity of Lacouture's point in the matter. Camirand's stance, then and later, was to encourage priests to attend the Lacouture retreats but "without swallowing everything" unthinkingly.[13]

In the same year, written retreat notes obtained from priest retreatants were collected by some of Lacouture's confreres and sent to the Jesuit minister general in Rome. From there they were submitted to an anonymous Jesuit censor, who in a one-page commentary stated the dangers in interpretation which the notes could furnish. The censorship appeared not to damage Lacouture's reputation at the time, for he continued to give his priestly retreats without hindrance. At the very least, however, the censorship illustrated that quite early in the decade bishops and other clergy were anything but unanimous in their opinion of Lacouture. Judging from the light of later events, Lacouture's biographer believed that authorities were on the alert from then on and that "the way was opened to those who searched for a way to reduce the preacher to silence."[14]

By 1936 Bishops Philippe Desranleau, Alfred Langlois, Alexandre Vachon, and Fabien-Zoël Decelles, all proponents of the Lacouture movement, commissioned Anselme Longpré to conserve and diffuse the retreat master's essential teachings. In a 1936 article which ten bishops later employed in their pastoral letters, Longpré defended the importance of promulgating the Jesuit's teaching:

> Armed with . . . the Word of God, he swooped upon our silver idols of well being, of comfort. He burned our Chesterfields [cigarettes], unmade our silken beds, disconnected our radios, threw in the fire our cushions and our silken fringes, preached to us to love the bare wood, because it resembled the cross of Jesus. [He spoke to us of] silence, solitude, a hidden life, according to the demands of our "death in Christ." During this . . . we lamented, we raged. . . . But it was necessary to pass through this: "The disciple is not greater than the Master." Is it not time that this doctrine be preached with force, to us who are the co-operators with Christ in the work of the salvation of souls? This preaching, besides, is inspired directly by the Gospel.[15]

Longpré concluded the article with an appeal that priests make the Lacouture retreat and argued that an example for so doing had already come from the hierarchy: the apostolic delegate and a dozen other bishops, among them Cardinal Rodrigue Villeneuve, who had already made two Lacouture retreats.[16]

Except for an interlude of six months, Lacouture continued to preach his retreats until December 1939. After giving his mid-December 1939 retreat at Hull, Ontario, a surprised Lacouture received an order to cease his retreat preaching both in Canada and in the United States. The order came from his provincial, after a stormy meeting of bishops some time prior to the event. At the episcopal meeting, Villeneuve, at one time a supporter of Lacouture, attempted to secure the departure of Lacouture but could not obtain sufficient support from the other bishops. Deadlocked, they sent the affair to Ildebrando Antoniutti, apostolic delegate to Canada, and submitted to his judgment. This resulted in Lacouture's exile, which lasted until his death in 1951. Still able to exercise his priestly functions, he was assigned at first to a distant Jesuit house in Santa Barbara, California. In the 1940s he was further restricted in his ministry and lived through a number of moves to Loyola University in Los Angeles, to Edmonton College in Alberta, to the Jesuit College at Sudbury in Ontario, and finally to the mission at St. Regis in the province of Quebec. In spite of his exile, however, the movement which he had begun continued to flourish both in Canada and in the United States through the work of his priest disciples, who were also drawn into the controversy. In coming to know the Lacouture retreat in the 1940s, Dorothy both benefited from and suffered because of it.[17]

Dorothy's Early Retreats (1933–1940)

Dorothy's gravitation toward the Lacouture movement may be traced both to her longstanding desire for heroic sanctity and more immediately to her retreat experiences during the 1930s. From the vantage point of adult retrospection, she had recalled the double effect which the life of friend Mary Harrington and the story of a saint had upon Dorothy at age eight:

> She [Mary Harrington] was a hard-working little girl, and naturally I had the greatest admiration for her on account of the rigorous life she led. I had a longing then, I can remember, for the rigorous life. . . . I do remember one occasion when she told me of the life of some saint. . . . I can only remember the feeling of lofty enthusiasm I had, how my heart semed almost bursting with desire to take part in such high endeavor. . . . I was filled with lofty ambitions to be a saint . . . a thrilling recognition of the possibilities of spiritual adventure.[18]

A text actually written when Dorothy was fifteen years old is testimony of the·strength of such preoccupation. Writing to her friend Henrietta, she had confided, "I know it seems foolish to try to be so Christlike — but God says we can — why else His command, 'Be ye therefore perfect.'"[19] Most likely it was from her reading of the *Imitation* that Dorothy had already identified sanctity with the following of Christ. Holiness viewed as a following of Christ, out of love for him, was to prove an important element in her later appreciation of the Lacouture retreat. Further development of Dorothy's capacity for reflection on the meaning and direction of her life was amply shown in the years that followed. Prayerful visits to the cathedral during her 1924 sojourn in New Orleans and her periods of solitude during her 1924–1929 stays at the beach are but two examples. Her later participation in retreats and days of recollection are to be seen as all of a piece with these earlier experiences.

Dorothy made her first formal retreat shortly after the publica-

tion of the May 1933 issue of the *Catholic Worker,* quite likely at the
recommendation of Paulist Father Joseph P. McSorley. He was at that
time her spiritual director. A few days spent in silence, and without
companionship, it was anything but a positive experience. Nearly twenty
years afterwards and many retreats later, Dorothy was able to express
this in writing:

> I should not have made a retreat by myself, I felt. I had been a Catholic
> only a few years and I was not ready for the long days of silence, of
> reading, of intimate colloquy with one of the nuns. If I had been with
> a group I might have enjoyed my stay. As it was I felt stifled, unable
> to comprehend what I was reading, unable to talk. It was a hard time.
> I do not remember now how many days I spent there. But when I left,
> I felt as though suddenly I was able to breathe again. The atmosphere
> had been too rarefied for me.[20]

Though Dorothy claimed in one account not to have thought
of retreats for a long time after her first experience, from then on retreat notices began to appear in the *Catholic Worker.* These recorded
a growing interest in and an awareness of retreats and retreat-study
weekends sponsored by various groups, including the Campions, at
that time identified closely with the Catholic Worker movement. By
February 1937 the New York Catholic Worker group was preparing a
one-day retreat for the unemployed, for which the preacher was Monsignor Fulton J. Sheen. By July of that year Catholic Workers themselves were invited to a one-day retreat directed by Missionary Servant
Father Joachim Benson. It was advertised as the first of a series of
Catholic Worker retreats and was favorably reviewed afterwards. Reports of Catholic Worker retreats in other cities followed in October
and November 1937. For the first, in Chicago, the time was divided
between instructions at Holy Trinity Church and informal discussions
at the Catholic Worker quarters. The second, in Washington, D.C., featured Paul Hanly Furfey as retreat master. Both of these were well received. By summer of 1939 Dorothy had organized and participated
in a three-day weekend retreat at the Catholic Worker farm at Easton.
The retreat was judged a successful event and was a move from retreat-
study weekends to retreat as a time of silent reflection. Dorothy wrote
a favorable report of the Easton retreat for the September issue of the
Catholic Worker:

> Last month, seventy-two of our fellow workers came together at
> Easton, at the Catholic Worker Farm, withdrawing themselves for a time
> from the work, to pray, to meditate, to listen to the teaching of Christ,
> and to build up the reserves of strength they need. The retreat was given
> by Fr. Joachim Benson, editor of the Preservation of the Faith, a mem-
> ber of the order of the Missionary Servants of the Most Holy Trinity.
> Fr. Joachim has long been a friend of the work. . . . For three days we
> had a closed retreat, silence was kept, as much as was humanly possible,
> no problems were discussed, no reading was done which was not spiri-
> tual. It was a time of real happiness.[21]

Further comments reveal her stance toward retreats at the time
and include an expressed appreciation for the role of silence. Dorothy
found a communal, fruitful silence during the 1939 Benson retreat,
unlike the silent aloneness felt at her first retreat. This is not surprising, given Dorothy's desire for a sense of community. The mental
stimulation offered in Benson's conferences and his ability to move and
enliven hearts were also important to her. In Augustinian fashion she
identified love with a strengthening of the will, enabling her to remain faithful to her vocation. Such love, encompassing both emotion
and the activity of the will for good, urged her beyond self in her quest
for Christ. To express this, she employed the language of the Canticles.
Christ was the beloved of her seeking, and it was for this reason that
she left her work aside for the time of retreat, knowing that "if we don't
find Him and hold Him, how are we to bring Him to the others?"[22]
Her attitude at the time of the 1939 retreat suggests both an awareness
of and affinity for the Lacouture movement. Among other things, she
later considered the Lacouture retreat as a course in love, and she thrived
on the multiple conferences and spirit of silence which it afforded.

Though existing evidence supplies a number of clues, the chronology of Dorothy's discovery of the Lacouture retreat can at best be only
approximated.[23] According to Dorothy's testimony, she first became
aware of what she referred to as *the retreat* through publisher friend
Maisie Ward. The context of Dorothy's accounts suggests 1938 or 1939
as the year when Ward informed her of an evangelical retreat given
by Abbé Saey, a disciple of Lacouture. Offered to workers in Montreal,
it was in French. Though people thronged to it, including Ward, it
was inaccessible to Dorothy because she did not understand the language. Subsequent exposures to the retreat were not lacking to her,

however, due to the resourcefulness of her friend Sister Peter Claver Fahy. A member of the Missionary Servants of the Blessed Trinity, Fahy had known Dorothy since 1933. The missionary served in numerous places, including New Jersey and Alabama, was acquainted with fellow missioner Pacifique Roy, worked with street preacher Father Frank Giri in Mobile, and at some point corresponded with Lacouture himself. Fahy obtained retreat notes from Giri, who had made the Lacouture retreat in Baltimore either in September 1938 or September 1939. These she shared with Dorothy. At the time, Dorothy was unimpressed and informed her friend that she preferred to take spiritual instruction directly from the New Testament and the lives of the saints. Her comment on the notes is telling: "The written word did not have the life and vitality of the spoken word, and perhaps it was the personality of the retreat master that made the teaching so powerful, I thought."[24]

Given the importance of personal encounter for Dorothy, it is not surprising that her appreciation of Lacouture was enhanced through an introduction to Father Pacifique Roy, a French-Canadian Josephite. Roy had been stationed in Baltimore at least since 1936 and was responsible for bringing Lacouture to that city for priests' retreats in 1938 and 1939. Dorothy first met Roy through Sister Peter Claver, who brought him one day to the Catholic Worker headquarters in New York. The chronology of this meeting is difficult to place, as existent evidence is conflicting. However, the ease with which Roy wrote to Dorothy on 6 February 1940 and other internal evidence in the letter suggests that they had met by this time. Once acquainted, Roy came as often as possible to the New York house, enthusiastically preaching the doctrine of the retreat as he had gleaned it from Lacouture. He often assisted at the newly established Catholic Worker house of hospitality in Baltimore, and Dorothy went to visit him whenever her travels took her to the area. It is certain that Roy was present at Furfey's last Catholic Worker retreat over Labor Day weekend, 1940. At this retreat within a retreat, Roy spontaneously began to preach the Lacouture doctrine between Furfey's regular conferences.[25]

By the summer of 1940 Sister Peter Claver had been transferred from Mobile, Alabama, to Gillette, New Jersey, where she began the establishment of a retreat center for the poor. Preparation required an immediate renovation of an old farmhouse, for which Dorothy recruited men from the Catholic Worker staff and breadline. Dorothy recalled a peaceful day of recollection spent with Sister Peter Claver at the completed retreat center. She placed the event at the end of December 1940, and the nature of her references to Lacouture in the next several issues of the *Catholic Worker* attest to a growing confidence in the retreat.[26]

INVOLVEMENT IN THE LACOUTURE MOVEMENT (1941–1955)

The next fifteen years of Dorothy's life were to be closely associated with the Lacouture movement. The retreat doctrine as she first heard it from Pacifique Roy impressed her, and the cumulative effect of Lacouture retreats, in which she later participated, enhanced the impact — so much so that in a November 1954 obituary written shortly after Roy's death, she recalled vividly his first visit to the New York house. The freshness of the recollection was in sharp contrast with the number of years that had elapsed:

> What he talked to us about was not the social order, but love and holiness without which man cannot see God. He spoke with such absorption that all who came, stayed to listen, and that day found him giving, and us receiving a little "retreat." It was the retreat of Fr. Lacouture, his fellow French-Canadian, which had inspired him as he inspired us that day so that we began "to see all things new." For me it was like falling in love again. I began to understand many things.[27]

Dorothy's recollection of this first meeting, as well as of later exposures to the retreat, revolved around the necessity for love and the call to holiness. She had begun by listening to Roy's repetitious conferences with enthusiasm. When quite early in their acquaintance he admitted that Father John Hugo was the person who could really give her the retreat, she set out immediately to find him.[28]

The Role of John J. Hugo

The story of Dorothy's involvement in the Lacouture movement would be incomplete without an indication of the role which Father John J. Hugo (1911–1985) played in it. A scholar and a gifted speaker, this priest of the Pittsburgh diocese was a key figure both in the promulgation of the retreat and in the controversy surrounding it. In September 1938 Hugo was initiated into the Lacouture movement through participation in a retreat given in Baltimore by Lacouture himself. The younger man, then ordained only two years, felt that through the retreat he was given a new perspective on Christian life. Hugo returned home to Pittsburgh determined to devote his life to preaching the retreat doctrine to the laity. He dreamt of being the counterpart of his adopted mentor, Lacouture, who had devoted most of his preaching efforts to priests. Beginning in fall 1938 Hugo immersed himself in an intense study of the Christian classics and introduced the retreat doctrine into a Scripture course he then taught at Seton Hill College. The following September he returned to Baltimore to make the retreat a second time, along with several priest friends, including Father Louis Farina, also of Pittsburgh. Inspired by Lacouture, Hugo and Farina began to give retreats to the laity at St. Anthony's Orphanage facilities in Oakmont, a suburb of Pittsburgh. It was at this location that Dorothy made her first full Lacouture retreat with Hugo in July of 1941. She participated also in the retreat he gave the following month at the Catholic Worker farm. Encouraged by Dorothy, Hugo shortly afterwards began a series of articles in the *Catholic Worker,* some of which developed the retreat teachings and others supported Dorothy's pacifism. Out of a desire to record accurately the teachings of the retreat, Hugo also wrote books and pamphlets. The most noteworthy of these was *Applied Christianity,* first published under the auspices of the Catholic Worker in 1944.[29]

Meanwhile, the Lacouture controversy had continued in Canada and by 1943 had begun to take hold in the United States as well. Hugo was drawn into the controversy and, in the process of defending and clarifying his own writings, became spokesman for proponents of the doctrine in the United States. Because of the controversy Hugo was sent to fill various pastoral positions in remote sectors of the Pittsburgh diocese and was effectively prevented from preaching the retreats for two decades. In the interim, Farina and other priest colleagues continued the retreats, though they were diminished in number and often in quality. During this period Dorothy and Hugo kept in touch and offered one another insight and encouragement. Once the major controversy had cleared, Hugo was assigned by Bishop John Dearden as founding pastor of St. Germaine's parish in Bethel Park, a suburb of Pittsburgh. This transfer was effected in June of 1957.

Tempered by his experience and strengthened by the confidence exhibited toward him in his new assignment, Hugo resumed preaching Lacouture retreats. For this purpose Hugo traveled again to the Catholic Worker farm in September 1964. In later years he offered retreats at centers in the Pittsburgh diocese, and it was there that Dorothy made her last Lacouture retreat in August of 1976. Among the tasks that Hugo still wished to complete was an updated account of the retreat doctrine and the history of the controversy. The new presentation of the doctrine, different in style from his earlier works though not in content, was published before his death in an automobile accident on 1 October 1985. The historical segment, substantially completed prior to this, was published posthumously. Taken together, they comprise his final word on the retreat and appear as a two-volume work, *Your Ways Are Not My Ways*.

The Retreat: Promulgation and Controversy

Promulgation

Dorothy had responded favorably to the first retreat she completed under the direction of John J. Hugo in July 1941. Made at the end of a speaking trip, she succeeded in encouraging eighteen Catholic Workers from various houses to join her for the retreat in Oakmont, Pennsylvania. Afterwards she informed her readers:

> We spent this period in complete silence, the day beginning at six and ending at ten. For spiritual reading at meals, we had the entire life of St. Francis by Jörgensen, and there were five conferences a day. These were so stimulating that not a moment dragged. We read nothing but the New Testament, and we all took copius [*sic*] notes. It was a time of real study, to put off the old man and on the new, and we came out with a real sense of renewal, a feeling that we had obtained a perspective, a point of view that gave balance to our outlook.[30]

In this first published account of the 3–11 July retreat, Dorothy concentrated on its external structure: the required silence, reading at meals, and the number of conferences. She made some essential observations as well and identified the Pauline admonition preached by Lacouture and his followers: to put on Christ. While her perception of the benefits of the retreat grew clearer as time went on, even from the beginning she thought of it as a course of study in Christian life, a synthesis of Catholic teaching which continued to give her direction.

At this point, a striking continuity emerges in Dorothy's life dating back at least as far as the year of her daughter's birth in 1926.

Feeling then that she had drifted along for nearly thirty years, she sought to have Tamar baptized Catholic and looked to the church as a guide in her daughter's religious development. She sought the same for herself through formal entry into the Catholic church in 1927. Later, she found recourse in Maurin and valued his indoctrination and suggestions for readings in church history, social encyclicals, and dogma. She gained instruction in the church's worship through contacts with leaders in the liturgical renewal, such as Virgil Michel, O.S.B., and she drew close to the monastic tradition through Maurin, Michel, and other Benedictines, eventually affiliating with them as an oblate. Without ever repudiating any of these influences, but basing insight upon former insight, she sought without ceasing, realizing this to be a part of her search for God, for the God-man Christ, whom she loved. Though sometimes inchoately, she sensed with Pascal that "you would not seek me if you had not already found me."[31]

Neither in summer 1941 nor later did Dorothy focus on the retreat for herself alone. Returning home to New York, she dispatched a lengthy 22 July letter to members of all Catholic Worker houses. Her readers were informed of a change in plans for the third annual Catholic Worker retreat at Easton. Unlike the 1939 and 1940 weekend retreats, it would be a week's duration, spent in strict silence. Taking note of the world at war, she called all Catholic Workers to turn even more fully to prayer and to realize what it could work in their lives. She urged all members to attend the retreat conducted by Hugo. In Benedictine fashion, she insisted that the retreat, as with the Mass and other prayer, is *the work.* She saw complementarity rather than dichotomy between moments of spiritual renewal and action for Christ:

> What we are aiming at is to bring men back to Christ, and it is presumption and effrontery and arrogance, if we try to do it without looking after ourselves first. . . . If St. Paul worried about being lost himself, in the effort to save others, how much more should we take care. Here is a time offered, to renew ourselves, to taste and see, that the Lord is sweet.[32]

This retreat, which began on 24 August, was a success by Dorothy's standards. In the September issue of the *Catholic Worker* she reported on it as a course of instruction in basic principles of Christian living in which she and her co-workers would learn to shun the "natural motive," working rather for the love of God. She had begun to use the language of the retreat, though still innocent of the fact that the term *natural motive* was a source of contention in the Lacouture controversy. For Dorothy, it meant an ordering of her life in response to God's love for her.[33]

Dorothy's serious efforts to promulgate the retreat may be dated from summer 1941. They soon included not only Catholic Workers and readers of the paper in general, but also other friends, priests, and bishops. The record of promulgation is valuable in that it provides insight into Dorothy's own participation in and growing perceptions of the retreat. Along with her September 1941 report of the retreat itself, Dorothy began with this edition to publish a series of Hugo articles, dealing first with retreat teachings and later with pacifism.[34] Between summer 1941 and summer 1942, she frequently brought the retreat to her readers' attention by references to Hugo, the publication of a letter on war by Lacouture, and by sharing her own interpretations. From examining these interpretations, it becomes clear that in accepting the dimensions of renunciation and detachment preached by the retreat, the manner in which Dorothy placed them in context was positive toward her own spiritual development. She shared with Lacouture a special compassion for the poor and was inspired by Lacouture's reminder that:

> If we cannot see Jesus in the poor man, we surely cannot see Him under the poverty-stricken veils of bread [Eucharist]. The reason the world does not love the poor is because the world does not see Jesus in [the] poor — no faith. Faith is finding God where the senses do not see Him and where they are least able to see him.[35]

Lacouture's witness and that of his disciples, Abbé Henri Saey, Pacifique Roy, and Sister Peter Claver, who likewise worked among the poor and loved them, spoke as strongly to Dorothy as did the preached doctrine. The message of detachment preached by the Lacouture retreat had not been heard in isolation but in the setting of Dorothy's own experiences. Before she knew of Lacouture, she and Peter had lived from the first days of the Catholic Worker in the midst of the poor and ministered to them. Both had embraced voluntary poverty in order that they might serve others in need. For Dorothy, the retreat confirmed their insight and provided her with a larger theological vocabulary with which to express it.

By April of 1942 Dorothy had news of the summer schedule at

Oakmont, where Hugo and Farina would again conduct retreats. Her reflections later that year indicate that she had attended at least one of them. Her third annual Lacouture retreat during the summer of 1943, also at Oakmont, marked a crucial time in her life. Though Dorothy would write of it only later, the controversy surrounding the retreat had begun to affect her directly, in that Hugo had been assigned to a country parish, as curate, in fall of 1942 and would be unable to preach any of the 1943 retreats. The largeness of his presence in the retreat movement had been important to her, and with his geographic removal, she was uncertain of its future. Second, Dorothy, then approaching her forty-sixth birthday, needed to deal with personal issues, including a felt urgency to guide her daughter in her final year before marriage to Catholic Worker David Hennessy. Third, the war and its consequences had taken a heavy toll on Dorothy. There was so little that she was able to *do* in face of all-out aggression; she believed in the power of prayer, though in the turmoil of those years her faith was sorely tested. Her pacifist stand remained unpopular and even divisive among Catholic Workers, and many of the houses had closed because there were so few able men left to staff them. She agonized over the numbers who had enlisted, realizing that many would return from the war maimed in body and in spirit or not return at all. Among the enlisted men were Catholic Workers such as Jack English, young men whom she loved and cared for deeply.[36]

Thus, it was with a heavy heart that she entered the July 1943 retreat at Oakmont. It was conducted by Louis Farina, with the assistance of Franciscan Father Oliver Lynch and a Father Corcoran, not an unusual arrangement, since Farina and Hugo had previously worked as a team. Dorothy was particularly impressed at this retreat by the warmth and ardor of Farina's preaching. The retreat overall had a lasting impact, and a good indication of Dorothy's thoughts during this time is preserved in personal notes written during the retreat. A certain thread runs throughout: the search for God continues as long as we live; the retreatant was to realize the sanctity God intended for each one, for "the only purpose for which we were made is to become saints"; we are to strive for a hidden sanctity, in which penance and prayer play an important part. On the eve of the retreat's close Dorothy recorded the crystalization of an idea which had been on her mind for some years. It was a firm decision to remove herself from the activities of the Catholic Worker so that she might spend more time in prayer and manual labor.[37]

In the September 1943 issue of the *Catholic Worker* Dorothy announced her decision, noting generally that there were both natural and supernatural reasons for the step she had taken. Arthur Sheehan was to replace her as editor and publisher and his work would be aided by Maurin and others. Her apologia for the departure included the reminder that St. Thomas Aquinas advocated action be added to the life of prayer, not taken from it. Dorothy envisioned herself living in solitude and quiet, neither seeing nor writing to friends but practicing penance and prayer, and writing articles to support herself. She expected to continue writing a book on Peter Maurin and to send in an occasional "Day by Day" column for the paper. She publicly gave voice to her hope of eventually establishing a retreat house for the poor and dreamt that it would be by the sea, with a farming commune attached. Its patrons were to be workers and poor people from the breadlines and mothers from the slums. She entered a query and a hope: "Where are the priests and where are the teachers to give these retreats for the integrated Christian life? God certainly will send them to us." Unknown to her readers, she and Pacifique Roy had already expended a good deal of energy in the hopes of both ministering to priests and providing retreat directors to staff the proposed retreat center. These efforts would multiply upon Dorothy's return to the Catholic Worker in 1944.[38]

The sabbatical gave Dorothy distance from the pressures of leadership in the Catholic Worker movement and freed her to concentrate on her personal and family life. With regard to retreats and days of recollection, the year was replete with them, not all of which were of the Lacouture orientation. Dorothy had set a precedent for this, one of her more recent ones having been a day of recollection with Benedictine Father Thomas Verner Moore on 11 July 1943. She spent the first month of her sabbatical year with the Ladies of the Grail in Wheeling, Illinois. Both she and Tamar participated in the final Grail course of the summer, which included instructions on prayer, liturgy, liturgical singing, rural living, long periods for prayer, and the learning of such skills as making butter, cheese, and bread. The integration between work and prayer appealed to Dorothy and remained important to her. Her October 1943 article for the paper informed her readers of the time spent at the Grail. And the benefit of the experience was not neglected in the next few years, when she attempted with Pacifique Roy to apply this monastic inspired pattern to the Catholic Worker farm at Easton. Decades later her 1943 notes from the Grail course appeared in the manuscript for "All Is Grace," the document in which she attempted to record her own spiritual journeying and synthesis.[39]

After leaving the Grail, Dorothy spent several months in comparative solitude, not far removed from Tamar, then a boarding student at the School of Agriculture in Farmingdale, Long Island. April 1944 found her and Tamar back at Easton, preparing for the daughter's 19 April marriage to Catholic Worker David Hennessy. Afterwards, Dorothy traveled to the small Grail farm in Foster, Ohio, where she lived for the month of May. Her notes indicate that she engaged in manual labor and spent a good portion of her time in reflection on the *Confessions* of Augustine. She pondered with him the mysteries of God, self, sin and goodness, the necessity for praise and, ultimately, union with God: "We are always striving towards that union which is the most intimate there is."[40]

Dorothy spent at least half of July at Oakmont, where she participated in the 2–8 July and 16–22 July Lacouture retreats for women. The first, offered by Franciscan Father Denis Mooney, assisted by Farina and Corcoran, was based on Lacouture's second series. Dorothy's lengthy notes for this retreat indicate a serious effort to follow the conferences. Yet her thoughts moved from consideration of the life of Christ to its application when the retreat would be over. She was concerned that "our work is to sow thoughts of [the] Gospel in the minds of others." Approaching the end of her sabbatical, she felt an intense pull between the hidden and active dimensions of her own life. By nature active, she feared having to make an either-or decision: to focus on her own sanctification or to lead others to God. She prayed to see her way clearly.[41]

Her decision was made in favor of an integration between the two. Like Maurin, she belived in a correlation between material and spiritual dimensions of human living. Herein lay the key to Dorothy's perception of an effective retreat movement: to bring together intellectual, spiritual, and material dimensions of living in a way befitting the innate dignity of the human person. She had lived for years among broken and desperate people who had been shattered by unemployment, addiction, and despair. Her experience taught her to be suspicious of gospel preaching that did not also provide a holistic way of living it. In her mind, opportunities for life on the land would ensure a harmony between preaching and life. After a year spent in rural settings Dorothy felt an even greater need to bring together the retreat and land movements. At the same time, she did not wish to incur the displeasure of retreat priests, some of whom thought she emphasized the material too much. However, following a conference on the biblical Martha and Mary toward the end of the retreat, she had resolved this and her contemplation-action dilemma for the moment, by asking Martha to be her patroness for the coming year. She had decided that "love is essentially energetic, but with many hours of prayer." This insight freed her to work toward the implementation of a retreat center which would be integrated with the land movement.[42]

Apparently the resolution in favor of a move toward activity brought her a sense of peace, for the tone of Dorothy's retreat notes for 16–22 July 1943 indicate a more settled frame of mind. Conducted at Oakmont by Father Joseph Meenan, with the assistance of Farina and Corcoran, this week was based on the usual first series of the Lacouture retreat. Dorothy remarked on conferences on the call to put on Christ, natural and supernatural motives, the necessity for prayer and detachment, and the saints' compunction for sin. As if for a watchword for the coming year, she wrote: "Every action must receive [the] touch of Christ. . . . The only way is to do it *for Christ*. Not for self. The only thing which gives importance to actions is Christ."[43]

Once returned to Easton, Pennsylvania, Dorothy wrote happily to friend Nina Polcyn that she was working to get the farm ready for retreats. The first, beginning on 10 September, would be conducted by [Joseph] Meenan. An integrative second week with Pacifique Roy would be "riotous with work and discussion." Over the next eleven years, first at Easton and then at Newburgh, Dorothy redoubled her efforts to promote an integration between land and retreat movements. Even during the retreat proper, she strove to encourage manual labor, in silence, as a part of the horarium. When first introduced to the retreat movement, Dorothy, like many of her thinking contemporaries, had been engaged in a task of social reconstruction, with emphasis on the human person and the necessity for all persons to place themselves in a community conducive to total growth. She felt this most especially for the desperate poor. From the early days of the Catholic Worker she had viewed life on the land as a proper environment for a healing of the human psyche, a reintegration of values distorted by twentieth-century fragmentation. As Dorothy had noted during the Catholic Worker's first summer at the Easton farm in 1936:

> In the country the material and the spiritual have their proper relationship. There one can wholeheartedly say that the material is good; that it is good to enjoy the material things of this world; that one can love the world and God Who made it, and not be a materialist and separated from Him.[44]

Similarly, the retreat taught a doctrine of samples—that is, that all persons and things reflect the glory and goodness of God. It was allied closely to Christian teachings on detachment, also preached by the retreat, which sought to assist in the ordering of all loves in God. While the retreat taught this by negation, stressing the spiritual separated from total human experience, Dorothy brought a larger perspective to bear upon her retreat experience. Her outlook compelled her to attempt an integration and a corrective through the Catholic Worker retreat center. Lacouture himself was aware of this and accepted Dorothy's insight.[45]

Extant correspondence and notices in the *Catholic Worker* chronicle the efforts expended at the Easton retreat center. A number of retreats and days of recollection were sponsored in the 1944–1945 season, followed by a summer of retreats in 1946. Beginning in late fall of 1944, Pacifique Roy worked closely with Dorothy, after having obtained authorization from his Josephite provincial, Edward V. Casserly. Though Roy continued to travel a great deal, he resided at the Easton farm until serious illness forced him to leave in 1946. In addition to serving as chaplain and sometimes as retreat director, he promoted a quasi-monastic atmosphere at the Easton farm. A versatile laborer himself, Roy recruited Catholic Workers to help restore the buildings, also installing electricity and making water more available. Dorothy often paid him tribute in later years, though she admitted that his joyous spirit was shadowed by an austerity which he tended to impose on the group. After Roy left Easton, chronic difficulties with families living on the upper property caused increasing disturbances for retreatants housed at the lower farm. In order to alleviate an intolerable situation as well as to provide better facilities for retreats, by February of 1947 Dorothy had begun to move the retreat facilities to a newly purchased farm at Newburgh, New York.[46]

In the years that they worked together, Roy and Dorothy shared the dream of also establishing a retreat center for priests. The main purpose of the proposed center was to provide a rural setting for renewal or rehabilitation for priests, notably those who were alcoholics. In order to function, the project required that three or four priests in good standing be released for the work. These men were to be well steeped in the spiritual life and, if possible, imbued with the Lacouture doctrine, for the center would provide retreats as well as an abundance of manual labor. Recovered priests would work among the poor, with the understanding that they were to preach the doctrine of the Lacouture retreat as well as assist in the rehabilitation of alcoholics among those to whom they ministered. This venture, if successful, would assist Dorothy in at least three ways. First, it would aid her unofficial ministry to priests, in an era when deviant behavior among them was little understood. A number of priests in difficulty had come to the Catholic Worker over the years. They were either in search of refuge themselves or were sent there by priests and bishops who were in a quandary as to how to help their brother priests. Surviving evidence points to a combination of compassion and firmness in Dorothy's own dealings with them. Second, a retreat center for priests, whether nearby or removed from the Easton farm, would guarantee the availability of directors for the Catholic Worker retreat center. Third, the ministry of recovered priests would help restore others to an awareness of their dignity, some through sobriety and all through spiritual nourishment. Though the idea for the priests' center may initially have been Roy's, it was Dorothy who persisted in requesting the support of bishops in several dioceses. This she pursued at least from March 1942 through the end of 1945. By then, accumulated responses warranted a conclusion that the project, no matter how well explained, would not receive the approval of the hierarchy she had consulted. Dorothy's 20 July 1942 letter to Bishop J. Francis A. McIntyre of New York is representative of her requests and argues for the connection which Dorothy saw between the house for priests and her retreat house for the poor. It reads in part:

> while this work [of rehabilitating priests at the proposed center] was going on, the work of giving retreats to the poor, the very poor would

[be] prepared and would take place. The very sufferings, the degradation undergone by these "other Christs" [priests] would make them more ready, would prepare them more thoroughly for this work of serving Christ in His Poor. The very fact that these two works would be combined—the work of taking care of priests in trouble, and the work of building up a retreat house for the very poor—would serve to bless the project.[47]

Of all those she approached, either in person or by letter, McIntyre was the most supportive. Unfortunately for Dorothy he did not have the final say in his archdiocese, nor did he have jurisdiction in the archdiocese of Philadelphia, where the Easton farm was located.

Meanwhile, Dorothy continued her efforts to further the Lacouture retreat. Among these was the promotion of a book written by Archbishop Norbert Robichaud, of Moncton, New Brunswick, who consciously sought to continue Lacouture's teachings. While Dorothy was aware in March 1944, through Roy, of a French version, *La Sainteté laïque,* it was not until she received an English translation, *Holiness for All,* late in 1945, that she had direct access to it. Never one to pass up an opportunity to further the retreat, Dorothy sent a copy as a Christmas gift to Cardinal Dennis Dougherty, archbishop of Philadelphia. In January 1946 she advertised the book in the paper, calling it "the retreat as given at Maryfarm [Easton]—the call to perfection of all Christians." While unable to carry out her intention to print all the chapters serially in the following months, she did print two of them: the introductory chapter and the fourth, entitled "The Model for Holiness: Jesus Christ." Shortly afterwards she reminded her readers that the retreats sponsored at Easton were very much in keeping with the practice of the works of mercy, for which the Catholic Worker was well known. Dorothy and her companions had consistently emphasized the corporal works, yet she belived that the spiritual works of mercy were as important: "The works of mercy include enlightening the ignorant, counseling the doubtful, comforting the afflicted, and to aid in this work we have retreats at Maryfarm, Easton, Pa."[48]

Dorothy kept abreast of developments in other retreat centers and brought them to her readers' attention. One of these was a March 1946 article on lay retreat houses, published as a supplement to *Blackfriars.* The accord which Dorothy gave to the article is evident in the June issue of the paper. In February 1947 she reported her retreat center's move to Newburgh, New York, and gave news of a recent visit to Roy at Hôtel Dieu, a Montreal hospital. In the course of this trip, she journeyed to Sudbury, Ontario, where Lacouture was then stationed, to meet him in person for the first time. She spoke with him of the activities and retreats of the Catholic Worker and requested an opportunity to make a retreat in Sudbury, given by him. While Lacouture admitted that he enjoyed her visit and encouraged her in her work, he declined to conduct a retreat, stating simply, "I may not do it." That summer, while retreats continued at Newburgh, Dorothy journeyed to New Kensington, Pennsylvania, for her own, also Lacouture-inspired. She later recommended the center to others, for she wished to reach as many as possible through the retreats. In April 1948, for instance, she reminded her readers:

> We cannot over-emphasize the importance of these retreats. . . . One must learn to love, and there is no place better than a retreat house to learn such lessons.
> The retreat house . . . is not just for our readers who can afford [it] . . . but it is also for the poor, the lame, the halt and the blind. So we recommend that you bring someone who could not otherwise make a retreat.[49]

By summer of 1948 a full schedule of retreats and study weeks was available at Newburgh, with opportunities for men and women separately, for mixed groups, and a Labor Day weekend retreat for families, in which babysitting services were provided. As at Easton, Dorothy fostered the Lacouture retreat but supplemented it with others, because of the unavailability of priests trained in the Lacouture movement.

Dorothy participated in the retreats as fully as possible, though as retreats at Newburgh began to multiply, especially during the summers of 1948 through June 1955, she often found herself as much a hostess as retreatant. Favorite retreat directors at Newburgh included Holy Spirit Father Francis Meenan and Father Marion Casey, who were both Lacouture oriented. After participating in an 18–23 August 1952 retreat with Casey, Dorothy reported an increasing hunger for the full retreat. Characteristically, she included an apostolic dimension: the need of retreats for others, who like her, were also called to holiness. As she admitted:

The more I make this retreat . . . the move convinced I am that it provides the answer. It is an Ignatian retreat, but only part of it, one third of it. When we spend five or six days on this part, I begin to long for the other two parts. . . . Many religious have the opportunity, but layfolk need it too.

The men on the breadline, those who live with us at St. Joseph's House on Chrystie street [*sic*], students, teachers, workers, all need it. Men are starving today for spiritual teaching.[50]

Because Dorothy considered Hugo and Farina two of the best preachers of the retreat, she had appealed repeatedly to Bishop Boyle to grant permission for them to direct an occasional retreat. This effort proved unsuccessful. However, in 1954, Hugo and Dorothy arranged to have days of recollection, during which the group present at the farm would listen to prerecorded conferences. The series was prepared and recorded by Hugo specifically for these occasions.[51]

The Catholic Worker had acquired a smaller tract of rich land on Staten Island by February 1950. Named the Peter Maurin farm, it was closer to the city than the one at Newburgh. Dorothy believed that the convenience of the location would encourage people to make use of more frequent opportunities for spiritual growth. Though projecting a complete move of the retreat facilities from Newburgh to Staten Island shortly after the purchase of the latter, it was not until the summer of 1955 that Dorothy succeeded in disposing of Newburgh. In the interim, Peter Maurin farm became the locus for conferences and days of recollection. Retreats continued at an undiminished pace at Newburgh, the final one being preached there by Marion Casey the week of 19 June 1955. A few months after the move to Staten Island was completed, Dorothy looked back fondly to the years at Newburgh. She remembered the occasions of retreat there as a joy, as a time when silence settled into receptivity, when the mind was stimulated, and when the heart expanded with "desire for God."[52]

In the preceding decade and a half, Dorothy had been stimulated and encouraged by the Lacouture movement in that it recognized the call of all persons to sanctity. She identified with the fact that it appealed to Catholic laity rather than simply limiting its attention to members of the clergy and religious orders. Dorothy found in the retreat a practical body of instruction which would enable her and other retreatants to cooperate more fully with God's grace in attaining holiness. Thus, her initiative in promoting Lacouturism arose from the belief that it made available needed spiritual formation for all. While Catholic Worker retreats were offered primarily for Catholic Christians, she also welcomed persons of other faiths to receive "this good news."[53]

Controversy

Dorothy's efforts to promulgate the retreat are best viewed in conjunction with the controversy surrounding it. While she was drawn into it primarily by association, the controversy affected her in several ways. First, on the most practical level, it limited the availability of priests familiar with the Lacouture doctrine for the retreats she sponsored at both Easton and Newburgh. Not that Dorothy was adverse to the preaching of other priests, for she herself had continued to take advantage of opportunities for days of recollection at other centers, notably those of a Benedictine orientation. However, since she viewed the Lacouture retreat as basic, she had hoped to provide its synthesis of the Christian life for all who came. Second, the circumstances surrounding the controversy released in Dorothy an energy, determination, and internal freedom which otherwise might not have been utilized. Because she believed in the retreat, Dorothy dealt directly with members of the hierarchy in efforts to establish and maintain successive Catholic Worker retreat centers, to seek permission for priests to preach the Lacouture retreat, and to persist for several years in the idea of a retreat house for priests. Her determination is particularly striking in relationship to Hugo and Roy. Because she looked upon the former as a fine preacher and writer, Dorothy not only approached Bishop Boyle to ask that Hugo might continue giving retreats, but she had also encouraged the younger man to write for the *Catholic Worker* and printed the first edition of his *Applied Christianity*.[54] Because Dorothy understood and appreciated Pacifique Roy, she strove to explain him to his provincial and collaborated with Roy on the hoped-for priests' center. In all of these instances, she saw a need and responded to it. Third, in giving her support and encouragement to the priests directly involved in the controversy, she found support for her own work as well, in which she frequently met with disagreement. Finally, the controversial attention given to the retreat gave Dorothy material for both immediate and later assessments of the Lacouture movement as a whole.

Dorothy followed the general lines of the controversy primarily through contacts with Lacouture, Hugo, and Roy, as well as through her own reading. A decade of correspondence with Lacouture and her recollection of a meeting with him in 1947 alone provide evidence that she was aware of his frequent moves and of the restrictions placed upon his ministry. In one of his letters, Lacouture reminded her that he had been forbidden to write for publication; nor was he allowed to preach or even to teach catechism to the native American children at St. Regis mission, where he resided in his last few years. Yet there is no hint of bitterness in his extant letters to Dorothy. Rather, after discovering in spring of 1942 that Hugo's "In the Vineyard" series was to be featured in the *Montreal Register,* he rejoiced and noted with some humor that the very doctrine which exiled him from that city was now being accepted by its diocesan paper. On another occasion, Lacouture suggested that Dorothy appeal directly to Archbishop Amleto Cicognani, apostolic delegate to the United States, on behalf of a priest then not in good standing. It appeared not to matter to the Jesuit that this same delegate had been one of the persons responsible for sending him into exile. On the contrary, a consistent thread that ran through Lacouture's letters to Dorothy was the reminder that those who strove to imitate Christ would also experience his cross. Whenever she faced opposition, as in events leading to the closing of the Baltimore house in 1942 and later during difficulties at Easton and Newburgh, he offered words of encouragement. His counsel "Do not yield to any discouragement" was typical.[55]

It was through Hugo, however, that Dorothy became more concerned over the ramifications of the controversy. She had deeply regretted his removal from the retreat circuit in the fall of 1942. Two years later, the publication of Hugo's *Applied Christianity* served as a catalyst for open criticism of the Lacouture retreat in the United States. The first response to the book occurred in Redemptorist Father Francis Connell's July 1945 critique in the *American Ecclesiastical Review.* Dorothy read the review, and followed Hugo's responses to it, as well as later criticisms. All of these hinged on an understanding of the relationship between nature and grace and drew particular attention to the supposed rigors that the retreat introduced. Dorothy considered it beyond her competence to attempt a direct answer to the critiques but continued to support the retreat both in public and in private.

At first Dorothy assured herself that the discussions provided opportunity "for clarification of thought."[56] As the controversy became protracted, however, assurance gave way to discouragement. It distressed her that a movement so vital to her own spiritual growth had become the cause of dissension. An article written for the July-August 1947 edition of the paper serves to illustrate her troubled frame of mind. In this writing, Dorothy dealt with three issues of conflict which had occurred in Catholic Worker history: precedence given to the works of mercy over indoctrination and organization, Dorothy's stand on pacifism, and the current retreat controversy. Her key points revolved around the necessity for sanctity, no matter what one endeavored to do in the material order. Her watchword was a line from Pius XII's writings that she had recently come upon: "In times during which it is the object of the world's hatred, Christianity is not a matter of persuasive words, but of greatness." With respect to the Lacouture movement, Dorothy observed that though the retreat had begun seven years previously for herself and other Catholic Workers, they had not yet begun to be holy, to do all for the love of God. She also considered that portion of the retreat which dealt with detachment. The illustrative example, abstention from smoking, was one over which many words were written in the course of the controversy. She wondered at the furor over so small a point, "except that it is a symptom of our self indulgence." Dorothy deemed the retreat controversy another war in their midst and stood amazed that participants themselves would sometimes judge the retreat directors as rigorists and Jansenists. [57] In spite of her grief over the controversy, Dorothy posited that suffering was a necessary part of their lives, controversy or not. The retreat taught that Christ was a sign of contradiction — that the disciple, in putting on Christ, would also embrace suffering. While in the retreat preaching much emphasis was placed on the cross, Dorothy did not lose sight of the fact that resurrection followed. It appears that in the course of the article, she had written her way out from despondency toward renewed hope:

> One might say that the retreat . . . is a basic retreat in that it makes man realize and face even with despair the work that is before him, the death to self, the chasm he must bridge, to reach God. We must begin sometime to aim at sanctity. The tragedy, Newman said, is never to begin. Or having put one's hand to the plough, to turn back. To become a tired radical. To settle down to relish comfortably past performances of self sacrifice and self denial. It is not enough, St. Ambrose remarks, to leave all our possessions, we must also follow Him, and that means to the Cross, to Gethsemene [sic] and Calvary, before one can share in the Resurrection and Ascension. [58]

Four years later Dorothy continued to reflect on all that the retreat had brought to those who made it in earnest. Without detracting
from the retreat itself, she was then able to admit that some of the
young priest directors had gloated over the difficulties of it. "Sometimes," she wrote, "I thought they were rubbing it in." At the time
of Pacifique Roy's death in 1954, Dorothy recognized that the controversy still raged but assured her readers that none of Hugo's works had
ever been formally condemned. She realized that sometimes persons
"went to extremes in their hatred of the world," but this was due to
misunderstanding rather than to the retreat doctrine itself.

Perhaps Dorothy's best attempt to objectively assess the controversy occurs as part of a simple meditation:

> Down through the ages there have been all kinds of theological
> controversies which become so bitter that the simple teaching of love
> is all but lost sight of. Yet these controversies are inevitable, if men are
> seeking truth and regarding truth as the most important thing in the
> world. They so respect and love truth, these controversialists, that they
> would not want to deviate by one hair's breadth from truth.[59]

It is not an objective statement, however. To a woman who envisioned
truth in the context of love — love for God, expressed concretely in genuine love for human persons — the concept of truth as an abstraction
had little appeal. Yet, in the midst of controversy, she listened, sometimes with pain, and considered the arguments. She remained mindful of human fallibility, including her own, and never lost sight of the
essential element of the retreat, namely, the universal call to holiness.

RETREATS IN LATER YEARS (1955–1980)

Period of Active Participation

After the disposal of Maryfarm, Newburgh, Dorothy hoped to
add retreats to the revised program at Peter Maurin farm. The initial
plan, drawn up prior to the November 1955 issue of the *Catholic Worker,*
included daily liturgy, regular days of recollection, retreats, farming,
and handicrafts on a small scale. In December, Dorothy alerted her
readers that three or four retreats at the farm were being planned
for the coming summer. One of these, conducted by Marist Father

Armand Guerin from 17–22 June 1956, became a reality. The following year, four retreats were scheduled there, and received a short notice in the June edition of the paper. Retreats at the farm were not mentioned for summer of 1958. As if in apology, "Peter Maurin Farm," a regular column in the *Catholic Worker,* later suggested other locations for retreat. Still desiring yearly participation in a retreat, Dorothy traveled the following year to Montreal with several other Catholic Workers in order to participate in a retreat with the Charles de Foucauld group. The eight-day retreat, which began the evening of 26 June 1959, was the longest that Dorothy had ever completed. She compared it favorably with Lacouture retreats she had made in the past and called attention to similarities between them: an emphasis on silence, recognition of the work of the Holy Spirit, teaching on prayer, and an hour of adoration before the Blessed Sacrament. In the September 1959 issue of the paper, Dorothy spoke with appreciation of a second retreat made that year, the Labor Day weekend retreat at the Maurin farm, conducted by Peter Minard, O.S.B. Pleased as she was by it, Dorothy still felt keenly the deprivation of the Lacouture retreat in the last few years. This was evident in the same article, in which she rejoiced over recent news of Hugo's recent good fortune:

> We heard from many . . . how Fr. Hugo was honored this month by the new Bishop, Bishop Wright. . . . He dedicated Fr. Hugo's new Church [St. Germaine] . . . and told of his happiness in finally meeting Fr. Hugo whom he had followed with interest over many years. Perhaps if he does not have to go on building, Fr. Hugo may be able to give retreats again — those famous retreats which "enlightened the mind and inflamed the heart" and "made all things seem new."[60]

Though subtly stated here, Dorothy frequently expressed irritation at any apparent priority given to building or other projects over people. Her immediate concern at the moment was the unavailability of a regular priest chaplain for the farm and, more so, of priests to direct retreats and days of recollection on a regular basis. This had become a growing problem, for she desired that the Maurin farm be a training center for lay Christian life and ministry, and she looked to priests to nourish groups by word and sacrament. While entertaining hopes for future retreats at Maurin farm, Dorothy continued to make yearly retreats elsewhere. For this purpose, she journeyed to Montreal at the end of summer 1960. She and six other Catholic Workers again joined the Charles de Foucauld Secular Fraternity for retreat at the beginning of September 1961. The site of this gathering was the Benedictine foundation of Mount Saviour at Elmira, New York.[61]

When in 1962 the Lacouture retreat was revived, Dorothy's announcement in the May issue of the paper was surprisingly subdued. That summer two Lacouture retreats were conducted by Marion Casey at Belle Plain, Minnesota, to which Dorothy invited her readers. For the following year, she had arranged with Casey that a retreat be given at the Maurin farm itself. Dorothy felt enriched by this retreat and eagerly noted, six months later, that John J. Hugo had begun to give retreats to his Pittsburgh parishioners. In January 1964 she informed her readers of another retreat-related event: the coming sale of Maurin farm and the Catholic Workers' move to another rural location, some ninety miles north of New York City. Though she had not long ago assessed the Maurin farm program as an attempt to do too much, she nonetheless had fond, broad hopes for the future Beata Maria farm, Tivoli. These included the implementation of retreats:

> We will have at last a Folk School . . . a place for study and discussion, . . . and a retreat house such as we have had several times in the past. The entire school will be staffed by our "community of need". . . . The scholars will become workers, and the workers scholars. . . .
>
> We are already planning our peace conference for the coming summer, and one on cooperatives; and several retreats, five or six days in silence, in work and in prayer.
>
> So the work develops, the works of mercy as the main work of our lives, the work our Lord told us to do in Matthew 25. The work of study, on all levels as Baron von Hugel suggested, to develop mind and spirit and to grow in the knowledge and love of God.[62]

While reality would fall short of the dream as in previous farm ventures, Dorothy was indeed encouraged by the restoration of the Lacouture retreat movement. That summer two Lacouture retreats were offered at the Tivoli farm. The first, given by Marion Casey 19–25 July 1964, attracted many persons who had made retreats at Easton and Newburgh. The second, conducted by John J. Hugo over the Labor Day weekend, was "great news" to Dorothy. Reflecting upon it afterwards, she proclaimed the subjects of the retreat preaching as:

the ideal, the goal, at which we aim. We fall far short of everything we profess, but we certainly don't want to water down the doctrine of Christ to fit ourselves. We can keep on striving toward it. "Lo, the Bridgroom [*sic*] cometh, go ye forth to meet him." We have to go towards him. We have to do our share. For the rest, "His grace is sufficient for us, we can be confident."[63]

Hugo returned to direct retreats at Tivoli for the next two summers. The following year's retreat, to be offered 25 June–1 July 1967, was moved to St. John's Church in Coylesville, Pennsylvania, where Hugo was then administrator. Notifying her readers of the change in the *Catholic Worker,* Dorothy noted simply that silence had been difficult to maintain at Tivoli, which was also a House of Hospitality. Hugo later put the silence issue in broader perspective. At the 1966 retreat he had agreed to permit discussion the last evening of the exercises. This change was made in order to accommodate retreatants who wished to introduce dialogue during the retreat. The discussion became bitter debate about the retreat and upset both Hugo and Dorothy. Each felt that the retreat's purpose was to present a picture of the Christian life and that afterwards each retreatant was to assess its value, rather than to give way to the opinion of a few outspoken persons. The incident at the 1966 gathering could not have failed to raise Dorothy's fears that the Lacouture retreat might again be eclipsed. Unfortunately for Dorothy, Hugo canceled the 1967 retreat at Coylesville. Dorothy appeared not to have immediate hopes for further retreats from Hugo, as he was then completing a study of St. Augustine for publication. However, the Lacouture retreat was never far from her mind. This may be adduced from her comments following a July 1968 retreat at Long Branch, New Jersey. It had been led by a group from the Lombardi Movement for a Better World. Using the Lacouture retreat as a yardstick, her single criticism revolved around the issue of silence. For her, the Lombardi retreat "was crowded with too much talk and discussion, and not enough time for reading and digesting the material we were studying. Living in community one hungers and thirsts for time alone, and silence, especially in a great diversified group such as this was."[64]

While no mention of current Lacouture movement retreats may be found for the next several years, Dorothy remained close to the movement through contacts with priest friends known to be sympathetic to the retreat. At Dorothy's invitation, Marion Casey gave conferences during the 9–15 June 1967 Catholic Worker summer school at Tivoli. Available evidence has shown that these talks incorporated retreat teachings. Casey's winter 1967–1968 and November 1968 visits to the Tivoli group were carefully noted. Again, no formal retreat was given, but his homilies provided Lacouture-oriented teaching. Pacifique Roy's nephew, Jesuit Father Leandre Plante, spent an extended time with the Catholic Worker group the winters of 1967–1968 and 1968–1969. In addition, Dorothy promoted a forthcoming book of Hugo's, which she realized was based directly upon retreat teachings. This she managed by printing forthcoming chapters in the October 1968 through June 1969 issues of the paper. An editorial comment accompanying one of these serially printed chapters connected Hugo's past writings on peace with the retreat itself. As a woman long and passionately involved in both the Lacouture retreat and peace movements, Dorothy viewed each as following gospel imperatives:

> He [Hugo] led the way among Catholics in the struggle for peace. It is because I am convinced that there can be no beginnings of peace in our hearts or in the world until we accept these hard sayings of the Gospel that I offer these articles to our readers.[65]

Frequent retrospects of past retreats and of priests formerly associated with the Lacouture movement also sustained Dorothy during these years. Retreat language continued to infiltrate her writings. While she wrote less frequently of participation in other, current retreats, evidence supports the fact that she continued to take such spiritual exercises seriously. She thought of retreats as grace-filled opportunities, which reminded her of the need for ongoing conversion of heart. In an Advent jotting, shared with her readers, she observed: "I am indulging myself in reading Scripture and *about* the spiritual life, the lives of the saints—instead of living it myself. I must make a retreat." Silence at retreats remained important to Dorothy. It was an element which drew her to participate in a Quaker-inspired retreat directed by Douglas Steere in February 1971 and to a 1975 pre-Christmas retreat at a Dominican monastery in New York City.[66]

When John J. Hugo resumed preaching the Lacouture retreat after a decade, Dorothy participated in one conducted by him in August 1976. It was to be her last. A fragile, ailing woman, she nonetheless traveled from New York by bus, carrying the brown bag lunch for which she was well known. Her short comment after the retreat is telling: "Fr. John J. Hugo gave a small group a week's retreat — a study of the Scriptures — in Pittsburgh, the third week in August. I left there refreshed and strengthened."[67] From first to last, Dorothy had viewed the Lacouture retreat as an exercise in gospel spirituality, as a putting on Christ. For this woman who considered the record of Christ's sayings in the New Testament as the greatest comfort of her life, any exercise which brought Christ closer to mind would serve to provide her with refreshment and peace.

The Retreat in Retrospect

Dorothy's direct experience of the Lacouture retreat spanned four decades. Retrospects from this period provide a good witness of its importance for her spirituality. Of these, material related to an unpublished manuscript, "All Is Grace," represents her most protracted effort to reflect on the retreat. This material may be divided into two sections: a lengthy manuscript and a related collection of written fragments. The manuscript consists of a series of unrefined notes taken during retreats, days of recollection, a Grail course in Christian living, and private reflections written during her sabbatical. Even though Dorothy wished to rework it, in its present state the manuscript is basically an unretouched record of her thoughts in the 1940s.[68] On the other hand, the fragment collection represents various later, disjointed efforts to write a reflective book based on the retreat experience. In all, Dorothy worked on her spiritual autobiography, titled "All Is Grace," for at least thirty years. The persistence of her efforts alone argue for the project's importance to her. Its main history may be traced from an October 1945 announcement to readers of the *Catholic Worker* that she hoped to write a book on retreats, to the September 1975 deposit of the material in the Marquette University archives.[69]

Dorothy had been drawn to the Lacouture retreat because of a perennial search for synthesis. Not only did she desire a greater understanding of her Catholic faith but the means which would aid her in living it. As she noted in a 1959 fragment:

> The convert wants a synthesis. He wants to be another Aquinas and relate his past knowledge to what he has learned as a Catholic, and do in his small way what Thomas did with Aristotle. But the layman con-

vert wants to make a synthesis too of the spiritual and material, the sacred and secular.[70]

The retreat itself was similarly contextualized. While the Lacouture retreat remained central to both manuscript and fragments, Dorothy focused her attention on other aids to holiness as well. Non-Lacouture retreats and days of recollection, priest confessors and directors whose orientation was different from that of Lacouture movement priests, reflections on the liturgy, on the saints, gratitude for the beauties of nature, and her concern for the world situation are all included. Even the title, "All Is Grace," which she wished to give the completed work, is illustrative of her intention. She derived it from Thérèse of Lisieux, who cried out the phrase in her last agony. Dorothy took the words to mean "what St. Paul said, 'that all things work together for good to those who love God.'"[71]

Dorothy looked consistently to priests as mediators of the good news of the Lacouture retreat. She often found, however, that the very men who preached a lofty doctrine of holiness failed in numerous ways to live up to the word they preached. In several fragments she dealt with the problem this had become for her. While she wished to give a faithful account of her dealings with priests, neither did she wish to compromise her purpose, which was to edify others. It appears that Francis of Assisi was instructive towards an acceptance and resolution of this dilemma. During a 1964 retreat with John J. Hugo she heard a few words from the Italian saint's *Testament* and recorded them as noteworthy:

> During our retreat we read Jörgensen's *Life of St. Francis,* and here are some less known words of the universally beloved St. Francis. "Then the Lord gave me and still gives me so great a confidence in priests, that if they even persecuted me, I would for the sake of their consecration say nothing about it. . . . And them and all other priests I will fear, love, and honor as my superiors, and I will not look at their faults, for I see God's Son in them. . . ."[72]

Though seven centuries of thought separated them, at some point in their lives both Francis and Dorothy had come to reconcile the gift of priestly ministry with the fragility of the human instrument. However, at no point did Dorothy relent in her expectation that the gospel be preached to the laity. She considered the retreat preaching an integral part of their ministry of the Word and felt herself fortunate to have heard some powerful preachers — Hugo being foremost — among the directors of the Lacouture retreat. Dorothy recalled with gratitude her 1944 retreat with Denis Mooney, O.F.M., and how he started all of the group reading the New Testament. She desired that priests "have enough faith in the power of the Holy Spirit to enlighten hearts so that we can accept the Word and be changed by it . . . have enough faith in us, the people, faith in our capacity to change."[73]

Perhaps a single vivid recollection of her first retreat, written in the 1960s, best illustrates its meaning for her life:

> I made this retreat, as the saying is, many times. The first time brought with it a shock of recognition that this was what I was looking for in the way of an explanation of the mystery of the Christian Life, the plan of God for us all. Though still I saw through a glass darkly, I saw things as a whole for the first time with a delight, a joy, an excitement, which is hard to describe. This is what I expected when I became a Catholic. This is what all my reading had led me to expect in the way of teaching and guidance in the spiritual life. I came away with what I can only consider to be an increased knowledge of the supernatural life, the feeling that I had grown in faith, hope and charity, that I had been fed the strong meat of the gospel and was now prepared to run the race, to journey onward with that food which would sustain me for forty days in any wilderness. I felt prepared for deserts and underground tunnels, for the dark night of the senses and of the soul. And I knew too that this strong light would dim with the ensuing months and that the next year I would again have to make the retreat, to adjust my vision to the blazing truth which was set before us, to get things into perspective once again.[74]

CONCLUSION AND ASSESSMENT

Two years before her friend's death, Sister Peter Claver Fahy observed that for Dorothy the Lacouture retreat "only gave consent to all the things that she had in her own heart."[75] This remark, while accurate, neither minimized the retreat nor Dorothy's response to it. It simply acknowledged that, in Dorothy's case, the retreat's importance lay primarily in the fact that it served as confirmation rather than as source of insight. The doctrine of the Lacouture movement articulated a reality of heroic Christianity that Dorothy had already begun to synthesize for herself in cooperation with God's grace at work within her. Her life experiences, a profound appreciation of Sacred Scripture, a wide range of reading, previous direction provided by early confessors and spiritual advisors such as Joseph McSorley, C.S.P., her interactions with Maurin and the Benedictine tradition, and her fidelity to the retreat, all provided parts of the framework for Dorothy's continued growth in holiness. To credit any of these in isolation would distract from her purpose in life in favor of the means she employed in achieving it. Stated abstractly, Dorothy's purpose was the attainment of sanctity. Stated in the concrete reality which was Dorothy's life, the attainment—which was also gift—was growth in love for Christ. Over and again, Dorothy had expressed her spirituality in terms of love for God and love for her neighbor. The meeting place for both was her ardent love for Christ: Christ as God made human and Christ within in every human being.

It is in this dimension—her love for Christ—that the retreat contains its greatest meaning for her spirituality. Dorothy regarded the retreat as a course in Christian living, which instructed and enabled the participant "to put on Christ" (Rom 13:14). For her, this was no figurative expression but indicated the depth of her identification with the person of Christ. A passionate woman, she recognized that hers was a lover's quest, that her life task was the ordering and enlargement of her capacity to love. Her reading of Dostoevsky and her own life experiences had prepared her well for the retreat teachings on love, detachment, and suffering for the sake of the Beloved.[76] Dostoevsky had taught her compassionate forbearance; her own experiences taught her how much she desired to love and to be loved. Her reflections on retreat teachings enabled her to place her life events in better perspective.

Among these was one of the greatest sacrifices of her life: leaving Forster Batterham at the time of her conversion to Catholicism. Writing in 1932, five years after the event, Dorothy recalled having been sick with the struggle to keep human love and love for God. It was not so much that she saw a dichotomy between the two but because she feared that in remaining with Forster she would in the end lack the courage to follow her vocation as a Catholic. Their mutual wrestling with the problem was resolved finally by Dorothy, who remarked, "I can say truthfully that I gave up human love when it was at its strongest and tenderest, because I had experienced the overwhelming conviction that I could not live [any] longer without God. There was no compromise possible."[77]

Her continued attempt to understand divine love in relation to human love was recalled more than thirty years later in two of Dorothy's accounts of hearing Lacouture teachings from Pacifique Roy. In the narratives, Dorothy connected Roy's preaching of God's love and Christ's teaching on the road to Emmaus with the ardent response of his disciples. She compared her own response to such teaching to falling in love again, with the composite understanding that love brings to mind and heart. As late as the 1970s she found herself still trying to explain what her identification with Christ meant. She admitted that in becoming Catholic she realized that she wanted "to put off the old man and put on Christ. I loved, in other words, and like all women in love, I wanted to be united to my love [, Christ]." It was not that she denied her love for Forster or any other person but that no human love alone could satisfy her hunger to be united with Christ. As she had noted elsewhere, Christ had truly been "bought . . . with my heart's blood."[78]

Perhaps it is because she loved so deeply that her interpretations of retreat teachings on suffering and detachment contain their own special poignancy. Dorothy frequently noted that the retreat taught that contradiction was necessary for sanctification. She believed that suffering purified and united one to Christ, and viewed it as a part of the human condition rather than as stoic endurance:

> Suffering borne with courage means to the devout mind a participating in the sufferings of Christ on the Cross and if bravely endured, can lighten the sufferings of others. It is not a cult of suffering. It is an acceptance of the human condition.[79]

Dorothy had long considered that the power of love enabled persons to desire to do great things for one another, and that in attempting to change the social order, no sacrifice and no suffering would ever seem too much, because all were united in God's love. At the end of her life she articulated a simple prayer expressing her desire to know, love, and serve God, a personal God known best through Christ, who took on human flesh and suffered and died for humanity. She prayed to find the way, not to the moon, but to God. This was her "real desire because of . . . [our] need for love, and God is love."[80]

Dorothy found meaning in retreat teachings on detachment, but brought a sense of discernment to her reflection. She did indeed accept the teachings of John of the Cross but was aware that a number of the early retreat directors preached the Carmelite's litany of renunciations out of context from the rest of his doctrine. One of her favorite passages from John of the Cross's ascetical treatise, *The Ascent of Mount Carmel,* had been neglected for the most part by retreat directors she had heard. On Dorothy's own admission, the passage in question presented the same teaching as those upon which the retreat priests relied. However, she felt that their focus opened the way to misunderstanding and that, as a consequence, renunciation would be valued for its own sake. She preferred that retreat preachers employ John's larger teaching, which made explicit the purpose of detachment, and of any ascetical exercise, as a continued movement from self-centeredness toward greater love for God. For Dorothy, attachment, in the sense of being an inordinate clinging to what one does not need, was the opposite of John's *nada,* or desire to have nothing in order to have God, who is All. It followed that in having God — the All — as her First Love, the created "all" was also hers to love freely and in proper perspective. This understanding she had found in John of the Cross's teaching and had applied it to herself:

> In order to arrive at having pleasure in everything,
> Desire to have pleasure in nothing.
> In order to arrive at possessing everything,
> Desire to possess nothing.
> In order to arrive at being everything,
> Desire to be nothing.
> In order to arrive at that wherein thou hast no pleasure,
> Thou must go by a way wherein thou hast no pleasure.
> In order to arrive at that which thou knowest not,
> Thou must go by a way that thou knowest not.
> In order to arrive at that which thou possessest not,
> Thou must go by a way that thou possessest not.
> In order to arrive at that which thou art not,
> Thou must go through that which thou art not.
>
> When thou thinkest upon anything,
> Thou ceasest to cast thyself upon the All.
> For, in order to pass from the all to the All,
> Thou hast to deny thyself wholly in all.
> And when thou comest to possess it wholly,

Thou must possess it without desiring anything.
For if thou wilt have anything in all,
Thou hast not thy treasure purely in God.[81]

Dorothy had long ago accepted the gospel teaching upon which the Carmelite's ascetical and mystical teachings were based: "Where your treasure is, there will your heart be also" (Mt 6:21). It was precisely because of her single-minded attachment to Christ that she found room for gratitude and ease in using simple gifts given her by others. Love for Christ expanded her heart rather than shrinking and withering it by scrupulous care over whether one or the other single material object kept her from God. Hers was a larger compass, a life of voluntary poverty which at the same time viewed all of creation as essentially good. Hers was a sacramental view of life, for she believed that "all things are His and all are holy."[82]

Dorothy's sacramental view of life is well illustrated by her relations with other persons. Not only have numerous contemporaries acknowledged the extent of her positive influence upon them, but Dorothy too found herself supported and inspired by various friends. An examination of her capacity for friendship invites an understanding of yet another dimension of Dorothy's spirituality.

5

Friends and Spiritual Guides

Dorothy perceived both canonized saints and contemporaries as friends and spiritual guides. Of those saints to whom she had special devotion, several entered her life more directly and had great impact upon her spirituality. A number of contemporaries, some of whom collaborated directly in her efforts to transform society, offered Dorothy the companionship of friendship and support, which she freely reciprocated. Interaction with these persons provided her with inspiration and an impetus for growth in the ways of the Spirit.

SAINTS IN ROMAN CATHOLIC TRADITION

The word saint is derived from the Latin, *sanctus,* which signifies one who is holy. In the Judeo-Christian scriptures, God is revealed as one whose holiness is without equal; the title Holy One is God's proper name (Is 1:4, 5:19, 6:3, 41:14). Through God's covenant with Israel, its people experienced a share in the very holiness of God (Ex 19:6). Later, the concept of the holy nation was applied by early Christians to the Christian community. Through union with Christ, the Holy One of Israel, members share in the divine holiness. The initial union, established by the grace of baptism, also demands personal moral effort for its growth in individuals. The universality of the call to holiness is recorded in the Sermon on the Mount, in which Christ called his followers without exception to holiness of life (Mt 5:6). Though its universal application was eclipsed in various periods of the church's history, the concept of holiness for all was accepted by Dorothy with refreshing insight.

Devotion to individual saints, a longstanding element in Catholic piety, derives from a recognition of persons believed to have attained outstanding holiness. In the first centuries after Christ's death the faithful venerated martyrs as saints and commemorated the anniversaries and places of their death. Living Christians believed that martyrs had shown the greatest proof of love in choosing to die at the hands of Roman persecutors rather than deny their faith in Christ. These early Christians invoked the intercession of the martyrs before God in order that they, the living, might remain strong in their own faith. In venerating the martyrs, members of the primitive church set a precedent for later Catholic devotion. It included the following elements: the veneration of deceased persons believed to be closely united to Christ, a regard for them as models for imitation, and intercessory prayer to the deceased that they may obtain favors and blessings from God. Toward the end of the Roman persecutions the title "saint" was applied not only to martyrs for the faith but was extended to those who, while not dying for the faith, had defended and suffered for it. Later, similar veneration was also accorded those whose lives as a whole were filled with heroic virtue. These included ascetics, great teachers or doctors of the faith, and persons who had excelled in charity or apostolic zeal.

In the first centuries, popular fame was the only criterion by which a deceased Christian's holiness was evaluated. Gradually, however, the ecclesiastical authority of a local bishop emerged to formalize popular recognition of later saints. This process of canonization, or formal recognition of sanctity culminating in decree, formed the beginnings of later juridical canonizations. Later the custom was introduced wherein the pope canonized newly recognized saints, whose veneration extended beyond the geographic boundaries of an individual bishop's jurisdiction. Through a multiplication of papal interventions, papal canonization received more definite structure and juridical value. Thus, by the thirteenth century canonical processes became the main source in investigation of a saint's life and miracles.[1] Dorothy recognized and respected this development, though she herself approached the saints within personal rather than juridical categories.

DOROTHY'S DEVOTION TO THE SAINTS

Spiritual Companions

Saints were as real to Dorothy as her visible friends.[2] A listing of those from whom she derived inspiration reads like a veritable litany, among them pacifists, socially active saints, and great mystics. The following catalogue is merely an indication: the Virgin Mother of Christ, Saints Joseph, Martin of Tours, Augustine, Benedict, Dominic, Clare of Assisi, Philip Neri, John of the Cross, Francis de Sales, Vincent de Paul, and John Bosco. Saints to whom she was particularly drawn and most beneficial for the direct development and expression of her own spirituality include: Francis of Assisi, Juliana of Norwich, Catherine of Siena, Teresa of Avila, and Thérèse of Lisieux.

Characteristically, Dorothy defined saints in terms of their capacity to love. She considered that "the saints are those who knew how to love, whose lives were transformed by love." She equated her own growth in holiness with growth in love, a love so strong that it would not hesitate in attempting to better social conditions. Already in 1917 an active advocate for the poor, Dorothy had searched for living saints to change the social order. Nor did this visionary impulse dim as she matured. She was conscious of it in 1948 when she asked, "Where are our saints to call the masses to God? Personalists first, we must put the question to ourselves." She felt a responsibility to cooperate fully with God's grace in order to become another saint who led others Godward. In her final decade she continued to look at the saints' example, and had no hesitation in sharing with her readers an article in which she found her situation, life, and work clarified:

> It is this earthy spirituality that Christians need to recover if the Church is to be prophetic, wild and holy, and not merely socially enlightened . . . it is time to take the lid once more off the well of truth from which the mystics and saints drew.[3]

Dorothy's interest in the saints may be traced to her eighth year, when she learned of them from a young Catholic friend, Mary Harrington. The experience was a comfort to a sensitive child who believed in God, yet was overwhelmed by a sense of Divine transcendence and impersonal majesty. As Dorothy later recalled:

> I loved the saints, and little Mary Harrington who lived on Cottage Grove avenue in Chicago, had told me of the saints and the Blessed Mother, and had so taken away all my fear of an awesome God and a vast and lonely heaven.[4]

Dorothy's early quest for God had begun in the midst of a religiously indifferent family. Her consequent sense of aloneness in this search was relieved by friendship with persons such as Mary Harrington but more so by the promise of saints' companionship. As persons who had lived heroically, they inspired Dorothy to imitation, and as human beings, they invited her to friendship. It was a friendship begun slowly, uneven in its development but ultimately never broken. As a teen and young adult Dorothy met the saints through her readings, notably those of Anatole France, George Eliot, and William James. While living with a Catholic milliner and a Catholic family in Chicago in the early 1920s she both admired and resented their confidence in the saints. During the years 1925–1932, Dorothy read various short works which brought to her attention the lives of a number of active saints, their social activities and their writings. She furthered her knowledge of specific saints through short readings in her daily missal and various biographies. As she willingly admitted, her openness to Peter Maurin's program in December 1932 had been partly determined by her then well-established interest in the saints.[5]

Good hagiography had been a critical issue with Dorothy, and she attempted to promote it through the *Catholic Worker* and other writings. This advancement derived from her own experience. Shortly after her conversion, Dorothy had felt her intelligence insulted by a confessor's recommendation of an insipid edition and translation of Thérèse of Lisieux's autobiography, *The Story of a Soul*. She believed that misrepresentation of the saints, either through faulty editing of their own writings or through poor biography, was a general deterrent to true appreciation of the saints:

> There are . . . the lives of the saints, but they are too often written as though they were not in this world. We have seldom been given the saints as they really were, as they affected the lives of their times. We get them generally [genuinely], only in their own writings. But instead of that strong meat we are too generally given the pap of [poor] hagiographical writing.[6]

By the first half of the 1940s, she had begun to appreciate the revised edition of Alban Butler's *Lives of the Saints*, which was better suited to contemporary taste than the earlier edition. She continued to discover other saints through these short biographies arranged according to the yearly calendar of their feast days. Her immediate impulse was to consider these holy men and women as "new companions to look forward to meeting some day." Decades and numerous biographical studies later, Dorothy spoke in positive, unqualified tones:

> It is not worthwhile writing or speaking unless you say what is in your heart and say it as you see things. This is the way. This is what converts expect when they come into the Church and they find it in the lives of the saints. . . .[7]

A woman of integrity herself, she admired that same quality in her friends, the saints.

Like them, Dorothy's purpose in life was to bear witness to Christ. Throughout her life she felt the need of contemporary saints who loved as Christ did, who embraced the whole world in their concern. With Léon Bloy, she considered the failure to cooperate with God's grace in becoming a saint the greatest unhappiness; with Charles Péguy, she felt a great responsibility to lead others to heaven. Mindful of this, Dorothy kept before her the importance of small, heroic measures, the discipline of daily duties lovingly performed. It was this single-mindedness that drew her to Francis of Assisi and other special patrons.[8]

Importance of Individual Saints

Francis of Assisi (1182–1226)

It is likely that Dorothy's first extended attempt to acquaint herself with the Poverello of Assisi occurred in the summer of 1928. She had recently come across a copy of *The Little Flowers of St. Francis* and delighted in it. The Christian classic provided Dorothy with a deeper appreciation for Francis than the synopsis she had already found in her *St. Andrew's Missal.* As with other works which she considered enriching, Dorothy reread *The Little Flowers* several times in subsequent years. It is obvious that chapter 8, "How St. Francis taught Brother Leo that perfect joy is only in the Cross," made a deep impression upon her. The story is based upon Francis' realization of the great love with which Christ gave himself to death on the cross. The Christian's spiritual participation in this mystery, whether the suffering arises from simple misunderstanding or ill will on the part of others, was for Francis an occasion of privileged imitation of Christ. As the saint is quoted having said to his friend Brother Leo:

if we endure . . . evils and insults and blows with joy and patience, reflecting that we must accept and bear the sufferings of the Blessed Christ patiently for love of Him, oh, Brother Leo, write: that is perfect joy![9]

Dorothy readily admitted that this lesson from *The Little Flowers* was a source of consolation over the years. She frequently recalled the refrain of the chapter, once remarking: "'This then is perfect joy.' How often that has been used around the Catholic Worker, making us laugh for joy at the sudden light and perspective given to our problems."[10]

In December 1932 or shortly afterwards, Dorothy was introduced by Peter Maurin to *Rite Expiatis,* the 1926 papal encyclical on Francis. This powerful work, issued by Pius XI in commemoration of the seventh centenary of the saint's death, concentrated on the active dimension of Francis' spirituality and proclaimed him an exemplar of Christian reform for all ages. The encyclical provided Dorothy with a clear presentation of Francis' striking fidelity to Christ, remarking on him as a "Second Christ," a man whose spirit was identical with that of the gospel. *Rite Expiatis* painted a picture of a thirteenth century in need of Christian reform, a youthful Francis converted to embrace the gospel fully, whose natural inclination to help the needy was transformed by grace. The document pointed out the saint's great love for poverty in imitation of Christ, the Poverello's humility and courtesy, his fidelity to the Church's teachings and his great respect for the clergy. Separate treatment was given to various branches of the Franciscan family, with attention given to the rise of the Third Order of Franciscan Tertiaries, now referred to as the Secular Franciscans. This group was established by Francis in response to people who wished to be affiliated with his movement but whom the saints recognized had responsibilities to spouse and family. Two aspects of this group were important to Dorothy: its definition, and its contribution to peace. In the words of the encyclical:

> the Third Order . . . was a religious order indeed, yet something unexampled up to that time, in as far as it was not bound by vows, while it offered all men and women living in the world a means both of observing the commandments of God and of pursuing Christian perfection. . . .
>   . . . Francis by his indomitable apostolate and that of his order, as well as by means of the Third Order, laid anew the foundations of

society, reforming it thoroughly according to the ideals of the Gospel.
. . . As the Tertiaries were classed with the clergy, it followed . . . that
the new religious enjoyed the same privileges and immunities as the
clergy. Thus very soon the Tertiaries neither took the solemn oath of
vassalage, nor did they take up arms when called to enlist as soldiers
or to wage war.[11]

The definition of the Secular Franciscans given in the encyclical assumed
Christian holiness as the end to which all persons were called, regardless of state of life. It provided Dorothy with an early affirmation of
the teaching she found stressed so well by the Lacouture retreat.

The question arises: if Dorothy knew of the Franciscan Secular
order as early as December 1932, why did she not become affiliated
with the Franciscan rather than with the Benedictine order? At least
two possibilities suggest themselves. While Maurin had great respect
for Francis, he was more attracted to the Benedictine tradition; it is
likely that his preference influenced Dorothy. Second, none of Dorothy's writings of this decade reveal that she had made the acquaintance of any single Franciscan or Franciscan group of the stature of
Virgil Michel and the Collegeville abbey. Whatever the case may be,
enough evidence appears in the *Catholic Worker* to warrant the conclusion that she remained interested in the Franciscan charism to the
end of her days. Indeed, Dorothy took frequent notice of the Franciscan contribution to peace, most directly through references to Francis and, in the early years of the *Catholic Worker,* through reminders
of the Secular Franciscans' contribution along the lines presented in
the 1926 encyclical.[12]

Rite Expiatis provided Dorothy with a strong foundation for
understanding the active dimension of the Franciscan charism. It was
clearly one that moved beyond the pious sentiment of Franciscan bird-
baths, which was a part of popular devotion to Francis. As Dorothy
had read in the 1926 document:

> what truly constitutes the entire Francis is the sum total of . . . heroic
> virtues, . . . his preaching of penance and mortification, . . . his
> manifold and energetic effort to reform society—it is all this that ren-
> ders him an object for Christianity to inspire imitation even more than
> admiration. . . . If he was apparently animated by a great tenderness
> toward created things, called even the lowliest among them "brother"
> and "sister" . . . yet it was only on account of his immense love of God

that he was moved to love the things which he knew had one and the same Author as himself, and in which he saw revealed the goodness of God.[13]

Dorothy did not take it upon herself to remove the accidents of a popular interpretation of Francis, but to enrich them by sharing the insights she had come upon.

Dorothy's exposure to Johannes Jörgensen's *St. Francis of Assisi,* an early twentieth-century biography based on solid scholarship, appears to be the third work which most influenced Dorothy's appreciation of the saint. Since Maurin first wrote of this work in "What St. Francis Desired," an essay published in the April 1934 issue of the paper, it is possible that she was introduced to it by Maurin. Dorothy referred to reading it in later years, frequently without further direct comment on its contents. However, her general knowledge of events in Francis' life, her appreciation of Francis' loving respect and compassion for the individual person, quotations from his Testament and Canticle of Brother Sun, all point to the Jörgensen biography as her major source.[14]

Over the years, Francis became the most-illustrated saint to appear in the *Catholic Worker.* Numerous essays, her own and others, gave an essentially authentic portrait of Francis. It was that of a man ardently in love with Christ, whose voluntary poverty, pacifism, manual labor, and personalism Dorothy found most attractive. Of these qualities, the connection she made between Francis' poverty and pacifism appeared to matter most to her; the topic runs as a thread through many of her writings. When first making the acquaintance of the de Foucauld-inspired Little Brothers in the 1950s, she readily compared them to Franciscans in their pacifism, poverty, and manual labor. In her mind, the one who was voluntarily poor worked to earn a living, freed from the insatiable hunger for power and possession over which wars were fought. On one occasion Dorothy quoted no less an authority than philosopher Paul Ricoeur to bolster her own opinion:

> Non-violence on the political plane has its complement in Franciscan poverty. Does not Franciscan poverty announce in an intemperate manner — out of season certainly with respect to every reasonable and ordered economy — the end of the curse which is attached to the private and selfish appropriation of goods? Doesn't a wide and generous vision

of the redemption teach us to read some signs of the Kingdom to come in the most absurd endeavors connected with the destruction of the Monster of capitalism and the Leviathan of the State?[15]

Dorothy realized the consequences of her pacifism, and strove to exercise her understanding of the gospel tradition in such a way as not to appear to pass judgment on others. This she did in conscious imitation of Francis, as she strove to win them "to another point of view, with love and with respect."[16]

Juliana of Norwich (ca. 1342–between 1416 and 1423)

Although she referred to the uncanonized Juliana of Norwich by November 1947, the date of Dorothy's introduction to this English mystic and to her revelations or *Showings* is uncertain. However, abundant evidence supports the fact that Dorothy found in it a source of consolation during the years that followed. As late as 1974 she listed *Showings* among her bedside books, a clear indication that she was then using the work for either morning or evening reflection. While she was aware of the work as a whole, Dorothy was drawn almost exclusively to a single passage within it. Dorothy's penchant for this selection, containing Christ's assurance to Juliana that all would be well, coincides with a decided emphasis already present in the English mystic's work. A study of the text reveals that while a positive tone pervades *Showings,* the work is punctuated by concern for the problem of sin and its punishment, which for Juliana appeared to be in conflict with God's love and goodness.[17]

Whenever Dorothy's thoughts turned to the threat of nuclear disaster, to other disturbing world events or to crises among the people with whom she lived and worked, she felt that she could take courage from Juliana. On one such occasion she quoted what had fast become her favorite passage, remarking that,

> I had been reading Juliana of Norwich, the old English mystic and she had reminded me that the worst that could have happened has already happened, and I do not mean the atom bomb.
> "I stood beholding generally, troublously and mourning, saying thus to our Lord, with full great dread: Ah, good Lord, how might all be well, for the great hurt that is come by sin to thy creatures? And to this our blessed Lord answered full meekly and with full lovely cheer,

and showed that Adam's sin was the most harm that was ever done, or ever shall be, to the world's end: and also he shewed that sin is openly known in all Holy Church on earth. Furthermore he taught that I should behold the glorious satisfaction; for this amends making is more pleasing to God and more worshipful, without comparison, than ever was the sin of Adam harmful. Then meaneth our blessed Lord thus in this teaching, that we should heed to this: 'For since I have made well the most harm, then it is my will that thou know thereby that I shall make well all that is less.'"

So in considering these things, there are these words to clutch to us, the words of our Lord to Juliana, the promise "that all shall be well, and all shall be well, and all manner of thing shall be well."[18]

Dorothy was mindful of Juliana when she spoke of the "glorious fact" of God's great compassion, forgiveness, and providence. When Dorothy found herself worrying, she looked to this insight of the *Showings*. It was to her always a fresh reminder that in the present life there were samplings of heaven — the state where *all* would be well — in love shared and in peace maintained.

Dorothy's later writings confirm that she continued to appreciate Juliana's profound assurance of a loving God's providence. Juliana's insight served as a reminder to Dorothy, and formed the basis for her gratitude to the woman who had lived six centuries before her and whose confidence in God's salvific love reached out to Dorothy in her own. It was their commonality of faith, transcending boundaries of time and place, which brought anchoress and activist together.[19]

Catherine of Siena (ca. 1347–1380)

Dorothy's frequent use of selected quotations derived from Catherine suggests that she read the saint's *The Dialogue* or, at the very least, a substantial biography which contained lengthy passages from the saint's written works. At the time of her first meeting with Maurin in December 1932, Dorothy's library included an unidentified life of Catherine. Seizing an opportunity to indoctrinate, Maurin exclaimed of Catherine, "Ah, there was a saint who had an influence on her times!" and proceeded to acquaint Dorothy with church history through further familiarizing her with noteworthy saints. Dorothy recalled that in the case of Catherine, Maurin eagerly discussed the saint's letters to popes and other fourteenth-century leaders, in which she corrected them for their failings. The Frenchman proposed to Dorothy that she fill the role of a twentieth-century Catherine, who would likewise influence both political and religious leadership. Dorothy believed that she fell short of his great expectaion:

> He [Maurin] would have liked to see in me another Catherine of Siena who would boldly confront bishops and Wall Street magnates. I disappointed him in that, preferring the second step in his program, reaching the poor through the works of feeding, clothing and sheltering, in what he called "houses of hospitality" (where the works of mercy could be carried out).[20]

Aside from Dorothy's modest assessment of her own influence, the question was one of emphasis in a far-reaching program. Maurin initially proposed a system of instruction for lay apostles, houses of hospitality, and participation in the land movement. Dorothy strove to implement it, without benefit of any substantial measure of practical assistance from her co-founder. In the process Dorothy dealt frequently with civil and religious leaders but, in the case of the latter, minus the anti-clerical attitude sometimes exhibited by Maurin himself. Moreover, she was sympathetic to Catherine's reference to the pope as "our dear, sweet Christ on earth."[21]

Although Peter familiarized her with the active dimension of Catherine's spirituality, Dorothy's response to the saint was a personal one. She found in the Italian a great impetus for perseverance in the face of difficulties and encouraged her readers to the same. A single insight from Catherine's writings predominates in Dorothy's reflections, namely, that "All the way to heaven is heaven, for He [Christ] said I am the Way." It is based on John's gospel (14:6) and adapted from *The Dialogue,* in which the saint uses her central image of Christ as the bridge between heaven and earth to admonish others toward proper Christian conduct. The way over the bridge (at the same time, Christ and the Christian way of perfection) is contrasted with the river which flows underneath it (the way of the devil, or nominal Christianity).[22]

Catherine's graphic portrayals of salvation and condemnation, reminiscent of Dante's *The Divine Comedy,* are left unexpressed in Dorothy's use of the image. Whereas with Juliana, Dorothy simply employed a single word of wisdom from a heavenly patron, she indicated a wider understanding of Catherine's text. The application was contemporary, yet intense, as was Catherine's. Like her Sienese patron

Dorothy focused her sight on heaven as her final end. With greater emphasis than her predecessor, however, she tried to make the present life a foretaste of the life to come. This realized eschatology is present in the tension Dorothy felt between proper attention given to better this world's conditions and an acknowledgment that the present was a pilgrimage, a preparation for the fullness of life to come:

> We are not expecting utopia here on this earth. But God meant things to be much easier than we have made them. A man has a natural right to food, clothing and shelter. A certain amount of goods is necessary to lead a good life. A family needs work as well as bread. Property is proper to man. We must keep repeating these things. Eternal life begins now. "All the way to heaven is heaven, because He said, 'I am the Way.'" The Cross is there of course, but "in the cross is joy of spirit." And love makes all things easy.[23]

In later years Dorothy clearly understood the nature of her vocation, one in which spiritual and corporal works of mercy were joined together. Like Catherine, Dorothy engaged in occasional confrontations — over issues such as the proliferation of arms and with city and state officials whose building codes and the like Dorothy felt hampered the Catholic Worker's direct action for the poor. On a more regular basis though, Dorothy's was a threefold ministry. First, it consisted of "counseling, consoling, comforting, holding out hope that 'all the way to heaven is heaven.'" Second, it included the work of feeding, sheltering, and clothing the poor. Third, through the *Catholic Worker*, it provided a form of direct action which Dorothy believed furthered Maurin's desire "to make people think."[24]

Dorothy supplemented the major imagery of Christ as the Way or Bridge, with a cluster of other passages from *The Dialogue*. Each bears the essential message that love for God is shown through love of neighbor. Dorothy printed an extended quotation in the May 1941 issue of the paper, which is representative of its variants appearing in later years. It reads as follows:

> St. Catherine of Siena records our Lord as speaking to her thus: "I require of you that you love Me with that love wherewith I love you. This you cannot do to Me, because I have loved you without being loved. All love that you bear Me you owe Me as a debt, and not as a free gift, because you are bound to give it to Me; and I love you freely, not in

duty bound. You cannot then, render to Me the love that I require of you; and therefore I have set you in the midst of others, in order that you may do to them what you cannot do to Me; that is, love them freely and without reserve, and without expecting any return from it; and then I consider done to Me whatever you do to them. So this love must be flawless, and you must love them with the love wherewith you love Me. For there is no love of Me without love of man and no love of man without love of Me; for the one love cannot be separated from the other."[25]

While in the *Dialogue* it is God as Father who speaks to Catherine of Christ, Dorothy frequently applied the dialogue directly to Christ as speaker. Living among the poor and ministering to their needs was for Dorothy a meeting with Christ in contemporary guise. She had found her first great reminder of this truth in the gospel teaching of Matthew 25:31–46. It was confirmed for her by the example of the Secular Dominican Catherine of Siena, who, as *mamma Caterina*, counseled members of her spiritual family and served the poor and despondent sick in her own day.[26]

Teresa of Avila (1515–1582)

Dorothy's predilection for Teresa of Avila is outstanding. Dorothy had been introduced to the Carmelite reformer and mystic through a pre-conversion reading of philosopher William James's *The Varieties of Religious Experience*. Dorothy read beyond the author's skepticism and found the work fascinating. In view of her perception of the book and consequent development in appreciation for the saint of Avila, James's treatment of Teresa merits some consideration. Though a number of his passing remarks contribute little toward an understanding of the saint, he did offer several substantive comments. The first, a quote from chapter 28 of Teresa's autobiography, illustrated James's point regarding the fruits of genuine mystical experience. Several other passages from Teresa's *Life* and from her *The Interior Castle*, quoted and commented upon later in the philosopher's work, served the same purpose. James found in Teresa's life and writings a correlation between prayer and personal life and action. This same correlation was of paramount importance to Dorothy. In her own later comments on the saint, Dorothy gave no attention to visionary language or to the detail of physical manifestations of ecstasy recorded by the saint, which she had first read in excerpted form in *Varieties*. She concentrated instead on

Teresa's teaching regarding the fruits of prayer. Dorothy's eventual definition of a mystic as a person deeply in love with Christ was in full accord with the teaching of Teresa and other Christian mystics. Its simplicity of expression, however, was more in keeping with the Benedictine tradition rather than the exuberant self-expression identified with Teresa and the Carmelite reform.[27]

Judging from her direct response to Teresa's works when she first read them, two other passages from James were more immediately important to Dorothy. In one of these, James presented Teresa as one of the ablest women on record. He remarked upon the saint's powerful, practical intellect, stressed her active temperament, at the same time offering the disparaging comment that it was a "pity that so much vitality of soul should have found such poor employment." Just prior to this the philosopher had spoken of a turn-of-the-century broadening of social consciousness. As if to confirm his point regarding efforts at social reform, James placed a similar reflection in proximity to Teresa's comment on Peter of Alcantara's asceticism. The philosopher's own remark reads as follows:

> the *Utopian dreams of social justice* in which many contemporary socialists and anarchists indulge are, in spite of their impracticability and non-adaptation to present environmental conditions, *analogous to the saint's belief in an existent kingdom of heaven.* They help to break the edge of the general reign of hardness, and *are slow leavens of a better order.* (Emphasis added.)[28]

William James made no attempt to further correlate the two passages. However, given Dorothy's early propensity to admire heroism in any worthy endeavor, it would not be difficult for her to associate dreams for a better social order with all that heroic sanctity encompassed. Later, she readily identified with Teresa's intelligence, activity, and reforming consciousness without explicitly referring to the narrowness of its scope.

Intrigued by a reading of *Varieties,* Dorothy set out to discover more about the saint who successfully integrated mystic experience with fruitful activity. A growing fondness for the Carmelite reformer is reflected in Dorothy's March 1926 decision to name her newborn daughter, Tamar Teresa. By this time she had read at least a biography of the saint, if not the actual autobiography. During the "idle, beautiful summer" of 1932 she read Teresa's *Life* and her *Foundations,* which

"led me on new paths, laid me open and receptive to strange advances."[29]
The new paths of which Dorothy spoke undoubtedly refer to the foundation of the Catholic Worker movement and its consequences for her
life. The receptivity to which she alluded points to her ability to take
Maurin seriously after meeting him in December 1932. Such openness, of which her readings were both a source and symbol, was ultimately the result of Dorothy's ongoing search to employ her gifts in
God's service.

A cursory examination of the *Life* and *Foundations* will indicate
the content of Dorothy's reading. The autobiography, written at the
express command of Teresa's confessors, traces the first fifty years of
the saint's life. It may accurately be assessed as the story of Teresa's search
for God, for it is a record of the manifestations of God's grace in the
writer's life. In the pages of the autobiography the saint traced her
early life, the origin of her Carmelite vocation, the experience of radical conversion after approximately twenty years as a nun, her growth
in and teachings on prayer, and events surrounding the establishment
of her first reformed Carmelite foundation, St. Joseph's, at Avila. The
Relations, bound with the autobiography in standard English translations, formed a complement to it. It covers the years 1560–1582 and
consists of five descriptions of Teresa's spiritual life to her confessors,
along with a number of shorter ones, many written after her reception
of the Eucharist. While these two works are primarily a record of Teresa's
inner history, the *Foundations* is principally a record of her practical
achievements. Related as closely to the history of the Carmelite reform
as it is to the life of the saint herself, the *Foundations* chronicled Teresa's
establishment of two monasteries for friars and fifteen additional con-
vents for nuns. Lenghty and arduous journeys are described, as are encounters with both opposition and support for the total project of reform.
Teresa's powers of organization, her business acumen, flashes of humor,
and her great faith despite having to face disapproval, jealousy, and
even ridicule emerge from a reading of the text.[30]

Taken collectively, the *Life, Relations,* and *Foundations* provided
Dorothy with a firsthand account of a saint with whom she could identify as an exemplar of all that she wished to be. Though her insights
would germinate only after the Catholic Worker movement began to
exist, Dorothy already looked to Teresa as a person who had sought
and found God. She recognized in this vibrant woman a warm and
integrated personality, someone with whom her twentieth-century pro-

tegée had much in common. Dorothy eventually shared with Teresa
an abiding desire for solitude, an intense and purposeful activity, an
ability to admit fright in the face of obstacles, a deep well of courage,
perseverance, and resourcefulness, and no less importantly, a subtle
and engaging sense of humor.[31]

Dorothy's self-education in the writings of Teresa continued beyond her initial introduction to them. Her article, written for the 14 July
1933 issue of *Commonweal,* indicates that she read a certain Father
Bruno's *St. John of the Cross* soon after its publication. Though a sizable
portion of the book is devoted to Teresa, it is primarily a study of Saint
John of the Cross, her fellow mystic and reformer. Dorothy's perspective on the material is revealed in her article, more than half of which
refers to Teresa. In a commentary on Teresa's esteem for voluntary poverty, Dorothy gave evidence for a continued use of the *Foundations.*
A number of other references and quotations employed by Dorothy
may be traced directly to Bruno's work and include mention of the
saint's devotion to St. Joseph. Like Teresa, Dorothy soon considered
Joseph both her banker and householder, a confidence which lasted
for the duration of her active years. In Bruno's work she had also come
upon illustrations of Teresa's irresistible sense of humor, which grace
had enhanced rather than destroyed. These Dorothy commented upon
in the 1933 article and remembered fondly in later years. One of the
most outstanding and complete of these recollections occurs in *The
Long Loneliness.* It preserves the immediacy of Dorothy's initial response to Teresa in 1932 and 1933 as well as the familiarity and friendship with her which had developed over the years:

> I had read the life of St. Teresa of Avila and fallen in love with her.
> She was a mystic and a practical woman, a recluse and a traveler, a
> cloistered nun and yet most active. She liked to read novels when she
> was a young girl, and she wore a bright red dress when she entered the
> convent. Once when she was traveling from one part of Spain to another
> with some other nuns and a priest to start a convent, and their way took
> them over a stream, she was thrown from her donkey. The story goes
> that our Lord said to her, "That is how I treat my friends." And she
> replied, "And that is why You have so few of them." She called life a
> "night spent at an uncomfortable inn." Once when she was trying to
> avoid that recreation hour which is set aside in convents for nuns to
> be together, the others insisted on her joining them, and she took
> castanets and danced. When some older nuns professed themselves

shocked, she retorted, "One must do things sometimes to make life more bearable." After she was a superior she gave directions when the nuns became melancholy, "to feed them steak," and there were other delightful little touches to the story of her life which made me love her and feel close to her.[32]

Frequent references to the saint over five decades attest to Dorothy's continued reliance on Teresa as a heavenly patron. Her fondness for a select number of Teresian texts is significant because it places in context Dorothy's attraction to the contemplative dimension of Teresa's life as well as to the active. In her published writings, Dorothy comfortably alluded to the active dimension by means of general recall and illustration. With respect to the saint's insights into prayer, however, Dorothy relied on Teresa to speak for herself, often printing the saint's words with little or no comment. That is not to say that either dimension was of lesser importance to Dorothy but that she manifested a greater reticence in speaking directly of her own experience of prayer.[33]

There is sufficient evidence to warrant the conclusion that Dorothy read Teresa's teachings on prayer as carefully as she did a work like the *Foundations,* or later, her *Letters.* During her 1943–1944 sabbatical, for example, Dorothy reflected on Teresa's "treatises on prayer, or some of them. Mostly I labored at watering the garden of my soul, with much toil." At the very least this reading included the chapters on prayer found in the *Life,* and quite possibly to the saint's *Way of Perfection* and *The Interior Castle.* This does not argue against a reading of the latter two works at an earlier date, but suggests a likely point for an extended meditation upon them. That she took the teachings seriously is reflected in numerous comments, such as one in the March–April 1975 edition of the paper: "St. Teresa wrote of the three interior senses, the memory, the understanding and the will, so even if one withdraws, as I am trying to do, from active work, these senses remain active."[34] The question for Dorothy was not that of disregarding the function of these faculties but their proper perspective in entering into focused attentiveness to God as loving Object of one's prayer.

One of Dorothy's favorite Teresian passages may be found in *Interior Castle.* The work as a whole represents the saint's mature thought on the evolution of personal spiritual development and comprises her most systematic teaching on prayer. The excerpt in question focuses on the two great commandments:

the Lord asks only two things of us: love for His Majesty and love for our neighbour. It is for these two virtues that we must strive, and if we attain them perfectly we are doing His will and so shall be united with Him. . . .

The surest sign that we are keeping these two commandments is, I think, that we should really be loving our neighbour; for we cannot be sure if we are loving God, although we may have good reasons for believing that we are, but we can know quite well if we are loving our neighbour. And be certain that, the farther advanced you find you are in this, the greater the love you will have for God; for so dearly does His Majesty love us that He will reward our love for our neighbour by increasing the love which we bear to Himself, and that in a thousand ways: this I cannot doubt.

It is most important that we should proceed in this matter very carefully, for, if we have attained great perfection here, we have done everything. . . . I do not believe we could ever attain perfect love for our neighbour unless it had its roots in the love of God.[35]

The context of Teresa's discussion was her teaching on the necessity for a proper understanding and integration between prayer and action. She believed that the nuns' attention to one another's needs, rather than diminishing an attitude of prayerful devotion, would serve only to increase it. Other instances given in this chapter of *Interior Castle* reveal Teresa's awareness that loving concern for others enables the Christian to move away from self-preoccupation into an identification with God's boundless love for all persons.

The relation between love of God and love of neighbor was as important for Dorothy as it had been for Teresa. While Dorothy frequently referred to it in passing, *From Union Square to Rome* (1938) provides an extended sampling of her incorporation of Teresian insights in this area. Dorothy's discussion in chapter 12 of the work revolved around the question of the failure of Christians to love others, a problem which had scandalized Dorothy in her teen years. Dorothy posited that while Christians professed belief, they deny and reject God *in fact* each time that they fail to recognize and respect the image and likeness of God found in every human being. This neglect, she argued, was at the root of social injustice, particularly toward the poor. She reminded herself and her readers that:

The first commandment is that we should love the Lord our God. We can only show our love for God by our love for our fellows. "If any man say, I love God, and hateth his brother he is a liar. For he that loveth not his brother, whom he seeth, how can he love God, whom he seeth not?" (1 John 4:20)[36]

While aware of a great lack of love in the world about her, Dorothy nonetheless believed that human beings are capable of much goodness, because Christ had taken upon himself human nature and exalted it. With this in mind she urged her readers not to discredit Christianity because of the faults of individual Christians.

In the course of chapter 13 Dorothy addressed three objections to Catholic Christianity. These revolve around: 1) the supposed morbidity of religion; 2) the Eucharist; 3) the problem of evil. Throughout her response, Dorothy employed Teresa as an authority. To deal with the objection that religion is morbid, Dorothy related Teresa's own movement toward joyful awareness of God as her beginning and last end. She explained to her readers the relative mediocrity of Teresa's first twenty years in religious life and her difficulties at prayer. A naturally attractive personality, Teresa felt that in then being drawn primarily to human companionship, she simultaneously turned away from God. Drawing her conclusions from Teresa's own retrospective, Dorothy posited that the Carmelite's struggle in the course of many years derived ultimately from a fear of total dedication to God:

> "I wished to live," she [Teresa] wrote, "but I saw clearly that I was not living, but rather wrestling with the shadow of death; there was no one to give me life, and I was not able to take it. . . ."
> The shadow of death that she spoke of was the life she was leading, purposeless, disordered, a constant succumbing to second-best, to the less-than-perfect which she desired. . . .
> As a convert I can say these things, knowing how many times I turned away, almost in disgust, from the idea of God and giving myself up to Him.[37]

The morbidity which Dorothy addressed had its roots in the fear of conversion and its consequences. Yet Dorothy argued that there was no hope of true happiness unless one is turned toward God. This orientation, rather than destroying or diminishing human affection, placed it in the perspective of God's infinite love and in so doing enhanced its meaning.

Dorothy called upon Teresa's assistance to answer a second objection, noting that the saint observed that Christ "is disguised as bread

so that we will not fear to approach Him." Dorothy believed that the
Eucharist was the great proof of God's love in Christ. Though she
found it difficult to fathom the depth of God's love for humanity, she
nonetheless sought to explain the mystery of human response to Infinite Love:

> We pray daily to increase in the love of God because we know that if we
> love a person very much, all things become easy to us and delightful.
> We want, rather unreasonably, sensible feelings of love. St. Teresa says
> that the only way we can measure the love we have for God, is the love
> we have for our fellows. So by working for our fellows we come to love
> them. . . .
>   And if you and I love our faulty fellow-human beings, how much
> more must God love us all?[38]

Dorothy found in the paradigm of human love a powerful though incomplete image for explaining the Divine capacity.

With regard to the problem of evil, Dorothy asked her readers
to consider the relationship between love and suffering. While for both
Dorothy and Teresa suffering entailed a willingness to suffer in the usual
sense of the word, it encompassed a much broader concept as well.
It involved a giving of self to God in great trust, a realization of the
necessity for continual conversion, and the joy of finding a greater self
than could ever be imagined without God. Most simply said, suffering
meant for them a readiness to do all for the sake of God, the Beloved,
a movement beyond self in love toward others. In the course of her
discussion, Dorothy noted again that "St. Teresa said that we can measure our love for God by our love for our fellow human beings." Dorothy's
reflection is quite personal, and reflects a great understanding of the
power of human affection. It is apparent that in the writing she was
overcome by a realization of what it means to be in love. References
to her own experience of loving is veiled, yet there is no doubt that
gratitude for the gift of human love had revealed to her the overwhelming experience of being loved by God. Her desire to return that love
to God, directed most often toward Christ, was no feeble, pious exercise, but a deep and ardent love for God as person. Her expression
is nearly ecstatic:

> Yes, love, great love—and who wishes to be mediocre in love?—
> brings with it a desire for suffering. The love of God can become so

overwhelming that it wishes to do everything for the Beloved, to endure hunger, cold, sleeplessness in an ecstasy of zeal and enthusiasm. There is a love so great that the Beloved is all and oneself nothing, and this realization, leading to humility, a real joyful humility which desires to do the least, the meanest, the hardest as well as the most revolting tasks, to crush the pride of self, to abandon oneself fully, to abandon even the desire for heroism. To prostrate oneself upon the earth, that noble earth, that beloved soil which Christ made sacred and significant for us by His Blood with which He watered it.[39]

As with Teresa there is no loss of human affection. Dorothy's great desire that in every circumstance she would continue to hold fast to God was accompanied by the concern that others share in the boundless goodness of that Love. Proof lay in the completion of *From Union Square to Rome* itself:

> Yes, I tell you, it has been hard to write all this. It has taken me more than a year to do it. All of it is addressed to you [her brother John] with love and with yearning and because there are many of *you,* and because God has given me writing to do as a vocation, I write.
>
> And I beg you to read and to believe me when I say that I believe that neither life nor death, nor things past nor things to come, can separate me from love of God [Rom 8:38–39], provided that by using that gift of free will, I direct my choice toward Him.[40]

Dorothy's choice, directed toward God, had freed her to love and set her on a path of dedicated ministry to those in whom the image of Christ was most hidden.

Thérèse of Lisieux (1873–1897)

Therese, written by Dorothy and first published in 1960, records her mature assessment of the French Carmelite. At the beginning of this narrative she recounted her introduction to the saint, which occurred during Dorothy's March 1926 hospitalization for the birth of her daughter, Tamar Teresa. While there, Dorothy and the young woman in the next bed discussed a name for Dorothy's newborn. When Dorothy mentioned the name Teresa, her hospital neighbor — knowing only of Thérèse of Lisieux — offered her a medal and synopsis of the newly canonized Thérèse's life. Dorothy held to her original intention of naming her child Tamar Teresa after the saint of Avila, with whom she was already familiar. Nonetheless, she decided that Tamar should have the protection of both saints:

> I decided that although I would name my child after the older saint, the new one would be my own Teresa's novice mistress, to train her in the spiritual life. I knew that I wanted to have the child baptized a Catholic and I wanted both saints to be taking care of her. One was not enough.[41]

Two years later, Dorothy learned more of Thérèse of Lisieux through her confessor, Augustinian Father Zachary. The priest gave her a copy of Thérèse's edited autobiography, *The Little White Flower, the Story of a Soul,* which she dutifully read. The flowery language of the autobiography, representative of nineteenth-century French piety, repelled Dorothy, as did her perception of the smallness of Thérèse's life and spiritual doctrine. An idealist and activist by temperament, Dorothy had readily found appealing socially active saints, like seventeenth-century Vincent de Paul, who worked with the poor of Paris. However, the fact that Thérèse was cloistered from the world was not in itself the actual deterrent. Already attracted to Teresa of Avila, also cloistered, Dorothy perceived in the Spanish Carmelite the accomplishment and largeness of heart which she found lacking in the nun of Lisieux.[42]

No evidence of an absorbing interest in Thérèse occurs in the 1930s, though the saint continued to occupy Dorothy's attention from time to time. Two instances deserve particular mention. A first account, apparently written by Dorothy between late summer and early fall of 1934, found its way into *House of Hospitality* (1939). It indicates a realization of the largeness of the Catholic Worker vision, the limitations of human instruments in carrying it out, and the necessity for great faith in God. As Dorothy wrote:

> Today we are not contented with little achievements, with small beginnings. We should look to St. Teresa [Thérèse], the Little Flower, to walk her little way, her way of love. We should look to St. Teresa of Avila who was . . . like those people who on their own account were greatly daring in what they wished to do for God. . . .
>
> Do what comes to hand. Whatsoever thy hand finds to do, do it with all thy might. After all, God is with us. It shows too much conceit to trust to ourselves, to be discouraged at what we ourselves can

accomplish. It is lacking in faith in God to be discouraged. After all, we are going to proceed with His help.[43]

There is an increased recognition of Thérèse's so-called Little Way, without any diminishment of regard for the Spanish saint. Though it is true that in this passage Teresa's influence is more obvious, the lesson Dorothy had drawn appropriately from each saint was a boundless confidence in God. Dorothy's desire to do great things remained, but it was now tempered by experience and the example of the saints — particularly Thérèse — that no matter how small, every effort for good bore fruit as God willed it.

A second instance of Dorothy's growing devotion to the French Carmelite may be traced to the International Seamen's Union east coast strike in spring 1936. Dorothy and her co-workers gladly offered hospitality to the men on strike. In her prayer at the time, she appealed boldly to the saint's sense of mission:

> You [Thérèse] pray for priests who have many to pray for them. But what about these 50,000 seamen on strike? Who is praying for them? St. Peter, St. James and John were men of the sea. Pray for these seamen.[44]

Dorothy knew by then of the saint's promise to spend her heaven doing good on earth, and was determined to hold her to it. It is quite possible that she had begun also to participate, perhaps unwittingly, in the rising devotion to the saint by members of the working class. Dorothy's eventual perception of Thérèse as a saint of the ordinary had its roots in Dorothy's direct participation in the lives of workers and in her efforts to promote just working conditions for them.

It was not until her 1943–1944 sabbatical, however, that Dorothy believed she began to understand the saint of Lisieux. The experience of greater solitude had confirmed community and active service as essential components of Dorothy's own vocation. Yet, by the same token, it had verified Thérèse's vocation as its necessary complement. A meditation on the sabbatical, written some years later, recalls Dorothy's realization of Thérèse's importance:

> I could see clearly the difference between the two Teresa's now, and came to the conclusion that St. Therese of Lisieux was the loftier vocation, the harder and more intense life. She did "nothing" but love.

The "nada" of St. John of the Cross was familiar to her. The older saint [Teresa] was gay, attractive, longing to love and be loved, by men and women alike. . . . St. Teresa set about teaching the science of prayer, and ended up by reforming the order so that it could blossom in a Little Flower. . . .

From that "year" I spent away from my work, I began to understand the greatness of the Little Flower. By doing nothing, she did everything. She let loose powers, consolations, a stream of faith, hope and love that will never cease to flow. How much richer we are because of her.[45]

Her juxtaposition of Teresa with Thérèse stands as a fitting symbol of Dorothy's entire spirituality. To understand this, it is necessary to remark upon the connection between Dorothy's vocation in its broadest terms, her attempts to integrate the two great commandments, and the importance of the contemplative and active dimensions of her spirituality. Dorothy's vocation was essentially a lifelong quest to put in order a great capacity for love. Hence the importance of her attempts to integrate the two great commandments, in which her emphasis was admittedly in favor of love for God expressed in love for other human beings. Her efforts followed scriptural teaching as well as that of saints like Teresa of Avila. Faithful exercise of the works of mercy, long a hallmark of Catholic Worker activities, was Dorothy's surest expression of her great love for other persons—for their own sakes as well as for the Christ disguised within.

Though she related more easily to love expressed in activity, the contemplative dimension of Dorothy's spirituality was more highly developed than is generally acknowledged. Among her natural endowments was a temperament suited for reflection. A consistent habit of journal-keeping from childhood, the quality of self-revelations found in her published writings, a natural alternation between solitude and companionship during her 1920s sojourn at the beach, the importance to her of reflective moments during retreats and her travels by bus are but selected instances of this tendency. Nor was this solipsism, for Dorothy's aloneness was related consciously to prayerful solitude in God's presence. She knew of and experienced the ultimate meaning of William Blake's fortuitous expression that "we are put on earth for a little space that we may learn to bear the beams of love."[46] To be still before God required courage of her, as of any human being. To be creature in the presence of the Creator meant that she was overwhelmed by the disparity between the two. It was to be placed in the presence of love so great that she was overcome by a realization of human incapacity to ever love enough in return. Yet in receiving such love, Dorothy's responsive heart sought to share it with others, simultaneously returning her love to God in some small way. Dorothy participated in the vocation of every contemplative who, no matter how small the province of her activity, is led from contemplation to action and back again to prayer.

Dorothy realized that both Carmelites were contemplative by vocation, yet initially identified more easily with Teresa's extroverted nature, with the activities related to her foundations, and with her way of relating to her sisters in community. Not that Dorothy lacked appreciation of Teresa's great teachings on prayer, including those of the *Interior Castle*. Yet even there, Dorothy had focused frequently on the saint's teaching on love of God being shown through love of neighbor. At the same time, Dorothy yearned to do what she felt Thérèse did so well: to love God and to experience God's love directly. The emphasis which Dorothy placed on each of these saints, while true to elements in their respective lives and teaching, is her own. While she was apparently aware that both women had set themselves to the same task of integration, dimensions of each of their spiritualities are left in shadow, according to Dorothy's chosen perspective. Teresa of Avila's actual integration of active and contemplative, love for God and love for contemporaries may be objectively a happier one. Dorothy's fondness for the Spanish saint never wavered. Yet, from the time of her sabbatical, Dorothy pursued a greater understanding of Thérèse of Lisieux. In the process she discovered that popular presentations of the saint had belied Thérèse's complexity and strength of character, which were to give Dorothy courage in later years.[47]

Articles written by Dorothy in the latter 1940s and throughout the 1950s indicate clearly the extent of her readings and reflections on Thérèse. For Dorothy this was both a personal task and a preparation for the writing and eventual publication of *Therese*. One of these, an article written for the October 1949 issue of the paper, indicates that she had begun in earnest to dispel a saccharine image of the saint. She quoted Thérèse's straightforward rather than flowery remarks and noted the strength of her faith during the physical and mental anguish of her last years. Dorothy's perspective, while true of the saint, is revelatory of the author. At the time of writing, Dorothy had reason to find her own faith shaken by current Catholic Worker circumstances. Peter Maurin had died that spring, and she felt herself very much alone in the task they had begun together. Her fall appeal, the tenor of which gives some indication of their "great and terrible work," concluded with a reminder that the breadline continued to grow and their house of hospitality remained full.[48]

Therese comprises Dorothy's only full-length biography of a saint. As she worked with primary texts in translation, Dorothy tested her insights against those of André Combes, Stéphane-Joseph Piat, and other Thérèsian scholars. She fully realized the wealth of literature already available but hoped to offer her perspective as a contribution towards popular understanding of the saint. Addressing the work to the masses, Dorothy held before these myriads of people a saint of the ordinary whom she believed could assist them in finding the deep significance of their own lives. She dealt with Thérèse's religious up-bringing, the closeness of her family, her position as youngest daughter, her mental illness in childhood, and the attacks of scrupulosity which were to plague her then and in later years. Dorothy wrote without embarrassment of the ardor of Thérèse's desires—to be another Joan of Arc, to be a great missionary—and the confines of their fulfillment within the Norman convent. Dorothy attempted to define for herself as well as for her readers the essence of Thérèse's Little Way. Deceptively simple, it presented the young nun's movement from self-preoccupation to freedom: freedom to love, to be about her daily activities with boundless confidence in God's goodness rather than in fear of judgment. In answer to her own question regarding Thérèse's appeal, Dorothy suggested:

> Perhaps . . . she was so much like the rest of us in her ordinariness. In her lifetime there are no miracles recounted, she was just good, good as the bread which the Normans bake in huge loaves, and which makes up a large part of their diet. Good as the pale cider which takes the place of the wine of the rest of France, since Normandy is an apple country. "Small beer," one might say. . . . She practiced the presence of God and she did all things—all the little things that make up our daily life and contact with others—for His honor and glory. She did not need much time to expound what she herself called "her little way," which she said was for all. . . .
>
> She speaks to our condition. . . . Is her little way a small contribution to the life of the spirit? It has all the power of the spirit of Christianity behind it.[49]

Though she had completed the book, Dorothy continued to maintain an active interest in Thérèse. "Love in Practice," an article she had written for *The Third Hour* (1961), aptly portrays this. In later years, she made frequent references to Thérèse's Little Way, that ordinary way of sanctity in which great desires are hidden, refined, and made attainable within the parameters of the human condition. Clearly, it had become Dorothy's way as well. Though even in the earliest days of the Catholic Worker she had worked with the materials at hand, from Thérèse she learned greater confidence in the ultimate effectiveness of small actions, when strengthened by prayer and the support of others. Dorothy found that communal efforts, no matter their seeming insignificance for promoting good, went far beyond great efforts expended in isolation. Her journey to Rome in autumn of 1965, during the Vatican Council's fourth session, is typical of Dorothy's expression of the Little Way. As a news release later reported: "while they debated . . . issues at the Second Vatican Council, Dorothy Day and her followers characteristically fasted and prayed in a convent on the outskirts of Rome."[50]

Because of Thérèse, Dorothy found meaningful an excerpt from one of William James's letters to a friend. She remarked upon the connection herself, and reprinted it on many occasions. It reads in part:

> The bigger the unit you deal with, the hollower, the more brutal, the more mendacious is the life displayed. So I am . . . against all big successes and big results; and in favor of the eternal forces of truth which always work in the individual and immediately unsuccessful way, underdogs always, till history comes, after they are long dead, and puts them on the top.[51]

From James she had learned of Teresa, whose daughter in religion Thérèse was, and through Thérèse had returned to James once more. Her reading of the philosopher forms a piece in the strong evidence of Dorothy's perennial quest for God. It is found in her intepretation of every work she read, and in her perceptions of every saint she came to know and love.

DOROTHY AS FRIEND

If friendship can be defined as a reciprocal relationship based on esteem, respect, and affection, then Dorothy's experience of friendship included many persons. Given the intensity of Dorothy's lifelong religious quest, it is not surprising that a strong religious dimension entered into most of these relationships. This includes those formed prior to her 1927 conversion as well as those begun in later years. For instance, childhood friend Mary Harrington had introduced Dorothy to the saints; University friend Rayna Simons Prohme, Dorothy believed, affirmed Christ by her actions while denying him by disbelief; radical friend Michael Gold teased Dorothy about her religiosity, yet was in sympathy with the Christian sensibilities of Tolstoy; and playwright Eugene O'Neill of her Greenwich Village days introduced her to Francis Thompson's religious poem "The Hound of Heaven." Dorothy valued friends for their own sake, certainly, for during the years 1927 through 1932, one of her most difficult experiences was the loss of contact with many of her radical friends. The alienation she felt during a three-month contract with Pathe studio in Hollywood, California, in 1929 taught her an important lesson about herself. Writing of those three months, she generalized:

> I was lonely, deadly lonely. And I was to find out then, as I found out so many times, over and over again, that women especially are social beings, who are not content with just husband and family, but must have a community, a group, an exchange with others. . . . Young and old, even in the busiest years of our lives, we women especially are victims of the long loneliness.[52]

The 1932 advent of Peter Maurin into her life marked a symbolic turning point away from loneliness to friendship and community. The Catholic Worker, which she and Maurin jointly founded, became a haven not only for those in dire physical need, but a forum for intellectual exchange, rooted deeply in religious belief. Dorothy's travels brought her into contact with persons as diverse as farmworker leader César Chávez, novelist Ignazio Silone, Jesuit Daniel Berrigan, Pope John XXIII and numerous others, both renowned and unknown, with whom she formed an expanded community of faith. She formed friendships of varying intensities with persons directly associated with the Catholic Worker. Among others, these included artists Ade Bethune and Fritz Eichenberg, monks Thomas Merton and Charles (Jack) English, and lawyer Charles Butterworth.

The volume of Dorothy's personal correspondence that has been preserved attests to the importance she attached to her friendships. In one of these letters, she wrote with gratitude of all those who had made of her life a community of friendships:

> Such *friendships* the Lord has sent us in this life. God is good. We can't thank Him enough. Thank you, thank you, Lord, for everything, but friendships especially. We are not alone.[53]

Representative of the most significant of her post-conversion friendships are those with Peter Maurin, Nina Polcyn Moore, and Helene Iswolsky. Each of these will be considered from the point of view of the manner in which they nourished and supported both the development and expression of Dorothy's spirituality.

Peter Maurin (1877–1949)

Peter Maurin wrote little beyond his so-called easy essays, which were intended to provide a vision for a new Christian social order. Other than noting an immediate itinerary and his current location, Maurin's few extant letters add little personal information. Thus, an understanding of the relationship between him and Dorothy relies heavily on the latter's writings. Because of her frequent protestations of the debt she owed Maurin, evidence of their friendship is easily overlooked. Nonetheless, Dorothy offered a significant commentary on their partnership which neither minimized her own contribution nor disregarded the vagaries of male-female role expectations. From her one discovers that it was the itinerant Maurin who sought out Dorothy and it was due to his persistence that they ultimately met. He had come across Dorothy's articles in *Commonweal* and obtained her address from George Shuster, then editor of the publication. On 8 December 1932, the very day on which Dorothy prayed for guidance in Washington, D.C., Maurin awaited her return to New York. He planned to urge a course of action upon her, namely that she use her journalistic training to start a paper in which his ideas would be expressed and illustrated. Her openness to him a few days later may be understood in light of the events that occasioned her prayer that early December morning.[54]

Dorothy's 1927 decision to become a Catholic had been a difficult one. Not only did she leave the man she loved and experience loss of contact with a number of radical friends, she was burdened also by the fear that in identifying herself with Catholicism she was betraying the poor. Prior to her conversion, she had recognized the church as the home of the poor. Only afterwards did she begin to realize both the complexity of her own desires and the limitations of the church's human dimension. Though socially active as a journalist before 1927, she now wished something more, and that was to be able to enlarge and integrate her work with her faith. Now, after nearly five years as a Catholic, Dorothy felt herself no closer to a way of exercising her vocation within the church. She had found in Catholicism a home, but no intellectual or programmatic impetus for action which would benefit the disadvantaged. True, she had been instructed by priests and directed by them to books which enlarged the understanding of her faith, yet in none of these did she find any plan of action to which she could apply her energies. As Dorothy was to discover afterwards, the failure lay not in the church's lack of social teachings based on the gospel, but in a lack of awareness on the part of priests and lay persons whom she had met before her encounter with Maurin.[55]

In fall 1932 Dorothy was engaged in free-lance writing of articles about the social order. These included a report on the hunger march of the unemployed for *America* and one on the Farmers' Conference for *Commonweal.* Coverage of the events, both Communist inspired, necessitated her trip to Washington, D.C. As she watched the marchers, Dorothy felt her helplessness and the disparity between her social action and that of Christ:

> I stood on the curb and watched them, joy and pride in the courage of this band of men and women mounting in my heart, and with it a bitterness too that since I was now a Catholic, with fundamental philosophical differences, I could not be out there with them. I could write, I could protest, to arouse the conscience, but where was the Catholic leadership in the gathering of bands of men and women together, for the actual works of mercy that the comrades had always made part of their technique in reaching the workers? . . . How our dear Lord must love them, I kept thinking to myself. They were His friends, His comrades, and who knows how close to His heart in their attempt to work for justice. I remembered that the first public act of our Lord recorded in the New Testament was the overthrowing of the money-changers' tables in the temple. The miracle at Cana . . . was the first miracle, . . . but it was not the social act of overturning the tables of the moneychangers, a divine courage on the part of this obscure Jew, . . .[56]

When finished writing her article on the marchers, Dorothy spent the morning of 8 December at the Shrine of the Immaculate Conception in Washington, D.C. There, in anguish, she offered a prayer that she would find a way to use her talents "for my fellow workers, for the poor."[57]

Once returned to New York, she found Peter Maurin, the French peasant-teacher whose spirit and ideas she claimed would dominate the rest of her life. More accurately, they found each other; from Dorothy one learns that Maurin personified the answer to her prayer. She agreed immediately to his suggestion that they publish a paper; however, practical necessity delayed publication until 1 May 1933. During the intervening months, Maurin sought to complete Dorothy's education in Catholicism through suggestions for reading and indoctrination, at any hour of the day or night. Dorothy saw the humor in this situation, much as she did throughout the twelve years that they actively collaborated. While Dorothy could wryly comment that Peter was someone "who talked you deaf, dumb and blind," she conceded that he was irrepressible, incapable of taking offense, and interested only in putting a theory of Christian revolution forward. She found in Maurin no self-seeking, only his Francis-like conviction that he was a troubadour of Christ.[58]

From the beginning, Maurin emerged as theorist and Dorothy as activist in their partnership. While he wandered about the state, all details of the paper, including its funding, fell to Dorothy. Maurin happily thought of Dorothy as editor and publisher for a new publication entitled *The Catholic Radical,* for which his essays would be the sole contribution. On the other hand, Dorothy's journalistic sense led her to report actual conditions in order to present a framework for Peter's essays, which she felt spoke of things as they should be. Sensing a need to address the working class, she entitled the publication, the *Catholic Worker.* When, in April, Maurin examined the actual paste-up for the first issue, he registered his disappointment to Dorothy, protesting that a paper with such broad appeal would have no real impact. Discussion, the first of many between them, replaced the former monologue of his indoctrination. Before leaving again for upstate New York, Peter clinched the situation with an aphorism of which he was fond: "Man proposes, but woman disposes."[59]

Dorothy insisted that Peter was a patient man, that they always disagreed with humor rather than with malice. Nonetheless, she found his absence for the next few weeks disconcerting and welcomed his return. By the June-July issue they had resolved their immediate dilemma. Maurin removed his name from the editorial board so that it would not be assumed that he sponsored or advocated reforms suggested within the paper. In an editorial for this second issue, Maurin noted that he would continue to sign his work so that his own ideas would be clearly evident. These included a three-point program of discussions, houses of hospitality, and a movement back to the land. The publication betrayed no indication of the tension that lay behind this decision, and the name of the paper itself remained unchanged. It was only after Maurin's death that Dorothy freely admitted that at first they found it difficult to understand one another. She frequently pointed to her initial overemphasis on a labor program, but it is evident that she found Maurin lacking in comprehension as well. Dorothy's comment on the summer 1933 editorial at a distance of nearly thirty years is interesting and to the point. A tempered criticism, it is also an honest appraisal of a friend she held dear:

> [Peter's] succinct listing of his aims was not even the lead editorial. [She planned the paper's layout.] Perhaps it sounded too utopian for my tastes; perhaps I was irked because women were left out in his description of a house of hospitality, where he spoke of a group of men living under a priest.[60]

Both of them had a penchant for hospitality, which immediately widened their horizons beyond the career in journalism both thought they had embarked upon. Before their eyes the *Catholic Worker* grew quickly from a paper into a movement. Their mutual generosity also occasioned frustration, sometimes coupled with humorous moments, and established a gentle repartee between the co-founders. In the very first months, Peter invited friends to Catholic Worker meals and shared his lodgings in the back of the Catholic Worker office. This was matched by Dorothy's successful efforts to provide a nearby house of hospitality for women as early as December 1933. An undated anecdote from the early years illustrates a potential hospitality disaster averted by her practicality, Peter's guileless fervor, and the solid underpinnings of their friendship:

> He [Peter] often brought people home with him for us to care for, and once, when it was a drug addict, I became impatient.

"Peter," I told him, "you teach personal responsibility and you bring home the hardest people to take care of. You can just take care of this man yourself." So Peter did, setting up a bed for him beside his own, tending to his needs, and certainly praying for him, because within a few days the man agreed to go to a hospital and submit himself to a cure.[61]

In his single-mindedness, Peter was often oblivious of the inconvenience and real burdens that he placed on others' time and energy, particularly on Dorothy's. Ultimately, the friendship between Dorothy and Maurin, like their partnership in the Catholic Worker, was based on shared gospel values rather than any innate compatibility of person. Dorothy never wavered in her conviction that Peter was a saint, yet she realized that saints, like persons in general, are not necessarily easy to live with. Dorothy permitted herself to wonder if she had really liked Peter sometimes. he valued few social amenities—cleanliness for example—nor did he share her passion for Dostoevsky's writings. However, their common love for Christ never failed to hold them together; he provided a vision of the gospel life which Dorothy needed to have articulated in order to act upon. Ever in search of integration, Dorothy appreciated the synthetic nature of Maurin's thinking, which valued both material and spiritual. Restless, she found in Maurin a man rooted deeply in the church's tradition and in devotion to the saints, whom both looked to as models to be imitated. A seeker after simplicity and peace, she found in Maurin an apostle of voluntary poverty, a man whose non-grasping approach to life she saw as necessary for a world of peace. Above all, Maurin was a Christlike figure who mirrored to her the ardor necessary to sustain a lifetime of devotion to Christ.[62]

During his active years, Maurin traveled about the country spreading the word of the Catholic Worker, as did Dorothy. Though the latter complained that he worried her by never letting Workers in New York know his itinerary, it must be said in fairness that when reminded, he did write home. With touching simplicity the man who first proposed *The Catholic Radical* would later conclude his letters to Dorothy with "Yours in Christ the Worker." While other examples abound to illustrate the influence Dorothy and Peter had upon one another, three may be mentioned briefly. First, over the years of their association, both continued to mature spiritually. Dorothy credited Maurin with having alerted her to encyclicals on the saints and the rightfulness of her desire to become holy; she also attributed to him her early effort to add a spiritual dimension to the paper. Yet it was she who introduced Maurin to the Lacouture retreat, in which he participated willingly on at least two occasions. Second, both were avid readers of noteworthy literature. While according to Dorothy the scale is balanced in favor of Maurin's contribution, they introduced works to one another. Admittedly, Maurin was no enthusiast of Dostoevsky, yet Dorothy prevailed upon him to summarize the Russian author's writings on occasion. Third, while he often supported Dorothy in the face of disappointment, she encouraged him when the more naturally pacific Peter was willing to be silent in the face of opposition. Here the visonary theorist was sustained by the determined woman who actually held the movement together. Speaking of two events in question, Dorothy's "we" stood for the Maurin-Day partnership:

> Peter may have been right on both occasions; silence may have been better. We have always acknowledged the primacy of the spiritual, and to have undertaken a life of silence, manual labor and prayer might have been the better way. But I do not know. God gives us our temperaments, and in spite of my pacifism, it is natural for me to stand my ground, to continue in what actually amounts to a class war, using such weapons as the works of mercy for immediate means to show our love and to alleviate suffering.[63]

As is frequently the case with people who work closely together, Dorothy felt that she had come to take Peter for granted. Her account of Maurin's attempts to practice an unasked-for breakfast speech for Tamar's April 1944 wedding is quite poignant. By following Dorothy around the kitchen the morning of the wedding, he provoked her anger. Peter turned away meekly; Dorothy felt doubly guilty. It was the first time, she admitted, that she had spoken so impatiently to *him*. Nonetheless, Peter gave his speech. Dorothy fondly remembered:

> We all laughed, but we all had to listen too. . . . There were no idle words with him. . . . but it took him a long time to say it.
> Our poor darling Peter! It was the last speech he made, as a matter of fact, because within a few months, he was stricken down, he lost his memory, and suddenly he could no longer "think," as he tried to tell us sadly.[64]

This illness, which lasted until Maurin's death on 15 May 1949, marked the end of his active days. His relative silence permitted Dorothy to gain a better perspective of their earlier times together. She missed his great faith and ready assurances, forgetting that she had brought the same to him. Though she had always shouldered the practical burdens of the movement, it was not the same, for they were soul mates, who had come to a deep understanding of one another. After 1949 she could no longer come home from one of her journeys and expect to find him there. He had in the past spoken in terms of principles rather than concrete answers. She had come to look forward to this solid nourishment, secure in the knowledge that application was her own particular gift. This she did with great resolve and courage, believing to the end of her days that, by God's grace, her friend Maurin had aided her in moving from theoretical compassion to its lived expression. Theorist and activist had not only been in partnership, but in the instance of Dorothy, the two had become integrated within a single person.[65]

Even before Maurin's death, Dorothy was aware that people thought her too modest when assessing their respective roles in the Catholic Worker movement. In at least one article she spoke of their relationship in a manner that neither denied nor inflated the importance of one to the other. From her perspective,

> many think I am engaging in a false humility in writing about him [Maurin], because I have been so much the active member of the team of Peter Maurin and Dorothy Day. My background as journalist and radical and convert to the faith enabled me to see and to popularize Peter's ideas. I have indeed tried to work them out. . . . I have learned, as St. Francis said was necessary, by doing. But the more we have worked, the more I have learned that one must *be* rather than *do*. The doing follows from the being.
>
> That is what people who do not recognize Peter's importance to this movement do not understand. It took a man of Peter's vision and integrity, a man who was the embodiment of what he talked about, to move the heart and the will to act. People respond to Peter. He has a childlike faith in people and always expects much of them. He may be disappointed often, but he continues in faith and hope. . . . We hope that those who come to us, as well as those who read the paper, will be led to examine their consciences on their work—whether or not it contributes to the evil of the world, to wars—and then to have the cour-

age and resolution to embrace voluntary poverty and give up their jobs, lower their standard of living and raise their standard of thinking and loving.[66]

Nina Polcyn Moore (1914–   )

Perhaps differences in gender, nationality and age had introduced a mentor element in the Day-Maurin friendship. This did not remain true of Dorothy and Nina Polcyn Moore, even though Dorothy was seventeen years Nina's senior. Bibliophiles as well as extensive travelers, the two women shared a lengthy friendship. It was sustained by correspondence and by numerous visits over a period of forty-five years, the highlight of which was a trip together to eastern Europe in 1971. Of the materials presently available, the women's written exchange remains important as a source for understanding Dorothy's way of friendship. Careful examination of the letters—especially those from the 1970s—provides insight into the nourishment which Dorothy and Nina each received when sharing thoughts, concerns, and aspirations with one other.[67]

Nina Polcyn, a native of Milwaukee and a 1935 graduate of Marquette University, had read the *Catholic Worker* since its first year of publication. At Nina's suggestion, sometime in 1934 Dean Jeremiah O'Sullivan invited Dorothy to speak at Marquette. The occasion provided the younger woman with a first opportunity to speak with Dorothy and to introduce the latter to her parents. Thereafter Nina's entire life was to be associated with the Catholic Worker in some manner. Immediately following her graduation, Nina spent the summer assisting at the New York Catholic Worker house. By October 1937 she and co-worker Leonard Doyle took the initiative in opening Catholic Worker Holy Family house in Milwaukee. When the center closed its doors early in 1942, the event provoked the first and probably greatest test of the Day-Polcyn friendship. The closing had been precipitated by a number of factors, including Dorothy's pacifism, the entry of the United States into the war, and the consequent scarcity of able-bodied men to assist female Catholic Workers. Though Nina had kept Dorothy informed of her group's consultations with John J. Hugo and the local hierarchy, especially on the pacifist issue, the actual closing of the house came as a blow. In a strongly worded telegram addressed to Nina, Dorothy chided:

you show lack of faith in men and God too. Why not yourselves [three women in charge] resign from position of responsibility with humility and turn house over to men [i.e., the men they served]. I do not believe there are no poor in Milwaukee. Love, Dorothy.[68]

Nina's lengthy response by mail stands as a masterpiece of diplomacy. She reviewed the situation, providing Dorothy with ample material for greater understanding. A gentle tone pervaded the letter, though Nina did not hesitate to make her own opinion known: "Not only do we need faith, but Leen says that God also requires us to use our intelligence in the situations we find ourselves."[69]

Obviously the point was well taken by Dorothy, as visits and letters continued as usual, with no noticeable change in the tone of the latter. In the early 1940s the two women regularly took time either before or after retreats to visit, and Dorothy established a pattern of staying with Nina when in the Chicago area. While throughout the decade Dorothy urged Nina to volunteer her services for an extended period at the Catholic Worker farm and retreat center, nothing ever came of the suggestion. However, as Nina moved more firmly into her own work, first as an employee and then as owner, by the mid-1950s, of Chicago-based St. Benet bookshop, Dorothy came to respect and affirm the validity of Nina's own vocation. It is during this period that their friendship appears to have come into its own as one of mutual respect and encouragement to live as Christ would have them do. To Nina's generous gifts of money and books at discount prices, Dorothy responded with gifts of the heart: an afghan or scarf handcrafted by herself, notices of meetings and developments within the Catholic Worker. They supported one another in prayer, offered consolation at moments of personal grief, and exchanged suggestions for spiritual reading. The two friends discussed world conditions and, especially after Nina's 1973 wedding to widower Thomas E. Moore, homey topics like children, grandchildren, and gardening tips.[70]

Along with chronicling Dorothy's decline in health, the correspondence of the 1970s provides a window into the activities, desires, and interests of Dorothy's final decade. In 1971 the trip to eastern Europe—which she and Nina had been planning with enthusiasm since the mid-1960s—finally became a reality. While their tour included short stays in Warsaw, Sofia, and Budapest, Dorothy's greatest delight was the few days spent in Leningrad and in Moscow. The trip remained a point of conversation for years afterwards. To record her immediate response to their summer travels, Dorothy wrote lengthy articles for the September and October–November 1971 issues of the *Catholic Worker*. Both of these testify that her interest in the tour was predominantly religious, and that it provided her with opportunity to reflect on the homeland, background, and religious motivation of favorite authors such as Dostoevsky, Chekhov, and contemporary author Solzhenitsyn.[71]

The following year Dorothy faced great fatigue and with it the discouragement of having to cancel many speaking engagements. Believing even a trip to Illinois too taxing, she declined Nina's invitations to come out to visit her. In spite of knowing that she would be guaranteed a genuine rest with Nina, Dorothy chose to remain in New York. Apparently Dorothy then struggled with the inevitability that it was time for her to relinquish the role of active leadership within the Catholic Worker movement. As a woman who had for so long cared for others, it was difficult for her to allow that the roles be reversed. Her resistance may be read in gracious refusals of Nina's invitations which are overshadowed by Dorothy's persistent mention of other persons' needs. One of these may be found in a letter requesting that Nina find Braille resources to aid blinded Catholic Worker friend Deane Mary Mowrer. Only reluctantly did Dorothy admit her own distress:

> Much love to you, Nina darling, and take care of yourself. Don't let yourself get down into such a valley of fatigue. It is hard to climb out again.[72]

Worn out as she was, Dorothy hesitated to travel to Notre Dame to receive the prestigious Laetare Medal at the University's commencement exercises on 21 May 1972. At one point she suggested that Nina accept the medal in her name. Not only illness, but a case pending between the Catholic Worker movement and the Internal Revenue Service weighed heavily on Dorothy that spring and early summer. Confident of her friend's concern, at one writing Dorothy requested simply: "Do call. I feel low."[73]

Dorothy rallied enough to attend the ceremony itself, at which time Nina photographed the event. That fall she recalled for Dorothy the joy that the award had given to others, particularly to Catholic Worker associates reunited at Notre Dame. In a fall 1972 letter to Dorothy,

Nina invited her friend to her forthcoming wedding to Thomas Eugene Moore. In describing her future husband she provided a listing of attributes which Dorothy found attractive in her own friends:

> Tom is such a wonderful person—I can hardly wait for you two to know each other. He is a man of deep integrity, a great love of the Lord, and a man of prayer.[74]

That Nina felt supported by Dorothy is clear from an allusion to their recent phone conversation. The uncertainty of entering into a first marriage at age fifty-eight was in itself overwhelming to Nina. That she would commit herself to a man with five grown children provided a great deal of additional uncertainty. In the face of this challenge, Dorothy encouraged her friend, so that both women were able to look to Nina's future as a great adventure in which the Lord would be lovingly present. From an October 1972 letter one may learn how greatly Dorothy anticipated the wedding. As preparation for the event, she intended to stay at Tivoli and try to build up her strength. By then she realized the need to remind herself to rest, yet she was "so used to thinking myself strong as a horse." Loyalty to her friend, along with determination and an increase of strength permitted Dorothy to attend the 3 February 1973 wedding.[75]

The tone as well as the contents of Dorothy's 27 March 1974 letter show her to be in good spirits again. The affection and ease with which she wrote to longtime friend Nina is very much in evidence in her comments:

> Voltaire said he believed in short letters and long friendships. That is us.
>
> You don't know how often I think of you. . . .
>
> Pray my strength holds out. Sometimes I think travelling is easier than staying home. . . .
>
> Anyway this is just to assure you I'm trying to get out to see you. I think of you so often and know you must miss Chicago. . . .
>
> Enough explaining! I love you. I love Tom. He was the best looking man in the church at the wedding.[76]

Alongside assurances of affection within this letter, Dorothy wrote of her unfailing concern for the poor. She observed that Catholic Worker lines continued to get longer, and considered sadly that malnutrition contributed to the alcoholism of the men and women they served.

She sounded a happier note in the mention of a generous abbot's $80,000 contribution which would enable her to buy an old settlement house with a view to providing hospitality for indigent old women.

Unfortunately, Dorothy's respite of improved health did not last. By summer of 1974 she had canceled all speaking engagements and was under a heart specialist's care. Almost jokingly, she asked Nina to "think of me as a silent contemplative for the next six months anyway." Though still recuperating, in early April 1975 she traveled to Montreal on an emergency visit to their mutual friend, psychiatrist Karl Stern. Noting the circumstances in a confidential letter to Nina, she wrote unassumingly yet truthfully of her anticipated journey to spend time with him. The letter reads as an outstanding testimony of Dorothy's compassion and her great faith in God and in the human person. Her conclusion to the account was a confident, "God *does* answer prayer."[77]

That strong faith was tested in the months to come. Dorothy had recovered some physical stamina and was again able to drive to Mass in the village near the Tivoli farm. At the same time she worried over the scandalous behavior of a priest who had been serving them at Tivoli and admitted fear that the bishop might rescind the privilege of having the Blessed Sacrament reserved in their farm chapel. Overall, Dorothy was concerned over the group of volunteers then working with them:

> Our young people are not of the highest caliber at the moment. First St. is good. Daily communicants. Here, out of 50, 8 come to Vespers at night. Good old Stanley [Vishnewski] and 6 others. Reading Pope John's letters comforts me.[78]

Nina's response was both positive and understanding. Again she invited Dorothy to visit as a respite from her present stress. In reminding her of her stepchildren's struggles, she offered a context for Dorothy to view those of would-be Catholic Workers. The quality of the Day-Moore relationship may be seen in Nina's expression of sympathy. As she comforted Dorothy:

> Sorry for all the struggles. Life is a struggle and my heart breaks for all the people who struggle so much. As Helen [Nina's sister] says, "We make our own hell." I guess we are here to help each other to cope.[79]

Dorothy's increasing weakness after a second heart attack made extended travel impossible in the last few years of her life. The two friends continued to keep in touch by mail and by phone however, and Nina came to visit Dorothy on at least three occasions. As incentives for Dorothy's recovery, Nina planned various trips, including one to Spain and another to London, always offering her services to Dorothy as tour guide. In addition, she offered many encouraging remarks such as:

> I hope your health continues to be sparkling. You are certainly sparkling in your correspondence and your column[.] I do believe your handwriting shows more strength too. . . . Thanks for sending the photo. It is darling and you look properly loved and cared for.[80]

Dorothy consistently responded to Nina's optimism with gratitude. At those times when she had greater strength her letters flashed with insight and lighthearted humor. In one written during her final year, Dorothy considered herself a treasured and pampered relic. Having lost none of her flair for descriptive detail, she continued in a similar vein:

> I wish you could see the luxury in which I live—large room and private bath, so much space it becomes a dumping ground. Where is my voluntary poverty? Two 5-shelf book cases crammed with books, good and bad. Everyone is always giving me things of beauty so I sometimes think that in addition to running a library, I am in a museum.
> After my morning psalms and sticky oatmeal breakfast I am looking at an . . . illustrated calendar and remembering . . . Rome, England, Australia, Africa—surely I've seen the beauty of the world! God has been good to me! How wonderful it is to travel.[81]

Dorothy took pleasure in traveling through books and within her memory in those final years. Just months before her death she recalled their trip to Russia and Poland, considering it a precious part of the "good lives you and I have both had." Encompassing that statement, as Dorothy well knew, was the fact that each had been enriched by the blessing of their lengthy friendship.[82]

Helene Iswolsky (1896–1975)

While living in France, Russian émigrée Helene Iswolsky had been an active participant in personalist discussions of the Maritain-Mounier circle during the 1930s. Among those with whom she became more closely associated was Russian philosopher Nicholas Berdyaev, to whose ecumenical spirit she felt a lifelong debt. Because of the precariousness of her position due to war conditions in France, Iswolsky fled the country with her mother in spring of 1941, arriving in New York City on 3 June 1941. In late fall of the same year, when visiting the Catholic Worker house for the first time, she and Dorothy became acquainted. At the time of their meeting, Dorothy already knew of the Russian scholar through Peter Maurin's recommendation of Iswolsky's *Soviet Man Now* and had very likely read her work. Though decades later Dorothy would believe that there was an almost instant rapport between them, her immediate remark after their first meeting was a cryptic, "Helene Iswoeski [*sic*], from Paris." Helene's impression of their first meeting, though viewed through the lens of a then decades-long friendship, offers some indication of the basis for their later importance to one another. As Iswolsky noted,

> During my first visit to the *Catholic Worker,* Dorothy talked about Dostoevsky. I discovered that she knew the great Russian classics and could quote them (in English, of course) as frequently as myself, and even more profusely than I did. But what impressed me most was not her culture, which was extensive, but her way of life, sharing the lot of the poorest, and not as an outsider, patronizing them, helping them at a distance, but as *one* of them, a member of that vast family living under the sign of destitution and misery.[83]

Having arrived in the United States almost penniless a few months before, it is not surprising that Helene would be attracted to Dorothy's manner of relating to the poor. That the American woman was also well versed in Russian literature was a comfort to an immigrant bereft of the familiar surroundings of both native and adopted countries. The two women gradually discovered that they had much in common: a grounding in personalist values, Helene at firsthand and Dorothy through Maurin; a lifelong love for learning; an outstanding love for Russian literature and the deep religious spirit of authors such as Dostoevsky, Tolstoy, and Soloviev; an ecumenical spirit, which led Dorothy to affirm and support Helene's efforts, particularly her Third Hour discussions and the journal by the same name; a pacifist stance, Dorothy's efforts remaining the more active of the two; compassion for the poor and suffering; a love for the liturgical and Benedictine traditions, which led to each being affiliated with separate abbeys as Benedictine oblates; and, above all, a passionate commitment to Christ, which is evident in their correspondence as well as in their independent writings.[84]

Judging from Dorothy's comments over the several years after their first meeting, theirs was a friendship that germinated slowly but steadily. In one recollection, Dorothy dated their friendship from the year 1947. By this time Iswolsky had begun publishing the *Third Hour,* to which Dorothy regularly contributed articles. Because of the journal's overall orientation toward religious and ecumenical endeavors and its concern for social justice, peace, and racial equality, it was a publication with which Dorothy could readily find concordances. Not only the work of the journal but nearly three decades of Helene's acceptance of invitations to speak to the Catholic Worker group brought the two women continually closer. Iswolsky's lectures encompassed various aspects of Russia's religious and literary heritage, frequently giving fresh perspectives on Berdyaev and Dostoevsky. Dorothy was nearly always present to hear her friend and to add her own insights to the discussions which followed.[85]

The pages of the *Catholic Worker* reflect Dorothy's longstanding interest in the Russian heritage, which had been stimulated anew by her friendship with Helene. At Dorothy's urging, Helene wrote for the paper, beginning with an article for publication in the May 1953 issue. Intended as a tribute to recently deceased French ecumenical leader Father Paul Couturier, it was a fitting debut for the Russian ecumenist. Helene's first contribution was followed by a dozen more articles and several book reviews over the next two decades, most of which carried a strong emphasis on religious dimensions of Russian literature and on the Russian Orthodox tradition. It was Dorothy's appreciation of efforts, such as Helene's, toward rapprochement between the Orthodox and Catholic churches that had initially attracted Dorothy to St. Procopius Abbey. She clearly stated her own ecumenical interests shortly after a visit to this abbey in the mid-1950s:

> I spoke at St. Procopius on Wednesday and Fr. Claude [Viktora, O.S.B.] who is novice master and has charge of the oblates (there is a group meeting in New York too) told me about the special mission of St. Procopius which is to work towards reunion. Due to my own interest

in *The Third Hour* and the articles Robert Ludlow has written on the
Eastern rites and reunion, and the Catholic Worker apostolate of peace
in general, I am very strongly attracted to this abbey. Our dear friend
Fr. Chrysostom [Tarasevitch, O.S.B.] teaches there and offers up the liturgy of St. John Chrysostom [Byzantine Catholic rite], and it was my
joy and privilege to be present. . . .[86]

Dorothy did more than participate in Eastern rite Catholic liturgies
when at St. Procopius, however. Due in part to her friendship with
Helene, who was a Byzantine rite Catholic, Dorothy was generally
familiar with the Eastern Catholic tradition. On one level, the richness
of its choral tradition attracted her, as did other appeals to the senses:
the celebrant's chanted prayers, elaborate liturgical gestures, and frequent use of incense, all of which were employed in the unhurried
liturgy. Beyond this, however, she treasured its belief in the inherent
unity of all peoples at prayer, especially prayer for peace, and recognized the frequency with which the Russian liturgy prays for peace.
Comments made during the 1950s indicate that Dorothy met Helene
for Sunday Mass at the Byzantine chapel of St. Michael's on a regular
basis. In later years, Dorothy participated in at least an occasional Byzantine rite liturgy.[87]

There were numerous times in the last twenty-five years of Helene's
life when the two women encouraged, supported and inspired one another. At the 1951 funeral of Helene's brother Grisha, for example,
Dorothy stood by her side, bringing the strength and peace which Helene
felt she always gave her in times of stress and suffering. Letters written
to Dorothy during the 1950s continued to express Helene's confidence
in Dorothy's concern. When forced to retire from her teaching and
related work at Fordham's Institute of Contemporary Russian Studies
in spring 1955, the scholar held a number of temporary positions prior
to her academic placement at Seton Hill in fall 1959. One of Helene's
choices, which was to spend the first three months of 1959 with com-
patriot Catherine de Hueck and her lay community in Combermere,
Ontario, appears to have dismayed Dorothy. While Helene planned
simply to rest, complete a book, and also offer lectures, the move
represented not so much a geographic journey to Dorothy as it did
a potential change of loyalty. Dorothy knew and respected Catherine
for her efforts, which included previous work with the blacks of Harlem,
but realized also her forceful character and powers of persuasion. In

letters to Helene currently available from this period, Dorothy repeatedly referred to Helene's stay as a visit, and stressed that she herself
missed her friend. In one letter she wrote:

> Living in community takes a lot of time — everything on schedule, and
> one is not as free as when one is alone. However, as a visit, it will be
> interesting, and comforable for a few of those winter months. . . . per-
> haps you will write all the better, on those memoirs of yours. Just the
> same we will miss you, even for such a leave of absence, and the Third
> Hour will miss you. . . . When you come back maybe you can spend
> a few days down here with me. I feel cheated what with being away
> during your visit this summer.[88]

Similar sentiments are expressed in two other letters:

> I have a feeling you will be home sooner than 3 months. We need to
> know you are here near us. And you are at home in N. Y.! . . .
>   Tonight my knee is so swollen with arthritis that I cannot get to
> the third hour meeting, but will most certainly get to the next one.
> You know how near the work is to my heart and it sounds like the meet-
> ing would be most interesting.
>   Much love to you, darling, and when you are rested work hard
> so that when you return you will come to the beach to rest and gaze
> out at the water there.[89]

In reality, Dorothy's fears were unfounded. While Combermere,
with its distinctively Russian spirituality, appealed to Helene, she
recognized her greater affinity for Dorothy and the Catholic Worker
staff. Not only did Helene consider the latter her adoptive family, but
she felt a call to continue her Third Hour work in the United States.
Thus, after completing the Labor Day weekend retreat at Peter Maurin
Farm, Helene began teaching at Seton Hill. Though living in Greens-
burgh, Pennsylvania, during the school term, Helene kept her New
York apartment and was warmly welcomed by Dorothy on regular visits
to the Catholic Worker during holidays.

Letters written in fall 1959 and January 1960 concern Dorothy's
care of Nanette, Forster Batterham's second common-law wife, recently
diagnosed as having terminal cancer. From Helene's remarks it is obvious that Dorothy had confided to her a great hesitation in under-
taking the care of the dying woman. It was not that Dorothy lacked

experience, for in her chosen ministry she cared frequently for sick and dying men and women. Rather, Dorothy resisted the painful memory of a decades-old break with Forster over their religious incompatiblity. Second, she resisted the painful experience of the present, in which she would care for Nanette, fearing that the woman would die without the consolation of firm belief in God. Finally, she resisted closer contact with Forster, though she had never ceased to love him and had never ceased to hope that he might someday share in the same faith. To Dorothy's resistance, Helene replied:

> How can you refuse a dying [woman], even if there was not all this concordance that links you to her. . . . every drop of water you have given her and every kind word spoken will lead her to Him, Whom she does not know yet. I had that problem with my brother [Grisha]. . . . The very fact that she wants you, dear Dorothy, is that you bring Christ with you, wherever you are. That I can tell you.
>
> Of course, these things can be decided only by you in your conscience. . . . I realize, that whatever you decide, it will not be easy to bare [bear] *either* of these crosses, or *both* of them. I will pray hard for you, dearest friend.[90]

It is clear from a letter written after Nanette's death that Helene was deeply moved by Dorothy's account of the sick woman's last moments. She rejoiced with Dorothy that Nanette had asked for baptism, believing that "all was just planned by God for you and Nanette. . . ."[91]

When the time drew near for Helene's summer 1966 retirement from Seton Hill, Dorothy extended to her an invitation to live at the Catholic Worker farm at Tivoli. She suggested also that Helene keep her New York apartment in order to give herself greater flexibility and a better atmosphere for concentration on scholarly endeavors. Accepting the suggestion as viable, Helene divided her time between the two locations for a number of years. Her affiliation with the Catholic Worker brought her the sense of community, which she so greatly desired. After one of her Catholic Worker talks on Solzhenitsyn, she wrote to a still itinerant Dorothy:

> I hope you got my letter in time for your birthday. . . . In any case, my thoughts were with you on that day more than ever, and so were our prayers . . . without that communal prayer and our masses [liturgy], I would be adrift in my old age. . . . I spoke again on Solzhenitsyn, but

on a different angle. I think I have found something new in his philosophy, and yet he has been saying it all the time: to be a community, as a whole, each of its members must strive for perfection, at least as much as possible. Then the community will be not a *mass,* but a cluster of shining crystals, each separate, yet becoming *one* in Christ. This is the Russian idea of *Sobornost,* in which every person is informed by the Holy Spirit, who is love of all.[92]

In the same letter, Helene reminded her friend of the words, "To Helene, my sister in Christ," which the author had written in a gift copy of *The Long Loneliness.* From these two references as well as Dorothy's own in various writings, it is clear that the doctrine of the Mystical Body of Christ held deep meaning for both women. While their friendship had a natural basis in a desire for rootedness, the tie that bound them ultimately was none other than their unity in Christ.

In the last two years of Helene's life, Dorothy's support and blessing enabled her to establish a permanent Ecumenical Center at Cold Spring, New York. Though failing health on the part of both women prevented frequent visits between them, Dorothy attended Third Hour meetings whenever possible and encouraged Catholic Worker friends to do the same. She wrote to Helene with affection and gratitude, of which the following remark may be considered typical: "We all miss you always. We love you — you enriched our lives much. Love always."[93]

That love was amply shown in the closing months of 1975. When a fall revealed Helene's serious health problems, Dorothy comforted her by frequent visits at her bedside. After her peaceful death on Christmas Eve, Dorothy wrote a moving tribute for the *Catholic Worker.* She strove to convey to her readers something of the affection and sense of privilege she experienced during her longtime association with the Russian expatriot. Her personalist association and her ecumenical endeavors were cited, which from Dorothy's perspective were works of peace. The simplicity of Helene's lifestyle, viewed in conjunction with her spirit of hospitality, illustrated the integration which Dorothy felt characterized Helene's life:

> Helene . . . cleared tables and often waited on guests, epitomizing Peter's edict—"The scholar must become a worker, and the worker a scholar"—as a way to overcome class war. I often thought of the phrase "noblesse oblige" in connection with Helene. She was a noble soul and set an example to us all in her disciplined life of work, translating,

teaching Russian and writing her memoirs, for which we hope to find a publisher.[94]

Dorothy survived Helene by almost five years. It was as though the older woman had gone before to prepare a fitting welcome for Dorothy who, when alive, had extended unfailing hospitality to the friend she loved so dearly.

CONCLUSION

Both Dorothy's devotion to the saints and her friendships with contemporaries exemplify her maintenance of an equilibrium between solitude and community. Solitude represented to her a communication with God's transcendence, an intense search for the experience of and response to God's love. Community, as its complement, represented the immanence of God, known through relationships with others, through love expressed toward persons for their own sake and for the image of Christ within them. Throughout her life Dorothy experienced a dynamic tension between this sense of aloneness before God and the interdependence of community. As a girl she had found solace in stories of the Virgin Mother of God and of the saints which relieved her image of a vast and lonely heaven. The religious odyssey of her childhood represents a solitary journey for the most part, in that her immediate family's religious expression was implicit at best. The assertion of independence attendant to her university and post-university years was also an intense quest for association with significant others, from Rayna Simons Prohme to Greenwich Village *literati* and Forster Batterham. She experienced her entry into the Catholic church and her nearly simultaneous departure from Batterham as a time of wrenching in human relations. The relative loneliness and searching of the years 1927–1932 were offset by the joys and demands of community, from the 1933 founding of the Catholic Worker until her death in 1980.

As Dorothy continued to mature spiritually, she came to a greater comprehension of the dynamic between solitude and community. Not only was her task the establishment of an equilibrium between the two, but an interpenetration of both spheres as well. To be alone was not to be separated from communion. Rather, to be in communion with others, to express love for them, was a way of loving and serving the God who made all that lives. Because the movements of Dorothy's heart were toward love, she learned ably from her heavenly patrons. From Francis, she imbibed continued lessons in poverty and peace and, inspired by his love for God and others, strove to promote justice and harmony among her contemporaries. From Juliana and Catherine, she absorbed a great confidence in God's care of the world and a firmer belief in Christ's presence in every situation. From the exuberant Teresa she found confirmed her own propensity for action grounded in fidelity to prayer. From her relationship to Thérèse she deepened her realization that small things done with great love surpass great deeds performed with lesser motivation.

Dorothy brought to her friendships with contemporaries the Augustinian insight that the human heart is never satisfied until it rests in God. The insight was explicit for Dorothy, shown through her selectivity toward those whom she received into her heart as close friends and the way in which she related to them. Not that she was exclusive in her human loves. Rather, her image of friendship was that of Emmaus, in which Christ spoke with and broke bread with his disciples. Christ was always in the midst of her friendships, the guide of how she was to relate to others. With Peter Maurin, intense and single-minded, she responded in kind and, with but a single known exception, always with good humor. With Nina Polcyn Moore, she learned to respect the younger woman's own search for a vocation and allowed herself to be rejuvenated by Nina's joyful spirit. To Helene Iswolsky she offered welcome, an open intelligence, and the richness of her own many enthusiasms. To all of her friends, she offered warmth, challenge, and unfailing loyalty.[95]

Singleminded in her devotion to Christ, Dorothy's large heart embraced all loves in Him. She struggled, yet offered the symbolic cup of water given in Christ's name. It is evident that she realized with Dante, whom she once quoted in the paper, that:

> Every movement of the heart is toward love. The human heart is incomplete alone. Whether in the order of nature or in the realm of mystic contemplation, it cannot attain to peace except in mingling with another being and life.[96]

Dorothy enfleshed that insight in her own life and encouraged others to do the same. Her friendships attest to this, as do her years of dedicated ministry among the poor. Through her writings she offered the fruit of a personal experience of the transforming power of all loves united in God, and in God in Christ. She urged readers of the paper to pray with her that all might

> be joined together in love, so strong a love in their march Godwards, that they will draw all with them, that all suspicion, anger, contention, bitterness and violence be burnt away in the fire of this love. And may it open their eyes, the brightness of this love, to the works we can all perform together in building up a new society, in our work for food, clothing, shelter, education and health for all. . . . And where there is no love, put love and we will find love; because love is the measure by which we shall be judged.[97]

CONCLUSION

The Final Word Is Love

Dorothy desired to be defined and remembered as a member of a particular Christian community and as a woman who had sought God ardently by following the example of Christ.[1] Her self-definition, while holding the key to her spirituality, seems inadequate because of its understatement. Dorothy *was* both community member and seeker, but the actual breadth and intensity of her commitment to each must be kept in mind to fully appreciate her contribution.

Dorothy's commitment to community is readily apparent in terms of her role as co-founder of the Catholic Worker movement and as a lay Catholic leader for nearly half of the century. An active and energetic woman, she brought to the Catholic Worker the experiences of an earlier radicalism which had both broadened and deepened her understanding of the Christian gospel and its lived implications. Ever a seeker of concordances, she continued to engage in the challenging task of synthesis and integration both for herself and for others, both within and outside of the Catholic Worker movement. As a Catholic Christian, she experienced a lived tension because of a perceptual fragmentation of reality into this-world and other-world concerns, which encouraged a spirituality separated from materiality. She had felt this tension as an adolescent and in mid-life began to deal creatively with the realization that the church as institution struggled throughout its history with the same preoccupation.

As a woman who realized intuitively the interrelation of the spiritual and the material, Dorothy had identified with and dedicated her life primarily to the working class, whom she felt was drawn away from religious practice because of the general inability of practicing

221

Christians and Christian leaders to view reality as a whole. She found this issue crucial when it came to addressing contemporary concerns:

> It is because we forget the Humanity of Christ . . . that we have ignored the material claims of our fellow man during this capitalistic, industrialist era. We have allowed our brothers and sisters, our fellow members in the Mystical Body to be degraded, to endure slavery to a machine, to live in rat-infested holes.
>
> This ignoring of the material body of our humanity which Christ ennobled when He took flesh, gives rise to the aversion for religion by many workers. As a result of this worshipping of the Divinity alone of Christ and ignoring His Sacred Humanity, religious people looked to Heaven for justice and Karl Marx could say—
>
> "Religion is the opium of the people."
>
> And Wobblies [IWW's] could say—"Work and Pray—live on hay; you'll get pie in the sky when you die."
>
> It is because we love Christ in His Humanity that we can love our brothers. It is because we see Christ in the least of God's creatures, that we can talk to them of the love of God and know that what we write will reach their hearts.[2]

Christ was reality and paradigm for Dorothy's understanding of an integrated faith and reached beyond a general appreciation of interrelationship between material and spiritual. Her lifelong quest for God—which was Trinitarian in understanding, though focused predominantly upon the person of Christ—had found early direction through her reading of Christian Scripture. A consistent and growing appreciation of the Word of God had continued to enliven and enrich the development of her spirituality from the time of her 1927 conversion to her death on 29 November 1980. So much so that by the last decade of her life Dorothy found that she could neither write nor express herself without using words and phrases of Scripture. Though it is impossible to determine when she most fully realized that a truly religious sensibility involves the total person—one burdened with fears, with sorrows, with guilt, as well as one uplifted by joy and beauty— in relationship to God, the fact remains that Dorothy did come to such recognition before her death:

> I know nowhere else to run except to Scripture—The Bible—to express exhuberant [sic] emotion—joy and sorrow, thanksgiving, adoration, or petition.

> So, this morning at seven o'clock, with the winter sun gilding the
> skies, I turn to the psalms to express my joy and thanksgiving.[3]

Dorothy's desire for synthesis was a driving force throughout various stages of her spiritual journey. She discovered God as she moved within currents of twentieth-century developments in Catholicism, which themselves arose out of efforts to revivify the practice of Christian faith within the contemporary situation. Among these developments the liturgical and retreat movements were greatly significant. The particular attraction of these for her—as with the Christian personalist movement—was the seriousness with which the universal call to holiness was applied to the laity as well as to professional religious. Dorothy recognized and defended the lay character of her own vocation, and that of others, particularly of Catholic Workers, "who felt that running hospices, performing the works of mercy, working on farms, was their vocation, just as definitely a vocation as that of the professed religious."[4] She viewed Catholic Worker houses as "cells" of Christian life, a term which may be applied readily to membership in the mystical body of Christ as well as to monasticism. Throughout her life Dorothy affirmed the laity's role as a leavening element for good in broader society, and nevertheless sought for herself monastic affiliation as a Benedictine oblate. While remaining essentially lay, Dorothy's oblate status provided her with a sense of further groundedness within the church's tradition, of which monasticism had played a large part. As an expression of gospel values, focused upon Christ as was her own spirituality, monastic affiliation gave a broad-based structure to her life while confirming and refining her natural gifts for companionship, hospitality, and compassion toward others, particularly the poor.

Like the saints whom she sought to emulate, Dorothy realized the deceptive simplicity of the Great Commandment: our love for God, which is itself a response to God's love for us, is expressed most fittingly in the quality of our love for other human beings. The woman who prayed that God "enlarge our hearts to love each other, to love our neighbor, to love our enemy as well as our friend," exhibited her own largeness of heart, both as a visionary and as a realist. With her friends and with those who came to the Catholic Worker, Dorothy shared her dream for a better world in which justice prevailed, a dream which she held in common with Peter Maurin. With her co-workers she strove to implement that vision: through her writings; through efforts toward reintegration and rehabilitation which the Catholic Worker farm ventures represented; through the promotion of lay retreats; through talks across the country and abroad; and through her efforts to promote peace. The enormity of the dream and the smallness of the tools at hand to implement it saddened Dorothy but did not deter her. She realized the value of every small action for good, keeping before her mind's eye the image of Christ's entire life, the whole of which she considered a "Passion" because of the energy, love, and attention he gave to so many people during his earthly ministry.[5]

Dorothy's spirituality was shaped by the religious and social sensibilities of her age. In responding to these she brought an extraordinary integrity to bear upon issues of the day, an integrity based upon her understanding of the Christian gospel and on the interrelationship of all persons because of Christ. Christ, as God made human, was the Way, the link between past, present and future, the bridge between material and spiritual, and the model for human integration. Dorothy searched for Christ and found him whom her heart loved. Christ was present to her in Word, in Sacrament and in the human sacrament of all those she loved. With an insight that had been tested by years of ministry to others, Dorothy realized:

> It is no use to say that we are born two thousand years too late to give room to Christ. Nor will those who live at the end of the world have been born too late. Christ is always with us, asking for room in our hearts.[6]

ABBREVIATIONS

AIG	All Is Grace Manuscript, Marquette University Archives, Catholic Worker papers, DD–CW, D–3, Box 6. See Appendix for further detail.
AIG fragm	All Is Grace fragment, Marquette University Archives, Catholic Worker papers, DD–CW, D–3, Box 6. Individual fragments identified by the present author as 1–11 and A–Y. See Appendix for further detail.
C–1.7, 2–WDM	Marquette University Archives. William D. Miller papers.
CW	*The Catholic Worker.*
"DAD"	Dorothy Day, "Day After Day," *Catholic Worker.*
"DBD"	Dorothy Day, "Day By Day," *Catholic Worker.*
DD–CW	Marquette University Archives. Dorothy Day–Catholic Worker Collection
HIP	Helene Iswolsky papers
MUA	Marquette University Archives
"NBTW"	Dorothy Day, "Notes By the Way," *Catholic Worker.*
SJAA	St. John's Abbey Archives. Collegeville, Minnesota
SJUA	St. John's University Archives. Collegeville, Minnesota
SPAA	St. Procopius Abbey Archives. Lisle, Illinois
TMSC, D–220	Thomas Merton Study Center. Dorothy Day–Thomas Merton Correspondence. Bellarmine College, Louisville, Kentucky
OF	*Orate Fratres*
"On P"	Dorothy Day, "On Pilgrimage," *Catholic Worker.*

NOTES

PREFACE

1. Cardinal [Emmanuel] Suhard, inset in *CW* 42 (January 1976): 6. Dorothy read the French Cardinal's writings and greatly admired him.

2. See Virgil Michel, "Mysticism and Normal Christianity: The Place of Liturgy in Mysticism," *Orate Fratres* 13 (October 1939): 548. For a survey of the evolution of the term *spirituality* and a presentation of contemporary understandings of Christian spirituality, see Sandra M. Schneiders, I.H.M., "Theology and Spirituality: Strangers, Rivals, or Partners?" *Horizons* 13 (Fall 1986): 253–274.

3. AIG fragm [N] provides a single instance of Dorothy's quotation of the passage from Pascal's *Pensées.*

4. In the course of completing the present work, the entire collection of materials housed at the John XXIII Ecumenical Center–Center for Eastern Christian Studies, Bronx, New York, was transferred to the present Center for Eastern Christian Studies at the University of Scranton, Pennsylvania. The Helene Iswolsky papers are an integral part of this collection.

1. A SPIRITUALITY IN CONTEXT

1. Jay P. Dolan, *The American Catholic Experience: A History from Colonial Times to the Present* (Garden City, N.Y.: Doubleday 1985; rpt. Notre Dame, Ind.: University of Notre Dame Press, 1992), pp. 313–314. The perspective was excerpted from an unnamed Baptist minister's 1894 sermon.

2. For a finely nuanced understanding of the Americanist vision, the debate and the condemnation of Americanism, see Joseph P. Chinnici, O.F.M., *Living Stones: The History and Structure of Catholic Spiritual Life in the United States* (New York: Macmillan; London: Collier Macmillan, 1989), pp. 119–133. The most complete account of the controversy is Thomas T. McAvoy, C.S.C., *The Great Crisis in American Catholic History, 1895–1900* (Chicago: H. Regnery Co., 1957).

3. See Dolan, *American Catholic Experience*, pp. 316–320; Thomas T. McAvoy, C.S.C., *A History of the Catholic Church in the United States* (Notre Dame & London: University of Notre Dame Press, 1969), pp. 346–352. By 1910 Pius required that all priests and candidates for the priesthood take an oath against modernism.

4. See Dolan, *American Catholic Experience*, pp. 321–346. For a positive perception of nineteenth-century Catholic devotionalism, see Chinnici, *Living Stones*, pp. 68–85. Though modified in the early twentieth century, the main strands remained in effect and were exemplified by the strong community sense inherent in Catholic devotion to the saints. For representative essays by John A. Ryan and Peter E. Dietz, see Aaron I. Abell, *American Catholic Thought on Social Questions* (New York & Indianapolis: Bobbs-Merrill, 1968), pp. 229–262. David A. O'Brien, *American Catholics and Social Reform: The New Deal Years* (New York: Oxford University Press, 1968) provides good background for John A. Ryan's efforts.

5. Dorothy Day, *From Union Square to Rome* (Silver Spring, Md.: Preservation of the Faith Press, 1938), pp. 19, 20. Dorothy recorded the attic experience in several places. I have also drawn from Dorothy Day, "July 30th" [after 1975], DD–CW, D–3, Box 7; AIG fragm [N & O]; Dorothy Day, *The Long Loneliness* (San Francisco: Harper & Row, 1952, 1981), pp. 17–20. Though Dorothy remarked in *Long Loneliness*, p. 19, that she was born in Bath Beach, Brooklyn, archivist Phillip M. Runkel noted in a 11 July 1991 conversation with the author that Dorothy was actually born in Brooklyn Heights.

6. Day, *Union Square to Rome*, p. 4. Compare with p. 21, in which she indicated that there were lapses of some years in her reading of Scripture. Another reference confirming Scripture reading since childhood occurs in Dorothy Day, "Obedience," *Ave Maria* 13 (17 December 1966): 20.

7. Dorothy Day, *The Eleventh Virgin* [autobiographical novel] (New York: Albert & Charles Boni, 1924), pp. 8–10. While Dorothy disguised proper names in this work, it is essentially accurate; Day, *Union Square to Rome*, pp. 18–24. Day, *Long Loneliness*, pp. 19–22.

8. Dorothy Day, "How many ways . . ." [ca. 1940], DD–CW, D–3, Box 7; "On P," *CW* 26 (March 1960): 6, in which she recalled contact with Barrett and Harrington during the year that she lived on the corner of Chicago's 37th Street and Cottage Grove Avenue. According to Oscar Theodore Barck, Jr., and Nelson Manfred Blake, *Since 1900: A History of the United States in Our Times* (New York: Macmillan; London: Collier-Macmillan, 1965), p. 128, Chicago's 1910 population was 36 percent immigrant and 42 percent second-generation stock.

9. Day, *Union Square to Rome*, p. 32. For an explicit statement on her learning to pray the Psalms, see "On P," *CW* 26 (March 1960): 6.

10. In AIG [N] and "On P," *CW* 45 (March–April 1979): 2, Dorothy

recalled wanting to become a Catholic at age twelve and her father's directing her toward the Episcopalian church. Day, *Union Square to Rome,* pp. 31–32, 159, telescopes her Episcopalian experience. A better picture may be gained by reading this in conjunction with Day, *Long Loneliness,* pp. 28–30 and "On P.," *CW* 26 (March 1960): 6. On her parents being non-churchgoers, on Dorothy's finding comfort in Scripture, and on fact that none of the Day children had been baptized due to their parents' thinking that religion was a strictly private affair, see Day, *Union Square to Rome,* pp. 20, 34, 36. The senior John Day professed to be an atheist, yet always carried a Bible with him.

11. See Day, *Long Loneliness,* pp. 30–39; quotation, p. 35.

12. Day, *Long Loneliness,* pp. 37–38; for shorter quotations, see pp. 36 and 37 respectively. While in this work Dorothy placed her first acquaintance with the *Day Book* in her last year in high school, in Day, *Union Square to Rome,* p. 39, she placed it during her first year in college. I use the *Long Loneliness* chronology, which fits better with her account, p. 38, of her senior essay on earlier Russian revolutionists.

13. Quotations from Day, *Long Loneliness,* pp. 36 and 39 respectively.

14. Day, "July 30th" [after 1975], DD–CW, D-3, Box 7.

15. Day, *Eleventh Virgin,* p. 49. Complete text of the letter, pp. 47–51; a lightly edited version occurs in Day, *Long Loneliness,* pp. 32–34.

16. Day, *Long Loneliness,* p. 39.

17. Day, *Union Square to Rome,* p. 119. The context suggests that Dorothy wrote the original while in high school.

18. Day, *Long Loneliness,* p. 43. See pp. 40–50 for her general account of her two years at the university. Similar accounts occur in Day, *Union Square to Rome,* pp. 37–60 and Day, *Eleventh Virgin,* pp. 61–87. For general background on the period 1890–1932, see Barck and Blake, *Since 1900,* pp. 1–453; Charles A. Beard and Mary R. Beard, *A Basic History of the United States* (New York: Doubleday, 1944), pp. 303–462. I have chosen this older work of two noted historians because of its chronological proximity to the period under discussion. The hope was to absorb a view of events that would relate more closely to Dorothy's experience of them. Mel Piehl, *Breaking Bread: The Catholic Worker and the Origin of Catholic Radicalism in America* (Philadelphia: Temple University Press, 1982), pp. 3–55, provides a cogent overview of the period in relationship to Dorothy Day.

19. Day, *Long Loneliness,* p. 41.

20. Ibid., p. 46.

21. William D. Miller, *Dorothy Day: A Biography* (San Francisco: Harper & Row, 1982), pp. 31–53, discussed Dorothy's association with the Scribblers and the *Daily Illini* in the context of her sojourn at the University and the development of her friendship with Rayna Prohme. Apparently Dorothy's articles were unsigned. See Nancy L. Roberts, *Dorothy Day and the Catholic*

Worker (Albany: State University of New York Press, 1984), p. 19, n. 16. In Day, *Long Loneliness,* pp. 47–50, Dorothy recalled her early friendship with Rayna Simons Prohme and remarked that in spite of brilliant scholarship and other fine qualities Rayna was not invited to join any of the sororities. Dorothy attributed the slight to anti-Semitism.

22. Day, *Long Loneliness,* p. 51. Though she made reference to 1917, the context is actually summer and fall, 1916.

23. Quotation, Day, *Union Square to Rome,* p. 67. See pp. 61–78 for her narration of the period June 1916–April 1917, which included her work for the *Call.* Compare with Day, *Long Loneliness,* pp. 50–68; Day, *Eleventh Virgin,* pp. 91–147. For evidence of Dorothy's later contact with Elizabeth Gurley Flynn, afterwards a Communist, see Dorothy Day, "Red Roses for Her," *CW* 31 (November 1964): 4; Roberts, *Dorothy Day,* p. 20. While at the *Call,* Dorothy met fellow writer Irving Granich (Michael Gold). The two became lifelong friends. For Dorothy's tribute to him, see Dorothy Day, "Michael Gold (April 12, 1894–May 14, 1967)," *CW* 33 (June 1967): 2, 8.

24. Quotation in Day, *Union Square to Rome,* p. 69. On Catholic involvement in World War I, see James Hennesey, S.J., *American Catholics: A History of the Roman Catholic Community in the United States* (Oxford, New York, Toronto & Melbourne: Oxford University Press, 1981), pp. 225–228.

25. Dorothy described events and her April–November 1917 experiences in Day, *Eleventh Virgin,* pp. 148–218; Day, *Union Square to Rome,* pp. 78–87; Day, *Long Loneliness,* pp. 67–83. For background on postal censorship see Barck and Blake, *Since 1900,* pp. 230–232. The protestors' imprisonment and hunger fast at Occoquan attracted the attention of President Wilson, who signed a pardon for the group after their sixteenth day of incarceration.

26. Day, *Union Square to Rome,* p. 6. On the sense of coming back to something lost, see p. 4; on the other two components of her suffering, see p. 87.

27. Dorothy Day, "A Human Document," *Sign* 12 (November 1932): 224.

28. Ibid. See also Day, *Long Loneliness,* p. 83.

29. The *Liberator* was the successor to the *Masses,* Dorothy recounted this period in Day, *Eleventh Virgin,* pp. 148–218; Day, *Union Square to Rome,* pp. 87–89; Day, *Long Loneliness,* pp. 83–87. While Dorothy frequently mentioned Eugene O'Neill in her later writings, one of her finest recollections occurs in Dorothy Day, "Told in Context" [ca. 1958], DD–CW, D–3, Box 7. In Day, "How many ways . . ." [ca. 1940], DD–CW, D–3, Box 7, she recalled visits to St. Joseph's Church with Agnes Boulton, who married O'Neill in 1918. For Boulton's perspective on Dorothy's winter 1917–1918 period see Agnes Boulton, *Part of a Long Story* (Garden City, N.Y.: Doubleday, 1958), pp. 40–91.

30. Quotation, Day, *Union Square to Rome,* p. 90. Dorothy described

the 1918 to summer 1921 period in Day, *Eleventh Virgin*, pp. 221–313 [1918–1919 only]; Day, *Union Square to Rome*, pp. 89–98; Day, *Long Loneliness*, pp. 87–95. Later, in *CW*, Dorothy continued to affirm Eugene Debs' place as an advocate for labor. The inclusion of R[obert] L[udlow]'s review of Ray Ginger, *The Bending Cross: A Biography of Eugene Debs*, *CW* 16 (October 1949): 6, is a single example.

31. Day, *Union Square to Rome*, p. 96, for quotation. Though difficult to date, the possibility of Dorothy's suicide attempt or attempts appears in friends' reminiscences of her involvement with Lionel Moise (1918–1923). Miller, *Dorothy Day*, pp. 136–137, draws upon a 1976 interview with Susan Light Brown and Malcolm Cowley, and such an attempt was suggested earlier by Jack (Father Charles) English in English-Deane Mowrer interview, September 1970, DD–CW, W–9, Box 1. English heard of it from Caroline Gordon Tate; since in Caroline's own interview with Deane Mowrer, May 1970, DD–CW, W–9, Box 1, she recalled having met Dorothy for the first time when the latter was living with Forster Batterham, Tate's knowledge of any suicide attempt was also derivative. Dorothy's experience, if actual, would be a factor in her deep understanding and compassion toward actual suicides of other persons she knew at various points in her life. From her comment in Day, *Union Square to Rome*, pp. 97–98, regarding her stay in Europe, it is probable that in 1920 Dorothy associated with American writers, disaffected by the war, who had emigrated to London and Paris.

32. Day, *Long Loneliness*, p. 108. A phone conversation with Marquette archivist Phillip M. Runkel, 11 July 1991, confirmed that in 1921 Dorothy resumed living with Moise in Chicago for about a year. After that, the Moise-Day affair was ended.

33. Reminiscences of her 1921–1923 period may be found in Day, *Union Square to Rome*, pp. 98–108; Day, *Long Loneliness*, pp. 95–108. Regarding Dorothy's visit to the IWW hotel, she was careful to note that Cramer, recuperating from a suicide attempt, had gone to the IWW hotel and was reluctantly allowed to stay there. For background on the postwar American fear of radicalism, identified as the "Red Scare," see Barck and Blake, *Since 1900*, pp. 276–280. Attorney General Mitchell A. Palmer initiated a number of raids in 1920, the tradition of which was carried into the 1920s.

34. Quotation from Day, "A Human Document," p. 224. For Dorothy's general reminiscences of the winter 1923–spring 1929 period, see Day, *Union Square to Rome*, pp. 108–142; Day, *Long Loneliness*, pp. 108–152. During her stay in New Orleans, both her sister Della and friend Mary Gordon lived with her; Miller, *Dorothy Day*, p. 159, wrote as though only Della were with Dorothy, and ascribed to Della some characteristics of Mary Gordon. For an overview of the American scene from 1920–1932 see Beard and Beard, *Basic History*, pp. 441–455, and Barck and Blake, *Since 1900*, pp. 281–

453. The economic boom of the 1920s was by no means fictitious, but certain developments proved unhealthy in the long run. Particularly distressful for the worker was the growth of technological unemployment: new machinery appeared to absorb jobs faster than it created them. This would permanently color Dorothy's attitude toward the machine and give an edge to her later understanding of the dignity of work.

35. Quotation from Day, *Long Loneliness,* p. 115. Dorothy's gradual disaffection with a round of parties may be traced in pp. 133–134.

36. Day, *Union Square to Rome,* p. 111; Day, *Long Loneliness,* p. 116.

37. Day, *Union Square to Rome,* pp. 121–122. See also Day, *Long Loneliness,* pp. 132–133.

38. AIG fragm [O]. In this manuscript, Dorothy claimed that she did not associate God with the 1906 earthquake but that she did associate God with creation in general. Compare her account in Day, *Long Loneliness,* pp. 19–21.

39. Day, *Union Square to Rome,* pp. 40–41; Day, *Long Loneliness,* p. 43.

40. AIG fragm [O]. The elements of joy and beauty were of lifelong importance for Dorothy's spirituality, though in later years her understanding was marked by a greater appreciation of their shadows: sorrow, ugliness, and dread.

41. Day, *Long Loneliness,* pp. 134–135. In an 11 July 1991 phone conversation, Phillip M. Runkel suggested that it is possible that Dorothy was not formally divorced from Tobey Berkeley when she was living with Batterham.

42. On Dorothy's continued scriptural reflection just prior to her conversion, see Day, *Union Square to Rome,* p. 136; Day, *Long Loneliness,* p. 142. Quotation, Day, *Long Loneliness,* p. 147. See Barck, *Since 1900,* p. 352, for background on the Sacco-Vanzetti case, which figured as part of the general suppression of radicals during the 1920s. In later years Dorothy frequently commemorated Sacco and Vanzetti in a summer issue of the paper, of which an inset in *CW* 25 (July–August 1958), 2, is a single example. According to a 14 January 1937 copy of her certificate of baptism, Dorothy received the sacrament on 29 December 1927 at Our Lady Help of Christians Church in Tottenville, Staten Island, DD–CW, D–6, Box 1. Baptism was administered conditionally because of her previous Episcopal baptism. In Day, *Long Loneliness,* pp. 148, 152, Dorothy remarked on "making her first confession" (Penance) that same day and receiving Eucharist the next morning. Her Catholic initiation was completed by her Confirmation on the feast of Pentecost [1928, from the context].

43. Dorothy Day, "Beyond Politics," *CW* 16 (November 1949): 1.

44. Quotation in Day, *Long Loneliness,* pp. 149–150. The church as an institution both attracted and troubled her over the years. Confirmed by Day, *Union Square to Rome,* pp. 132–134, 138–140, 151; Day, *Long Loneli-*

ness, pp. 107, 139–140, 149–151; Robert Coles, *Dorothy Day: A Radical Devotion* (Reading, Mass.: Addison-Wesley, 1987), p. 11. See Piehl, *Breaking Bread,* p. 30, for the observation that "as late as 1940 two-thirds of the Catholics in one religious survey were described as lower class, rather than middle or upper class."

45. Quotation in "On P.," *CW* 22 (January 1956): 2. See Day, *Long Loneliness,* pp. 149–166, for Dorothy's general recollection of the years 1928–1932. The year of her summer at the Marist novitiate was confirmed in "On P.," *CW* 21 (April 1955): 7. Dorothy Day, "The Brother and the Rooster," *Commonweal* 10 (18 September 1929): 501–503, is a fictionalized account of one of the older Marist brothers she met that summer. Dorothy traveled to Mexico with Tamar in order to escape nearness to Forster; her desire for him, as she admitted, was very strong. Articles written during her stay in Mexico include: Dorothy Day, "Guadalupe," *Commonweal* 11 (26 February 1930): 477–478; Dorothy Day, "A Letter from Mexico City," *Commonweal* 11 (16 April 1930): 683–684; Dorothy Day, "Spring Festival in Mexico," *Commonweal* 12 (16 July 1930): 296–297.

46. See Barck and Blake, *Since 1900,* pp. 400–423; Beard and Beard, *Basic History,* pp. 452–462.

47. Day, *Long Loneliness,* pp. 158–159.

48. For text of the 1931 encyclical, see Joseph Husslein, S.J., ed. *Social Wellsprings,* 2 vols. (Milwaukee: Bruce, 1940–1942), 2: 178–234. Dolan, *American Catholic Experience,* p. 402, provides general commentary on the encyclical in relationship to John A. Ryan's work. For a discussion of American Catholic response to *Quadragesimo Anno* during the 1930s, see Aaron I. Abell, *American Catholicism and Social Action: A Search for Social Justice, 1865–1950* (Garden City, N.Y.: Doubleday, 1960), pp. 234–263.

49. Dorothy Day, "Peter Maurin[,] 1877–1977," *CW* 43 (May 1977): 1. See Dorothy Day, "Hunger Marchers in Washington," *America* 48 (24 December 1932): 277–279. Dorothy Day, "Real Revolutionists," *Commonweal* 17 (11 January 1933): 293–294. See Dorothy Day, *House of Hospitality* (New York & London: Sheed & Ward, 1939), pp. v–xiii, for details of her Washington, D.C., experience.

50. Robert Ellsberg, Introduction to *By Little and By Little: The Selected Writings of Dorothy Day* (New York: Alfred A. Knopf, 1983), p. xv.

2. LITERARY INFLUENCES ON THE SPIRITUALITY OF DOROTHY DAY

1. Quotation from Day, *Union Square to Rome,* p. 28. Dorothy agreed with her friend Malcolm Cowley that "the central function of literature is to broaden or deepen our sense of life." See "On P.," *CW* 25 (November 1958): 6.

2. "On P.," *CW* 39 (May 1973): 8. In AIG fragm [T] Dorothy reflected

that her interpretation of John of the Cross's doctrine of detachment was flexible, and "so I hang on to my book, my books, which are the voices of friends and teach."

3. AIG fragm [O]. See "On P.," *CW* 14 (April 1948): 2. Ashcroft was from the Benedictine foundation in Newton, New Jersey.

4. Day, "July 30th" [after 1975], DD–CW, D–3, Box 7. In this manuscript, Dorothy mentioned her conversion being in her mid-twenties. She was actually thirty. This is an example of Dorothy's penchant for forgetting precise dates long after the fact, and sometimes, not so far removed from the fact. For assigning dates relative to Dorothy, I rely on cross-reference checks wherever possible. On the association made between reading and the Benedictine ideal of *lectio divina,* see "DAD," *CW* 10 (June 1943): 4. An account of table reading at Mott St. occurs in Day, "Feast . . ." [8 September] 1948, DD–CW, W–4.2, Box 1. In AIG fragm [W], Dorothy referred to opening Scripture in the [medieval] manner of Francis.

5. "On P.," *CW* 39 (July-August 1973): 2. "Reading is prayer" refers to *lectio divina.* See also Dean Brackley and Dennis Dillon, "An Interview with Dorothy Day," *National Jesuit News* 1 (May 1972): 8–10. On the power of the Word, see Dorothy Day, "What Do the Simple Folk Do?" *CSCW [Church Society for College Work] Report* 31 (November 1973): 5.

6. "On P.," *CW* 40 (September 1974): 2. Dorothy frequently mentioned Scripture as one of her bedside books. See, for example, "On P.," *CW* 41 (March–April 1975): 2.

7. "On P.," *CW* 46 (June 1980): 1. "Daily reading of the Psalms of David" here refers to Dorothy's praying of the Liturgy of the Hours.

8. Day, *Union Square to Rome,* p. 84.

9. "On P.," *CW* 38 (October–November 1972): 2. On Dorothy's dependence on C. S. Lewis's interpretation of the warlike psalms, see "On P.," *CW* 32 (March 1966): 2. The psalms to which Dorothy referred are those prayed as part of the Liturgy of the Hours, a form of which is found in both Episcopal and Roman Catholic worship.

10. "On P.," *CW* 34 (September 1968): 2.

11. "On P.," *CW* 38 (June 1972): 7.

12. Day, *Union Square to Rome,* p. 12.

13. Day, *Long Loneliness,* p. 60. One example of Dorothy's use of Mt 25:40 as shorthand for the entire passage, 25:31–46, may be found in Day, *Union Square to Rome,* p. 147.

14. Elliot Ross, "Christ in His Poor," *CW* 1 (October 1933): 7, 9.

15. The advisability of Houses of Hospitality had first been noted in "Catholic Worker Program," *CW* 1 (15 December 1933): 4. An actual listing of the corporal and spiritual works by name first appeared in "A Long Editorial—But It Could Be Longer," *CW* 2 (February 1935): 7. They include: [cor-

poral] to feed the hungry, to give drink to the thirsty, to clothe the naked, to harbor the harborless, to ransom the captive, to visit the sick, to bury the dead; [spiritual] to instruct the ignorant, to counsel the doubtful, to admonish the sinner, to bear wrongs patiently, to forgive offenses willingly, to comfort the afflicted, to pray for the living and the dead. Practice of the works of mercy had been noted explicitly as part of "Catholic Worker Program of Action," *CW* 3 (September 1935): 4.

16. [Dorothy Day] "Look on the Face of Thy Christ," *CW* 5 (December 1937): 4. Throughout the present work I have positively identified Dorothy's authorship for unsigned articles in all instances where internal and/or external evidence warranted my conclusion.

17. Quotations from [Dorothy Day] "An Appeal," *CW* 7 (February 1940): 4, and "On P," *CW* 45 (February 1979): 7, respectively. For Dorothy, the spiritual works of mercy included the availability of retreats, especially for the poor. See "On P," *CW* 13 (May 1946): 2.

18. [Dorothy Day] "Look on the Face of Thy Christ," *CW* 5 (December 1937): 1. For *CW* and *OF* articles which are not listed individually in the bibliography I list the complete reference each time they are cited.

19. Dorothy Day, "The first plank . . ." [1961?], DD–CW, D–3, Box 7. Shorter quotations from "On P," *CW* 39 (May 1973): 8; Dorothy Day, *An Answer to Some Charges against the Catholic Worker* (pamphlet, 1937), p. 8; "On P," *CW* 42 (June 1976): 8.

20. Quotation in Day, *Union Square to Rome*, p. 7. See also pp. 34–36. Further background on her early use of the *Imitation* in Day, *Eleventh Virgin*, p. 41; Brackley and Dillon, "Interview with Dorothy Day," p. 8; Dorothy Day, "A Reminiscence at 75," *Commonweal* 98 (10 August 1973): 424; AIG fragm [11]; Day, "July 30th . . ." [after 1975], DD–CW, D–3, Box 7.

21. Day, *Union Square to Rome*, pp. 108–109 (*Imitation*, bk. IV, ch. 4).

22. Thomas à Kempis, *The Imitation of Christ*, ed. Harold C. Gardiner, S.J. (New York: Doubleday/Image Books, 1955), p. 213. The arrangement in sense lines is my own.

23. AIG fragm [11]. This retrospect recalls her agreement with Father [James T.] McKenna, who befriended her as a Catholic neophyte in summer 1929. On Dorothy's reading of the *Imitation* between summer 1925 and December 1927, see Day, *Union Square to Rome*, p. 127. See also Day, *Long Loneliness*, p. 142.

24. Retreat notes for 20 July 1943 in AIG, pp. 21–32. For sample references to bk. III, ch. 5, see Dorothy Day, "Random Reflections," *CW* 11 (June 1944): 1; [Dorothy Day,] "Love Is the Measure," *CW* 13 (June 1946): 2. Dorothy Day, untitled booklist in *Christian Century* 80 (13 March 1963): 337. "On P," *CW* 42 (July–August 1976): 2. "On P," *CW* 45 (January 1979): 2, for quotation; "On P," *CW* 45 (May 1979): 2.

25. Thomas à Kempis, *Imitation*, bk.I, ch.3, p. 35.

26. Day, *Long Loneliness*, p. 34. See p. 36 to confirm that she was then reading Augustine. Dorothy often spoke of reading Scripture, the *Imitation*, and the *Confessions* in conjunction with one another. Examples occur in AIG fragm [N]; Day, *Union Square to Rome*, p. 136; Dorothy Day, *Therese* (Springfield, Ill.: Templegate Publishers, 1960, 1979), p. vii.

27. Day, *Long Loneliness*, p. 35.

28. AIG fragm [N]. As elsewhere, Dorothy considered 1924–1927 as the conversion years. Also found in AIG fragm [X].

29. Dorothy Day, "Bread for the Hungry," *CW* 42 (September 1976): 1, in which she recalled: "There is a beautiful passage in St. Augustine, whose *Confessions* I read at this time [at the beach]. 'What is it I love when I love Thee,' it begins, and goes on to list all the material beauty and enjoyment to be found in the life of the senses." Dorothy frequently associated joy, love and beauty, for which an example occurs in AIG fragm [O].

30. AIG fragm [X].

31. Ibid. Dorothy had been reflecting on the passage from *Confessions*, X.11. On *Confessions*, X.6 being her favorite passage from Augustine, see "On P," *CW* 46 (September 1980): 6.

32. AIG fragm [X].

33. See "On P," *CW* 37 (July–August 1971): 2. See Day, *Union Square to Rome*, p. 18; Dorothy Day, "Khrushchev and Alexander Nevsky," *CW* 27 (October 1960): 1; Day, *Long Loneliness*, p. 87. The lesson of the wise elder Zossima's conversion to love had a good deal to do with Dorothy's later life.

34. Quotation in Day, *Union Square to Rome*, p. 8. See Day, *Long Loneliness*, pp. 34, 42–43; Day, *Eleventh Virgin*, p. 49.

35. Day, *Long Loneliness*, p. 107.

36. Ibid., p. 142. See p. 114 regarding her winter reading.

37. Maurin's arrangement of the sayings of Zossima appeared in Peter Maurin, "The Wisdom of Dostoeivsky," *CW* 2 (May 1934): 1, 2. See Dorothy Day, *Loaves and Fishes* (San Francisco: Harper & Row, 1963, 1983), p. 101, for the conclusion that Maurin would not have read Dostoevsky on his own. "On P," *CW* 46 (October-November 1980): 2. This was the last column she wrote for the paper and consisted of short diary entries.

38. "On P," *CW* 39 (May 1973): 8. Dorothy frequently alluded to Dostoevsky's works as spiritual reading. One instance found in Day to Merton, 4 June [1962?], TMSC, D-220. For background on Dostoevsky, see Denis Dirscherl, S.J., *Dostoevsky and the Catholic Church* (Chicago: Loyola University Press, 1986); Piehl, *Breaking Bread*, pp. 72–73. Dorothy's spelling of Dostoevsky's name varied according to the source she was using.

39. Day, *Loaves and Fishes*, p. 71.

40. "On P.," *CW* 40 (February 1974): 8. See also Day, *Long Loneliness*, pp. 204–205.

41. "On P.," *CW* 40 (January 1974): 8. The word *library* here is not to be taken formally, but in the sense of a home library, with books often getting lost, taken, or misplaced. Dorothy had favorite editions, such as the Garnett translation of Dostoevsky, but used whatever edition of a work was available to her at the time.

42. Dorothy Day, "Suicide or Sacrifice?" *CW* 32 (November 1965): 1. Other examples of her similar reflection on Kirilov occur in AIG fragm [R]; Dorothy Day, "O Death in Life" [n.d.], DD–CW, D–3, Box 7. Remarks on suicide in general occur in "On P.," *CW* 35 (March-April 1969): 2; "On P.," *CW* 44 (February 1978): 2; "On P.," *CW* 46 (July–August 1980): 2.

43. Dorothy Day, "Suicide or Sacrifice?" *CW* 32 (November 1965): 1.

44. AIG fragm [R].

45. Ibid.

46. See Day, *Long Loneliness*, p. 108; Dorothy Day, "Obedience," p. 22; "On P.," *CW* 41 (December 1975): 2.

47. [Dorothy Day] "It Is the Revolution," *CW* 12 (January 1946): 2. See also Dorothy Day, " A People's Movement," *Third Hour* 2 (1947): 89–90.

48. "On P.," *CW* 34 (February 1968): 8. Similar references occur in Day to Fritz Eichenberg, 3 June 1960, obtained from Eichenberg; "On P.," *CW* 27 (December 1960): 7; Dorothy Day to Nina Polcyn Moore, postmarked 25 February 1978, DD–CW, W–17, Box 1; "On P.," *CW* 37 (October–November 1971): 6; "On P.," *CW* 39 (January 1973): 2; "On P.," *CW* 40 (September 1974): 2; "On P.," *CW* 42 (February 1976): 4; "On P.," *CW* 45 (February 1979): 7; "On P.," *CW* 45 (June 1979): 6.

49. [Dorothy Day] "Room for Christ," *CW* 12 (December 1945): 2. The article was reprinted in *CW* 46 (December 1980): 7–8. For the shorter quote, see Dorothy Day, "Spring Appeal," *CW* 24 (April 1958): 2.

50. See "On P.," *CW* 27 (December 1960): 7.

51. Day, *Union Square to Rome*, p. 47.

52. "On P.," *CW* 32 (March 1966): 1. See also Day, *Union Square to Rome*, p. 170.

53. Brackley and Dillon, "An Interview with Dorothy Day," p. 8.

54. Dorothy Day, "How to get all these ideas . . ." [early 1950s], DD–CW, D–3, Box 7.

55. Ibid. Dorothy rightfully referred to the mysterious visitor as friend, because he was so considered by Dostoevsky. She quoted the Constance Garnett translation (frequently reprinted), which was her favorite version. See Fyodor Dostoyevsky, *The Brothers Karamazov*, trans. Constance Garnett (New York: Modern Library, n.d.), pp. 317–318.

56. Ibid.

57. [Dorothy Day], "Why Do the Members of Christ Tear One Another?" *CW* 9 (February 1942): 4; "NBTW," *CW* 11 (March 1944): 2; "Dostoeievsky," *CW* 14 (June 1947): 2; untitled selection from *The Brothers Karamazov, CW* 30 (February 1964): 6.

58. Dostoyevsky, *The Brothers Karamazov,* pp. 52–58, for the entire pericope and p. 57 for the passage often quoted by Dorothy. Dorothy referred to the saying being ascribed to her rather than to Dostoevsky in her 26 September 1972 and 28 October [1972] letters to William D. Miller, C–1.7, 2–WDM; "On P," *CW* 37 (July–August 1971): 2. The scriptural passage in question is 1 John 4:20.

59. [Dorothy Day] "Hell Is Not to Love Anymore," *CW* 6 (May 1939): 4. In "Pray," the last subsection of the article, she used an unidentified quotation from the *Imitation,* bk. 3, ch. 5, pp. 110–112, which follows the tone of her reflection on Zossima. Dorothy's insight and desire to integrate divine and human love are evident here; there is no condemnation of the flesh in her writing. Employment of the terms *natural love, supernatural love, grace,* and *nature* were common to Catholic vocabulary of the day.

60. "On P," *CW* 42 (May 1976): 2, 10. On the saint as a lover in the context of Zossima's counsel, see Dorothy Day, "Spring Appeal," *CW* 24 (April 1958): 2. In Day to Charles Butterworth, 10 January 1976, DD–CW, W–13, Box 1, Dorothy admitted that "Love in practice, etc. gets harder." Dorothy made numerous references to love in practice, as for instance, "NBTW," *CW* 11 (January 1944): 1; [Dorothy Day] "Love Is the Measure," *CW* 13 (June 1946): 2; [Dorothy Day] "'The Communion of Distrust,'" *CW* 22 (September 1955): 2; D[orothy] D[ay], "In Peace Is My Bitterness Most Bitter," *CW* 33 (January 1967): 2.

61. Day, *Long Loneliness,* pp. 42–43. See also Day, *Union Square to Rome,* p. 40.

62. Day, *Long Loneliness,* p. 71. Later remarks which attest to the perduring impact of Tolstoy may be found in Day, *Union Square to Rome,* p. 68; Day, *Loaves and Fishes,* p. 177; Dorothy Day, "The Meaning of Poverty," *Ave Maria* 13 (3 December 1966): 21.

63. Day, *Union Square to Rome,* p. 81; see also p. 88. In Day, *Long Loneliness,* p. 71, Dorothy noted only Gold's sympathy with Tolstoy. From the context of her general thinking in 1917, the version I have quoted appears to be more accurate.

64. Day, *Union Square to Rome,* p. 81, in which she also remarked: "We used to pick up people we encountered in the parks and bring them home with us."

65. Ibid., p. 104.

66. Day, *Long Loneliness,* p. 114, on her novel reading at the beach. Her comment regarding *Anna Karenina* occurs in "On P," *CW* 37 (July–August

1971): 2. For confirmation that she was rereading the work in 1978, see "On P," *CW* 44 (February 1978): 2. Representative remarks on *Resurrection* and *War and Peace* may be found in Day to William Oleksak, 4 April 1972, DD–CW, W–6.4, Box 1; Day to Nina Polcyn Moore, 16 February 1978, DD–CW, W–17, Box 1; "On P," *CW* 26 (April 1960): 7.

67. "On P," *CW* 16 (October 1949): 3. Helene Iswolsky, whose homeland was Russia, spent some years in personalist circles in Paris before settling in the United States.

68. Dorothy kept close tabs on the paper almost until the end of her life. Even after resigning as editor in 1975 she still gave advice. See for example the editorial note introducing a reprint of Dorothy Day, "Ammon Hennacy—A Christian Anarchist," *CW* 44 (January 1978): 5. A[mmon] H[ennacy], "Leo Tolstoy," *CW* 27 (November 1960): 1, is among the *CW* features which commemorate the fiftieth anniversary of Tolstoy's 10 November 1910 death.

69. [Dorothy Day] "Hell Is Not to Love Anymore, III," *CW* 8 (April 1941): 7.

70. Ibid.

71. "On P," *CW* 26 (April 1960): 7, 8. Dorothy was familiar with the Maude translation, though incorrectly gave Aylmer Maude credit rather than Louise Maude. Dorothy visited the Doukhobors at Ammon Hennacy's request. The Doukhobors, a Russian sect, lived originally as a commune devoted to living out early Christian ideals as they understood them. She again recalled Tolstoy's aid to the Doukhobors in "On P," *CW* 44 (March–April 1978): 2.

72. Dorothy Day, "What Does Ammon Mean?" *CW* 31 (June 1965): 7. Ammon Hennacy, a convert to Catholicism in 1952, had left the church by 1965. Dorothy remarked that he was an admirer of Tolstoy, having been converted to a Tolstoyan Christianity when reading the author while serving a term in the Atlanta Penitentiary as a young man. This was during World War I, when Hennacy had been jailed as a conscientious objector.

73. Dorothy Day, "Introduction" [ca. 1975], DD–CW, D–3, Box 7. This is a draft for her foreword to Dorothy Gauchat, *All God's Children* (New York: Ballantine Books, 1976). This portion of the draft was not published.

74. "On P," *CW* 44 (March–April 1978): 2; "On P," *CW* 44 (June 1978): 2.

75. Quotation in Dorothy Day, "It is not with any spirit of complaint . . ." [unpublished 1964 article for *Commonweal*], DD–CW, D–3, Box 7. Day to Fritz Eichenberg [internal evidence confirms 1964 as the year of writing], per Eichenberg. For the hunting scene, see Leo Tolstoy, *War and Peace*, trans. Constance Garnett (New York: Modern Library [1931]), pp. 460–473; a later source which Dorothy probably also used is Leo Tolstoy, *War and Peace*,

trans. Louise and Aylmer Maude (New York: Simon & Schuster, 1942, 1958), pp. 545–559.

76. "On P.," *CW* 34 (June 1968): 2.

77. Dorothy Day, "What Dream Did They Dream? Utopia or Suffering," *CW* 14 (July–August 1947): 4. In this article, Dorothy made a direct reference to Marya's service to the poor. The pilgrim theme related to Marya was also noted in "On P.," *CW* 18 (October 1951): 2.

78. "On P.," *CW* 42 (July–August 1976): 2. See also Dorothy Day, "A Reminiscence at 75," p. 425.

79. Tolstoy, *War and Peace*, trans. Garnett, p. 324. See also Tolstoy, *War and Peace*, trans. Louise and Aylmer Maude, p. 385. Pierre took to his reading the memory of a recent conversation with Freemason leader Osip Alexyevitch Bazdyev.

80. See William D. Miller, *A Harsh and Dreadful Love: Dorothy Day and the Catholic Worker Movement* (New York: Liveright, 1973), pp. 5–7; Piehl, *Breaking Bread*, pp. 69–71.

81. Emmanuel Mounier, *Manifeste au service du personnalisme* (1936) in *Oeuvres*, vol. 1 (Paris: Editions du Seuil, 1961), p. 493. Translation is my own.

82. See Emmanuel Mounier, *La Révolution personnaliste et communautaire* (1935) in *Oeuvres*, vol. 1, p. 149.

83. Mounier, *Manifeste*, p. 526. Translation is my own.

84. See ibid., especially pp. 534, 535, 539, 540. A particular tension which appears in Mounier's writings is an awareness that it is necessary to distinguish between person and community in the realm of language. However, the reality that he perceived was the necessity of respect for the person, who, as person, is already in relationship (communion, community) with others.

85. Peter Maurin, " A Letter to John Strachey and His Readers," *CW* 2 (April 1935): 8. See also [Dorothy Day], "Days with an End," *CW* 1 (April 1934): 3–4; A. H. Coddington, "Notes on the Catholic Press," *CW* 2 (March 1935): 10. Maurin recommended *Révolution personnaliste* in *CW* 3 (September 1935): 8.

86. [Dorothy Day] "Leadership," *CW* 3 (October 1935): 4. Dorothy frequently credited Maurin with introducing the Catholic Worker to French personalist thought and explicitly considered herself a personalist. See for example, Dorothy Day, "A People's Movement," pp. 84, 90.

87. [Dorothy Day] "Food," *CW* 4 (May 1936): 4. For an interesting example of how the personalist movement was applied retroactively by the *CW*, see "Blessed Martin Revolutionary Personalist," *CW* 4 (May 1936): 6.

88. See Peter Maurin, "Communism of Communitarianism," *CW* 4 (May 1936): 1. For evidence of his personalist indoctrination of the monks and students at Collegeville, see "Study Personalism [letter]," *CW* 4 (January

1937): 5; "Book Reviews [Sociology]," *CW* 4 (March 1937): 6. For the English translation of Mounier's *Manifeste au service du personnalisme* (1936), see Emmanuel Mounier, *A Personalist Manifesto,* trans. Monks of St. John's Abbey (New York: Longmans, Green, 1938). In Dorothy Day, "Acceptance Speech" [Liturgical Conference at Collegeville, Minnesota], August 1968, DD–CW, D–5, Box 4, she attributed the translation to Peter Maurin and Virgil Michel; in "On P," *CW* 39 (May 1973): 1, she credited Maurin with its initial translation. The work in question was recommended by Maurin in his columns. See for example, Peter Maurin, "Easy Essays," *CW* 6 (October 1938): 8.

89. Peter Maurin, "Personalist Communitarianism [Easy Essays]," *CW* 6 (June 1939): 7.

90. [Dorothy Day] "What We Are Doing in Town and Country," *CW* 4 (September 1936): 2. For related information on the farming commune, see D[orothy] D[ay], "Farming Commune," *CW* 6 (October 1938): 8; "DAD," *CW* 10 (January 1943): 4. For her comments on Father [Monsignor Nelson H.] Baker, see [Dorothy Day], "Personal Responsibility," *CW* 4 (August 1936): 3. This priest had died on 10 July 1936. See *Official Catholic Directory,* 1937, p. 1030.

91. "DAD," *CW* 10 (February 1943): 4.

92. See "Emmanuel Mounier," *CW* 16 (April 1950): 2; Joseph E. Cunneen, "Cross Currents," *CW* 17 (October 1950): 8. Representative articles on personalism include: Jack English, "Personalism and the Apostolate," *CW* 15 (June 1948): 5; Robert Ludlow, "Personalist Revolution," *CW* 18 (November 1952): 1, 4–5; Stanley Vishnewski, "Bishops Uphold Personalism," *CW* 27 (December 1960): 5; Joseph Geraci, "Personalist Approach," *CW* 41 (May 1975): 9. Among Dorothy's numerous later references to personalism may be cited "On P," *CW* 25 (July–August 1958): 7; "On P," *CW* 37 (December 1971); 2. Among the reviews may be found: Michael Harrington, "Emmanuel Mounier [review of Emmanuel Mounier, *Be Not Afraid*]," *CW* 18 (March 1952): 4; Ed Turner, "Book Reviews [Turner review consists almost completely of a long quote from Emmanuel Mounier, *The Spoil of the Violent*]," *CW* 28 (June 1962): 7; Jacques Travers, "Book Reviews: Yoder, Merton and Mounier [Turner review of Eileen Cantin, *A Personalist View of History*]," *CW* 40 (September 1974): 4–5, 7; Joseph Geraci, "Personalists [review of Joseph Amato, *Mounier and Maritain: A French Catholic Understanding of the Modern World*]," *CW* 41 (October–November 1975): 7.

93. "On P," *CW* 42 (May 1976): 2. As late as the summer of 1978, Dorothy recalled the importance of Mounier to the Catholic Worker movement. See "On P," *CW* 44 (July–August 1978): 2: "Jacques [Travers] once gave a great talk on Emmanuel Mounier (one of Peter Maurin's favorite philosophers) at Tivoli, on Sunday afternoon, with Mary Lathrop Pope giving readings from Mounier, to illustrate the points Jacques made."

94. This is generally evident in Dorothy's writings, as well as in her talks given across the country. Examples of the latter include: "The Pacifist's View of the Catholic Worker," talk given at Marquette University (7 February 1958); untitled talk given at the University of Santa Clara, Santa Clara, California (21 March 1960); "Poverty and the Christian Commitment," talk given at the Social Action Forum, New York University (12 November 1965). Audiotape collection, Marquette University Archives, Milwaukee, Wisconsin.

95. See Joseph Amato, *Mounier and Maritain: A French Catholic Understanding of the Modern World* (University, Ala.: University of Alabama Press, 1975); Dorothy Day, "A People's Movement," p. 84; Julie Kernan, *Our Friend, Jacques Maritain: A Personal Memoir by Julie Kernan* (New York: Doubleday, 1975), p. 97; Stanley Vishnewski, "J. Maritain: An Appreciation," *CW* 39 (June 1973): 1.

96. Jacques Maritain, *Art and Scholasticism* [trans. of *Art et Scolastique*], trans. J. F. Scanlan (London: Sheed & Ward, 1930) was featured in "Books Recommended by *The Catholic Worker* for Study Groups," *CW* 1 (December 1933): 2; Jacques Maritain's *Three Reformers: Luther, Descartes, Rousseau* was featured in "The Catholic Worker and His Books," *CW* 1 (February 1934): 2. "Jacques Maritain in the *Colosseum*," *CW* 2 (December 1934): 7. A shorter, variant translation of this excerpt may be found in *CW* 4 (October 1936): 2. Both of these are from the same work, of which the latter translation may be found in Jacques Maritain, *Freedom in the Modern World*, trans. Richard O'Sullivan (New York: Scribner's, 1936), p. 135.

97. "Professor Jacques Maritain Writes Characteristically to Peter Maurin," *CW* 2 (December 1934): 8. For background on Maritain's first visit in November 1934, see Kernan, *Our Friend*, pp. 94–97. For Dorothy's representative reminisences, see "DBD," *CW* 12 (June 1945): 3; Day, *Long Loneliness*, p. 186; Day, *Loaves and Fishes*, p. 30; Day, "Obedience," p. 22; "On P," *CW* 42 (May 1976): 2.

98. See Peter Maurin, "On the Use of 'Pure' Means," *CW* 2 (January 1935): 5, and *CW* 2 (March 1935): 4, where the work, still untranslated, was referred to as "The Temporal Regime and Liberty." It was recommended and referred to as "Society and Liberty" in Peter Maurin, "A Program for Immediate Needs," *CW* 2 (January 1935): 7 and as "The Temporal Regime and Liberty" in Peter Maurin, "The Communism of the Catholic Worker," *CW* 3 (September 1935): 8. The official translation of J. Maritain's *Du Regime temporel et la liberté* appeared as Jacques Maritain, *Freedom in the Modern World*.

99. "Jacques Maritain, Noted Philosopher, Is Guest of Paper," *CW* 3 (January 1936): 1, 5. Maritain's concern for the primacy of the spiritual is particularly evident in Jacques Maritain, *The Things That Are Not Caesar's* (London: Sheed & Ward, 1930), a translation of *Primauté du spirituel*. Among Maurin's recommendations may be noted: J. Maritain, *The Things That Are*

Not Caesar's in Peter Maurin, "Colonial Expansion," *CW* 3 (April 1936): 8; J. Maritain, *Humanisme Intégral* in Peter Maurin, "Communism of Communitarianism," *CW* 4 (May 1936): 8 and in Peter Maurin, "Radicals of the Right [Nos. 5–7]," *CW* 4 (July 1936): 4. [J. Maritain's *Humanisme Intégral* was twice translated into English. For the first, see Jacques Maritain, *True Humanism,* trans. Margot Adamson (New York: Scribner's 1938). For the second, see Jacques Maritain, *Integral Humanism: Temporal and Spiritual Problems of a New Christendom,* trans. Joseph W. Evans (New York: Scribner's 1968). J. Maritain, *Freedom in the Modern World* recommended in Peter Maurin, "Easy Essays" and "So-Called Communists," *CW* 4 (January 1937): 7 and 8 respectively; Peter Maurin, "Caesarism or Personalism," *CW* 4 (March 1937): 2; Peter Maurin, "Fighting Communism [Easy Essays]," *CW* 5 (July 1937): 7; Peter Maurin, "Unpopular Front [Easy Essays]," *CW* 5 (September 1937): 4; Peter Maurin, "Business and Such [Easy Essays]," *CW* 6 (October 1938): 8.

100. Dorothy herself recommended *Freedom in the Modern World* in "DAD," *CW* 5 (February 1938): 2. She had also approved a number of repeated excerpts from the work. See for example, *CW* 4 (October 1936): 2; *CW* 4 (March 1937): 1. For Dorothy's consideration of "The Pure Mean[s] of Love," see [Dorothy Day] "Our Stand," *CW* 7 (June 1940): 4. For Maritain's consideration of the end of *a* world, see J. Maritain, *Freedom in the Modern World,* p. 131.

101. Dorothy Day in Coles, *Radical Devotion,* pp. 62–63. For Dorothy's quote from Maritain's *Art and Scholasticism,* see "DBD," *CW* 3 (January 1936): 6.

102. Dorothy Day, "In Peace Is My Bitterness Most Bitter," *CW* 33 (January 1967): 1–2. She also recalled Maritain's words on the transfiguration in "On P," *CW* 39 (October–November 1973): 8.

103. Jacques Maritain, "Maritain on Spain," *CW* 5 (November 1937): 4. "Jacques Maritain," *CW* 6 (December 1938): 8. See also "Re Jacques Maritain," *CW* 6 (January 1939): 3. It must be acknowledged that Maritain did not classify himself as a pacifist, as is evident from a reading of his works. See for example the argument in J. Maritain, *Freedom in the Modern World,* pp. 184–188, in the context of his discussion "On the Purification of the Means."

104. Maritain was personally influenced by his love for and association with his wife, Raïssa, and his sister-in-law, Vera Oumansoff. Both women were Russian-born converts from Judaism. Dorothy experienced persuasive personal encounters with numerous Jews, including her college friend Rayna Prohme, and a life-long friendship with Michael Gold. These were formative for her ecumenical spirit in general.

105. See "Prejudice," *CW* 3 (September 1935): 5; reprinted in *CW* 4 (April 1937): 6. "Maritain Criticizes Anti-Semitism," *CW* 6 (January 1939):

2. Dorothy Day, untitled review of Jacques Maritain's *A Christian Looks at the Jewish Question* in *CW* 7 (November 1939): 7.

106. "DAD," *CW* 10 (June 1943): 4. From AIG, p. 32, it is clear that at the time Stanley Vishnewski had been reading the work on St. Paul as table reading at the New York house. The work in question is Jacques Maritain, *The Living Thoughts of St. Paul* (New York & Toronto: Longmans, Green, 1941).

107. Jacques Maritain, as excerpted in "Reaching the Masses," *CW* 5 (June 1937): 3; reprinted in *CW* 5 (January 1938): 2; *CW* 5 (April 1938): 5; *CW* 6 (May 1938): 5; abbreviated and untitled in *CW* 14 (January 1948): 1.

108. "Book Reviews," includes Jacques Maritain, *Man and the State*, reviewed by Michael Harrington in *CW* 17 (May 1951): 4 and Jacques Maritain, *The Range of Reason*, reviewed by Francis Murphy in *CW* 19 (April 1953): 4; "Maritain," on Jacques Maritain, *Approaches to God*, reviewed by Natalie Darcy in *CW* 21 (November 1954): 4, 5.

109. "DAD," *CW* 6 (December 1938): 1. On Raïssa Maritain, *We Have Been Friends Together*, trans. Julie Kernan (New York: Longmans Green, 1942), see "DAD," *CW* 9 (January 1942): 4; "DAD," *CW* 9 (February 1942): 4; "DAD," *CW* 10 (June 1943): 4.

110. "NBTW," *CW* 12 (July–August 1945): 2. See Raïssa Maritain, *Adventures in Grace*, trans. Julie Kernan (New York: Longmans, Green, 1945).

111. Coles, *Radical Devotion*, p. 143.

112. From the tone of his 4 August 1934 letter to the Catholic Worker, DD–CW, W–2.2, Box 1, Furfey had become acquainted with the movement, but had not yet visited any of the houses. In Paul Hanly Furfey, *The Morality Gap* (New York: Macmillan, 1969), p. 100, the author recollected that Agnes Regan, then assistant director of the National Catholic School of Social Service in Washington, D.C., had told him about the Catholic Worker house in New York. This was in 1934, most likely during the summer. Furfey confirmed this and other pertinent information in Furfey-Merriman correspondence, May-December 1984, and during the Furfey-Merriman interview in Washington, D.C., 20 November 1984. In his published works, Furfey offered several reminiscences which relate to his contacts with the Catholic Worker movement. In addition to Furfey, *The Morality Gap*, pp. 99–113, see Paul Hanly Furfey, "From Catholic Liberalism to Catholic Radicalism," *American Ecclesiastical Review* 166 (1972): 678–686; Paul Hanly Furfey, "From a Catholic Liberal into a Catholic Radical," *America* 127 (11 November 1972): 391–392; Paul Hanly Furfey, *Love and the Urban Ghetto* (Maryknoll, N.Y.: Orbis Books, 1978), pp. 111–130. Several articles by Charles E. Curran assess Furfey's Christian radical period. In chronological order, these are: Charles E. Curran, "Paul Hanly Furfey: Theorist of American Catholic Radicalism," *American Ecclesiastical Review* 166 (1972): 651–677; Charles E. Curran, "The Radical Catholic

Social Ethics of Paul Hanly Furfey," in *New Perspectives in Moral Theology* (Notre Dame, Ind.: University of Notre Dame Press, 1974), pp. 87–121; Charles E. Curran, "The Catholic Worker and Paul Hanly Furfey," in *American Catholic Social Ethics* (Notre Dame, Ind.: University of Notre Dame Press, 1982), pp. 130–171. The last named is particularly insightful.

113. Robert D. Cross, *The Emergence of Liberal Catholicism in America* (Cambridge: Harvard University Press, 1958), p. vii, described Catholic liberalism as the tendency to promote a friendly interaction between Catholicism and American life. Furfey assessed his so-called Comtean approach in Paul Hanly Furfey, *Three Theories of Society* (New York: Macmillan, 1937), pp. 56–67 and in Paul Hanly Furfey, *The Mystery of Iniquity* (Milwaukee: Bruce, 1944), pp. 69–70. He described it as a system developed by Auguste Comte (1798–1857) which emphasized observed facts and their relationships, accompanied by a corresponding contempt for theological or metaphysical doctrine which sought any deeper reality beneath the facts.

114. Furfey, "From Catholic Liberalism to Catholic Radicalism," p. 683.

115. The first *CW* mention of the Campion Propaganda Committee occurred in "Catholics to Show Solidarity against Mexican Atheism," *CW* 2 (December 1934): 1. See also, "DBD," *CW* 3 (May 1935): 3; "Farming Commune," *CW* 3 (May 1935): 3; "Speakers-Organizers!" *CW* 3 (May 1935): 5. Dorothy Weston had been on the *CW* staff since the June–July 1933 issue; Coddington had joined the movement no later than December 1934. See A. H. Coddington, "Book Reviews," *CW* 2 (December 1934): 8. The unsigned "Book Reviews," *CW* 2 (November 1934): 8, has a distinctively Coddington flavor.

116. Coddington left after the April 1936 issue and Dorothy Weston after the May 1936 issue, and went their own separate way. See the mastheads for *CW*, April 1936 through June 1936, inclusive. Background on the Campion difficulty may be found in Miller, *Harsh and Dreadful Love*, pp. 69–70, 106. Miller, p. 106, mistakenly claims that the Campions left CW in 1935. Further information from Dorothy Weston Coddington to Paul Marx, 18 October 1952, SJAA, Z–37:2; [Dorothy Day] to Brendan [O'Grady], n.d., but in response to O'Grady's 2 June 1954 letter to Day, DD–CW, W–10, Box 1; Joseph and Alice Zarrella–William D. Miller interview, 10 July 1967, DD–CW, W–9, Box 2.

117. See Day, *Long Loneliness*, pp. 180–181, 183; Dorothy Day, "What Dream Did They Dream? Utopia or Suffering?" *CW* 14 (July–August 1947): 4; "DBD," *CW* 3 (April 1936): 4, in which she apologized: "We regret any hurt feelings of our readers by the comments in Varia in the last issue." For the article in question, see A. H. Coddington, "Notes on the Catholic Press [subtitle, 'Varia']," *CW* 3 (March 1936): 5.

118. On Furfey's popularity, see Stanley Vishnewski, *Wings of the Dawn* (New York: Catholic Worker Press, 1984), pp. 89–90.

119. *Pace* Vishnewski, p. 89, Furfey's was the *second* weekend conference at the Staten Island farm [garden] commune in 1935. Gerald Ellard,
S.J., presented the first weekend conference. See "Campion Propaganda Committee," *CW* 3 (July-August 1935): 2. The commune is to be distinguished
from Maryfarm at Easton, Pennsylvania, purchased in spring 1936. See Dorothy Day, "To Christ—To the Land!" *CW* 3 (January 1936): 1. For Furfey-
Campion activities during 1935, see "Campion Propaganda Committee," *CW*
3 (June 1935): 8; Elizabeth G. Lamb, "Campion Propaganda Committee,"
CW 3 (July–August 1935): 2; "Campion Propaganda Committee," *CW* 3
(September 1935): 6; D. I. Mahler, "Campion Propaganda Committee," *CW*
3 (October 1935): 3. From the last named, it is evident that Dorothy Day
also spoke to the Campions as a group. For late 1935 and 1936 Furfey-Campion
activities, see A. H. Coddington, "Campion Propaganda Committee," *CW*
3 (January 1936): 7; A. H. Coddington, "Campion Propaganda Committee,"
CW 3 (February 1936): 7, 8.
120. See Jane A. Marra, "Boston Letter," *CW* 4 (October 1936): 3. Jane
Marra had been a Campion activist at the Boston house and remained with
the Catholic Worker after the Coddington/Weston–Day/Maurin rift.
121. Note the inclusion of "Il Poverello" house in "Catholic Worker
Branches," *CW* 4 (April 1937): 6. From A. H. Coddington to Virgil Michel,
29 July 1937, SJAA, Z–23:7, it is clear that Coddington anticipated that Furfey would present a two-week summer institute at the Campion farm, beginning on 15 August 1937. In the same letter Coddington referred to having
written to a number of people, Dorothy Day included, to enlist their financial aid for the Campion farm venture[!]
122. On the 29 September 1937 and 2 November 1937 addresses, see
Joseph J. O'Connor, "Washington Group Hears Fr. Furfey, Holds Retreats,"
CW 5 (November 1937): 2; Marie Connolly, "Father Furfey, Callahan Talk
at Pittsburgh," *CW* 5 (December 1937): 6.
123. [Dorothy Day] "'Hell Is Not to Love Any More,'" *CW* 6 (May
1939): 4.
124. See Paul Hanly Furfey, "Unemployment on the Land," *CW* 7 (October 1939): 8; John J. Hugo, "Capitalism Impractical," *CW* 7 (November
1939): 8; Ray Scott, "Accepts the Challenge," *CW* 7 (November 1939): 8; John
Harrington, "Free Land," *CW* 7 (November 1939): 8; Paul Hanly Furfey, "There
Are Two Kinds of Agrarians," *CW* 7 (December 1939): 7, 8; John Harrington
(letter), *CW* 7 (December 1939): 7; John J. Hugo, "In Defense of the Romantic Agrarians," *CW* 7 (January 1940): 8. When the first Furfey article on the
agrarian movement was published, Dorothy remained impartial in print, simply
inviting other contributions for clarification of thought. See [Dorothy Day]
untitled, *CW* 7 (October 1939): 8.
125. [Dorothy Day] "C.W. Holds '40 Retreat at Easton," *CW* 7 (Sep-

tember 1940): 2. Pertinent correspondence prior to the retreat includes Dorothy Day to Catholic Workers, 25 July 1939, DD–CW, W–4.2, Box 1; Paul Hanly Furfey to Dorothy Day, 8 August 1940, DD–CW, W–4.2, Box 1; Margaret V. Killian to CW staff, 13 August 1940, DD–CW, W–4.2, Box 1. For announcement prior to retreat, see S[tanley] V[ishnewski], "Retreat," *CW* 7 (July–August 1940): 2. During the Furfey-Merriman interview, 20 November 1984, Furfey recalled that his conferences were scripturally oriented, one in particular being devoted to a literal interpretation of the Our Father. Furfey considered his scriptural approach to be linguistic and used it as an effort to get at the root meaning of the text.

126. The Roy incident and other 1940 retreat reminiscences were reported factually by Dorothy in 1947 and sadly by Furfey some forty-four years after the event. See Dorothy Day, "What Dream Did They Dream? Utopia or Suffering?" *CW* 14 (July–August 1947): 1, 4, 6. Furfey-Merriman interview, 20 November 1984. *Pace* Miller, *Dorothy Day,* pp. 336–337, the 1940 gathering was not planned as a Lacouture-type retreat.

127. Paul Hanly Furfey to Dorothy Day, 9 December 1935, DD–CW, W–2.2, Box 1. He heard of the personalist-inspired Les Compagnons de Saint-François from his colleague Louis Achille of Howard University. In the summer of 1938 Furfey arranged a trip to France in order to study the personalist movement, or, as Furfey termed it, the new social Catholicism, at first hand. Though unable to arrange a meeting with Emmanuel Mounier, he did meet the Jeunesse Ouvrière Chrétienne (Jocistes), who were under the influence of Mounier, as well as a group of Les Compagnes de Saint-François, the female branch of Les Compagnons. Furfey-Merriman interview, 20 November 1984. See Furfey, *Morality Gap,* pp. 104–107.

128. Paul Hanly Furfey to Robert Ellsberg, 9 February 1978, DD–CW, W–2.2, Box 1. Shorter quotation, Furfey, *Fire on the Earth,* p. vii. See also Curran, "American Catholic Social Ethics," p. 64. In addition to being a theorist of Catholic radicalism, Furfey was personally involved with the radical movement. He lived a life of voluntary poverty and worked with the poor in the Washington, D.C., black ghetto for a number of years. Confirmed by Curran, "Catholic Worker and Paul Hanly Furfey," p. 134, and Furfey-Merriman interview, 20 November 1984. Other Furfey works which explored the theory of Christian radicalism include: *Three Theories of Society* (1937), *This Way to Heaven* (1939), *A History of Social Thought* (1942), *The Mystery of Iniquity* (1944), *The Respectable Murderers* (1966), and *The Morality Gap* (1969). It was not until *Love and the Urban Ghetto* (1978) that Furfey moved explicitly away from Christian radicalism to embrace what he termed a Christian revolutionism, the latter being based on his understanding of South American liberation theology.

129. Furfey, *Fire on the Earth,* p. 15. Later, in *The Mystery of Iniquity*

(1944), p. 114, he criticized the lack of organization in the Catholic Worker movement, the implication being that seeing God in the poor was not enough. At no time did Furfey actually abandon sociological methods. See Curran, "Catholic Worker and Paul Hanly Furfey," pp. 160–161.

130. Furfey, *Fire on the Earth*, p. 35. In his writings, Furfey referred more frequently to the Sermon on the Mount (Matthew, chs. 5–7) than to Matthew 25. With Dorothy, the emphasis was reversed. Furfey consistently recognized charity as the virtue which encompasses all the others.

131. One example of Dorothy's understanding of Matthew 25 occurs in The Editor [Dorothy Day], *An Answer to Some Charges against the Catholic Worker* (pamphlet), 1937. In this pamphlet Day lists Furfey as one among many priest-advisors to the Catholic Worker. On several occasions, Dorothy recalled a point once made by Furfey, directed to Christ's remonstrance in Matthew 25. See Dorothy Day, "Letter on Hospices," *CW* 14 (January 1948): 2; D[orothy] Day, "Wise as Serpents, Simple as Doves," *CW* 17 (March 1951): 2; "On P," *CW* 33 (September 1967): 7.

132. Quotation, Furfey, *Fire on the Earth*, p. 127. See Dorothy Day, "Farming Commune," *CW* 6 (October 1938): 8.

133. W[illiam] M. C[allahan], "Books," *CW* 4 (August 1936): 2, 4; the reviewer quoted passages from Furfey's *Fire on the Earth*, pp. 74, 84–85, 110–112. Peter Maurin, "Communitarian Personalism [no. 8]," *CW* 4 (September 1936): 1. Paul Hanly Furfey, "No Compromise with Mammon," *CW* 4 (October 1936): 2, which consisted of an excerpt from Furfey's *Fire on the Earth*, pp. 76–78. E[dward] K. P[riest], "Book Reviews" (includes review of Paul Hanly Furfey, "Catholic Extremism"), *CW* 4 (November 1936): 4. An earlier article, related to the thought of *Fire on the Earth*, had been printed: Paul Hanly Furfey, "Maximum-Minimum," *CW* 3 (May 1935): 5.

134. C[larence] D[uffy], "Book Review [Paul Hanly Furfey, *A History of Social Thought*]," *CW* 10 (April 1943): 7. For Dorothy's reference to the work, see Dorothy Day, "Peter the 'Materialist,'" *CW* 12 (September 1945): 6.

135. John Doebele, "Book Review [Paul Hanly Furfey, *The Mystery of Iniquity*]," *CW* 12 (February 1945): 8. Overall, the reviewer was positive, but took exception to Furfey's remark on the [Lacouture] retreat, arguing that Furfey misrepresented it. For Furfey's actual statement see his *Mystery of Iniquity*, pp. 43–45, which is presented in the context of a discussion of "exaggerated supernaturalism." See "On P," *CW* 23 (December 1956): 1.

136. See Paul Hanly Furfey, *The Respectable Murderers* (New York: Herder & Herder, 1966). For the reviews, see Stanley Vishnewski, "Book Review," *CW* 33 (December 1966): 7; Gordon C. Zahn, "Book Reviews," *CW* 33 (February 1967): 8.

137. It was not until the 1970s that Furfey gave a nuanced understand-

ing of bearing witness and nonparticipation. See Paul Hanly Furfey, *Love and the Urban Ghetto,* pp. 116–119.

3. THE IMPACT OF MONASTICISM

1. Dorothy most likely read the following editions: J[oris] K. Huysmans, *The Cathedral,* trans. Clara Bell (London: K. Paul, Trench & Trübner, 1922); J[oris] K. Huysmans, *En Route,* trans. C. Kegan Paul (London: K. Paul, Trench & Trübner; New York: E. P. Dutton, 1918, 1920). The earliest English language edition of *The Oblate* is: J[oris] K. Huysmans, *The Oblate,* trans. Edward Perceval (London: Kegan Paul, Trench, Trübner; New York: E. P. Dutton, 1924). The monastic orders Huysmans named are all branches of the Benedictine family. See Day, *Long Loneliness,* pp. 107, 142, for her comments about Huysmans.

2. Day, "A Reminiscence at 75," p. 424.

3. Erwin Iserloh, "Movements within the Church and Their Spirituality," in *History of the Church,* ed. Hubert Jedin, Konrad Repgen, and John Dolan, vol. 10: *The Church in the Modern Age,* trans. Anselm Biggs (New York: Crossroad, 1981), p. 299. See pp. 624–626 and pp. 653–654 for respective comments on the English Distributists and on Dorothy Day.

4. Abbot Deutsch's November 1933 contribution confirmed by Catholic Worker staff member's October 1934 annotation on Alcuin Deutsch, O.S.B., to Editors, *Catholic Worker,* 13 October 1934, DD–CW, W–2.2, Box 1. When the *CW* became more firmly established, generous responses to Dorothy's first appeals as well as spontaneous donations made by *CW* readers provided important monetary support to the movement. Abbots of various Benedictine and Cistercian abbeys and members of the diocesan hierarchy were notable among the regular financial contributors over the years. Clear evidence found in DD–CW, W–2.2, Box 1. I am indebted to Michael J. Blecker, O.S.B., a monk of Collegeville, for an introductory overview of the abbey's history and spirituality. Personal interview, 12 September 1984, at which time Blecker, now deceased, was President of the Graduate Theological Union, Berkeley, California.

5. Dorothy Day, "Fellow Worker in Christ," *OF* 13 (January 1939): 139–140.

6. Virgil Michel, O.S.B., to Dorothy Day, 14 February 1934, DD–CW, W–2.2, Box 2. The first contact with Virgil Michel was quite likely in December 1933 when he returned permanently to Collegeville from the Indian Missions. See Paul Marx, O.S.B., *Virgil Michel and the Liturgical Movement* (Collegeville, Minn.: Liturgical Press, 1957), pp. 163, 176. Deutsch's remark that he introduced Michel to the *CW* in Abbot [Deutsch] to [*CW*] Editors, 2 March 1934, SJAA, 91–13, AA–11A. This is a carbon copy of the original, which was sent to *CW* staff.

7. [*CW*] Editors to Deutsch, 26 February 1934, SJAA, 91–13, AA–11A. Peter Maurin, "The Spirit for the Masses," *CW* 1 (October 1933): 2. Maurin, at one time a member of the Brothers of the Christian Schools (Christian Brothers), absorbed some of his thinking from this group. The Eucharist was an important dimension of the Christian Brothers spirituality. See David Peter, F.S.C., "John Baptist de LaSalle, Priest," *OF* 19 (July 1945): 397–399.

8. Deutsch gave Michel a copy of Guardini's work in 1920. The first English translation was Romano Guardini, *The Spirit of the Liturgy* (London: Sheed & Ward, 1930). Michel reviewed a later edition in *OF* 10 (March 1936): 236–238. Prior to 1924, Michel studied primarily English literature and philosophy. His English dissertation, completed at the Catholic University of America, treated the philosophy of Orestes Brownson. While at the University, Michel fell under the influence of Father Thomas Edward Shields, an educator with an intuitive grasp of liturgy. See Marx, *Virgil Michel,* pp. 10–11. For further background on Deutsch's European experience, see Alcuin Deutsch, O.S.B., "Tenth Anniversary Issue: Introduction," *OF* 10 (October 1936): 481, and Colman J. Barry, O.S.B., *Worship and Work* (Collegeville, Minn.: St. John's Abbey, 1956), pp. 257–258.

9. Dom Lambert Beauduin, O.S.B., to Paul B. Marx, O.S.B., 27 September 1952, in Marx, *Virgil Michel,* p. 28. See Dom Lambert Beauduin, O.S.B., *Liturgy the Life of the Church,* trans. Virgil Michel, O.S.B. (Collegeville, Minn.: Liturgical Press, 1926). This translation heralded the establishment of Collegeville's Liturgical Press.

10. Beauduin, engaged for eight years in social work as a diocesan priest, had become firmly convinced that his ministry to others must be rooted in the liturgy. In order to better enable him in popularizing liturgical interest, he subsequently became a Benedictine of Mont César Abbey. In 1909 he founded *La Vie Liturgique,* the popular missal that started the Belgian liturgical movement. An ecumenist as well, Beauduin took part in the Malines Conversations (1921–1926) organized by Cardinal Mercier as an effort to bridge the gap between Catholics and Anglicans. In 1924 Pius XI appointed the monk to found a center at Amay-sur-Meuse (transferred in 1939 to Chevetogne) in Belgium to train monks in the Eastern liturgical rites as an effort toward rapprochement between the Roman Catholic and Russian Orthodox churches. For background on Beauduin see Marx, *Virgil Michel,* p. 27; J. Hajjar, "From Pius XII to the Second Vatican Council," p. 501, and Roger Aubert, "The Life of the Church," p. 603 in *The Christian Centuries,* vol. 5: *The Church in a Secularised Society,* ed. Louis J. Rogier, Roger Aubert, David Knowles, A.G. Weiler, John Tracy Ellis (New York, Ramsey, N.J., Toronto: Paulist Press; London: Darton, Longman & Todd, 1978); Louis Bouyer, *Liturgical Piety* (Notre Dame, Ind.: University of Notre Dame Press, 1955), pp. 58–64. Mutual influence between Dom Columba Marmion, abbot of Louvain's Maredsous

Abbey, and Dom Lambert Beauduin of Louvain's Mont César Abbey noted by Gerald Ellard, S.J., in his letter to Paul Marx, O.S.B., 23 March 1955, SJAA, Z–24:7.

11. See Virgil Michel to Abbot Alcuin Deutsch, 29 September 1924, in Marx, *Virgil Michel,* p. 46, note 29.

12. Michel had called for a Scholastic movement as early as 1921. See Marx, *Virgil Michel,* p. 35.

13. See excerpts of Michel's 3 April 1925 and 25 April 1925 letters to Deutsch from Louvain and Maredsous in Marx, *Virgil Michel,* pp. 38–39.

14. See "Foreword," *OF* 1 (November 1926): 2. The unsigned article was most likely written by Virgil Michel himself. Michel was editor-in-chief for nearly seven of the first twelve years of the journal's existence. *Orate Fratres* drew the cooperation of a number of Collegeville monks as well as eleven associate editors, among whom were Gerald Ellard, S.J., of St. Louis, Missouri, and Donald Attwater, then a resident of Wales. Attwater's numerous articles gave a distinctly ecumenical flavor to the journal. He helped to make the review and Liturgical Press literature known in England, in addition to relaying to Michel the contributions of Attwater's artist friend, Eric Gill. See Marx, *Virgil Michel,* p. 118. A sense of the fine Michel-Ellard collaboration may be found in extant letters of Gerald Ellard, S.J., to Virgil Michel, 5 November 1925–5 January 1938, SJAA, Z–24:7.

15. See the review of available literature for this period in Joseph J. Bluett, S.J., "The Mystical Body of Christ: 1890–1940," *Theological Studies* 3 (May 1942): 261–289. Emphasis on the doctrine of the Mystical Body did much to overcome a strictly juridical notion of the church as the perfect society and assisted in the formulation expounded by Vatican II that the church is the people of God. Though Beauduin did much to familiarize Virgil Michel with the doctrine of the Mystical Body while the latter was in Europe, Michel had already come across the doctrine in Guardini's *Vom Geist der Liturgie.* It is possible, of course, that it did not strike Michel at the time.

16. Michel and his collaborators, like Beauduin, drew their inspiration from Pius X's 1903 *motu proprio* in which he recommended the laity's active participation in the liturgy. On the dialog Mass and the *missa recitata,* see "The Apostolate," *OF* 1 (December 1926): 62, and [adapted from] Dom Bernard de Chabannes, "The Dialog Mass," *OF* 12 (March 1938): 225. In the first two decades of the liturgical movement, there were some reflections on and use of the vernacular in worship and the evening Mass.

17. Dorothy Day, "Observations of a Traveler," *Worship* [formerly *OF*] 35 (May 1961): 385–387 gives evidence that from early 1934 on, Dorothy faithfully read this journal and other publications related to the liturgy. Evidence for initiation of *OF* subscription and a copy of all Liturgical Press publications to date donated to Dorothy found in Virgil Michel to Dorothy Day, 14 Feb-

ruary 1934, DD–CW, W–2.2, Box 2; [*CW*] Editors to Alcuin Deutsch, O.S.B., 26 February 1934, SJAA, 91–13, AA–11A; Abbot [Deutsch] to [*CW*] Editors, 2 March 1934 [copy], SJAA, 91–13, AA–11A.

18. See Virgil Michel, O.S.B., "The Liturgy the Basis of Social Regeneration," *OF* 9 (November 1935): 536–545; Virgil Michel, O.S.B., "The Scope of the Liturgical Movement," *OF* 10 (October 1936): 485–490. Michel's study of *Quadragesimo Anno* resulted in the publication of Virgil Michel, O.S.B., *Christian Social Reconstruction* (Milwaukee: Bruce, 1937).

19. Michel's support of the cooperatives and land distribution movement may be seen in Virgil Michel, "The Cooperative Movement and the Liturgical Movement," *OF* 14 (February 1940): 152–160; Virgil Michel, "Timely Tracts: City or Farm," *OF* 12 (June 1938): 367–369. For Catholic Worker examples, see Dorothy Day, "To Christ—To the Land!" *CW* 3 (January 1936): 1, 2; "Ten Monks Popularizing Consumer Cooperatives," *CW* 6 (February 1939): 6; "NBTW" *CW* 11 (May 1944): 2, where Dorothy spoke of Maurin's conversation with a Father Magee of Easton regarding Benedictinism and the rural life movement; "Catholic Worker Positions" *CW* 34 (November 1968): 2, which addressed the issue of a distributist economy.

20. For background, see Dom Hubert Van Zeller, O.S.B., *The Benedictine Idea* (London: Burns and Oates, 1959), pp. 1–52.

21. *The Rule of St. Benedict*, 4:21, ed. Timothy Fry, O.S.B. (Collegeville, Minn.: Liturgical Press, 1981), p. 183. This is the critical edition. Except where noted in the present work, all quotations from the *Rule* are taken from this edition.

22. [Dorothy Day] "Midwinter," *CW* 2 (January 1935): 4. Her reflection is based on 1 Cor 12:26. Dorothy associated her insights on the Mystical Body with the IWW slogan: An injury to one is an injury to all. For this, see "On P.," *CW* 36 (January 1970): 2, and "On P.," *CW* 41 (February 1975): 2. While Dorothy drew on her own knowledge of Scripture and her former affiliation with the non-Christian IWW's in order to understand the doctrine of the Mystical Body, she learned also from the teachings of liturgists such as Virgil Michel and Gerald Ellard, S.J., and relied, as did many of the Catholic Workers, on presentations given to them in 1930s by Benedict Bradley, O.S.B., of Newark, N.J.

23. "On P.," *CW* 15 (May 1948): 3.

24. Dorothy Day, "Fall Appeal," *CW* 30 (October 1963): 2.

25. Day, *Long Loneliness*, p. 179, where she recalled Peter's counsel. In Day, *Union Square to Rome*, p. 28, Dorothy remarked that she had a very close family life, but knew little about the broader community as a child.

26. Dorothy Day, "Meditation" [n.d.; internal evidence suggests the early 1940s], DD–CW, D–3, Box 7.

27. [Dorothy Day] "Peter's Program," *CW* 21 (May 1955): 2. See also

[Dorothy Day] "What We Are Doing in Town and Country," *CW* 4 (September 1936): 2.

28. Day, *Long Loneliness,* p. 243. See also, pp. 222–224, 244, 285–286. Note the Augustinian implication, regarding our hearts resting only in God, in Dorothy Day, "Month of the Dead," *CW* 26 (November 1959): 6.

29. "DAD," *CW* 10 (June 1943): 4. Dorothy was actually quoting or paraphrasing Maurin in this portion of her article, though her references to the unsigned article, "Self-Sufficiency" (*Blackfriars* [April 1943]: 122–125), may lead the reader to wonder whether she was quoting Maurin or "Self-Sufficiency." Dorothy recalled Maurin's conversations with Virgil Michel in "On P," *CW* 20 (October 1953): 6.

30. Dorothy Day, "Poverty Is the Face of Christ," *CW* 18 (December 1952): 6. In this article, she noted that Maurin was interested in communal farms for the family, for the laity, because he was interested in the Benedictine community and the entire tradition of communal living, which she referred to as "religious communism." Dorothy viewed the possibility of such communities in the United States as an answer to the problem of the machine and unemployment, and to the depression which she feared, "once we stop this mad race for armaments."

31. Dorothy Day, "Farming Commune," *CW* 11 (February 1944): 8. On Dorothy's interchangeable references to family and community, see Dorothy Day, "And for Our Absent Brethren," *CW* 10 (December 1943): 2, "A house of hospitality is a family and as such is a small community"; "On P," *CW* 22 (May 1956): 7, where she referred to herself as the mother of a [large] family. For one of her comments on sharing voluntary poverty, see "On P," *CW* 13 (October 1946): 8.

32. [Dorothy] D[ay], "Community Conference," *CW* 22 (April 1956): 6. See Dorothy Day, "Have We Failed in Peter Maurin's Program?" *CW* 20 (January 1954): 6. On the foundation based on Acts 2:42–47 (and repeated in 4:32–35), see "On P," *CW* 22 (December 1955): 6.

33. "On P," *CW* 26 (December 1959): 2. Also see "On P," *CW* 30 (May 1964): 2.

34. Dorothy Day, "Community of Brothers," *CW* 22 (December 1955): 1, 7. In this article she reminded readers that Maurin "urged study of religious community, especially of Benedictine monasteries as models of community life, . . ." Dorothy considered Buber's *Paths in Utopia* as a book from which she gained much encouragement in her work toward community. See "On P," *CW* 25 (September 1958): 1. Articles on other intentional communities abound in the pages of the *CW* from the 1950s through the 1970s, of which Dorothy Day, "Hutterite Communities [derived from the Anabaptist movement]," *CW* 35 (July–August 1969): 2, 7, 8 is an example.

35. Dorothy Day, "What Do the Simple Folk Do?" p. 4. For an indica-

tion of Dorothy's greater peace regarding the Catholic Worker reality, see "On P," *CW* 31 (January 1965): 6, 8. Note also the tone in Dorothy Day, "On Pilgrimage—Our Spring Appeal," *CW* 36 (May 1970): 1, 2, 11. She stated, p. 11: "We are, too, a community of need, rather than what sociologists call an 'intentional community.'"

36. See Henri J. M. Nouwen, "The Faces of Community," *CW* 44 (March–April 1978): 7. Though no longer editor of the paper, Dorothy approved this selection for inclusion in the paper.

37. *Rule,* 53.15. Dorothy used favorite quotations from the *Rule* as filler in *CW.* She used whatever translation was on hand. On at least one occasion she quoted from Benedict's chapter on hospitality. See *CW* 7 (October 1940): 3, "Let all guests who come be received as Christ Himself, for He will say: 'I was a stranger and you took me in'" (Mt 25:35; *Rule,* 53:1).

38. Dorothy's interest in the sayings of the Fathers of the Church is confirmed by frequent, short excerpts from their writings which appeared in *CW.* The following from the writings of Basil, found in *CW* 17 (December 1950): 7, is typical: "The bread you hoard belongs to the hungry; the cloak in your wardrobe belongs to the naked; the shoes you let rot belong to the barefoot; the money in your vaults belongs to the destitute."

39. *CW,* vols. 1–7, Introduction by Dwight MacDonald and Preface by Dorothy Day (Westport, Conn.: Greenwood Reprint Corporation, 1970), p. 12, n. 7. Regarding Dorothy's experience of living on the lower east side in her earlier years, see Day, *Loaves and Fishes,* p. 8. In the second issue of the paper, see [Dorothy Day] "Maurin's Program" and Peter Maurin, "Easy Essays," *CW* 1 (June-July 1933): 4 and 1, respectively. See also [Dorothy Day] "On the Love of God," *CW* 1 (September 1933): 6; Peter Maurin, "To the Bishops of the U.S.: A Plea for Houses of Hospitality," *CW* 1 (October 1933): 1.

40. "Houses of Hospitality," and "Call for Catholic Houses for Needy Women and Girls," in *CW* 1 (November 1933): 7 and 1, respectively.

41. On the 11 December 1933 opening of the hospitality center, see [Dorothy Day] "Co-operative Apartment for Unemployed Women Has Its Start in Parish," *CW* 1 (December 1933): 1, 5. On her dream and search for larger quarters, see [Dorothy Day] "The Teresa-Joseph Cooperative," and [Dorothy Day] "Commentary Column," *CW* 1 (February 1934): 5 and 3, respectively.

42. [Dorothy Day] "Apartment [Teresa-Joseph Cooperative] in Immaculate Conception Parish Shelters Many in Last 10 Months," *CW* 2 (October 1934): 5.

43. [Dorothy Day] "Houses of Hospitality," *CW* 4 (December 1936): 4. See also [Dorothy Day], "Again an Appeal—Please!" *CW* 3 (December 1935): 8; [Dorothy Day] "What We Are Doing in Town and Country," *CW* 4 (September 1936): 2.

44. On small beginnings, see [Dorothy Day] "Houses of Hospitality,"

CW 4 (December 1936): 4. The term *Ambassadors of God* was used by Maurin in his "Easy Essays." For an example, see Peter Maurin, "To the Bishops of the U.S.: A Plea for Houses of Hospitality [#1]," *CW* 1 (October 1933): 1.

45. [Dorothy Day] "'They Knew Him in the Breaking of Bread,'" *CW* 4 (February 1937): 1. For other early accounts of their work of hospitality, see Dorothy Day, "Houses of Hospitality," *Commonweal* 27 (15 April 1938): 683–684; Dorothy Day, "The House on Mott Street," *Commonweal* 28 (6 May 1938): 37–39; Dorothy Day, *House of Hospitality* (New York & London: Sheed & Ward, 1939). In the 15 April 1938 *Commonweal* article, Dorothy observed that approximately a thousand men came for breakfast at the New York house. She pleaded again for parish centers and for parish priests who would minister closely to the needy, arguing what a difference this would bring about in the outlook of the poor. The 6 May 1938 *Commonweal* article gave a realistic picture of the tasks at hand. From [Dorothy Day] "'And There Remained Only the Very Poor,'" *CW* 7 (July–August 1940): 2, it is evident that the New York house was serving lunch and supper in addition to breakfast. For evidence of Dorothy's awareness that they were then unable to realize Maurin's vision, see "DAD," *CW* 9 (September 1942): 4. Stanley Vishnewski, a Catholic Worker from 1934 until his death in November 1979, maintained that taking care of the poor "obscured" the final stage of Maurin's program, which "was the establishment of thousands of cells of Christian living throughout the world." From Stanley Vishnewski–Deane Mowrer interview, 1969, DD–CW, W–9, Box 2. For a recap of Maurin's vision, see Dorothy Day, "The Scandal of the Works of Mercy," *Commonweal* 51 (4 November 1949): 99–102.

46. "Catholic Worker Ideas on Hospitality," *CW* 7 (May 1940): 10. See Jean Danielou, S.J., "Toward a Theology of Hospitality," *CW* 18 (June 1952): 4, for a historical survey of the Christian tradition of hospitality.

47. "DAD," *CW* 9 (September 1942): 4. Dorothy used the term *rum hound* in "DAD," *CW* 8 (May 1941): 1.

48. [Dorothy Day] "Room for Christ," *CW* 12 (December 1945): 2. Dorothy frequently referred to Christ disguised in ordinary human beings and events. Thus, the fact that the pericope of Emmaus was one of her favorite New Testament passages is no surprise. For one of her references to Emmaus, see [Dorothy Day] "Homes for the Homeless," *CW* 21 (May 1955): 7.

49. Editors [Dorothy Day], "We Need Your Help," *CW* 16 (May 1949): 3. Dorothy acknowledged with gratitude her debt to Peter Maurin, even to her last years. See for example, Dorothy Day, "Peter Maurin[,] 1877–1977," *CW* 43 (May 1977): 1.

50. "On P," *CW* 22 (May 1956): 7. On Dorothy's long-standing identification with the poor prior to meeting Maurin, see Dorothy Day, *House of Hospitality,* p. xiii: "I felt that they were my people, that I was a part of them."

51. "On P.," *CW* 26 (August 1959): 8. On a band-aid being applied to a cancer, see "On P.," *CW* 35 (December 1969): 1.

52. See "On P.," *CW* 44 (June 1978): 2; "On P.," *CW* 45 (February 1979): 7.

53. "Going to the Roots . . . Questions and Answers," *CW* 44 (May 1978): 6.

54. Chrysostom Tarasevitch, O.S.B., was a monk of St. Procopius Abbey in Lisle, Illinois, to which Dorothy was affiliated as a Benedictine oblate.

55. See *Rule,* chs, 8–19 inclusive. Other concerns which relate to the Divine Office may be found in chs. 42, 43, 47, and 48.

56. Ibid., 19.6–7; 4.21; 43.3.

57. On *lectio divina,* see ibid., 4.55; 8.3; 42.3; 48 passim; 73.2–6. On petitionary and devotional prayer, see 4.56–57; 20 passim; 52 passim. Reference to Mass on Sundays and festivals in 35.14. See related note in David Parry, O.S.B., *Households of God,* (Kalamazoo: Cistercian Publications, 1980), p. 107, n. 4.

58. See *Rule,* ch. 48, on harvesting in the context of manual labor. Chs. 32, 55, and 57, with their respective mention of tools, stylus and writing tablets, and craftsmen, provide evidence of other types of labor in which early monks engaged.

59. Ibid., ch. 4, where representative spiritual and corporal works of mercy were listed among the tools of good works. See ch. 36.2–3 where priority was given to the care of the sick brethren as a work of mercy and was performed in conscious compliance with the injunction of Mt 25:36,40.

60. Ibid., 48.1; 49.1–2.

61. Ibid., Prologue.2–3 on the toil of obedience. A positive theology of labor remained latent, and it was not until the twelfth century that human work was viewed in the West also as a participation in God's creativity. See Jacques Le Goff, *Time, Work and Culture in the Middle Ages,* trans. Arthur Goldhammer (Chicago: University of Chicago Press, 1980), pp. 77–81, 107–115.

62. Rembert Sorg, O.S.B., *Towards a Benedictine Theology of Manual Labor* (Lisle, Ill.: St. Procopius Abbey Press, 1949) [p. 1], and quoted with slight textual variations in Dorothy Day, "Work," *CW* 16 (October 1949): 4, 6. For a literal translation of the passage, also differing from Dorothy's version, see Sorg, p. 18.

63. Sorg, *Benedictine Theology,* p. 9. The entire sentence is underlined in the original, with the word *work* being twice underlined.

64. Ibid., pp. 11–16, especially the section on "The New Lordship." For another commentary on later interpretation see Jean Leclercq, O.S.B., "The Monastic Tradition of Culture and Studies," *American Benedictine Review* 11 (March-June 1960): 99–131.

65. Sorg, *Benedictine Theology,* pp. 16–17.

66. Ibid., p. 31 for Sorg's statement of the ideal. In the examination proper, Sorg presented the positions of two contemporaries, Dom Paul Delatte and Abbot Cuthbert Butler. Sorg's own position combined the two. Delatte, then abbot of Solesmes, argued that Benedict's concept of work was larger than manual labor; this accorded with the highly developed intellectual tradition of Solesmes. Abbot Cuthbert proposed that Benedict required his monks to do some form of manual labor. The works in question are Paul Delatte, O.S.B., *The Rule of St. Benedict,* trans. Dom Justin McCann (London: Burns, Oates, & Washbourne, 1921); Cuthbert Butler, O.S.B., *Benedictine Monachism* (New York: Longmans, Green, 1924).

67. Sorg, *Benedictine Theology,* p. 36.

68. Dorothy Day, "Work," *CW* 16 (October 1949): 6.

69. Ibid. Sorg's discussion of his "deeper" theology of manual labor is found in his *Benedictine Theology,* pp. 12–16.

70. Dorothy referred to Maurin's horarium in her article, "Work," *CW* 16 (October 1949): 6; an expanded form of it appears in Day, *Loaves and Fishes,* p. 96; for another comment on his horarium, with Dorothy's stress on time for prayer, see "On P," *CW* 19 (June 1953): 6. Maurin frequently expressed his synthesis in terms of the slogan, "Cult, Culture, and Cultivation."

71. Some years before Maurin's novitiate, the Cardinal Protector of the Christian Brothers had been Jean Baptiste-François Pitra (1812–1889), a learned Benedictine of Solesmes and co-worker with famed liturgist Dom Prosper Gueranger. Among those Pitra had influenced was Brother Joseph Josserand, superior general of the Christian Brothers during Maurin's afffiliation with the order. A generation before Maurin, Pitra came to the Paris novitiate periodically to speak to the congregation about their vocation. Maurin's biographer, Arthur Sheehan, who relied extensively on his subject's own testimony, has written of these conferences: "So inspiring were his [Pitra's] counsels and so sound his wisdom that the Brothers regarded him almost as St. Benedict back again in the flesh." See Arthur Sheehan, *Peter Maurin: Gay Believer* (Garden City, N.Y.: Hanover House, 1959), p. 44.

72. "On P," *CW* 40 (February 1974): 8; "On P," *CW* 42 (June 1976): 2.

73. "Primer of Prayer by Father McSorley" (ad for Joseph McSorley, C.S.P., *Primer of Prayer* [New York & London: Longmans Green, 1934]), *CW* 2 (November 1934): 6.

74. Virgil Michel to P. Adalbert Callahan, O.F.M., 6 February 1936, carbon copy, SJAA, Z-23:7.

75. [Dorothy Day] "A New [Liturgical] Year Begins," *CW* 8 (December 1940): 4. Dorothy noted Gill's references to work as prayer in [Dorothy Day] "Eric Gill Letters," *CW* 8 (February 1941): 6; Dorothy Day, "The Church and Work," *CW* 13 (September 1946): 7; For comment on "Laborare est orare," see Josephine Drabak, "Love Made Visible," *CW* 12 (November 1945): 11.

For a report on Dorothy's talk to would-be Catholic Workers, see Will Woods, "Mass-Hands," *OF* 16 (May 1942): 320–322.

76. Dorothy Day, "The Council and the Mass," *CW* 29 (September 1962): 2.

77. "On P," *CW* 32 (March 1966): 6.

78. "DAD," *CW* 8 (April 1941): 4. For her series treating industrial issues, see Dorothy Day, "The Church and Work," *CW* 13 (September 1946): 1, 3, 7–8; Dorothy Day, "Reflections on Work," *CW* 13 (November 1946): 1, 4; Dorothy Day, "Reflections on Work: Blood on Our Coal," *CW* 13 (December 1946): 1, 4; Dorothy Day, "Reflections on Work," *CW* 13 (January 1947): 1, 2; Dorothy Day, "Reflections on Work," *CW* 14 (March 1947): 2, 4. Sample articles illustrating her advocacy of Chávez and the farm workers include Dorothy Day, "The Organizer," *CW* 32 (February 1966): 1, 6; Dorothy Day, "Strike Leader Comes East," *CW* 33 (May 1967): 1, 9; "On P," *CW* 38 (January 1972): 1, 2, 4; "Boycott Lettuce" [includes letter from César Chávez], *CW* 38 (June 1972): 1, 5; César Chávez, "Always There" [tribute to Dorothy], *CW* 46 (December 1980): 7.

79. Dorothy frequently noted that all work should be considered in the light of the works of mercy, an insight which she shared with Father James Tompkins of Nova Scotia. An instance may be found in Dorothy Day, "Education and Work," *CW* 20 (September 1953): 2. A good statement on how she related the primitive and later Benedictine theology of work may be found in [Dorothy Day], "The Poor Could at Least Keep Clean," *CW* 9 (September 1942): 7. The fact of the 1942 statement verifies that Sorg's *Benedictine Theology* confirmed her thinking rather than offering fresh insight. Dorothy invoked Maurin as her authority for her theology of work in Day, *Long Loneliness,* p. 227.

80. *Rule of St. Benedict,* Prologue.20–21.

81. Development of oblate tradition confirmed by 23 January 1988 telephone conversation with Vitus Buresh, O.S.B., archivist of St. Procopius Abbey; Placid [J.] Cormey, O.S.B., Newsletter to Oblates of St. Gregory's Priory, Portsmouth, Rhode Island, 9 October 1946, DD–CW, D–5, Box 1; Barry, *Worship and Work,* pp. 150, 261, where the author noted American abbots' efforts to revive the institution of secular oblates.

82. Virgil Michel to [CW] Friends, 4 May 1935, DD–CW, W–2.2, Box 2. Letters which provide evidence of Michel's sponsorship of Benedictine oblates in New York, known to Dorothy, include: Tom (A. H.) Coddington to Virgil Michel, 4 February 1936, SJAA, Z–23:7; Mary Moriarty to Virgil Michel, 18 February [1937], SJAA, Z–25:10; Sylvia Batdorf to Virgil Michel [spring 1937], SJAA, Z–22:4.

83. Raïssa Maritain, *We Have Been Friends,* p. 176, where she noted 11 June [1906] as the date of their conversion to Catholicism; pp. 192–193,

where she noted Jacques Maritain's first visit, in August 1907, to the Benedictines of Solesmes, then in exile on the Isle of Wight, purportedly to relate news of Bloy's conversion. Raïssa Maritain, *Adventures in Grace,* p. 13, where she remarked on the joy of their spiritual director, Father Humbert Clerissac, O.P. [friend of Dom DeLatte, abbot of exiled Solesmes community], at their becoming Benedictines; since Clerissac died on 16 November 1914, their conversion as oblates occurred sometime between mid-1906 and late 1914.

84. "DAD," *CW* 3 (February 1936): 5. Rt. Rev. Alcuin Deutsch, O.S.B., *Manual for Oblates of St. Benedict* (Collegeville, Minn.: St. John's Abbey Press, 1937). This work was reviewed by G[odfrey] L. D[iekmann], *OF* 12 (November 1937): 44–45.

85. Ade Bethune to Virgil Michel, 8 April 1936, SJAA, Z–22:4, at which time she still lived in New York City. An ad entitled "Christmas Cards," *CW* 4 (November 1936): 8, lists Bethune's new address at Newport. In Ade Bethune to Virgil Michel, 15 March 1938, SJAA, Z–22:4, she observed: "I am teaching on Mondays at Portsmouth Priory School!" Placid [J.] Cormey, O.S.B., Newsletter to Oblates, 9 October 1946, DD–CW, D–5.1, identified both Bethune's 1940 affiliation and Dorothy's 1942 affiliation. J. Hugh Diman, O.S.B., to [*CW*] Editor, printed in *CW* 4 (February 1937): 5. Pertinent references to Joseph Woods, O.S.B., include: "DAD," *CW* 5 (September 1937): 2; [Dorothy Day] "First Mass," *CW* 6 (October 1938): 4; "DAD," *CW* 6 (June 1939): 4; "DAD," *CW* 6 (July–August 1939): 3, with picture on p. 8; Erwin Mooney, "Peter Maurin Begins Summer School," *CW* 7 (July-August 1940): 3; "DAD," *CW* 8 (October 1941): 7; "DAD," *CW* 10 (December 1942): 6; "DAD," *CW* 10 (July–August 1943): 1, 3; AIG, pp. 216–225, consists of Dorothy's notes on conferences given by Woods on 9 and 13 June [1943]. In Dorothy Day to Thomas Merton, 17 March 1963, TMSC, D–220, she recalled being directed by Woods to Hosea many years ago; Brackley and Dillon, "Interview with Dorothy Day," p. 9; "On P," *CW* 41 (March–April 1975): 8, in which she recalled the recent death of Woods.

86. Dorothy Day, "Views and News," *CW* 8 (January 1941): 1. She may have been thinking of later desert dwellers such as de Foucauld, since the rosary is a Catholic devotion which achieved widespread popularity in the Middle Ages. Dorothy knew that Cassian, though of Eastern origin, was a bridge to Western monasticism.

87. *The Desert Fathers,* trans. and introduction Helen Waddell (New York: Sheed & Ward, 1942). Except when noted, page numbers refer to this American edition. "DAD," *CW* 10 (June 1943): 4, "I was converted to being an oblate by reading and re-reading *The Fathers of the Desert* (you can get it from Sheed and Ward, 63 Fifth Avenue, for seventy-five cents)." From the information given in the June 1943 column as well as her later references, she meant to say *"The Desert Fathers."* Dorothy occasionally misquoted titles

when giving them from memory. In "NBTW," *CW* 10 (October 1943): 1, she explicitly associated her sabbatical with her desire for a desert experience. "DAD," *CW* 10 (September 1943): 1, 2. On rereading *Desert Fathers* and often unnamed other works on Eastern monachism, see "DAD," *CW* 10 (February 1943): 4; "NBTW," *CW* 11 (March 1944): 2; AIG fragm [A & S]; "On P," *CW* 30 (November 1963): 6, where she noted a visit with Donald Attwater and his gift to her of Donald Attwater, *Saints of the East.* It is obvious from the column that she read this work on Eastern (Orthodox) monasticism. In Dorothy Day to Thomas Merton, 17 March 1963, TMSC, D–220, she spoke with appreciation of his gift: *The Wisdom of the Desert,* trans. Thomas Merton (New York: New Directions, 1960). She read this work, which consists of 150 excerpts from fourth-century hermit Fathers of the Desert. In "On P," *CW* 37 (September 1971): 7, Dorothy recorded her visit to Dostoevsky's grave at the Alexander Nevsky Lavra (monastery) in Leningrad. This visit was in keeping both with her love for Dostoevsky and for Orthodox monasticism, an outgrowth of early Eastern monachism.

88. *Desert Fathers,* p. 274.

89. As quoted in "On P," *CW* 46 (February 1980): 7. The prayer, as it reads in full, may be found in *Desert Fathers,* p. 287. Dorothy's previous excerpts of the prayer appeared in much the same completeness as the February 1980 quotation. Some examples occur in "Prayer of St. Ephraim," *CW* 9 (September 1942): 4; "Prayer to St. Ephraim," *CW* 21 (December 1954): 5; "Prayer of St. Ephraim the Syrian," *CW* 29 (January 1963): 6. She sometimes printed another prayer of St. Ephraim, also a prayer of repentance, which she had come across in Nadejda Gorodetzky, *The Humiliated Christ in Modern Russian Thought* (London: Society for Promoting Christian Knowledge, 1938). One example may be found as "Lenten Prayer of St. Ephrem [Ephraim]," *CW* 16 (April 1950): 5. This issue lists the source, not quite accurately, as "*The Humiliated Christ in Russian Thought.* Gordetsky."

90. As noted in *The Desert Fathers,* trans. & introduction Helen Waddell (London: Constable, 1936), p. viii, "I have left on one side the spectacular austerities which Gibbon and his successors have made sufficiently familiar: they are the commonplaces of controversy. These I had expected to find; and they were the least part of what I found. It is forgotten that inhumanity to one's self had often its counterpart in an almost divine humanity towards one's neighbour: and the crazed figure of the decadence, St. Simeon Stylites, has overshadowed the quiet men who founded the Desert rule. The Desert has bred fanaticism and frenzy and fear: but it also bred heroic gentleness."

91. Placid [J.] Cormey, O.S.B., Newsletter to Oblates of St. Gregory's Priory, Portsmouth, 9 October 1946, DD–CW, D–5, Box 1.

92. Helene Iswolsky, *No Time to Grieve: An Autobiographical Journey* (Philadelphia: Winchell, 1985), p. 241. For early references to St. Procopius

in *CW*, see "Book Reviews," *CW* 3 (June 1935): 7; "DAD," *CW* 8 (December 1940): 7.

93. On Helene Iswolsky's first meeting with Dorothy, see *No Time to Grieve*, p. 235. "Slavonic Mission," *CW* 10 (September 1943): 3. Notices of Michael Kovalak's death appeared, with biographical data, in "On P," *CW* 43 (June 1977): 2; Brian Terrell, "Michael Kovalak," *CW* 43 (June 1977): 2; Mary Lathrop Pope, "Thank You, Mike," *CW* 43 (July–August, 1977): 7. Vitus Buresh, O.S.B.—Brigid Merriman telephone conversation, 23 January 1988; Christian Ceplecha, O.S.B., to Brigid Merriman, 12 February 1988. "On P," *CW* 18 (November 1951): 6.

94. Father Rembert Sorg [O.S.B.], "Manual Labor as Mortification," *CW* 14 (March 1948): 2; Dorothy Day, "Work," *CW* 16 (October 1949): 4, 6. Rembert Sorg, O.S.B., "On Meditating Like a Dove," *OF* 19 (December 1944): 13–17; Rembert Sorg, O.S.B., "Timely Tracts: In Defense of Latin," *OF* 19 (January 1945): 113–119; Rembert Sorg, O.S.B., "This Year's Paschal Mystery," *OF* 22 (March 1948): 193–200. Rembert Sorg, O.S.B., "The Spirituality of the Psalms," *OF* 22 (October 1948): 529–541. Rembert Sorg, O.S.B., "The Way of the Mystics," *OF* 23 (February 1949): 150–153. "Sunday Conferences, 4 p.m. at Peter Maurin Farm, Staten Island," *CW* 17 (April 1951): 3. Waclaw Zajaczkowski, "Benedictines and the Catholic Worker Movement," *CW* 19 (March 1953): 3, 6. "Labor Is Life" (review of Rembert Sorg, O.S.B., *The Mass for Labor Day*), *CW* 24 (May 1958): 6.

95. "A Benedictine Writes" (Father Chrysostom Tarasevitch, O.S.B., to "Dear Friends"), *CW* 15 (June 1948): 8; "War and Peace" (Father Chrysostom Tarasevitch, O.S.B., to "My Dear Friends," 24 August 1948), *CW* 15 (October 1948): 3; Father Chrysostom Tarasevitch, O.S.B., to [CW] Friends, 23 December 1948, *CW* 15 (January 1949): 4. Chrysostom Tarasevitch, O.S.B., "Church in Russia," *CW* 16 (May 1949): 1, 5, 8 and *CW* 16 (June 1949): 4. Vitus Buresh, O.S.B., to Brigid Merriman, 3 February 1988, in which he noted that Tarasevitch was among the monks of St. Procopius who conducted days of recollection for the New York group of oblates. Instances of Tarasevitch giving retreats and talks to the Catholic Worker group may be found in: "On P," *CW* 16 (May 1949): 2, which lists him as director for the 17–23 July 1949 retreat to be given at the Newburgh farm; Tom Sullivan, "Mott Street," *CW* 16 (July–August 1949): 3, notes that Tarasevitch recently spoke at the New York house on "The Proper Attitude of a Christian Towards Russia." From "Maryfarm Retreats." *CW* 17 (November 1950): 2, and "Maryfarm Retreats," *CW* 17 (December 1950): 8, it is evident that he gave a Thanksgiving weekend retreat that year at the Newburgh farm. Chrysostom Tarasevitch, O.S.B., "A Treasury of Russian Spirituality," *OF* 23 (November 1948): 18–21. Chrysostom Tarasevitch, O.S.B., "Church Unity," *OF* 23 (May 1949): 297–302. One instance of Dorothy's communication with Tarasevitch whenever she was in

the Chicago area may be found in "On P.," *CW* 24 (December 1957): 2.

96. [Dorothy Day] "Peter's Program," *CW* 21 (May 1955): 2. On her speaking with Claude [Viktora, O.S.B.] and her [17] November 1954 lecture at St. Procopius, see "On P.," *CW* 21 (December 1954): 2, 6.

97. "On P.," *CW* 23 (April 1957): 6. Information on Dorothy's oblate profession and ratification obtained from SPAA, courtesy of Christian Ceplecha, O.S.B., 12 February 1988.

98. Stanley Vishnewski to Brother Benet Tvedten, O.S.B., 14 August 1968, DD–CW, W–12.3, Box 3.

99. Dorothy Day to Colman J. Barry, O.S.B., 6 April 1966, SJAA, 91–13, AA–11A. It is evident from the letter that she still visited Collegeville whenever speaking trips took her in that direction.

100. Comment made in Dorothy's then shaky handwriting on envelope in which the 2 September 1976 letter of Charles Finnegan, O.F.M., to Dorothy Day was enclosed. Because Dorothy was quite ill at the time, at her request Stanley Vishnewski wrote a formal reply to Finnegan on 4 October 1976. On 11 October 1976, since the provincial was on his way to a general chapter in Assisi, the vicar provincial, Alban A. Maguire, O.F.M., acknowledged Vishnewski's reply. In his letter Maguire clarified that the invitation was to become affiliated with the first order (friars) rather than by the usual lay membership in the third order (Secular Franciscans). There is no evidence of a further reply from Dorothy. Letters and Dorothy's written comment, DD–CW, D–5, Box 3.

101. A 1 October 1947 letter survives to Dorothy from Mother (then Sister) Benedict Duss, O.S.B., DD–CW, D–5, Box 1. Sister Benedict had shortly before obtained Rome's final approval for the abbey of cloistered Benedictine nuns, located in the Hartford, Connecticut, diocese (now an archdiocese); it is apparent from the letter that a friendship existed between Dorothy and the Benedictine nun. Dorothy referred to trips to see Mother Benedict in several instances, of which "On P.," *CW* 23 (October 1956): 2, is an example. In a letter dictated by Dorothy on 12 April 1971 to organizer Father Myron B. Bloy, DD–CW, D–5, Box 2, she replied positively to an invitation to attend a conference of the Church Society for College Work. Of the Benedictine also planning to attend, she said: "Brother David Steindl-Rast, of Mt. Savior, is one of my favorite people."

102. In 1098, reformer St. Robert of Molesmes and twenty-one Benedictine monks journeyed to Citeaux to establish what eventually became the motherhouse of the Cistercian order. These monks endeavored to return to the exact observance of the *Rule* of Benedict. The Englishman Stephen Harding, who became abbot in 1109, and Bernard, who entered in 1112, were among the most renowned early leaders of the reform. The only later reform that has survived to the present was that of La Trappe, an abbey in France.

It was led by the mature Armand Jean le Bouthillier, the Abbé de Rancé, who in 1638 at age twelve had been appointed abbot *in commendam.* Though La Trappe was suppressed in 1791, it survived through the leadership of novice master Dom Augustin de Lestrange, who returned to France with his monks in 1815 and re-occupied some of the ancient abbeys. For several decades the Trappists formed three groupings, each following a slightly different version of the regulations of either De Rance or Lestrange. In 1892 the three congregations united under one superior general to form the Order of Cistercians of the Strict Observance. See André Louf, *The Cistercian Way,* trans. Nivard Kinsella (Kalamazoo: Cistercian Publications, 1983), pp. 23–43.

103. Frederic M. Dunne, O.C.S.O., to *CW* Editors, 15 April 1936, DD-CW, W–2.2, Box 1. Abbot Dunne–Dorothy Day correspondence, 4 January 1939–2 March 1948, DD–CW, W–2.2, Box 1. See Abbot Frederic M. Dunne, O.S.C.O., to Miss Day, printed in *CW* 15 (May 1948): 5, for which no manuscript copy survives; Dorothy Day, "When we were children, . . ." [1943], DD–CW, D–3, Box 7, remarks on Dunne's friendship. Dorothy Day to Thomas Merton, 4 June [1960], TMSC, D–220.

104. Thomas Merton, "Clairvaux Prison," *CW* 14 (January 1948): 5; "Salute to Merton," a review of Thomas Merton, *Figures for an Apocalypse,* reviewed by Raymond E. F. Larssen [Larsson], *CW* 14 (April 1948): 11; Thomas Merton, "Poverty" (excerpt from *Seeds of Contemplation*), *CW* 15 (April 1949): 3.

105. Thomas Merton, excerpt from *The Sign of Jonas, CW* 23 (September 1956): 1; Thomas Merton, excerpt from *The Sign of Jonas, CW* 23 (October 1956): 1; Thomas Merton, excerpt from *Thoughts in Solitude, CW* 24 (June 1958): 1. The themes of commitment to Christ and the freedom proper to the Christian, found in these three excerpts, appeared frequently in the Day-Merton correspondence.

106. Merton to Day, 9 July 1959, in *The Hidden Ground of Love: The Letters of Thomas Merton on Religious Experience and Social Concerns,* ed. William H. Shannon (New York: Farrar, Straus, Giroux, 1985), p. 136. Wherever available to me, I use and note the archival copies of his letters to Dorothy rather than this work, as Shannon omits portions of several letters. Day to Merton, Feast of the Sacred Heart (June 1959), TMSC, D–220. Merton's gifts ranged from copies of his works to clothes, Trappist cheese, and a Christmas gift of smoked bacon. See James H. Forest, "Thomas Merton and the Catholic Worker Ten Years After," *CW* 44 (December 1978): 4.

107. Merton to Day, 4 February 1960 in *Hidden Ground,* p. 137. Day to Merton, 23 December [1959], TMSC, D–220. Dorothy and Merton frequently spoke of their concern for perseverance. Some of these include Day to Merton, 4 June [1960], TMSC, D–220; Merton to Day, 17 August 1960

in *Hidden Ground,* p. 138; Day to Merton, 17 March 1963, TMSC, D–220; Merton to Day, 5 September 1963, DD–CW, D–1.1, Box 8.

108. Day to Merton, 4 June [1960], TMSC, D–220. Merton to Day, 17 August 1960 in *Hidden Ground,* pp. 137–138.

109. Day to Merton, 10 October [1960], TMSC, D–220. Excerpts include Thomas Merton, "Detachment" (passage from "Notes for a Philosophy of Solitude" in *Disputed Questions* [New York: Farrar, Straus & Giroux, 1960], p. 173), *CW* 27 (May 1961): 7; Thomas Merton, "The Rule of Christ" (passage from "Christianity and Totalitarianism" in *Disputed Questions,* pp. 138–139), *CW* 28 (February 1962): 4.

110. Merton to Day, 23 July 1961, DD–CW, D–1.1, Box 8.

111. Quotation in Day to Merton, Feast of the Assumption [15 August], 1961, TMSC, D–220. Dorothy's remark on Juliana of Norwich as a favorite of Merton's in "On P.," *CW* 40 (January 1974): 2. See Thomas Merton, "Chant to be Used in Processions around a Site with Furnaces," *CW* 28 (July–August 1961): 4.

112. Merton to Day, 23 August 1961 in *Hidden Ground,* p. 139.

113. Merton to Day, 22 September 1961 in *Hidden Ground,* p. 140. Thomas Merton, "The Root of War," *CW* 28 (October 1961): 1, 7–8. This article, minus the first three paragraphs, appeared as Thomas Merton, "The Root of War Is Fear," in *New Seeds of Contemplation* (New York: New Directions, 1962, 1972), pp. 112–122.

114. Thomas Merton, "The Shelter Ethic," *CW* 28 (November 1961): 1, 5. "On P.," *CW* 28 (December 1961): 2. Merton to Day, 20 December 1961, DD–CW, D–1.1, Box 8.

115. Thomas Merton, "Christian Ethics and Nuclear War," *CW* 28 (March 1962): 2, 7; Thomas Merton, "Ethics and War: A Footnote," *CW* 28 (April 1962): 2. The second is a corrective to the first, due to the fact that the March article mistakenly got printed from a first, uncorrected draft copy. Merton to Day, 21 March 1962, DD–CW, D–1.1, Box 8. The recent contribution Merton discussed in this letter appeared as Thomas Merton, "We Have to Make Ourselves Heard," *CW* 28 (May 1962): 4–6 and *CW* 28 (June 1962): 4–5. It is a revised and greatly expanded version of an article previously published as Thomas Merton, "Nuclear War and Christian Responsibility," *Commonweal* 75 (9 February 1962): 509–513. Merton to Day, 9 April 1962 in *Hidden Ground,* pp. 144–145.

116. Day to Merton, 4 June [1962], TMSC, D–220.

117. Merton to Day, 16 June 1962, DD–CW, D–1.1, Box 8.

118. Merton to Day, 11 August 1962 in *Hidden Ground,* p. 147. Other midsummer letters include Merton to Day, 12 July 1962 in ibid., pp. 146–147; Day to Merton, 23 July 1962, TMSC, D–220.

119. Day to Merton, 23 August 1962. Dorothy and Merton were both

sponsors for the American Pax group from its beginnings. See "Announcing the Formation of the American Pax Association," *CW* 29 (October 1962): 3. In Day to Merton, 12 November [1962], TMSC, D–220, Dorothy gave further encouragement to Merton through her enthusiasm over the publication of representative selections of his works. These appeared in *A Thomas Merton Reader,* ed. Thomas P. McDonnell (New York: Harcourt, Brace and World, 1962).

120. Review of Thomas Merton, ed. and introduction, *Breakthrough to Peace* (New York: New Directions, 1962). Reviewed by Thomas Cornell in *CW* 29 (January 1963): 5, 8. Review of Ignace Lepp, *The Christian Failure,* reviewed by Benedict Monk [Thomas Merton], in *CW* 29 (January 1963): 5, 8. Benedict Moore [Thomas Merton], "Danish Non-violent Resistance to Hitler," *CW* 30 (July-August 1963): 1, 3. Merton referred to the last named in Merton to Day, 5 September 1963, DD–CW, D–1.1, Box 8. Quotations from Merton's works at this period include: "Pasternak" (Merton, *Disputed Questions,* pp. 11–12), *CW* 29 (March 1963): 7; "On Writing," *CW* 30 (July-August 1963): 6; "God Is Not Mocked" (Merton, *New Seeds of Contemplation,* pp. 119–120), *CW* 30 (October 1963): 6. Reviews include: review of *The Prison Meditations of Father Delp,* with introduction by Thomas Merton, reviewed by Thomas Cornell, *CW* 29 (April 1963): 5; Thomas Merton, translator and commentary, *Clement of Alexandria: Selections from the Protreptikos,* reviewed by James Forest, *CW* 29 (April 1963): 5.

121. Day to Merton, 17 March 1963, TMSC, D–220. The work in question is *The Wisdom of the Desert,* translated and introduced by Thomas Merton.

122. Day to Merton, St. John's Day [24 June 1965], TMSC, D–220. Merton to Day, 16 July 1965, DD–CW, D–1.1, Box 8. The Maximus article was published as Thomas Merton, "St. Maximus the Confessor on Non-violence," *CW* 32 (September 1965): 1–2. The texts presented, debated, revised, and sometimes promulgated at Vatican Council II were identified as schemata. Schema 13 (which had originally borne the number 17), dealt with the relationship of the church and the world. The final revision of schema 13 was promulgated on 7 December 1965 as the *Pastoral Constitution on the Church in the Modern World (Gaudium et Spes).* Chapter 5 of part II treats the issue of war and peace.

123. Merton to James Forest, typed copy of telegram, 11 November 1965, TMSC, D–220. Merton to Day, Western Union Telegram, 11 November 1965, DD–CW, D–1.1, Box 8. Quotations from Day to Merton, 15 November 1965, TMSC, D–220. The Cardinal's speech was published as Paul-Emile Léger, "War, Racism and Mass Media," *CW* 32 (December 1965): 5, 7.

124. Merton to Day, 22 November 1965, DD–CW, D–1.1, Box 8, where Douglass's insistence is mentioned. Douglass wrote frequently for *CW* but

did not consider himself a Catholic Worker. Day to Merton, 2 December 1965, TMSC, D–220.

125. Merton to Day, 20 December 1965, DD–CW, D–1.1, Box 8. Dorothy herself marked off the quoted section as important.

126. Merton to Day, 29 December 1965, DD–CW, D–1.1, Box 8. In his letter he refers to Dorothy's 1965 Christmas card to him, which is no longer extant.

127. Thomas Merton, "No More Strangers," *CW* 32 (February 1966): 5. The work in question is Philip Berrigan's *No More Strangers,* with an introduction by Thomas Merton (New York: Macmillan, 1965).

128. Merton to Day, 12 September 1966, DD–CW, D–1.1, Box 8. Thomas Merton, "Albert Camus and the Church," *CW* 33 (December 1966): 1, 4–5, 8.

129. Day to Merton, 29 January [1967], TMSC, D–220. See Dorothy Day, "'In Peace Is My Bitterness Most Bitter,'" *CW* 33 (January 1967): 1–2.

130. Merton to Day, 9 February 1967, DD–CW, D–1.1, Box 8. The articles on native Americans include: Thomas Merton, "Ishi—A Meditation," *CW* 33 (March-April 1967): 5–6; Thomas Merton, "The Shoshoneans (A Review-Article)," *CW* 33 (June 1967): 5–6; Thomas Merton, "War and Vision: The Autobiography of a Crow Indian," *CW* 33 (December 1967): 4, 6.

131. Quotation from Merton to Day, 18 August 1967, DD–CW, D–1.1, Box 8. Day to Merton [summer 1967, prior to 18 August], TMSC, D–220. The groups meeting that summer included Pax, which met at CW farm at Tivoli, 28–30 July 1967; Peacemaker, planned for 19 August–1 September 1967 at Tivoli; War Resisters League and Catholic Peace Fellowship. For meetings of the first two groups, see "Summer Conferences 1967," *CW* 33 (June 1967): 6.

132. Quotation from Merton to Friends, Advent-Christmas Letter 1967, DD–CW, W–6.4, Box 1. Day to Merton, 13 September 1967, TMSC, D–220. Thomas Merton, "Auschwitz: A Family Camp," *CW* 33 (November 1967): 4–5, 8. Merton to Day, 19 September 1967, DD–CW, D–1.1, Box 8. Day to Merton, 28 September 1967, TMSC, D–220.

133. Merton to Day, 20 December [1967], DD–CW, D–1.1, Box 8. Thomas Merton, "The Sacred City," *CW* 34 (January 1968): 4–6. Thomas Merton, "The Vietnam War: An Overwhelming Atrocity," *CW* 34 (March 1968): 1, 6–7. The last-named appeared later as Thomas Merton, "Vietnam—an Overwhelming Atrocity," in his *Faith and Violence: Christian Teaching and Christian Practice* (Notre Dame, Ind.: University of Notre Dame Press, 1968), pp. 87–95. Dorothy also published a lengthy excerpt from his essay, "Religion and Race in the United States" (*Faith and Violence,* p. 143), in *CW* 34 (November 1968): 1.

134. Thomas Merton, "The Wild Places," *CW* 34 (June 1968): 4, 6.

In Merton to Friends, Midsummer Letter 1968, DD–CW, W–6.4, Box 1, he spoke of the critical problem of violence in society. Merton to Day, 25 July 1968, DD–CW, D–1.1, Box 8. In the 25 July letter, Merton requested Dorothy's prayers for his forthcoming trip to Asia. Its main purpose was to attend a meeting with Roman Catholic monks who would discuss monasticism in the Orient. The Pax conference paper mentioned by Merton was published as Thomas Merton, "Peace and Revolution: A Footnote to Ulysses," *Peace* (quarterly magazine of Pax group) (February 1969) and was advertised in *CW* 35 (March–April 1969): 8.

135. Day to Merton, 19 August 1968, TMSC, D–220.

136. Dorothy Day, "Thomas Merton, Trappist (1915–1968)," *CW* 34 (December 1968): 1, 6. The excerpts Dorothy used in this obituary article have all been discussed.

137. Thomas Merton, "Technology and Hope," *CW* 35 (May 1969): 5.

138. Quotation from Merton, untitled, *CW* 41 (June 1975): 8; reprinted, *CW* 43 (December 1977): 2. Dorothy Day, "Rabbi Heschel said . . ." DD–CW, D–3, Box 7 (MS for Dorothy Day, "Adventure in Prayer," *The Third Hour* 9 [1970]: 39–45). Representative excerpts from Merton include: Thomas Merton, "Feet on the Ground, Hands In the Dirt (passages from his "Ecumenism and Monastic Renewal," *Journal of Ecumenical Studies*, 5 [Spring 1968]: 275–276)," *CW* 36 (May 1970): 6; Thomas Merton, unidentified excerpt on Christian nonviolence, *CW* 36 (June 1970): 3; Thomas Merton, untitled, on Freedom (*Conjectures of a Guilty Bystander* [Garden City, New York: Doubleday Image paperback 1968], *CW* 38 (June 1972): 2; Thomas Merton, untitled on Christ's rejection (*Raids on the Unspeakable*) *CW* 39 (December 1973): 1; Thomas Merton, untitled on resurrection (*The Sign of Jonas*), *CW* 40 (September 1974): 5.

139. Quotation from Merton's *The Sign of Jonas* in *CW* 40 (September 1974): 5. "On P," *CW* 41 (June 1975): 6, where she remarked on working on the forthcoming introduction by rereading Merton's four long reviews on native American civilizations. These had originally been printed in *The Catholic Worker*. The book appeared as Thomas Merton, *Ishi Means Man: Essays on Native Americans*, foreword by Dorothy Day (Greensboro, N.C.: Unicorn Press, 1976). "On P," *CW* 44 (December 1978): 6, where she also noted, "Trappists have always been our friends; Trappists in Kentucky, Georgia, Massachusetts, New York, Utah, Virginia."

140. For background on de Foucauld, see Charles de Foucauld, *Inner Search: Letters (1889–1916)*, trans. Barbara Lucas (Maryknoll, N.Y.: Orbis Books, 1979); René Bazin, *Charles de Foucauld*, trans. Peter Keelan (London: Burns Oates and Washbourne, 1923); Anne Fremantle, *Desert Calling: The Life of Charles de Foucauld* (London: Hollis and Carter, 1950); Peter F. Anson, *The Call of the Desert: The Solitary Life in the Christian Church* (London: S.P.C.K.,

1964): 209–211; Little Brother of Jesus, *Silent Pilgrimage to God,* trans. Jeremy Moiser with a preface by René Voillaume (Maryknoll, N.Y.: Orbis Books, 1975). For a short commentary on de Foucauld's development of an ideal for the Little Brothers, see René Voillaume, *Seeds of the Desert,* trans. Willard Hill (London: Burns & Oates, 1955): 20–23. On the development of de Foucauld-inspired groups, see Michel Lafon, *Vivre Nazareth aujourd'hui* (Vitry-sur-Seine: Librairie Arthème Fayard, 1985): 29–79.

141. AIG, pp. 96, 238; "NBTW," *CW* 12 (March 1945): 2; Tom Sullivan, "Mott Street," *CW* 16 (March 1950): 2, which reported a recent talk on the Little Brothers given by Jacques Maritain at the Catholic Worker house; "St. Francis," *CW* 18 (September 1952): 3, which compared the Little Brothers to the Franciscans in their pacifism, poverty, and manual labor; George Carlin, "Art Student in Paris," *CW* 18 (September 1952): 4; Dorothy Day, "Poverty Is the Pearl of Great Price," *CW* 20 (July–August 1953): 7; Ad for "The Third Hour," *CW* 20 (November 1953): 8, which noted the inclusion of an article by Anne Fremantle, "The Little Brothers"; Dr. S. Bolshakoff, "Conversion of the Working Class," *CW* 20 (December 1953): 1, 8; Dorothy Day, "French Worker Priests and the Little Brothers of de Foucauld," *CW* 20 (March 1954): 2, 4.

142. Dorothy Day, "Help Wanted," *CW* 20 (April 1954): 2.

143. "On P.," *CW* 21 (June 1955): 6. She noted that some of the Little Sisters were waiting to receive visas to the United States in order that they might establish a house in Chicago.

144. "On P.," *CW* 25 (October 1958): 1. In "On P.," *CW* 25 (January 1959): 2, Dorothy referred to two articles by Voillaume, printed in the quarterly, *Jesus Caritas,* a publication of the de Foucauld Association. In "On P.," *CW* 25 (July 1959): 6, she referred to René Voillaume, *Seeds of the Desert,* as "the best spiritual reading for our time that I have come across." In the same column, she remarked that Jack English (then Father Charles), had sent her translations of chapters from the French edition of Voillaume's work which had been omitted from the English edition; she also noted the forthcoming June 1959 retreat.

145. Directives and schedule regarding the 26–30 June 1959 retreat, DD–CW, D–5, Box 1. Day to Merton, Feast of the Sacred Heart [1959], TMSC, D–220. She described the retreat in Dorothy Day, "Retreat," *CW* 26 (August 1959): 2, 7. See also Charles Butterworth, "Benedict Labré House, Montreal," *CW* 26 (August 1959): 1.

146. See "On P.," *CW* 26 (December 1959): 6, for her reference to a current reading of Fremantle's work. List of works recommended for reading by the Jesus Caritas Fraternity, DD–CW, W–6, Box 3. Day to Merton, 22 January 1960, TMSC, D–220. Postulancy comprises the initial formative period before incorporation into a religious group. See "On P.," *CW* 28 (October 1961): 2, on the Labor Day retreat.

147. "On P.," *CW* 29 (June 1963): 1, 2, 6, 8; "On P.," *CW* 30 (October 1963): 6. See "On P.," *CW* 32 (October 1965): 8, for her later comment.

148. Montreal Little Sister Claude Gervais to Day, 28 February 1960 and 11 June 1961, DD–CW, D–5, Box 1, indicate respectively Gervais's flexibility and an admitted failure within the Fraternity to meet Dorothy's vocational needs. Circumstances of Dorothy's withdrawal from the secular fraternity and support indicated in André and Cinette Ferrière to Day, 8 August 1963, DD–CW, D–5, Box 1. Dorothy continued to print the fraternity logo by hand on many letters to Merton and to Charles Butterworth. Day to Charles and Bernice Butterworth, 10 January 1976, DD–CW, W–13, Box 1, is an example.

149. "On P.," *CW* 30 (October 1963): 6; Day to Butterworth, postmarked 27 October 1963, DD–CW, W–13, Box 1; "On P.," *CW* 32 (October 1965): 8; Day to Merton, 28 September 1967, TMSC, D–220, where she offered special tribute to the Little Brothers of Jesus; "On P.," *CW* 35 (Jan 1969): 6; "On P.," *CW* 39 (July–August 1973): 7.

150. "On P.," *CW* 43 (October–November 1977): 2. See also "On P.," *CW* 41 (March–April 1975): 2. "Friday Night Meetings," *CW* 42 (December 1976): 7. "On P.," *CW* 44 (February 1978): 5. "On P.," *CW* 46 (September 1980): 6.

4. SIGNIFICANCE OF THE RETREAT MOVEMENT

1. Twentieth-century movements for spiritual renewal included the liturgical, scriptural, and retreat movements, among others. See Erwin Iserloh, "Movements within the Church and Their Spirituality," in *History of the Church,* ed. H. Jedin, et al., vol. 10, pp. 299–336. Also Roger Aubert, "The Life of the Church," in *Christian Centuries,* ed. L. J. Rogier, et al., vol. 5, pp. 574–606. Retreat descriptions occur in Pope Pius XI, *Mens Nostra* (20 December 1929), in Claudia Carlen, I.H.M., ed., *The Papal Encyclicals: 1903–1939* ([Wilmington, N.C.]: McGrath Publishing Company, 1981), pp. 335–343. Also in Pius XII, *Menti Nostrae* (23 September 1950), #54, pp. 20–21, in *Selected Documents of His Holiness, Pope Pius XII.* For an overview of the twentieth-century retreat movement in the United States, see Chinnici, *Living Stones,* pp. 157–171. While the author does not consider the Lacouture movement itself, the chapter provides a helpful context. See also Thomas C. Hennessy, S.J., ed. *The Inner Crusade: The Closed Retreat in the United States* (Chicago: Loyola University Press, 1965).

2. Pius XI, *Quas Primas* (11 December 1925), #1, in Carlen, ed., *Papal Encyclicals: 1903–1939,* p. 271.

3. Pius XI, *Mens Nostra,* #4 in Carlen, ed. *Papal Encyclicals: 1903–1939,* p. 337. While Pius XI used the terms *retreats* and *spiritual exercises* interchangeably and affirmed the value of retreats in general, he especially

wished to promulgate the Ignatian form of the retreat. See for instance, ibid., #16, p. 341, where he reiterated his 1922 proclamation of Ignatius of Loyola as the patron of all retreats. The original promulgation occurred on 22 July 1922 in Pius XI's Apostolic Constitution, *Summorum Pontificum.*

4. *Mens Nostra,* #11, p. 340. On the extension of retreats to the laity, see ibid., #3, p. 336.

5. Ibid., #17, p. 342. On retreats for working people, see ibid., #12, p. 340. On days of recollection, see ibid., #17, pp. 341–342. Regarding retreats, Pius XII shared sentiments similar to those of Pius XI. See *Meditator Dei* (20 November 1947), ##178–181, in *Selected Documents of His Holiness, Pope Pius XII,* pp. 61–62.

6. General background on Lacouture obtained through John J. Hugo–Brigid Merriman interview, 18–19 November 1984. Other material in Dorothy Day, "Death of Father Onesimus Lacouture, S.J.," *CW* 18 (December 1951): 1, 6; Jean-Claude Drolet, "Un Mouvement de spiritualité sacerdotale au Québec au XXe siècle (1931–1965): Le Lacouturisme," *Canadian Catholic Historical Association: Study Sessions, 1973* (Ottawa, 1974): 55–87; Anselme Longpré, *Un Mouvement spirituel au Québec (1931–1962): au retour à l'Evangile* (Montreal: Fides, 1976); John J. Hugo, *Your Ways Are Not My Ways,* vol. 1 (Pittsburgh: Encounter With Silence, 1986). Translations from Longpré and Drolet are my own.

7. For Lacouture's own statistics on his 1931–1939 retreats to priests, see Longpré, *Un Mouvement spirituel,* pp. 67–73. These confirm and give the starting dates for the six retreats he presented in the United States: at Mount St. Charles, Woonsocket, Rhode Island (30 August 1937), at the Sulpician Seminary in Washington, D.C. (9 September 1937), at [St. Mary's] Seminary in Baltimore (5 September 1938 and 4 September 1939), at Notre Dame University, Indiana (11 June 1939) and to the Oblates of St. Francis de Sales in Philadelphia (13 July 1939). See Longpré, p. 37, for evidence that Lacouture preached periodically to religious and lay groups from 1931 to 1939.

8. The Ignatian week is to be understood as a flexible period of time. Most frequently it comprises a period approximating an actual week. Lacouture's retreat weeks consisted of eight full days. Comparison of Ignatius' and Lacouture's weeks obtained from *The Spiritual Exercises of St. Ignatius,* trans. Anthony Mottola (Garden City, N.Y.: Image Books, 1964) and an examination of Lacouture's notes, DD–CW, W–6, Box 3. Corroborated by Longpré, *Un Mouvement spirituel,* pp. 23–27.

9. See Lacouture's statistics in Longpré, *Un Mouvement spirituel,* pp. 67–73 and Longpré's comments, pp. 25–26. According to Drolet, "Un Mouvement de spiritualité sacerdotale," p. 62, Lacouture recommended that his retreatants make the first series several times before passing on to the others.

On p. 66 Drolet claimed that while Lacouture did not give the third series, he nonetheless outlined its general themes at every retreat that he offered.

10. Ignatian principle and foundation forms part of the first week. Quotation is from *Spiritual Exercises of St. Ignatius*, p. 47. For his doctrine on detachment, Lacouture depended not only on Ignatius but leaned heavily on John of the Cross, the latter having taught that a single voluntary attachment sufficed to block the Christian's way to perfect union with God. See comments in Longpré, *Un Mouvement spirituel*, pp. 27–29 on the consequences of loving Christ.

11. Longpré, ibid., p. 30.

12. Lacouture wrote out his retreat notes in greater detail during the 1940s as part of an effort to clear up misunderstandings. This is reported by John Hugo, *A Sign of Contradiction*, 2 vols. in 1 (New York: published privately by the author, 1947), pp. 109–112.

13. Longpré, *Un Mouvement spirituel*, pp. 42–43. Quoted phrase, p. 43, my translation. Excerpts of the October 1933 letter appear in Drolet, "Un Mouvement de spiritualité sacerdotale," p. 67.

14. Ibid., p. 44, my translation. Drolet, "Un Mouvement de spiritualité sacerdotale," p. 68, took a calmer view of the 1933 situation.

15. Anselme Longpré, "Que penser des retraites du Père Lacouture?" *Revue eucharistique du Clergé* (January 1936): 5, 6 [excerpts] in Longpré, *Un Mouvement spirituel*, pp. 41–42. Other excerpts were printed by Drolet. Translation is my own. The burning of the priests' cigarettes, disconnecting of radios and the like are to be taken figuratively.

16. Longpré, "Que penser des retraites," in Drolet, "Un Mouvement de spiritualité sacerdotale," p. 70. Drolet claimed that some bishops went so far as to impose the Lacouture retreat on all the priests in their dioceses and that quite likely this intensified the climate of uneasiness.

17. Lacouture noted that a six months' rest was imposed on him for the first half of 1938, at which time he visited the Holy Land. In Longpré, *Un Mouvement spirituel*, p. 70. Hugo, *Your Ways Are Not My Ways*, vol. 1, p. 298, considered this rest as part of the mounting opposition. Longpré, *Un Mouvement spirituel*, pp. 44–45, described the meeting of bishops and on pp. 45–46 noted in fairness to Antoniutti that in 1939 he thought the exile would be temporary. On restrictions placed upon Lacouture, see pp. 44, 53. Drolet, "Un Mouvement de spiritualité sacerdotale," p. 71, lists various locations after Santa Barbara to which Lacouture was assigned. This is in accord with Dorothy Day, "Death of Father Onesimus Lacouture, S.J.," *CW* 18 (December 1951): 6, and Hugo *Your Ways Are Not My Ways*, vol. 1, pp. 23–27, though there are minor discrepancies. Hugo noted, p. 25, that when at St. Regis, Lacouture was under the jurisdiction of his friend and supporter, Bishop Alfred Langlois.

18. Day, *Union Square to Rome*, pp. 25-27. A similar account appears in Day, *Long Loneliness*, pp. 23-24.

19. Day, *Long Loneliness*, p. 34.

20. Ibid., p. 244. Dorothy again recalled this retreat in 1978, though with less detail. See "On P," *CW* 44 (December 1978): 6. Dorothy noted on a number of occasions that Joseph P. McSorley, C.S.P., was her first spiritual advisor or director. See for instance, Day, *Loaves and Fishes*, pp. 123-124 and "On P," *CW* 32 (March 1966): 1. While summer 1933 marked her first formal retreat, Dorothy was positively disposed to the concept of a religious retreat through her pre-conversion reading. Noted in AIG fragm [Q]: ". . . long before I had become a Catholic . . . I had laughed with joy over the retreat or mission described in James Joyce's *Portrait of the Artist as a Young Man*. It has been long since I read it but I can still remember the thrill I had as I read through that incredible sermon."

21. [Dorothy Day] "C.W. Retreat" *CW* 7 (September 1939): 4. See Day, *Long Loneliness*, p. 245, regarding the early 1930s: "I did not think of retreats for a long time again." Despite Dorothy's protestation, at her encouragement Catholic Workers and their associates had already participated in weekend retreats and days of recollection given by priests such as Virgil Michel and Paul Hanly Furfey. Dorothy printed notices of other retreats in the *Catholic Worker* from its first year of publication. Some of these include: "K. of C. Distribute *Catholic Worker* at Manresa Retreat," *CW* 1 (July-August 1933): 3; "News from Manresa," *CW* 1 (September 1933): 3; "Montreal Seamen's Retreats Successful," *CW* 2 (January 1935): 5; "Towel Workers Retreat," *CW* 3 (October 1935): 1. A 1937 winter retreat sponsored by the Catholic Worker was advertised in "Msgr. Sheen to Conduct Retreat for Unemployed," *CW* 4 (February 1937): 2. The 1937 Benson retreat at Stirling, New Jersey, was advertised in "Catholic Worker One-Day Retreat," *CW* 5 (July 1937): 1. Reviewed in James F. Montague, "Farming Commune," *CW* 5 (Aug 1937): 4. Reports of Catholic Worker retreats in other cities include: "Chi CW Holds Retreat, Makes Plea for Poor," *CW* 5 (October 1937): 2; "Washington Group Hears Fr. Furfey, Holds Retreats," *CW* 5 (November 1937): 2. Prior to the 1939 Benson retreat, Dorothy had sent out a letter to all the houses encouraging all Catholic Workers to attend the three-day event at the CW farm in Easton. Letter in question is Dorothy Day to Fellow Workers in Christ, 25 July 1939, DD-CW, W-4.2, Box 1: "I cannot urge you strongly enough, to make every effort to be with us."

22. [Dorothy Day] "C.W. Retreat," *CW* 7 (September 1939): 4. Dorothy tried to bring Christ to others in many ways, including the promotion of a one-day retreat specifically for men on the New York breadline. See "Retreat on Mott Street," *CW* 7 (June 1940): 6.

23. I have used primary materials as much as possible. However, sec-

ondary sources have been consulted regularly. In the present instance, these include: Miller, *A Harsh and Dreadful Love;* Miller, *Dorothy Day;* William D. Miller, *All Is Grace* (Garden City, N.Y.: Doubleday, 1987). Miller's use of and interpretation of primary materials regarding the retreat and other items of interest contain a number of chronological and factual errors. This is unfortunate, because several other writers have accepted him as a reliable authority.

24. Quotation from Day, *Long Loneliness,* p. 246. In AIG fragm [R] and in Day, *Long Loneliness,* pp. 245–246, she recalled the Saey retreat which Ward attended. Dorothy generally used an emphasized form for her term *the retreat* when referring to the Lacouture retreat, to distinguish it from all others. This she adopted from Pacifique Roy, S.S.J. See ibid., p. 254.

25. On Roy's responsibility for bringing Lacouture to the United States, see Hugo, *Your Ways Are Not My Ways,* vol. 1, p. 236 and Day, *Long Loneliness,* p. 246. Pacifique Roy to Dorothy Day, 6 February 1940, DD–CW, D–1.1, Box 10. See Miller, *Dorothy Day,* p. 336, on Dorothy's 19 June 1940 journal entry relative to Roy. Dorothy Day to Bishop Francis A. McIntyre, 6 March 1942, DD–CW, W–6, Box 3: "He [Roy] has been my spiritual adviser [*sic*] since I met him in August, 1940." On Roy's early association with the Catholic Worker group, see Day, *Long Loneliness,* pp. 246–254. On p. 250, she identified this with the year 1939. Though stationed in Mobile from 1936 to summer 1940, Sister Fahy traveled frequently and often stayed at her Philadelphia motherhouse and other locales in the northeast. For Dorothy's remarks on the 1940 Labor Day weekend retreat, see [Dorothy Day] "CW Holds '40 Retreat at Easton," *CW* 7 (September 1940): 1, 2; Dorothy Day, "What Dream Did They Dream? Utopia or Suffering?" *CW* 14 (July–August 1947): 1, 4, 6, 8.

26. Evidence for Sister Fahy's summer 1940 transfer from Mobile to Gillette, New Jersey found in Onesimus Lacouture, S.J., to Peter Claver Fahy, 16 July 1940, DD–CW, D–1.1, Box 10. Growing confidence in Lacouture seen in Dorothy Day "Views and News," *CW* 8 (January 1941): 4; "DAD," *CW* 8 (February 1941): 1, 4; publication of Onesimus Lacouture, "Thoughts on Poverty," *CW* 8 (April 1941): 1, 3.

27. Dorothy Day, "Requiem for Father Roy," *CW* 21 (November 1954): 1, 6. Similar accounts of Pacifique Roy's contacts with the Catholic Worker may be found in Day, *Long Loneliness,* pp. 246–254; Day, *Loaves and Fishes,* pp. 124–130.

28. Day, *Long Loneliness,* p. 254; Day, "Requiem for Father Roy," *CW* 21 (November 1954): 6. I accept the accuracy of Dorothy's testimony, even though Sister Fahy claimed credit for sending Dorothy to Hugo. Fahy testimony in Sister Peter Claver–Marc Ellis interview, June 1978, DD–CW, W–9, Box 1 and Sister Peter Claver, "Reminiscence" presented at "The Catholic Worker: Fifty Years," conference at Holy Cross College, Worcester, Massachusetts, 1–

2 May 1983. Reminiscence transcript obtained from John J. Hugo, 18 November 1984. Internal evidence strongly suggests that Sister Fahy's recall here is faulty. Sister Fahy repeated her testimony in her 20 April 1985 notes given to William D. Miller. See Miller, *All Is Grace,* p. 41.

29. Sources include Hugo-Merriman interview, 18–19 November 1984; J. J. Hugo, "Chronology: Father John J. Hugo," given to me by the author; Hugo, *Your Ways are Not My Ways,* vol. 1, passim. See John J. Hugo, *Applied Christianity* (New York: privately printed [Catholic Worker press], 1944).

30. "DAD," *CW* 8 (July–August 1941): 3.

31. Dorothy Day, *On Pilgrimage* (New York: Catholic Worker Books, 1948), p. 157, and AIG fragm [N]. Variants in Day, *On Pilgrimage,* p. 39; Day, *Long Loneliness,* p. 139; "On P.," *CW* 32 (December 1965): 2.

32. Dorothy Day to Catholic Workers, 22 July 1941, DD–CW, W–4.2, Box 1. Her stance echoes Pius XI in *Mens Nostra.*

33. "DAD," *CW* 8 (September 1941): 1, 3.

34. John J. Hugo, "In the Vineyard," a ten-part series (later issued as a pamphlet), printed in *CW* 8 and 9, September 1941 through July–August 1942. John J. Hugo, "The Weapons of the Spirit," a six-part series (later issued as a pamphlet), printed in *CW* 9 and 10, November 1942 through April 1943. John J. Hugo, "Catholics Can Be Conscientious Objectors," *CW* 10 (May 1943): 6–8 and *CW* 10 (June 1943): 6–9. John J. Hugo, "The Superficial 'Realist,'" *CW* 10 (July–August 1943): 4. John J. Hugo, "The Gospel of Peace," a seven-part series (later issued as a pamphlet), printed in *CW* 10 and 11, September 1943 through April 1944. John J. Hugo, "Going My Way," *CW* 11 (July–August 1944): 1, 6. John J. Hugo, "The Immorality of Conscription," *CW* 11 (November 1944): 3–10; reprinted in *CW* 12 (March 1945): 3–10 and *CW* 14 (April 1948): 3–10. John J. Hugo, "Conscience Vindicated," *CW* 12 (April 1945): 1–3. John J. Hugo, "Peace without Victory," *CW* 12 (September 1945): 1, 2, 8. John J. Hugo, "Fathers of the Modern Desert" also titled "A Father of the Modern Desert," a four-part series, printed in *CW* 12 and 13, October 1945 through March 1946.

35. Lacouture in "DAD," *CW* 9 (April 1942): 4. Lacouture's experiences with the poor included his work among the Eskimos and the native Americans of Eastern Canada. Sample references to Hugo and sharing of her own interpretations include "DAD," *CW* 8 (October 1941): 7; "DAD," *CW* 9 (January 1942): 4; [Dorothy Day] "Stephen Hergenhan," *CW* 9 (March 1942): 6, 8. See Onesimus Lacouture, S.J., "On War," *CW* 9 (November 1941): 1, 2.

36. "DAD," *CW* 9 (April 1942): 4. "DAD," *CW* 10 (December 1942): 6. Hugo's transfer to St. Mary's, Kittanning, was effective 15 October 1942. This is confirmed by his own *vita,* given to me on 18 November 1984, though in some accounts Hugo mistakenly gave fall 1944 as the time of his transfer. The *Official Catholic Directory,* 1943, p. 1058, confirms that Hugo was al-

ready stationed at Kittanning. Tamar had been pressing her mother for an early marriage but reluctantly agreed to wait until after her eighteenth birthday (4 March 1944).

37. Oliver Lynch, O.F.M.–Brigid Merriman interview, 15 May 1984. Oliver Lynch, a Franciscan of the St. Barbara province, spoke before his death of the powerful impact the Lacouture retreat had on members of the clergy. He himself was much impressed with the evangelical nature of the retreat in an era when Catholic teaching was predominantly apologetic rather than scripturally oriented. During the Hugo-Merriman interview, 18–19 November 1984, Hugo recalled that he and Farina had worked as a team at Oakmont. Apparently Hugo's presence dominated, for in "On P," *CW* 26 (November 1959): 8, Dorothy recalled Farina giving retreats at Oakmont only after Hugo was stopped from doing so. Dorothy's notes for her 18–25 July 1943 retreat are available in AIG, pp. 1–81. Quotation is from AIG, p. 15. Dorothy published an expanded version of her notes for the first day of this retreat in D[orothy] Day, "On Retreat," *CW* 10 (July–August 1943): 2, 3. Internal evidence strongly suggests that she also incorporated some of her 1941 and 1942 retreat notes in the article. While access to Dorothy's total retreat notes is presently restricted, available materials provide ample resources for research. In AIG, pp. 76–77, Dorothy noted that she had entertained the idea of time away from the CW for several years. Day, *House of Hospitality,* pp. 100–101, indicates a previous feeling that she was engaged in too much activity and too little prayer.

38. "DAD," *CW* 10 (September 1943): 1, 2, 6. Quotation from p. 2. While the idea of the leave was formed during her July retreat, it is likely that Dorothy conferred with Hugo during her visit with him at Kittanning on 25 July 1943 and with Maurin when he returned to New York after his 29 August–4 September 1943 retreat in Oakmont. For confirmation of Maurin's presence at the week conducted by Farina, see David Mason, "Hegira with Peter," *CW* 10 (September 1943): 8.

39. Dorothy recorded notes from the 11 July 1943 day of recollection with Thomas Verner Moore, then a Benedictine, in AIG, pp. 258–262. See her reference to the same Moore conferences in "DAD," *CW* 10 (September 1943): 1. Moore, formerly a Paulist who later became a Benedictine and then a Carthusian, was a good friend of Paulist Joseph McSorley, an early advisor of Dorothy's. Her experiences at the Grail in September 1943 are recorded in "NBTW," *CW* 10 (October 1943): 1, 2 and AIG, pp. 268–294.

40. On Dorothy's stay at Farmingdale, see Dorothy Day, "And for Our Absent Brethren," *CW* 10 (December 1943): 2, 3. On the 19 April 1944 wedding, see "NBTW," *CW* 11 (May 1944): 1, 2. In Dorothy Day to Nina Polcyn, 24 August 1944, DD–CW, W–17, Box 1 and "DBD," *CW* 11 (November 1944): 2, Dorothy recalled spending the month of May at the Grail in

Foster, Ohio. May 1944 notes in AIG, pp. 298–299, with quotation from p. 299.

41. There is strong external and internal evidence that a complete version of Dorothy's notes for the 2–8 July 1944 retreat may be obtained by combining AIG fragm [W], numbered pp. 57–86, with AIG, pp. 81–166. Quotation is from AIG, p. 117. The dilemma Dorothy felt is most evident in the first segment. See Appendix for details on the AIG collection.

42. AIG, p. 93, where Dorothy named Father [George] Garrelts as one of the priests who faulted her for concentrating on the material. Her preoccupation with an integration between the retreat and land movements is evident in her AIG notes for 4, 5, and 6 July [1944]. On p. 128 (6 July), she queried: "How can this retreat be preached without 'Land Movement'[?]" The conference on Martha and Mary was presented on Thursday evening, 6 July 1944. Quotation is from p. 132.

43. Dorothy remarked on her activities in the interim between the two retreats in AIG, p. 166. These included a visit to Hugo, to friends in Pittsburgh, and an afternoon meeting with Bishop Hugh C. Boyle of Pittsburgh. It is likely that the meeting with Boyle provided Dorothy with an opportunity for one of her frequent requests that Hugo be permitted again to give retreats to the Catholic Worker group. Dorothy's notes for the 16–22 July 1944 retreat found in AIG, pp. 166–213. Quotation is from pp. 173–174.

44. Quotation from Day, *House of Hospitality,* p. 159; internal evidence indicates that this passage represents an unedited diary entry from summer 1936. Dorothy Day to Nina Polcyn, 24 August 1944, DD–CW, W–17, Box 1, which includes her comment on Roy. Retreat date confirmed by [Dorothy Day], "The Catholic Worker Retreat House," *CW* 11 (October 1944): 2. This issue marked Dorothy's return as editor and publisher of the paper. That retreat master was Father [Joseph] Meenan of Pittsburgh derived from Cletus J. Benjamin, vice-chancellor of Philadelphia, to Dorothy Day, 4 September 1944. This and following 5 items in DD–CW, W–4.2, Box 1. Evidence for fact that manual labor was part of the retreat horarium in Dorothy Day to Fellowworkers (*sic*) in Christ, 1 March [1945]; Dorothy Day to Father [Francis M.] Ott, 15 October 1945; Maryfarm at Easton Retreat schedule, 1946; Maryfarm at Newburgh Retreat brochure, spring and summer, 1948; Dorothy Day to Catholic Workers [8 September] 1948, p. 3. For published reference, see [Dorothy Day] "The Catholic Worker Retreat House," *CW* 11 (October 1944): 2.

45. See Dorothy Day, "The Eightieth Birthday of Don Sturzo," *CW* 18 (December 1951): 7.

46. "DBD," *CW* 11 (November 1944): 1, indicates that Roy was working at the Easton farm and probably already residing there. Dorothy Day to Rev. Casserly, Provincial, 15 January 1945, DD–CW, W–6, Box 3, indicates

that Roy had been at Easton for some time. Tributes to and remembrances of Roy at Easton may be found in Dorothy Day, "Requiem for Father Roy," *CW* 21 (November 1954): 1, 6; Day, *Loaves and Fishes,* pp. 124–130. Compare with Stanley Vishnewski, "Life in Community," *Catholic World* 185 (August 1957): 346–351. On difficulties at the Easton farm and the move to Newburgh, see Day, *Long Loneliness,* pp. 259–263. Both farms were christened "Maryfarm." On the move to Newburgh, see "Retreats," *CW* 13 (February 1947): 1. Dissension due to demands of married couples also haunted the group at Newburgh and came to a head in 1948. Dorothy addressed and took firm measures to resolve the issue, September 1948. Evidence in Dorothy Day to Catholic Workers [8 September] 1948, DD–CW, W–4.2, Box 1.

47. Quotation from Dorothy Day to Bishop [J. Francis A.] McIntyre, 20 July 1942. Except where indicated, all items in this note from DD–CW, W–6, Box 3. Other indications of Dorothy's consultations for the proposed retreat center for priests include: Day to McIntyre [New York], 6 March 1942; McIntyre to Day, 14 March 1942; Day to McIntyre, 20 March 1942; McIntyre to Day, 3 August 1942; Day to Father Benjamin, chancellor [Philadelphia], 30 September 1944; Day to Casserly, provincial, 15 January 1945; Day to Bishop [Hugh C.] Boyle [Pittsburgh], 24 October 1945; Boyle to Day, 3 November 1945; Cletus J. Benjamin, chancellor, to DD, 19 November 1945, DD–CW, W–4.2, Box 1; "A Proposed Retreat House for Priests," undated; "Plan Suggestions," undated, DD–CW, W–6.4, Box 1. Dorothy also corresponded with Lacouture on this matter, as in Lacouture to Day, 22 March 1942, DD–CW, D–1.1, Box 6.

48. Quotation from "On P," *CW* 13 (May 1946): 2. Pacifique Roy to Dorothy Day, 26 and 30 March 1944, DD–CW, D–1.1, Box 10. The French edition, circulating in Canada, first appeared in 1943. See Longpré, *Un Mouvement spirituel,* p. 46, n. 13. Gift to Cardinal Dougherty acknowledged in Joseph J. McGlinn, secretary to the archbishop, to Dorothy Day, 21 December 1945, DD–CW, W–2.2, Box 1. The work in question is Norbert Robichaud, *Holiness for All,* trans. by a member of the Congregation of the Brothers of Christian Schools (Westminster, Md.: Newman Bookshop, 1945). From information given in Roy to Day, 31 August 1944, DD–CW, D–1.1., Box 10, Christian Brother Luke probably translated the work. See [Dorothy Day] "Called to Be Saints; Or Go to Hell," *CW* 12 (January 1946), 2, where she first remarked on Robichaud's book. Norbert Robichaud, "Holiness for All," *CW* 13 (February 1946): 4; Norbert Robichaud, "Holiness for All—The Model for Holiness: Jesus Christ," *CW* 13 (April 1946): 4.

49. Extended quotation from "On P," *CW* 14 (April 1948): 11. See Barbara Fry, "Retreat Houses, Religious and Lay," *Blackfriars* [Supplement] 47 (March 1946): 44–49. "On P," *CW* 13 (June 1946): 2. [Dorothy Day] "Retreats," *CW* 13 (February 1947): 1; "On P," *CW* 13 (February 1947): 2. After

her return from Montreal and Sudbury, Dorothy wrote to Lacouture, who responded in Lacouture to Day, 8 February 1947, DD–CW, D–1.1, Box 6. On Dorothy's retreat at New Kensington, see "On P," *CW* 14 (September 1947): 2.

50. "On P," *CW* 18 (September 1952): 6.

51. Instances of Dorothy's appeals to Bishop Boyle occur in Day to Boyle, 24 October 1945, DD–CW, W–6, Box 3; Day to Boyle, 19 April [1946], DD–CW, W–6, Box 3. She referred to one of these appeals in AIG fragm [1]. On the Hugo conference recordings—audiotape and phonodisc—see Dorothy Day, "Peter Maurin Farm," *CW* 20 (April 1954): 5. The Hugo days of recollection were scheduled at the Maurin farm on Staten Island. Confirmed by Hugo in Hugo-Merriman interview, 18–19 November 1984.

52. Jane O'Donnell, "Maryfarm," *CW* 16 (February 1950): 3. On the disposal of Newburgh and the completed move to the Maurin farm, see "On P," *CW* 21 (June 1955): 1; "On P," *CW* 22 (July-August 1955): 3. Cited recollection in [Dorothy Day] "Fr. Paul Judge," *CW* 22 (November 1955): 3.

53. Dorothy Day, "Death of Father Onesimus Lacouture, S.J.," *CW* 18 (December 1951): 6, which indicates that Catholic Worker retreats were open to non-Catholics.

54. Hugo, *Applied Christianity*, 1944. Dorothy frequently referred to this work as "Fr. Hugo's notes of Fr. Lacouture's retreat." One such instance is Day to Rev. Casserly, provincial, 15 January 1945, DD–CW, W–6, Box 3.

55. Extant letters from Lacouture to Day include: 16 January 1941; [between July–November 1941]; 28 February 1942; 22 March 1942; 21 April 1942; 2 July 1942; 28 February 1945; 8 February 1947; 11 May 1950; 26 November 1950. Quotation is from the 11 May 1950 letter. These letters, DD–CW, D–1.1, Box 6. The Catholic Worker location in Baltimore was an interracial house; racial prejudice led to its closing. Extant correspondence with Pacifique Roy provides evidence that Dorothy was familiar with a good deal more of the Canadian controversy than she wrote of publicly. For instance, Roy to Day, 16 January 1942, DD–CW, D–1.1, Box 10, mentioned that he was sending her fifty copies of the 30 August 1941 letter of Archbishop Philippe Desranleau of Sherbrooke to Sulpician R. Lesieur, superior of the major seminary in Montreal. The complete French text of this letter, supportive of Lacouture, is printed in Longpré, *Un Mouvement spirituel*, pp. 75–80.

56. Quoted phrase, originally Maurin's, used by Dorothy in Day to Father [William R.] O'Connor, 15 October 1945, DD–CW, W–4.2, Box 1. See Francis J. Connell, C.SS.R., review of *Applied Christianity* by John J. Hugo, in *American Ecclesiastical Review* 113 (July 1945): 69–72. "NBTW," *CW* 12 (October 1945): 2, encouraged readers to write to CW staff to receive a copy of Hugo's response to the Connell article. That Dorothy continued to follow the controversy is certain; however, evidence has not shown that she read all the major articles and Hugo's responses in full. On a number of occasions

Dorothy alluded to a felt lack of competence in addressing the controversy directly. Two of these are Day, *On Pilgrimage*, p. 65; Day, *Long Loneliness*, p. 258.

57. Quotations from Dorothy Day, "What Dream Did They Dream? Utopia or Suffering?" *CW* 14 (July–August 1947): 4, 6, respectively. Interviews with persons variously associated with the Catholic Worker indicate a wide range of perceptions regarding the Lacouture movement. Transcripts, DD–CW, W–9, Boxes 1 and 2. Some of these include: Mary Durnin–Deane Mowrer interview, n.d.; Durnin was positively disposed to the retreat. Karl Stern–Deane Mowrer interview, July 1968; Stern, a convert-friend of Dorothy's who lived in Canada, appears not to have made the retreat, but was knowledgeable of its history. He noted that Dorothy was not one to engage in controversy. Stanley Vishnewski–Deane Mowrer interview, 1969; Vishnewski, who was himself negative toward the retreat, nonetheless attempted to give it a fair assessment. Caroline Gordon [Tate]–Deane Mowrer interview, 19 May 1970; Gordon, who made retreats directed by Fathers Marion Casey and John Hugo, accepted the retreat without question. Ade Bethune–Nancy L. Roberts interview, 26 April 1983; Bethune made at least one retreat with Hugo at Easton. While she vigorously opposed the asceticism preached by the retreat, she did observe that Dorothy "got the good out of it and she quit smoking." The outspoken Bethune was open with Hugo about her reservations. Written examples include: Ade Bethune to Father Hugo, 23 February 1942; Ade Bethune to Father Hugo, 27 March 1942. Both letters, DD–CW, W–2.2, Box 1.

58. Dorothy Day, "What Dream Did They Dream? Utopia or Suffering?" *CW* 14 (July–August 1947): 1, 4, 6, 8. Extended quotation is from p. 4. On 18 April 1948, Dorothy commented on the continuing retreat controversy in her journal. This was later printed, along with a lengthy excerpt from John J. Hugo, *Sign of Contradiction* (privately printed by the author, 1947), pp. 115–125, in Day, *On Pilgrimage*, pp. 65–74. Her comments on the controversy which reached a wider audience may be found in Day, *Long Loneliness*, pp. 258–259.

59. Extended quotation from Dorothy Day, "Meditation" [n.d.], DD–CW, D.3, Box 7. For shorter passages see Dorothy Day, "Death of Father Onesimus Lacouture, S.J.," *CW* 18 (December 1951): 6, and Dorothy Day, "Requiem for Father Roy," *CW* 21 (November 1954): 6, respectively.

60. "On P," *CW* 26 (September 1959): 2, 6. In this article, the Benedictine was referred to as Fr. Menard of Mt. Saviour. In Elizabeth Rogers, "Peter Maurin Farm," *CW* 26 (October 1959): 8, the priest was referred to as Father Peter Minard. He is the same as Pierre Minard, O.S.B., listed in the *National Catholic Directory*, 1959, p. 625. He and CW friends Placid J. Cormey, O.S.B., and Damasus Winzen, O.S.B., were then attached to Mount Saviour monastery in Elmira, New York. [Cormey incorrectly listed as Corney in *Official Catholic*

Directory for 1959 and 1960. Correctly listed as Cormey in ibid., 1961, p. 636.] See Beth Rogers, "Peter Maurin Farm," *CW* 22 (November 1955): 2; "On P," *CW* 22 (December 1955): 6. Notice of 17–22 June retreat in "Retreat in June," *CW* 22 (June 1956): 6; on Dorothy's preparation for this retreat, see "On P," *CW* 23 (July-August 1956): 7. For dates of summer 1957 retreats, see "Retreats," *CW* 23 (June 1957): 1. It is likely that Dorothy was unable to participate in any retreats that summer because of events following her third annual protest on 12 July 1957, during the civil defense drill. See "Dorothy Day among Pacifists Jailed," *CW* Special Edition (17 July 1957). Dorothy's twenty-five-day internment in July and August with other pacifists is recorded in Dorothy Day, "Vocation to Prison," *CW* 24 (September 1957): 1, 2, 6. Stanley Vishnewski, "Peter Maurin Farm," *CW* 25 (December 1958): 8. On the 1959 de Foucauld retreat, see Dorothy Day, "Retreat," *CW* 26 (August 1959): 2, 7, 8.

61. AIG fragm [N]; "On P," *CW* 23 (January 1957): 8. On her journey to a 1960 retreat in Montreal, see "On P," *CW* 27 (September 1960): 2. For the 1961 retreat, see "On P," *CW* 28 (September 1961): 3; "On P," *CW* 28 (October 1961): 2.

62. On the sale of Peter Maurin farm and for her quoted hopes for Tivoli, see "On P," *CW* 30 (January 1964): 8. A good assessment of Peter Maurin farm found in Day, *Loaves and Fishes,* p. 200. See "The Retreat," *CW* 28 (May 1962): 2; further information given in "Retreat," *CW* 29 (July–August 1962): 2. The retreats were the week of 5 July 1962 and 26 August –1 September 1962. The 1963 Casey retreat was announced in "Retreat," *CW* 29 (June 1963): 3; "On P," *CW* 30 (September 1963): 6, confirms that Dorothy made this retreat. Her notes form a part of AIG fragm [4], in which she remarked that the retreat lasted from Monday evening through Saturday morning. By piecing together information from this document and the one previously cited, the dates of the retreat may be determined as 22–27 July 1963. Hugo mentioned in "On P," *CW* 30 (December 1963): 2.

63. Quotation, "On P," *CW* 31 (September 1964): 8. On the 1964 Casey retreat, see "On P," *CW* 30 (May 1964): 8. Dorothy Day to Nina Polcyn, 17 July 1964, DD–CW, W–17, Box 1, for the "great news" of Hugo's retreat.

64. Quotation from "On P," *CW* 34 (July–August 1968): 8. On Hugo's 1965 retreats at Tivoli, see Dean Mary Mowrer, "Farm with a View," *CW* 31 (July–August 1965): 5. On Hugo's 19–25 June 1966 retreat at Tivoli, see "Summer Conferences, 1966," *CW* 32 (June 1966): 7; Dean Mary Mowrer, "A Farm with a View," *CW* 32 (July-August 1966): 8; Day to Nina Polcyn, 19 July 1966, DD–CW, W–17, Box 1, where Dorothy noted, "A young priest from Chicago, only ordained a year, came to our retreat—don't know whether he got much." For the proposed 1967 retreat at Coylesville and Dorothy's comments on recent retreats at Tivoli, see "On P," *CW* 33 (May 1967): 10. Hugo's perspective on the 1966 retreat given in Hugo-Miller interview, 1976, DD–CW, W–9, Box 1

and Hugo, *Your Ways Are Not My Ways,* vol. 1, pp. 222–225. Cancellation notice of 1967 Coylesville retreat given in "On P.," *CW* 33 (June 1967): 8. Other information on the 30 June–6 July 1968 Lombardi retreat at the Redemptorist retreat house, Long Branch, in DD–CW, D–5, Box 2. According to Felix Zubillaga, S.J., "The Church in Latin America," in *History of the Church,* ed. H. Jedin, et al., vol. 10, p. 682, the "Movement for a Better World" was initiated by Riccardo Lombardi, S.J., in 1960. Its goal was to provide assistance to all persons engaged in church-related ministry. In later years, Dorothy frequently compared other spiritual renewal movements to the Lacouture retreat. In addition to the Lombardi Better World movement, these included the Pentecostal or Charismatic movement and the Cursillo. Dorothy saw a resemblance between the Lacouture and Pentecostal movements because of their emphasis on Scripture. One of Dorothy's references to the Pentecostal movement occurs in "July 30" [after 1975], DD–CW, D–3, Box 7. The Cursillo, or "Little Course in Christianity," she considered an extension of the retreat, insofar as it developed the experience of community living beyond the time spent in retreat. Two of her references to the Cursillo occur in AIG fragm [Q & U].

65. Quotation from Dorothy's editorial comment, p. 4, which was printed with John J. Hugo, "Thy Will Be Done," *CW* 34 (December 1968): 4, 5. On Casey's summer 1967 conferences, see Deane Mary Mowrer, "A Farm with a View," *CW* 33 (July-August 1967): 3. On his winter visits, see Deane Mary Mowrer, "Tivoli: A Farm with a View," *CW* 34 (January 1968): 3; *CW* 34 (November 1968): 3. On Plante's extended stays with the Catholic Worker group, see Deane Mary Mowrer, "Tivoli: Farm with a View," *CW* 34 (January 1968): 3; *CW* 34 (April 1968): 6; *CW* 34 (December 1968): 3; *CW* 35 (January 1969): 3; *CW* 35 (March–April 1969): 3; *CW* 35 (May 1969): 6. John J. Hugo, *Love Strong as Death: A Study in Christian Ethics* (New York: Vantage Press, 1969), appeared serially before publication as John J. Hugo, "Love Strong as Death," *CW* 34 (October 1968): 4, 6; "The Plan of Salvation," *CW* 34 (November 1968): 4, 5; "Thy Will Be Done," *CW* 34 (December 1968): 4, 5; "Transformation through Holiness," *CW* 35 (January 1969): 5; "Nature and Grace," *CW* 35 (February 1969): 4; "A Time for Pruning," *CW* 35 (March–April 1969): 4; "The Wheat and the Vine," *CW* 35 (May 1969): 4; "Life and Holiness," *CW* 35 (June 1969): 4. Though the language and themes of *Love Strong as Death* bore the strong imprint of the retreat, its only direct link with it—and that an implicit one—lay in its dedication: "to the memory of a beloved teacher, Onesimus Lacouture, S.J."

66. Quotation from "On P.," *CW* 41 (January 1975): 1, 2; it is based on her diary entries for December 1974. Mention of some priests formerly associated with the Lacouture movement include: "On P.," *CW* 37 (December 1971): 2, where she remarked happily on a current meeting with Franciscan

Father Alan McCoy and his involvement with the retreat in the "golden era" of the 1940s; Day to Hugo, 15 November [1972], DD–CW, W–6.4, Box 1, in which she informed him of Monsignor [Dominic J.] Fiorentino's recent death; "On P," *CW* 40 (March–April 1974): 8, where she remarked on a recent visit to Franciscan Father Denis Mooney's grave in Washington, D.C., "remembering gratefully the retreats [retreat?] he gave us in Pittsburgh. . . ." Regarding Dorothy's use of retreat language, Day to Nina Polcyn Moore, 5 November 1974, DD–CW, W–17, Box 1, on pain involved in Christian detachment, is but a single instance. Dorothy participated in a "Withdraw and Renew" retreat led by Douglas V. Steere at Rye, New York, 19–21 February 1971; information found in Dorothy's annotated copy of program and schedule notes, DD–CW, D–5, Box 2. On the 17–20 December 1975 retreat as a guest of Dominican nuns, see "On P," *CW* 41 (January 1975): 2.

67. "On P," *CW* 42 (September 1976): 2. For Hugo's recall of August 1976, see John J. Hugo, *Your Ways Are Not My Ways,* vol. 1, pp. 225–228. The present writer participated in the revived Lacouture retreat, presented by John J. Hugo, 11–18 November 1984, at the same location (Sisters of the Holy Family of Nazareth Motherhouse) as Dorothy's 1976 retreat.

68. See Appendix for retreat and conference directors, dating of events, and division of the AIG manuscript and AIG fragments, based on a close study of the manuscripts.

69. For her 1945 announcement, see "NBTW," *CW* 12 (October 1945): 2. A notation on the AIG manuscript indicates that it was deposited at Marquette University archives on 22 September 1975. The AIG fragment collection was later pulled together by archivist Phillip M. Runkel and consists of retreat-related fragments of Dorothy's writings which had been sent to the archives over the years. When taken together, the AIG fragments comprise approximately as much text as the lengthy AIG manuscript. In a good portion of the AIG fragments, Dorothy gave a synopsis both of the history of the Lacouture movement as well as her introduction to it. They offer variant accounts and differing levels of completion, but in essentials agree with one another. In the AIG fragments Dorothy frequently referred to writing what she variously termed, her spiritual adventures, her spiritual autobiography, or "All Is Grace." Of the thirty-five fragments in the present collection — I exclude fragment W which I believe belongs to the larger manuscript — only four offer no positive clues for dating, but these too were most likely written prior to 1975. AIG fragm [11] appears to be her last formal attempt at writing "All Is Grace" and may be positively dated 27 February 1975. Extant letters, written between 27 December 1963 and 8 July 1965, DD–CW, D–3.6, from Eugene Exman and Erik A. Langkjaer, both of Harper and Row publishers, to Dorothy reveal that she was then under contract to write "All Is Grace"; her own comments in Dorothy Day to "Dearly Beloved" (Occasional Letter),

January 1973 — found on reverse side of Day to Bill [William D. Miller], n.d.— indicate that she was still under contract to write another book; "All Is Grace" is the most likely effort. All Day-Miller correspondence cited in this note, is found in C–1.7, 2–WDM. In Day to William D. Miller, Ash Wednesday [12 February], 1975, she still spoke of writing "a real or a spiritual autobiography." In Day to William D. Miller, 10 April 1975, she hinted that "with your help, I could have another book with little effort." Miller visited Dorothy in May 1975, at which time she left with him materials related to "All Is Grace," to be deposited eventually at Marquette. See Miller, *All Is Grace,* pp. 1–4. Nothing more came of the materials, even though Dorothy was still concerned about her inability to complete the project. In Day to Miller, 26 January 1976 and 10 June 1976 she referred to diary pages from her notebooks, which Miller's daughter Carol Miller had promised to type. In the 26 January letter Dorothy called them "notes for a continued autobiography which I will do myself." These notes are distinct from the present AIG manuscript and AIG fragments. There is no evidence available to suggest that Dorothy did anything with the materials referred to in the 1976 Miller correspondence.

70. AIG fragm [1].

71. Quotation from AIG fragm [V]. The same fragment shows Dorothy's awareness that Bernanos used the words at the end of one of his novels [*The Diary of a Country Priest*], and that he in turn derived them from the saint of Lisieux. Both the lengthy AIG manuscript and the AIG fragments reveal Dorothy's wide interest. The scriptural text is from Romans 8:28.

72. Quotation from "On P," *CW* 31 (September 1964): 2. The words apparently struck Dorothy anew. It was not Dorothy's first exposure to the *Testament,* since she read Jörgensen's life of Francis in the 1920s. She had printed a nearly identical quotation from the *Testament* as early as *CW* 5 (April 1938): 7. Dorothy's hesitation in writing of priests and her desire to edify is noted in AIG fragm [1], although Dorothy wrote of priests in nearly every fragment. While she was attracted to Lacouture, Abbé Saey, and Father Paul Judge because of their loving identification with the poor, Dorothy found instances where those who preached warmly of the love of God appeared rigid or haughty in their own dealings with others. Sources: AIG fragm [A & Q]. Dorothy noted men who preached identification with Christ in suffering who nonetheless balked at the criticism directed at them during the retreat controversy. This was particularly true of Hugo, whom she felt to be defensive and proud, though she did credit him with some mellowing in later years. Source: AIG fragm [Y]. She felt the dichotomy of priests who preached detachment yet lived lives of bourgeois comfort. Sources: AIG fragm [1 & E].

73. Quotation from AIG fragm [N]. Dorothy frequently emphasized priests' ministry of preaching to the laity, the need for priests to believe both in the laity's call to holiness and in the laity's ability to become holy. Instances

include: AIG fragms [K, N, Q]. For Dorothy's recollection of Mooney, see Brackley and Dillon, "Interview with Dorothy Day," p. 8. Though the priest's name was printed as Dennis Rooney, the reference is unmistakably to Denis Mooney, O.F.M.

74. AIG fragm [U].

75. Sister Peter Claver Fahy — Marc Ellis interview, June 1978, DD–CW, W–9, Box 1.

76. One instance where Dorothy acknowledged her debt to Dostoevsky's writings may be found in "On P," *CW* 39 (May 1973): 8. Here she noted, "I do not think I could have carried on with a loving heart all these years without Dostoyevsky's understanding of poverty, suffering and drunkenness. The drunken father of Sonya in *Crime and Punishment,* the story Grushenka told in *The Brothers Karamazov* about the depraved sinner 'who gave away an onion,' the little tailor who took in the honest thief, sharing his corner of a room — all of this helped me to an understanding of St. Paul's 'folly of the cross' . . ." The Lacouture retreat was also termed the "folly of the cross" retreat.

77. Day, "A Human Document," *Sign* 12 (November 1932): 224. Though Dorothy ceased living with Forster Batterham after her conversion, she continued to love him and maintained contact with him in later years. She comforted him and assisted in nursing Nanette, his second common-law wife, during her terminal illness with cancer (fall 1959 through January 1960). Dorothy wrote of this period in AIG fragm [3]. Also referred to by Caroline Gordon in Gordon–Dean Mary Mowrer interview, 19 May 1970, DD–CW, W–9, Box 1; Miller, *Dorothy Day,* pp. 457–459.

78. The two accounts of Roy's teaching include Day, *Long Loneliness,* pp. 246–251; Dorothy Day, "Requiem for Father Roy," *CW* 21 (November 1954): 1, 6. Quotation about putting on Christ and being united to her love in Day, *Long Loneliness,* p. 149. In the early 1970s, Robert Coles engaged Dorothy in conversation on the importance of this passage to her. See Coles, *Radical Devotion,* pp. 60–63. On Christ being bought with her heart's blood, see Dorothy Day, "Michael Gold," *CW* 33 (June 1967): 2.

79. Quotation from Day, "What Do the Simple Folk Do?" p. 5. One instance of Dorothy's reflection on retreat teaching on contradiction and suffering in AIG, pp. 191–192. Reflection on her desire to share in the sufferings of Christ in AIG, pp. 241–242.

80. Quotation from Dorothy Day, "On Simple Prayer," *CW* 42 (March–April 1976): 4. The role of suffering in attempts to change the social order expressed in Day, *House of Hospitality,* pp. 255–256.

81. AIG fragm [4], read with AIG fragm [5]. Translation is from an unidentified edition. A more recent translation of this passage, from John of the Cross's *The Ascent of Mount Carmel,* Book I,13.11, may be found in

The Collected Works of St. John of the Cross, trans. Kieran Kavanaugh, O.C.D., & Otilio Rodriguez, O.C.D. (Washington, D.C.: Institute of Carmelite Studies, 1979), pp. 103–104.

82. Quotation from Day, *On Pilgrimage,* p. 41. Dorothy reflected on the passage from Matthew 6:21 in AIG, p. 128. One of her frequent notes of gratitude for gifts occurs in AIG, pp. 42–43.

5. FRIENDS AND SPIRITUAL GUIDES

1. By 1234, during the pontificate of Gregory IX, this practice became the standard form of inquiry and remains in effect to the present. For background on saints in Roman Catholic tradition see Peter Brown, *The Cult of the Saints: Its Rise and Function in Latin Christianity* (Chicago: University of Chicago Press, 1981, 1982); "Saints, Devotion to the," "Beatification," and "Canonization," in Elizabeth A. Livingstone, ed. *The Concise Oxford Dictionary of the Christian Church* (Oxford: Oxford University Press, 1977); C. O'Neill, "Saint," in *New Catholic Encyclopedia,* 1967; P. Molinari, "Canonization of Saints (History and Procedure)," *New Catholic Encyclopedia,* 1967. See Eberhard Bethge, "Modern Martyrdom," in *Bonhoeffer: Exile and Martyr,* ed. John W. de Gruchy (New York: Seabury Press, 1975), pp. 155–166, for a view of contemporary martyrdom.

2. Coles, *Radical Devotion,* pp. 141–143; Tom Sullivan, "Remembering Dorothy With Love," *CW* 46 (December 1980): 9; Dorothy Day to John J. Hugo, 15 November [1972], DD–CW, W–6.4, Box 1: "Ever since [I read that] St. Therese wrote 'I will spend my Heaven doing good upon earth,' I have felt even closer to all the saints. Love in Christ—and pass on my greetings to Cecilia [Hugo's sister]. Can't do much letter writing,—hope they (Dorothy [Gauchat], Cecilia [Hugo] and others) understand. I feel so close to them all."

3. Extended quotation from "On P," *CW* 38 (January 1972). 1; ellipses are Dorothy's own; she was quoting Rosemary Haughton, "Signs in the Wind," *New Blackfriars* 52 (May 1961): 204. On saints as persons who knew how to love, see [Dorothy Day], "November, Month of Remembrance," *CW* 22 (November 1955): 1; Dorothy Day to Charles Butterworth, Saturday 5 April [Saturday 4 April 1964], DD–CW, W–13, Box 1: "I do trust we will all grow in sanctity or rather in love, which is the same thing." On her early desire for saints to change the social order and her 1917 advocacy for the poor, see Day, *Long Loneliness,* pp. 45, 61–62. Quotation from 1948 in Day, *On Pilgrimage,* p. 90; [identical in Dorothy Day, "A People's Movement," p. 90].

4. Dorothy Day, two-page fragment [December ca. 1943, with later revisions superimposed on text], DD–CW, D–3, Box 7.

5. For her reflection on the early 1920s, see Day, *Long Loneliness,* pp. 105–107; Dorothy remarked on a mid-1920s reading of various short works

on the saints in AIG fragm [O]; see also Day, *Therese,* pp. vii–viii. On her 1932 openness to Maurin, see Day, *House of Hospitality,* p. xvii.

6. Day, *On Pilgrimage,* p. 90. Dorothy attempted to promote good hagiography and an awareness of the need for contemporary saints through incidental comments, articles, and numerous book reviews featured in *CW*. An example of the first may be found in "NBTW," *CW* 11 (March 1944): 1, where she spoke of "the splendid hagiography of Fr. Thurston and Donald Attwater [editors of the revised edition of Alban Butler, *Lives of the Saints*], Gheon, Ida Coudenhove, Margaret Monroe [*sic*] and other modern writers [of saints' biographies]." Among the articles may be found: Raymond Larsson, "The Fruits of Wonders in the Lives of the Saints," *CW* 17 (March 1951): 3, 8; Dorothy Day, "The Race of Heroes and Saints," *CW* 18 (January 1953): 1, 7, 8; Pat Jordan, "Thomas More: God's Loyal Servant," *CW* 41 (February 1975): 8. Review of Margaret T. Monro, *A Book of Unlikely Saints* (New York: Longmans, Green, 1943) in *CW* 10 (December 1943): 7, is representative. On Dorothy's first reading of Thérèse's autobiography, see Day, *Therese,* p. viii.

7. Quotation from Dorothy Day, "Fear in Our Time," *CW* 34 (April 1968): 7. Evidence for Dorothy's growing appreciation of Butler's work, through reading the revised edition, in two-page fragment [December, ca. 1943 with later revisions superimposed on text], DD–CW, D–3, Box 7. The work in question is *The Lives of the Saints* (originally compiled by the Rev. Alban Butler), ed. and revised Herbert Thurston, S.J., and Donald Attwater, 12 vols. (London: Burns, Oates & Washbourne, 1931–1942).

8. See Coles, *Radical Devotion,* p. 97, in which he quoted Dorothy: "We are here to bear witness to our Lord. We are here to follow His lead. We are here to celebrate Him through these works of mercy." See also Day, *House of Hospitality,* p. 267: "As Léon Bloy wrote: 'There is only one unhappiness, and that is — *not to be one of the Saints'* [said by the figure Clotilde in Léon Bloy, *The Woman Who Was Poor*]. And we could add: the greatest tragedy is that not enough of us desire to be saints."; "NBTW," *CW* 11 (January 1944): 2, in which she quoted Charles Péguy: "I am afraid to go to heaven alone. God will say to me, 'Where are the others?'" Similar reflections on Péguy in AIG fragm [1] and Dorothy Day, "Fall Appeal," *CW* 34 (October 1968): 2. Dorothy Day, "Inventory — January 1951," *CW* 17 (January 1951): 2: "We are all waiting like Lord Jim, in Conrad's story, for great opportunities to show heroism, letting countless opportunities go by to enlarge our hearts, increase our faith, and show our love for our fellows, and so for Him."

9. Quotation from "The Little Flowers of St. Francis," in *St. Francis of Assisi: Writings and Early Biographies. English Omnibus of the Sources for the Life of St. Francis,* ed. Marion A. Habig, 3rd rev. ed. (Chicago: Franciscan Herald Press, 1973), p. 1320. To date, I have been unable to determine which translation Dorothy used. *The Little Flowers (Fioretti),* a popular four-

teenth-century biography, is a classic of world literature and the most widely read account of the Poverello of Assisi in the last century. While the work rested firmly on oral tradition, its value lay beyond the confines of strict biographical accuracy and gives an indication of interpretive struggles over the question of voluntary poverty among Franciscans in the first century after Francis' death. From evidence found in Day, *Long Loneliness*, p. 132, it is likely that Dorothy came across *The Little Flowers* (*Fioretti*) early in the 1920s. Summer 1928 as a time of extended reflection is suggested by means of cross-referencing data given in Day, *Long Loneliness*, p. 153, and Dorothy Day, "Remembering St. Francis," *St. Anthony's Messenger* 73 (October 1965): 38. In 1928 as well as in later years, Dorothy took pleasure in reading the anecdotes of the *Fioretti* to children under her care.

10. "On P.," *CW* (May 1976): 10.

11. Quotations from "St. Francis: Herald of the Great King, #12 (*Rite Expiatis*)," 30 April 1926, in *Social Wellsprings*, vol. 2, pp. 62, 63. The Tertiaries' refusal to bear arms is generally acknowledged as being instrumental in the breakdown of the feudal system. Four recollections of Maurin's promotion of *Rite Expiatis* include: [Dorothy Day], "Days With an End," *CW* 1 (April 1934): 3; Dorothy Day, "Peter Maurin, Agitator," *Blackfriars* 30 (September 1949): 412; draft copy of Day to Father [Theodore] Hesburgh, 27 March 1972, DD–CW, D–5, Box 4.; "On P.," *CW* 40 (February 1974): 8.

12. Some of Dorothy's references to the Franciscan contribution to peace include: [Dorothy Day], "Why Write about Strife and Violence?" *CW* 2 (June 1934): 1; [Dorothy Day], "Fight Conscription," *CW* 7 (September 1939): 1 [later reprinted as Catholic Worker pamphlet, "Fight Conscription," DD–CW, D–7, Box 1]; Dorothy Day, "Beyond Politics," *CW* 16 (November 1949): 2.

13. *Rite Expiatis*, #14 in J. Husslein, S.J., *Social Wellsprings*, vol. 2, pp. 65–66.

14. Johannes Jörgensen, *St. Francis of Assisi*, trans. T. O'Conor Sloane (New York: Longmans, Green, 1912, 1913, 1939). Peter Maurin, "Easy Essays" [includes "What St. Francis Desired"], *CW* 1 (April 1934): 3.

15. Paul Ricoeur, "'The Image of God' and the Epic of Man," *Cross Currents* 11 (Winter 1961): 48–49, in *CW* 28 (July–August 1961): 5. The second sentence of the *CW* quote is terminated after "goods?" In the original the sentence is completed as: ". . . goods, an act which generates hardheartedness and solitude?"

16. Dorothy Day, "The Case of Cardinal McIntyre," *CW* 31 (July–August 1964): 8.

17. Little is known of the English anchoress beyond the information provided in two versions of Juliana's only known work, *Showings*. The name given her is derived from the church, St. Julian in Norwich, England, where she lived in a cell attached to the church structure. The shorter version of

Showings, written by Juliana shortly after her great mystical experience of 13 May 1373, contains her first reflections on its meaning. The second, a longer text presently divided into eighty-six chapters, was concluded in 1393 and represents a mature interpretation of the 1373 experience. It relates a total of sixteen revelations or insights into Christian teachings. A noteworthy translation of both versions appears as *Julian of Norwich: Showings,* trans. with an introduction by Edmund Colledge, O.S.A., and James Walsh, S.J., and Preface by Jean Leclercq, O.S.B. (New York: Paulist Press, 1978). Dorothy's first known reference to Juliana occurs in [Dorothy Day], "Be Kind, Cain," *CW* 14 (November 1947): 6. Dorothy consistently alluded to Juliana by name rather than by the title of her work, *Showings,* or variants of the title such as *Revelations of Divine Love* and *Comfortable Words for Christ's Lovers.* The following are representative: D[orothy] D[ay], "The Satan Bomb," *CW* 16 (March 1950): 2; Dorothy Day, *Therese,* p. 147, in which she referred to God's father-mother love "as Juliana of Norwich calls it."; Day to Merton, 15 August 1961, TMSC, D–220; "On P," *CW* 40 (January 1974): 2; "On P," *CW* 43 (March–April 1977): 2. Dorothy referred to "a Julian of Norwich" (*Showings*) as a bedside book in "On P," *CW* 40 (May 1974): 1.

18. [Dorothy Day], "Be Kind, Cain," *CW* 14 (November 1947): 6. Dorothy quoted from the Hudleston translation of the long text. She lightly edited the translation, as she was often wont to do. Currently available in *Revelations of Divine Love: Shewed to a Devout Ankress by Name Julian of Norwich,* ed. and introduction Dom Roger Hudleston, O.S.B., (London: Burns Oates, 1927, 1935 [1st ed.]; 1952 [2nd ed.]). The 1952 postscript to the original introduction indicates no textual changes for the second edition. In the 1947 issue of *CW,* Dorothy first quoted from chapter 29 (Hudleston, 1952 ed., pp. 51, 52) and concluded her article with a quote from chapter 27 (Hudleston, 1952 ed., p. 49). Chapter 29 of the long text essentially corresponds with chapter 14 of the short text. For comparison of the two, see *Julian of Norwich: Showings,* ed. Colledge and Walsh, pp. 149–151, 227–228.

19. A typical example occurs in: Dorothy Day, "O Death in Life!" [November 1950 or later], DD–CW, D–3, Box 7: "'The worst has already happened and has been remedied,' Juliana of Norwich said, and she meant the Fall and Christ's redeeming of us all. Once this glorious fact shines upon us, once we dwell with the saints in the timeless life of the Christian, joy can once again flood our hearts." See "On P," *CW* 33 (September 1967): 2.

20. "On P," *CW* 39 (May 1973): 8. For Dorothy's description of her first meeting with Maurin, his subsequent indoctrination and hope that Dorothy would follow directly in Catherine of Siena's footsteps, see Day, *Loaves and Fishes,* p. 12 and Day, *Long Loneliness,* p. 172.

21. For a sense of Maurin's program and Dorothy's practicality, see Day, *Long Loneliness,* pp. 172–175. On Catherine's reverence for priests and her

reference to the pope as *il dolce nostro Christo in terra* see Fabian Parmisano, O.P., *Catherine of Siena: 600 Years Later* (Mission San Jose, Calif.: Mater Dei Press, 1980), p. 21. An instance of Dorothy's knowledge of Catherine's phrase, "our dear, sweet Christ on earth," found in Day to Nina Polcyn Moore, postmarked 21 March 1979, DD–CW, W–17, Box 1.

22. Instances of Dorothy's use of Catherine's "All the way to heaven . . ." in AIG, p. 8; "On P," *CW* 13 (February 1946): 1; Dorothy Day, "A People's Movement," p. 88; Day, *On Pilgrimage,* pp. 17, 59, 97, 102; "On P," *CW* 17 (February 1951): 6; Dorothy Day, "Peter Maurin Farm," *CW* 20 (April 1954): 3; Day to Charles Butterworth, 10 June 1959, DD–CW, W–13, Box 1; Day, *Therese,* p. 121; AIG fragm [V]; Dorothy Day, "All the Way to Heaven Is Heaven," (reference is in the title only) *CW* 28 (February 1962): 2; "On P," *CW* 33 (September 1967): 2; DD, "On P," *CW* 36 (May 1970): 2; "On P," *CW* 37 (December 1971): 2; Day, "What Do the Simple Folk Do?" p. 6. See *Catherine of Siena: The Dialogue,* trans. and Introduction by Suzanne Noffke, O.P. (New York, Ramsey, N.J., & Toronto: Paulist Press, 1980).

23. Day, *On Pilgrimage,* p. 102.

24. "On P," *CW* 37 (December 1971): 2.

25. "Love of God," *CW* 8 (May 1941): 5. Cf. *Catherine of Siena,* trans. Noffke, pp. 121, 36, respectively. See Parmisano, *Catherine of Siena,* p. 12. Some variant, abbreviated forms of the *CW* 8 (May 1941): 5, text appear in Editors [Dorothy Day], "Our Fall Appeal," *CW* 13 (October 1946): 2; 1954 MS for *The Gospel in Action* (1955), p. 30, DD–CW, D–3, Box 3; "St. Catherine of Siena," *CW* 30 (January 1964): 6. For the last named, cf. *Catherine of Siena,* trans. Noffke, p. 45. Confirmation of Dorothy's propensity for quoted text found in Eileen Egan, "What Shall We Say?" *CW* 46 (December 1980): 8.

26. See Parmisano, *Catherine of Siena,* p. 5.

27. William James, *The Varieties of Religious Experience* (New York, London, & Bombay: Longmans, Green, 1902). See especially pp. 20–21 and 408–415. Dorothy's references to the work, some supplying clues to when she read it, include: AIG fragm [O], which indicates that she read it during her 1920s stay at the beach; Day, *Union Square to Rome,* p. 136, infers that she read the work before December 1927; Day, *Long Loneliness,* p. 140, suggests that she read the work prior to March 1926; AIG fragm [S], notes that she found the work fascinating; AIG fragm [4]; "On P," *CW* 36 (January 1970): 8. For a study which distinguishes between theological and psychological approaches to mysticism, see Anselm Stolz, O.S.B., *The Doctrine of Spiritual Perfection,* trans. Aidan Williams, O.S.B. (St. Louis, Missouri, & London: B. Herder Book Co., 1938). He identifies the theological with a Benedictine approach to prayer; the psychological with the sixteenth-century Carmelites John of the Cross and Teresa of Avila.

28. For James's comments on early twentieth-century awareness, Teresa's

abilities and their "poor employment," see James, *Varieties,* pp. 346–347. The author's assumption in referring to Teresa's narrow range of activity, while valid on its own terms, neglected to take into account a different historical milieu. Extended quotation, ibid., p. 360. Note 1 for James's next section contains Teresa's comment on Alcantara, ibid., pp. 360–361.

29. On Dorothy's decision to name her daughter Tamar Teresa, see Day, *Long Loneliness,* pp. 140–141. In this passage Dorothy commented that she "had read the life of St. Teresa of Avila. . . ." She frequently referred to Teresa's autobiography as "the life." Dorothy chose for herself the name Maria Teresa for her confirmation on Pentecost [1928]. See ibid., p. 152. Dorothy's descriptions of her summer 1932 reading are found in ibid., p. 161, and AIG fragm [A]. Quotations are from AIG fragm [A].

30. Standard English language editions of the *Life* and *Foundations* which were easily accessible to Dorothy in the 1920s and 1930s include the following: *Collected Works of St. Teresa,* 6 vols. in 9, trans. John Dalton (London: Thomas Baker, 1912–1924); *The Book of the Foundations of St. Teresa of Jesus,* written by herself, revised edition (London: Thomas Baker, 1913); *The Life of St. Teresa of Jesus,* written by herself, trans. David Lewis, 5th ed. (London: Thomas Baker, 1932). Dorothy used the Lewis translation of the *Foundations* in the mid-1930s as shown in Day, *House of Hospitality,* p. 135. This portion of Dorothy's book was written between October 1935 and April 1936 and was very likely unretouched prior to its 1939 publication. I consider it probable that Dorothy read the *Relations* in summer 1932. Dorothy noted in AIG fragm [S] that she was drawn to the *Relations* by a reading of the *Life.*

31. Teresa's humor is freely expressed in her letters, which Dorothy read by the time of writing AIG fragm [S]. Standard collections of these in English translation include: *The Letters of Saint Teresa,* trans. and annotated by the Benedictines of Stanbrook and Introduction, Cardinal Gasquet, 4 vols. (London: Thomas Baker, 1919–1924); *The Letters of Saint Teresa of Jesus,* trans. and edited by E. Allison Peers, 2 vols. (London: Burns Oates & Washbourne, 1951).

32. Day, *Long Loneliness,* pp. 140–141. See Dorothy Day, "Saint John of the Cross," *Commonweal* 18 (14 July 1933): 287–288. Father Bruno, O.D.C., *St. John of the Cross,* ed. Fr. Benedict Zimmerman, O.D.C., with Introduction by Jacques Maritain (New York: Sheed & Ward, 1932). In the 1933 *Commonweal* article, Dorothy quoted directly from chapter 15 of Teresa's *Foundations.* An outstanding example of Dorothy's devotion to St. Joseph, in conscious imitation of Teresa, may be found in [Dorothy Day], "With Thanks to Our Readers," *CW* 3 (April 1936): 4, which includes an excerpt from the saint's *Life,* ch. 6: 9, 11. A sample of Day's references to the saint's humor might include: (a) Life as a night at an uncomfortable inn, in AIG, pp. 70, 103; "On P," *CW* 13 (Feb 1946): 1; Day, *On Pilgrimage,* p. 175; Doro-

thy Day, "Maryfarm," *CW* 20 (March 1954): 3; Day, *Loaves and Fishes,* p. 215. (b) Teresa of such a grateful disposition that she could be bought by a sardine, in "DBD," *CW* 1 (March 1934): 5; "On P," *CW* 16 (October 1949): 1; Dorothy Day, "Fall Appeal" *CW* 30 (October 1963): 2; "Thank you, thank you!" *CW* 34 (December 1968): 1. (c) Steak to be given to melancholy nuns in "On P," *CW* 25 (June 1959): 1; "On P," *CW* 42 (May 1976): 2. (d) Dancing to make life bearable in "On P," *CW* 40 (Jan 1974): 2; "On P," *CW* 42 (May 1976): 2.

33. I believe that Dorothy's reticence accounted in part for her inability to complete the AIG manuscript for publication.

34. "On P," *CW* 41 (March-April 1975): 2. Comment regarding her 1943–1944 sabbatical in AIG fragm [A]. At the very latest, Dorothy had read Teresa's *Way of Perfection* and *The Interior Castle* by the mid-sixties; confirmed by AIG fragm [S].

35. *Interior Castle,* 5th Mansions (*sic*), ch. 3 in *The Complete Works of Saint Teresa of Jesus,* vol. 2., trans. and ed. E. Allison Peers (New York: Sheed & Ward, 1946), pp. 261–262. It is likely that Dorothy found this Teresian insight in a secondary source during the 1930s, but it is not impossible that she had read *Interior Castle,* then available in the Dalton or Lewis translations.

36. Day, *Union Square to Rome,* p. 148. See entire discussion for ch. 12, pp. 143–151. Dorothy frequently quoted Teresa by name, using variant forms of "We can only show our love for God by our love for our fellows." Some examples include: AIG, p. 296; "NBTW," *CW* 11 (January 1944): 1; [Dorothy Day], "An Appeal to Women," *CW* 12 (November 1945): 1; Dorothy Day, Preface to an unpublished book by Robert Ludlow, 1948, DD–CW, D–3, Box 7; Dorothy Day, "The Scandal of the Works of Mercy," p. 99; AIG fragm [A]; 1954 MS for *The Gospel in Action* (1955), p. 30, DD–CW, D–3, Box 3; "On P," *CW* 33 (September 1966): 2; Day, "What Do the Simple Folk Do?" p. 4.

37. Day, *Union Square to Rome,* pp. 154–155. See entire discussion, pp. 152–173. Dorothy quoted from the Lewis translation of Teresa's *Life,* ch. 8.18.

38. Day, *Union Square to Rome,* p. 162. See p. 160 for Teresian concept of Christ disguised as bread. Teresa treated this at length in her *Life* (ch. 38, Lewis edition).

39. Day, *Union Square to Rome,* pp. 171–172. Shorter quotation, p. 170. See p. 151 for Dorothy's reflection on human love leading to an appreciation of God's love.

40. Ibid., p. 173.

41. Day, *Therese,* pp. vi–vii. See also Day, *Long Loneliness,* pp. 140–141.

42. See Day, *Therese,* pp. vii–x; Day, *Loaves and Fishes,* pp. 122–123.

At Thérèse's request, all early editions of the autobiography had been edited for publication by her blood sister, Carmelite Mother Agnes. Available early data strongly suggests that in 1928 Dorothy read the Taylor edition, which included the autobiography as well as other primary documents. Editions then in print were *Soeur Thérèse of Lisieux, The Little Flower of Jesus,* ed. T. N. Taylor (London: Burns, Oates & Washbourne, 1922) and *Saint Thérèse of Lisieux, The Little Flower of Jesus,* ed. Rev. Thomas N. Taylor (New York: P. J. Kenedy & Sons, 1926). The "Note to the Eighth Impression [1922 British edition]" indicates that this translation was published separately as "A Little White Flower," and was available from both London: Burns, Oates & Washbourne and New York: Kenedy & Sons.

43. Day, *House of Hospitality,* pp. 74–75. A short reference to Thérèse also occurs on p. 131. In "On P," *CW* 43 (February 1977): 2, Dorothy recalled that when Peter Maurin first came to her, he showed her the Little Way, though she did not think much of the Little Flower and her Little Way at the time.

44. AIG fragm [A], in which she recorded her 1936 prayer. For background on the strike, see "Seaman's Strike Called Off; Union Heads Refuse Support," *CW* 4 (June 1936): 1, 4.

45. AIG fragm [A].

46. Dorothy Day, "Rabbi Heschel said . . ." DD–CW, D–3, Box 7, published as "Adventure in Prayer," *Third Hour* 9 (1970): 39–45. Dorothy acknowledged that she came across the quotation in Douglas Steere's foreword to Thomas Merton, *Contemplative Prayer* (New York: Herder & Herder, 1969), which she had just begun to read.

47. A three-page fragment, "How to get all these ideas down . . ." ca. 1951, DD–CW, D–3, Box 7, illustrates Dorothy's struggle to understand how Thérèse lived out the two Great Commandments. It reads in part: "I used to think in my ignorance, twenty-three years ago when I first read the story, that she [Thérèse] may have loved God but that she did not love her brothers, except of course inside herself, in her desire to serve them. But I was all tangled up on the subject as most people are, thinking that love of God, such a burning love of God, consumed altogether the love of brother so that the two were merged and in the contemplative life one withdrew entirely from any realization of brotherhood."

48. "On P," *CW* 16 (October 1949): 1; Editors [Dorothy Day], "Fall Appeal," *CW* 16 (October 1949): 2.

49. Day, *Therese,* pp. 174–175. For translations of the autobiography, Dorothy relied on the *Autobiography of St. Thérèse of Lisieux,* trans. Ronald Knox (New York: P. J. Kenedy & Sons, 1958) and *The Story of a Soul,* trans. Michael Day (London: Burns, Oates, 1951); for her letters, on André Combes, ed., *Collected Letters of St. Thérèse of Lisieux,* trans. F. J. Sheed (New York: Sheed & Ward, 1949); for Thérèse's conversations from May–September

1897, on *Novissima Verba*, trans. Carmelite nuns of New York (New York: P. J. Kenedy & Sons, 1951). The secondary work on which she relied the most was Stéphane-Joseph Piat, O.F.M., *The Story of a Family*, trans. Benedictine of Stanbrook Abbey (New York: P. J. Kenedy & Sons, 1947). The Piat work was also Dorothy's source for quotations from Zelie Guerin's letters.

50. Richard W. Conklin to Editors, University of Notre Dame News, 8 March 1972, for release in a.m. papers, Sunday 12 March, DD–CW, D–5, Box 4. War and peace were among the key issues debated before the final text of the conciliar document, "The Church in the Modern World," was promulgated on 7 December 1965. Dorothy Day, "Love in Practice," *Third Hour* 8 (1961): 15–21, available to me in MS form, "Love in Practice," ca. 1961, DD–CW, D–3, Box 7.

51. Inset, *CW* 39 (March–April 1973): 6. [Original source: William James to Mrs. Henry Whitman in *The Letters of William James*, vol. 2, ed. Henry James (Boston: Atlantic Monthly Press, 1920), p. 90.] For an indication of its importance, see "On P," *CW* 40 (March–April 1974): 8, "We reprinted the William James card, on smallness, because of Therese. . . ."

52. Day, *Long Loneliness*, pp. 157–158.

53. Dorothy Day to Patrick and Kathleen Jordan (n.d.), in Pat Jordan, "Illuminating Dark Times," *CW* 46 (December 1980): 8. Dorothy had a high regard for Fritz Eichenberg and his work. They carried on an extended correspondence which, judging from extant letters, began in spring of 1949. Day letters to Eichenberg, sent by Eichenberg to Marquette University for examination per Merriman request, 9 June 1984. Catholic Worker Jack (Father Charles) English became a Trappist monk in 1951 but, until his death on 9 December 1972, remained close to Dorothy and other Catholic Workers, especially Tom Sullivan. Charles Butterworth, a graduate of Harvard Law School, was listed as an associate editor of the *Catholic Worker* from January 1959 through October–November 1977. He died of leukemia on 8 February 1978 at the age of fifty-one. Day-Butterworth correspondence reveals their close association and the confidence Dorothy had in his ability to manage the Catholic Worker house, especially when she was away on speaking trips in the first half of the 1960s, DD–CW, W–13, Boxes 1 and 3; DD–CW, D–1.1, Box 1.

54. For background on Dorothy's first meeting with Maurin, see Day, *Long Loneliness*, pp. 166, 169; Dorothy Day, "I Remember Peter Maurin," *Jubilee* 1 (March 1954): 34; Dorothy Day, draft copy of article on the Catholic Worker Movement, DD–CW, D–3, Box 7, written for *The Catholic Youth Encyclopedia* (1961). For background on Maurin, see Arthur Sheehan, *Peter Maurin: Gay Believer*; Marc H. Ellis, *Peter Maurin: Prophet in the Twentieth Century* (New York & Ramsey, N.J.: Paulist Press, 1981); Marc Ellis, "The Legacy of Peter Maurin," *Cross Currents* 34 (Fall 1984): 294–304. For another per-

spective on the relationship between Dorothy and Maurin, see Mel Piehl, *Breaking Bread* (1982), pp. 58–66 and passim.

55. Day, "A Reminiscence at 75," p. 424; Brackley and Dillon, "Interview with Dorothy Day," p. 10; Day, *Long Loneliness,* pp. 161–162; Day in Coles, *Radical Devotion,* p. 11; Dorothy Day, "The Case of Cardinal McIntyre," *CW* 31 (July–August 1964): 6.

56. Day, *Long Loneliness,* pp. 165–166. See also Day, *Loaves and Fishes,* pp. 12–13.

57. Day, *Long Loneliness,* pp. 166. Closer to the event, Dorothy remembered that she had prayed more specifically for a way "to do the work that I wanted to do for labor." See [Dorothy Day], "Progress," *CW* 1 (December 1933): 4.

58. Day, "I Remember Peter Maurin," p. 34; on this same page she credited Maurin as being the answer to her prayer. See also Day, *Long Loneliness,* pp. 166, 169–174; Day, *Loaves and Fishes,* pp. 4–16.

59. Maurin's aphorism quoted in Day, *Long Loneliness,* p. 175; see also, pp. 173–174. Day, "I Remember Peter Maurin," p. 36; Day, *Loaves and Fishes,* pp. 15–16.

60. Day, *Loaves and Fishes,* p. 22; see pp. 18–20, where she related missing Maurin and her joy on his return.

61. Day, "I Remember Peter Maurin," p. 39.

62. Day, *Loaves and Fishes,* pp. 101–102.

63. Day, *Long Loneliness,* p. 181. Sometimes Dorothy expressed her worry over Maurin's location in open letters to him, published in the paper. See "DAD," *CW* 6 (Jan 1939): 1, 4; "Open Letter to Peter Maurin from Editor: DAD," *CW* 6 (June 1939): 1, 4. Maurin's extant correspondence with Dorothy, written between 19 January 1936 and 7 September 1942, DD–CW, W–10, Box 1. Introduction to encyclicals on the saints noted in Day, "Peter Maurin, Agitator," pp. 412–413: "He called our attention to one on St. Francis of Assisi, and one on St. Francis de Sales especially, quoting: 'Let no one think that the command, "Be ye perfect as your heavenly Father is perfect," is addressed to a select few and that others are permitted to remain in an inferior degree of virtue. The law obliges, it is clear, absolutely everyone in the world without exception.'" See [Dorothy Day], "On the Love of God," *CW* 1 (September 1933): 6, where, at Maurin's suggestion, she consciously introduced devotional matter into the paper. Michael G. I. Callanan to Dorothy Day, 10 July 1949, DD–CW, W–10, Box 1, provides evidence that Maurin made at least two Lacouture type retreats with Louis Farina; his attendance at one of these is noted in David Mason, "Hegira with Peter" *CW* 10 (September 1943): 8. Peter Maurin, "The Wisdom of Dostoievsky," *CW* 2 (May 1934): 1, 2; Peter Maurin, "Forced Labor by Fiodor Dostoievski," *CW* 5 (January 1938): 3.

64. Day, *Long Loneliness*, p. 242. For a reflection on her "neglect" of Maurin, see Day, *Loaves and Fishes*, p. 93.

65. Striking reflections on how much Dorothy missed Peter and her desire to continue their work occur in the following: "Families and the Retreat House," [8 September] 1948, DD–CW, W–4.2, Box 1; "On P," *CW* 17 (September 1950): 2; "On P," *CW* 27 (June 1961): 2.

66. Dorothy Day, "The Catholic Worker," *Integrity* 1 (November 1946): 17–19.

67. Aside from shared Christian values, the women's friendship was sustained by their mutual love for travel. As Dorothy wrote to Nina Polcyn, 17 July 1964, DD–CW, W–17, Box 1: "Travelling is a great recreation, and a great enlightener. I do enjoy it so and am glad you get the same kick out of it." Nina married Thomas Moore on 3 February 1973. For correspondence prior to this time, she will be referred to as Polcyn; afterwards as Polcyn Moore.

68. Day telegram to Polcyn, 19 February 1942, DD–CW, W–17, Box 2. Sources for Polcyn background and 1937–1942 period include: Nina Polcyn Moore, "A Month at the Catholic Worker in 1935," unpublished manuscript [1980], DD–CW, W–17, Box 1; Nina Polcyn, "Milwaukee," *CW* 5 (October 1937): 3; Leonard Doyle, "Milwaukee CW Going to Town with House, School, Propaganda," *CW* 5 (November 1937): 2; Nina Polcyn, "Milwaukee," *CW* 6 (October 1938): 5; Nina Polcyn, Margaret Blaser, Florence Weinfurter, "Credo" [1939], DD–CW, W–17, Box 2; Dorothy Day to Catholic Workers, 10 August 1940, DD–CW, W–17, Box 2; Nina Polcyn, "Holy Family House in Milwaukee Has New Site," *CW* 8 (December 1940): 6; Mario Echer, "Milwaukee Group Reports Moving," *CW* 8 (January 1941): 5; Fr. [John J.] Hugo to Friends [Polcyn et al.], 20 December 1941, DD–CW, W–17, Box 2; Polcyn et al. to Father Hugo, 23 December 1941, DD–CW, W–17, Box 2.

69. [Polcyn] to Day, Third Sunday of Lent [8 March 1942], DD–CW, W–17, Box 2. The Leen to which Polcyn referred was the spiritual writer, Edward Leen, C.S.Sp. (1885–1944).

70. Day-Polcyn [Moore] correspondence, 1942–1980, DD–CW, W–17, Box 1 and DD–CW, D–1.1, Box 8.

71. A sample of their dreams for travel to Russia may be found in Day to Polcyn, 17 July 1964, DD–CW, W–17, Box 1. Their 15 July–5 August 1971 tour, sponsored by Promoting Enduring Peace Incorporated, was led by Dr. Jerome Davis, retired theology professor of Yale Divinity School. This and further background provided by materials dated between 31 March–25 August 1971, DD–CW, D–5, Box 2. Dorothy and Nina frequently recalled the trip, of which Day to Polcyn Moore, postmarked 4 February [1977?], DD–CW W–17, Box 1, is typical: "When we went to Russia together, I felt the same age as you. We had such a holiday — never laughed so much. A joyous mem-

ory." For an article in which Dorothy anticipated the trip, see "On P.," *CW* 37 (July–August 1971): 2, 8. For immediate recollections of the trip see Dorothy Day, "On Pilgrimage: First Visit to Soviet Russia," *CW* 37 (September 1971): 1, 7, 8; Dorothy Day, "Russia, II: On Pilgrimage," *CW* 37 (October–November 1971): 3, 6.

72. Day to Polcyn, 6 April 1972, DD–CW, W–17, Box 1.

73. Day to Polcyn, Saturday [early May 1972], DD–CW, W–17, Box 1. In the same letter, Dorothy informed Nina that she had asked Hesburgh to have either Nina or William Storey of Notre Dame accept the award for her. Information on events related to Dorothy's 1972 reception of the Laetare Medal, DD–CW, D–5, Box 4; this includes news release, news articles, correspondence between Notre Dame President Theodore Hesburgh and Dorothy, as well as other materials. That Dorothy actually attended the 21 May event confirmed by Polcyn to Day [between 17 August–7 September 1972], DD–CW, D–1.1, Box 8. Dorothy's concern over the IRS case expressed in Day to Polcyn, Saturday [early May 1972], DD–CW, W–17, Box 1, and in Dorothy Day, "We Go on Record: CW Refuses Tax Exemption," *CW* 38 (May 1972): 1, 3, 5. Her relief over the case's resolution expressed in Day to Polcyn, 17 August 1972, DD–CW, W–17, Box 1, and in "On P.," *CW* 38 (July–August 1972): 1, 2.

74. Polcyn to Day, 3 November 1972, DD–CW, D–1.1, Box 8.

75. Day to Polcyn, 28 October 1972, DD–CW, W–17, Box 1. Confirmation that Dorothy actually attended the wedding found in Polcyn Moore to Day, 10 March 1973, DD–CW, D–1.1, Box 8. Once Nina was firmly established in her marriage, she would comment with wry humor in Polcyn Moore to Day, 30 July 1974, DD–CW, D–1.1, Box 8: "My joke is that Jane Frances Chantal my patron (Aug 21) left 5 children to found an order. And I left order to found five children."

76. Day to Polcyn Moore, 27 March 1974, DD–CW, W–17, Box 1.

77. Day to Polcyn Moore [June 1974], DD–CW, W–17, Box 1, at which time Dorothy anticipated a 5 July appointment with a heart specialist. In Day to Polcyn Moore, 3 April 1975, DD–CW, W–17, Box 1, she recounted Karl Stern's trials and her anticipated journey, the next day, to visit him in Montreal.

78. Day to Polcyn Moore, 1 July [1975], DD–CW, W–17, Box 1.

79. Polcyn Moore to Day [July 1975], DD–CW, D–1.1, Box 8. By the time of her 23 July 1975 letter to Polycn Moore, DD–CW, W–17, Box 1, Dorothy, who then felt better physically, had worked her way out of her discouraged mood. In Day to Polcyn Moore, 3 November 1975, DD–CW, W–17, Box 1, Dorothy commented that she was pleased with the good staff then at the New York and Tivoli houses. This change is understandable in light of the fact that volunteers at the Catholic Worker houses came and went frequently, particularly before and after the summer months.

80. Polcyn Moore to Day, Easter Thursday [30 March 1978], DD–CW, D–1.1, Box 8. Between 1977 and 1980, Nina visited Dorothy on at least three occasions. Confirmed by Polcyn Moore to Day, 22 September 1977, DD–CW, D–1.1, Box 8, and Day, "On P," *CW* 43 (September 1977): 2; Polcyn Moore to Day, 2 December [1978], DD–CW, D–1.1, Box 8, and "On P," *CW* 44 (December 1978): 6; "On P," *CW* 46 (June 1980): 4.

81. Day to Polcyn Moore, postmarked 21 March 1979, DD–CW, W–17, Box 1.

82. Day to Polcyn Moore, 21 February 1980, DD–CW, W–17, Box 1. This is Dorothy's latest extant letter to Nina.

83. Helene Iswolsky, *No Time to Grieve,* p. 235. This work provides a good overview of Iswolsky's life and background. For more information on her personalist associations, see Helene Iswolsky, *Light Before Dusk: A Russian Catholic in France, 1923–1941* (New York: Longmans, Green, 1942). See "DAD," *CW* 9 (December 1941): 4, for her comment after Iswolsky's first visit to the Catholic Worker.

84. Of the materials currently available for this section of the chapter, extensive lacunae exist in the collection of Dorothy's letters to Helene. As much as is possible, this lack is remedied through the use of Helene's letters to Dorothy, Dorothy's comments about Helene in letters to Nina Polcyn Moore, and through pertinent articles written both by Day and by Iswolsky.

85. Dating of the friendship supplied in "To the Friends of Helene Iswolsky" from Brother Victor Avila, O.S.B., Dorothy Day, and Marguerite Tjader, 10 January 1976, found on reverse of Day to Polcyn Moore, 17 January 1976, DD–CW, W–17, Box 1. The 1947 dating coincided with the publication of Dorothy's first article for *Third Hour.* Elsewhere Dorothy counted their friendship from the year of their first meeting in 1941; see "On P," *CW* 42 (January 1976): 2. Dorothy Day wrote the following articles for Helene's journal: "A People's Movement," *Third Hour* 2 (1974): 84–90; "Idea of an Agronomic University," *Third Hour* 5 (1951): 55–59; "The Prayer of Jesus," *Third Hour* 6 (1954): 13–18; "Prophet Without Honor," *Third Hour* 7 (1956): 10–17; "Love in Practice," *Third Hour* 8 (1961): 15–21; "Adventure in Prayer," *Third Hour* 9 (1970): 39–45 [reprinted in *Third Hour* 10 (1976): 120–124]; "Helene Iswolsky Dies," *Third Hour* 10 (1976): 8–11. Iswolsky's acceptance of invitations to speak to the Catholic Worker group is chronicled by notices and comments printed in the paper. Typical of these is a report on her presentation on the pacifist strain found in Russian literature. See A[mmon] H[ennacy], "Labor Day Conference," *CW* 22 (October 1955): 2, 7.

86. "On P," *CW* 21 (December 1954): 2, 6. Helene Iswolsky's articles for the paper include: "Msgr. Paul Couturier Dies: Apostle of Unity," *CW* 19 (May 1953): 2, 8; "The Third Hour, issue VI," *CW* 20 (July–August 1954): 4; "Only Prisons Have Bars," *CW* 21 (January 1955): 2, 8; "Bakunin Revisited,"

CW 22 (February 1956): 5; "Good-Bye, Philip!" *CW* 23 (April 1957): 3, 8 [internal evidence suggests that Helene wrote the insert section and Dorothy wrote the rest]; "Heaven Knows, Mr. Khrushchev!" *CW* 23 (June 1957): 1, 7; "Farewell to Father [H. A.] Reinhold, Friend and Teacher," *CW* 34 (March 1968): 8; "The Spiritual Homecoming of Nicolas Berdyaev," *CW* 35 (February 1969): 1, 6; "The World of Alexander Solzhenitsyn," *CW* 36 (June 1970): 4, 7; "New Russian Saints," *CW* 36 (December 1970): 4, 6, 8; "Solovyev and the Jews," *CW* 38 (January 1972): 2; "Solzhenitsyn and the Artist's Vocation," *CW* 39 (March–April 1973): 7; "W. H. Auden: Faith and the Ironic Hero," *CW* 40 (January 1974): 7. The following is typical of her reviews: Helene Iswolsky, untitled review of Konstantin Mochulsky, *Dostoevsky: His Life and Work, CW* 34 (January 1968): 7.

87. Among Dorothy's references to her regular participation in Byzantine rite liturgies, the most indicative are found in "On P," *CW* 25 (November 1958): 6. "On P," *CW* 33 (December 1966): 2, provides evidence that she still attended Byzantine rite liturgies, at least on occasion.

88. Day to Iswolsky, undated [between 8 October and 30 December 1958], Helene Iswolsky papers. Helene recalled the importance of Dorothy's presence at her brother's funeral in Helene Iswolsky, *No Time to Grieve,* p. 264. Helene's extant dated letters to Dorothy range from 1947 through 1975, DD–CW, D–1.1, Box 6.

89. Day to Iswolsky, 30 December [1958] and 23 January [1959], Helene Iswolsky papers. The beach reference is an invitation for Helene to stay for a time at one of the Catholic Worker bungalows on Staten Island, near Peter Maurin farm.

90. Iswolsky to Day, Feast of the Holy Rosary [7 October 1959], DD–CW, D–1.1, Box 6. Background for Dorothy's care of Nanette may be found in Miller, *Dorothy Day,* pp. 457–459, and in Caroline Gordon [Tate]–Deane Mowrer interview, 19 May 1970, DD–CW, W–9, Box 1.

91. Iswolsky to Day, 21 January [1960], DD–CW, D–1.1, Box 6.

92. Iswolsky to Day, 22 November [1971], DD–CW, D–1.1, Box 6.

93. Day to Iswolsky, 19 August [1975], Helene Iswolsky papers.

94. "On P," *CW* 42 (January 1976): 2. Quite fittingly, Helene was clad in a Benedictine habit and buried in the Catholic Worker plot at St. Sylvia's Cemetery, Tivoli. In Day to Polcyn Moore, 8 December 1975, DD–CW, W–17, Box 1, Dorothy explained the reason for her delayed visit to Nina: "My main delay is Helene Iswolsky's illness which is likely to be terminal. We are her family so I've been spending 2 days a week near her, so I can visit 3 times a day briefly. . . . She is my age, and I think closer to me than to anyone else. So I must stand by."

95. One illustration of Dorothy's accord with Augustine seen in Dorothy Day, "Month of the Dead," *CW* 26 (November 1959): 6: "I called my

last book, 'The Long Loneliness' . . . because I tried to point out with St. Augustine, that no matter how crowded life was with activity and joy, family and work, the human heart was never satisfied until it rested in God, the absolute Good, absolute Beauty, absolute Love." A reflection, based on her appreciation of the Emmaus pericope (Luke 24:13–35) is recorded in Day, *Long Loneliness,* pp. 285–286.

96. "Takes Two Hearts," *CW* 20 (September 1953): 6, attributed to Dante.

97. "On P," *CW* 29 (January 1963): 6. Dorothy's last sentence, though not identified by her, is derived from John of the Cross. See *The Collected Works of St. John of the Cross,* p. 672, #57 of "Sayings of Light and Love [re: judged on love]" and p. 703, John of the Cross to María de la Encarnación, 6 July 1591.

CONCLUSION

1. Coles, *Radical Devotion,* p. 159. The title for these concluding pages is taken from Day, *Long Loneliness,* p. 285.

2. [Dorothy Day], "The Humanity of Christ," *CW* 3 (June 1935): 4.

3. "On P," *CW* 41 (February 1975): 2. The immediate occasion for her joy was the birth of a great-granddaughter.

4. Day, *Long Loneliness,* p. 187.

5. Quotation in [Dorothy Day], "Love Is the Measure," *CW* 13 (June 1946): 2. On Dorothy's perception of Christ's passion, see Day in Cole, *Radical Devotion,* p. 117.

6. [Dorothy Day], "Room for Christ," *CW* 12 (December 1945): 2. Reprinted in *CW* 46 (December 1980): 7.

APPENDIX

"All Is Grace" Manuscript Contents and
Chronology for "All Is Grace" Fragments

A. The AIG Manuscript

Evidence found within the AIG manuscript as well as external data provided by other archival materials, the *Catholic Worker,* and the *Official Catholic Directory* strongly suggest the following retreat and conference directors, dating of events, and division of the text:

pp. 1–81 notes from 18–25 July 1943 Lacouture retreat at Oakmont, Pennsylvania with Fathers Louis Farina, Oliver Lynch, O.F.M., and Corcoran

[pp. 57–86 of AIG fragm [W] comprise notes from 2–3 July of 2–8 July 1944 Lacouture retreat at Oakmont with Fathers Denis Mooney, O.F.M., and Louis Farina]

pp. 81–166 notes from 4–8 July of 2–8 July 1944 Lacouture retreat at Oakmont with Fathers Denis Mooney, O.F.M., and Louis Farina

pp. 166–213 notes from 16–22 July 1944 Lacouture retreat at Oakmont with Fathers Joseph Meenan and Louis Farina

pp. 214–215 notes from 6 August of 1–6 August 1949 Lacouture retreat at Newburgh with Father Paul Judge

pp. 216–222 notes from 9 June 1943 non-Lacouture Day of Recollection at Newport, Rhode Island, with Father Joseph Woods, O.S.B. [p. 216: "Benedictine most opposed to retreat"]

pp. 222–225 notes from 13 June 1943 non-Lacouture Day of Recollection at Portsmouth Priory, Rhode Island, with Joseph Woods, O.S.B.

pp. 225–226 notes from 20 June 1943 non-Lacouture Day of Recollection. Location undetermined. Reads like a conference given by a Benedictine.

pp. 226–258 personal notes from 11, 14–18 February 1944. Is in rural setting; Farmingdale, Long Island is likely. Notes include reflection on earlier non-Lacouture conferences given by Joseph Woods, O.S.B.

pp. 258–262 notes from 11 July 1943 non-Lacouture Day of Recollection at the Cenacle [628 W. 140th St., New York City?] with Father Thomas Verner Moore, then a Benedictine pp. 262–265 notes from 6 August 1944 non-Lacouture conference given by Joseph Woods, O.S.B. Location undetermined.

pp. 265–268 notes from 13 August 1944 non-Lacouture conference given by Joseph Woods, O.S.B. Location undetermined.

pp. 268–294 notes from September 1943 Grail course at Wheeling, Illinois. Non-Lacouture speakers, some of whom were Father Ermin Vitry, O.S.B., Dr. Lydwine van Kersbergen, Janet Kalvan, Msgr. Luigi Ligutti, Joan Overboss, and Father Michael A. Mathis, C.S.C.

pp. 295–297 personal notes written between 28 November 1943 and January 1944. Likely location: Farmingdale, Long Island.

pp. 298–299 personal notes written on 10–11 May 1944 at the Grail farm in Foster, Ohio

[At some point Dorothy had inserted between pp. 3 & 4 of the manuscript a one-and-a-half page excerpt from Henri de Lubac, *The Discovery of God,* 1960.]

B. *The AIG Fragments*

Evidence found within the fragments as well as external data provided by other archival materials and the *Catholic Worker* suggest the following chronology. Italicized suggestions are those the present writer considers certain.

The fragments have been designated by the present writer with numbers 1–11 (DD–CW, D–3.6, folder 1) and letters A–Y (DD–CW, D–3.6, folder 2). I retain the 1984 order in which the fragments were filed within the archive folders. Date suggestions have been provided by Marquette archivists for items in folder 1. Dating agreement or disagreement for numbers 1–11 indicated below.

1	1959 [MUA same]
2	1959 [MUA same]
3	*late 1959* [MUA ca. 1959]
4	*July 1963* [MUA 1963]
5	July 1963 [MUA not designated]
6	1964 or more likely, 1965 [MUA 1964 or 1965]
7	written February 1964 and retyped August 1966 [August 1966 designated on the original before deposit at MUA]
8	retyped copy of John J. Hugo, *A Sign of Contradiction* (1947), ch. 5 [August 1966 designated on this copy before deposit at MUA]
9	*between late 1963 and 1968* [MUA not designated]
10	1966 or, more likely, 1967, a later version of 6 [MUA 1967?]
11	*27 February 1975* [date designated on the original before deposit at MUA]

A   *between April 1951 and 10 July 1953*
B   *n.d.* can be derived
C   copy of Lacouture's letter to his mother, 8 September 1916
D   *after 1961*
E   mid-1960s
F   *n.d.* can be derived
G   ca. 1965
H   *1963 or later*
I   after 1940s
J   *after 1955*
K   after March 1960
L   between January 1961 and November 1963
M   *May 1964 or later*
N   *1963 or later*
O   *n.d.* can be derived
P   *n.d.* can be derived
Q   mid-1960s
R   *after 9 November 1965*
S   *after 1961*
T   after September 1957
U   *1960s*
V   1960s
W   *1944* [belongs with AIG manuscript]
X   *April 1963 or later*
Y   between 1955 and mid-1962

BIBLIOGRAPHY

PRIMARY SOURCES: ARCHIVES AND UNPUBLISHED MATERIALS

Collegeville, Minn. St. John's Abbey Archives.
   Abbot Alcuin Deutsch Papers.
   Paul Marx Dissertation Papers.
   Virgil Michel Papers.

Collegeville, Minn. St. John's University Archives.
   Virgil Michel Papers.

Lisle, Ill. St. Procopius Abbey Archives.
   Benedictine Oblate Papers.

Louisville, Ky. The Thomas Merton Study Center.
   Thomas Merton–Dorothy Day Correspondence.

Milwaukee, Wis. Marquette University Archives.
   Dorothy Day–Catholic Worker Papers.
   William D. Miller Papers.
   Audiotapes of Dorothy Day's talks (arranged chronologically)

   "The Pacifist's View of the Catholic Worker." Talk given at Marquette University. Milwaukee. 7 February 1958.
   Untitled talk given at the University of Santa Clara. Santa Clara, California. 21 March 1960.
   Untitled talk given at joint meeting of Franciscan Fraters of Old Mission Santa Barbara and Catholic Human Relations Council of Santa Barbara. Santa Barbara, Calif. 12 March 1965.
   "Poverty and the Christian Commitment." Talk given at the Social Action Forum. New York University. 12 November 1965.
   "Who Is My Brother's Keeper?" Talk given at the State University of New York at Geneseo. 6 October 1966.
   "The Urban Poor." Talk given at the Peacemaker Conference. Tivoli, N.Y. Summer 1967.

305

"The Grapepickers: Nonviolence in Social Change." Talk given at PAX Conference. Tivoli, N.Y. August 1969.

Untitled talk given at Casa Maria House of Hospitality. Milwaukee, Wis. 24 September 1969.

Untitled talks given at Peacemaker Conference. Tivoli, N.Y. 26 May 1974 & 24 June 1975.

Oral History transcripts of Ade Bethune, Father Marion Casey, Mary Durnin, Edmund J. Egan, Fritz Eichenberg, Father Charles (Jack) English, Sister Peter Claver Fahy, Caroline Gordon, Thomas Hoey, Father John J. Hugo, Dr. Karl Stern, Thomas C. Sullivan, Stanley Vishnewski, Joseph and Alice Zarrella.

Peace Dale, R.I. Fritz Eichenberg residence.
Fritz Eichenberg papers. (Temporarily housed at Marquette University Archives per Brigid Merriman, O.S.F., request.)

Scranton, Pa. University of Scranton. Center for Eastern Christian Studies. (Formerly located at Bronx, New York. John XXIII Ecumenical Center-Center for Eastern Christian Studies.)
Helene Iswolsky Papers.

Interviews and Correspondence

Blecker, Michael J., O.S.B.–Merriman, Brigid, O.S.F. Personal Interview, 12 September 1984.

Buresh, Vitus, O.S.B.–Merriman, Brigid, O.S.F. Telephone conversation, 23 January 1988.

Buresh, Vitus, O.S.B.–Merriman, Brigid, O.S.F. Personal Correspondence, January–February 1988.

Ceplecha, Christian, O.S.B.–Merriman, Brigid, O.S.F. Personal Correspondence, February–March 1988.

Furfey, Paul Hanly–Merriman, Brigid, O.S.F. Personal Correspondence, May–December 1984.

Furfey, Paul Hanly–Merriman, Brigid, O.S.F. Personal Interview, 20 November 1984.

Hugo, John J. "The Deliverance of Onesimus: A History of 'The Famous Retreat.'" Typewritten manuscript obtained from the author, July 1984.

Hugo, John J.–Merriman, Brigid, O.S.F. Personal Correspondence, 1984–1985.

Hugo, John J.–Merriman, Brigid, O.S.F. Personal Interview, 18–19 November 1984.

Hugo, Cecilia–Merriman, Brigid, O.S.F. Personal Interview, 19 November 1984.

Lynch, Oliver, O.F.M.–Merriman, Brigid, O.S.F. Personal Interview, 15 May 1984.

PRIMARY SOURCES: PUBLISHED WORKS OF DOROTHY DAY

Arranged according to date of first publication.

The Eleventh Virgin (autobiographical novel). New York: Albert & Charles Boni, 1924.

"Brother and the Rooster." *Commonweal* 10 (18 September 1929): 501–503.

"Guadalupe." *Commonweal* 11 (26 February 1930): 477–478.

"A Letter from Mexico City." *Commonweal* 11 (16 April 1930): 683–684.

"Spring Festival in Mexico." *Commonweal* 12 (16 July 1930): 296–297.

"A Human Document." *Sign* 12 (November 1932): 223–224.

"Hunger Marchers in Washington." *America* 48 (24 December 1932): 277–279.

"Real Revolutionists." *Commonweal* 17 (11 January 1933): 293–294.

"St. John of the Cross." *Commonweal* 18 (14 July 1933): 287–288.

The Mystical Body of Christ (pamphlet). East Orange, N.J.: Thomas Barry, August 1936.

An Answer to Some Charges against the Catholic Worker (pamphlet). 1937. Reprint of letter in *Brooklyn Tablet* (5 October 1935).

From Union Square to Rome. Silver Spring, Md.: Preservation of the Faith Press, 1938.

Folly of Force (pamphlet). New York: Catholic Worker, ca. 1938.

"Houses of Hospitality." *Commonweal* 27 (15 April 1938): 683–684.

"The House on Mott Street." *Commonweal* 28 (6 May 1938): 37–39.

House of Hospitality. New York & London: Sheed & Ward, 1939.

"Fellow Worker in Christ." *Orate Fratres* 13 (22 January 1939): 139–141.

Fight Conscription! (pamphlet). New York: Catholic Worker, 1942.

"The Catholic Worker." *Integrity* 1 (November 1946): 16–21.

"Peter and Women: Fragment from an unpublished manuscript." *Commonweal* 45 (6 December 1946): 188–191.

"A People's Movement." *Third Hour* 2 (1947): 84–90.

On Pilgrimage. New York: Catholic Worker Books, 1948.

"Peter Maurin, Agitator." *Blackfriars* 30 (September 1949): 409–415.

"The Scandal of the Works of Mercy." *Commonweal* 51 (4 November 1949): 99–102.

"Traveling by Bus." *Commonweal* 51 (10 March 1950): 577–579.

"Blood, Sweat and Tears." *Commonweal* 53 (29 December 1950): 300–301.

"Idea of an Agronomic University." *Third Hour* 5 (1951): 55–59.

The Long Loneliness. Illustrated by Fritz Eichenberg. Introduction by Daniel Berrigan. San Francisco: Harper & Row, 1952, 1981.

"The Prayer of Jesus." *Third Hour* 6 (1954): 13–18.

"I Remember Peter Maurin." *Jubilee* 1 (March 1954): 34–39.

The Gospel in Action (pamphlet). St. Paul: Catechetical Educational Society, 1955.

"Prophet Without Honor." *Third Hour* 7 (1956): 10–17.

"Priest of the Immediate." *Commonweal* 65 (28 December 1956): 331–333.

"Apostolate to the Worker." In *Lay Workers for Christ,* pp. 125–135. Edited by George L. Kane. Westminster, Md.: Newman Press, 1957.

"Abbé Pierre and the Poor." *Commonweal* 71 (30 October 1959): 146–148.

"The Neglected." In *Who Is My Neighbor?* pp. 51–60. Edited by Esther Pike. Greenwich: Seabury Press, 1960.

Therese. Springfield, Ill.: Templegate Publishers, 1960, 1979.

"Love in Practice." *Third Hour* 8 (1961): 15–21.

"Observations of a Traveler." *Worship* 35 (May 1961): 385–387.

Loaves and Fishes. Introduction by Robert Coles. San Francisco: Harper & Row, 1963, 1983.

[Booklist]. *Christian Century* 80 (13 March 1963): 337.

"Pope John XXIII: The Papacy and World Peace." *American Dialogue* 1 (July–August 1964): 8–10.

"Comment: Dorothy Day writes about Francis Cardinal McIntyre, and the duties of the lay Catholic." *Jublilee* 12 (September 1964): 38–40.

"Remembering St. Francis," *St. Anthony Messenger* 73 (October 1965): 38.

"The Meaning of Poverty." *Ave Maria* 13 (3 December 1966): 21–22, 29.

"Obedience." *Ave Maria* 13 (17 December 1966): 20–23.

"'A.J.': Death of a Peacemaker." *Commonweal* 86 (24 March 1967): 14–16.

"Dorothy Day on Hope." *Commonweal* 91 (14 November 1969): 217–218.

"Adventure in Prayer." *Third Hour* 9 (1970): 39–45 (reprinted in the 1976 issue).

Meditations. Edited by Stanley Vishnewski. Illustrated by Rita Corbin. New York: Paulist Press, 1970.

"An Interview with Dorothy Day." Interviewed by Dean Brackley and Dennis Dillon. *National Jesuit News* 1 (May 1972): 8–10.

On Pilgrimage: The Sixties. New York: Curtis Books, 1972.

"A Reminiscence at 75." *Commonweal* 98 (10 August 1973): 424–425.

"What Do the Simple Folk Do?" *CSCW [Church Society for College Work] Report* 31 (November 1973): 3–6.

"Helene Iswolsky Dies." *Third Hour* 10 (1976): 8–11.

Foreword to Gauchat, Dorothy, *All God's Children.* New York: Ballantine Books, 1976.

By Little and By Little: The Selected Writings of Dorothy Day. Edited with an Introduction by Robert Ellsberg. New York: Alfred A. Knopf, 1983.

PRIMARY SOURCES: PERIODICALS AND GENERAL REFERENCES

America
American Benedictine Review
American Ecclesiastical Review
Ave Maria
Blackfriars
Catholic Worker
Commonweal
Christian Century

Emmanuel
Homiletic and Pastoral Review
Journal of the History of Ideas
Jubilee
Orate Fratres
Theological Studies
Thought
Worship (formerly Orate Fratres)

Dorothy Day and the Catholic Worker: A Bibliography and Index. Compiled by Anne Klejment & Alice Klejment. New York & London: Garland Publishing, 1986.

National Union Catalog
—pre-1956 imprints
—1956–1980 listings

Official Catholic Directory, 1930–1988

PRIMARY SOURCES: BOOKS

Autobiography of St. Thérèse of Lisieux. Translated by Ronald Knox. New York: P. J. Kenedy & Sons, 1958.

Bazin, René. *Charles de Foucauld.* Translated by Peter Keelan. London: Burns, Oates & Washbourne, 1923.

The Book of the Foundations of S. Teresa of Jesus. Written by herself. London: Thomas Baker, rev. ed. 1913.

Boulton, Agnes. *Part of a Long Story.* Garden City, N.Y.: Doubleday, 1958.

Bouyer, Louis. *Liturgical Piety.* Notre Dame, Ind.: University of Notre Dame Press, 1955.

Bruno, Father, O.D.C., *St. John of the Cross.* Edited by Fr. Benedict Zimmerman, O.D.C. Introduction by Jacques Maritain. New York: Sheed & Ward, 1932.

Butler, Rev. Alban. *The Lives of the Saints.* Edited and revised by Herbert Thurston, S.J., and Donald Attwater. 12 vols. London: Burns, Oates & Washbourne, 1931–1942.

Carlen, Claudia, I.H.M., ed. *The Papal Encyclicals: 1903–1939.* [Wilmington, N.C.]: McGrath Publishing Company, 1981.

Catherine of Siena: The Dialogue. Translated with an Introduction by Suzanne Noffke, O.P. New York, Ramsey, N.J., and Toronto: Paulist Press, 1980.

The Collected Works of St. John of the Cross. Translated by Kieran Kavanaugh, O.C.D., & Otilio Rodriguez, O.C.D. Washington, D.C.: Institute of Carmelite Studies, 1979.

The Collected Works of St. Teresa. 6 vols. in 9. Translated by John Dalton. London: Thomas Baker, 1912–1924.

Combes, André, ed. *Collected Letters of St. Thérèse of Lisieux.* Translated by F. J. Sheed. New York: Sheed & Ward, 1949.

The Complete Works of Saint Teresa of Jesus. 3 vols. Translated and edited by E. Allison Peers. New York: Sheed & Ward, 1946.

The Desert Fathers. Translated, with Introductions by Helen Waddell. London: Constable, 1936.

The Desert Fathers. Translated, with sectional introductions by Helen Waddell. Tutorial Introduction by F. J. Sheed. New York: Sheed & Ward, 1942.

Deutsch, Alcuin, Rt. Rev., O.S.B., *Manual for Oblates of St. Benedict.* Collegeville, Minn.: St. John's Abbey Press, 1937.

Dostoyevsky, Fyodor. *The Brothers Karamazov.* Translated by Constance Garnett. New York: Modern Library, n.d.

Foucauld, Charles de. *Inner Search: Letters (1889–1916).* Translated by Barbara Lucas. Maryknoll, N.Y.: Orbis Books, 1979.

Furfey, Paul Hanly. *Fire on the Earth.* New York: Macmillan, 1936, 1943.

———. *Love and the Urban Ghetto.* Maryknoll, N.Y.: Orbis Books, 1978.

———. *The Morality Gap.* New York: Macmillan, 1969.

———. *The Mystery of Iniquity.* Milwaukee, New York & Chicago: Bruce, 1944.

———. *The Respectable Murderers.* New York: Herder & Herder, 1966.

———. *Three Theories of Society.* New York: Macmillan, 1937.

Gorodetzky, Nadejda. *The Humiliated Christ in Modern Russian Thought.* London. Society for Promoting Christian Knowledge, 1938.

Guardini, Romano. *The Spirit of the Liturgy.* London: Sheed & Ward, 1930.

The Hidden Ground of Love: The Letters of Thomas Merton on Religious Experience and Social Concerns. Edited by William H. Shannon. New York: Farrar, Straus, Giroux, 1985.

Hugo, John J. *Applied Christianity.* New York: Privately printed [Catholic Worker press], 1944.

———. *Dorothy Day, Apostle of the Industrial Age.* Privately published by the author, [1980].

———. *Love Strong as Death: A Study in Christian Ethics.* New York: Vantage Press, 1969.

———. *Nature and the Supernatural: A Defense of the Evangelic Ideal.* For private use; duplicated by the author, after February 1949.

————. *A Sign of Contradiction.* 2 vols. in 1. Typed and duplicated by the author, [1947].

————. *You Are Gods!* Typed and duplicated by the author, n.d.

————. *Your Ways Are Not My Ways: The Radical Christianity of the Gospel.* Vol. 1: The Deliverance of Onesimus; The Retreat: Its Story. Pittsburgh: Encounter with Silence, 1986.

————. *Your Ways Are Not My Ways.* [Vol. 2] Pittsburgh: Encounter with Silence, 1980. [1st ed.]

————. *Your Ways Are Not My Ways: The Radical Christianity of the Gospel.* Vol. 2: The Retreat. Pittsburgh: Encounter with Silence, 1984. [2nd ed.]

Huysmans, J[oris] K. *The Cathedral.* Translated by Clara Bell. London: K. Paul, Trench & Trübner, 1922.

————. *En Route.* Translated by C. Kegan Paul. London: K. Paul, Trench & Trübner; New York: E. P. Dutton, 1918, 1920.

————. *The Oblate.* Translated by Edward Perceval. London: Kegan Paul, Trench, Trübner; New York: E. P. Dutton, 1924.

Iswolsky, Helene. *Light before Dusk: A Russian Catholic in France, 1923–1941.* New York: Longmans, Green, 1942.

————. *No Time to Grieve: An Autobiographical Journey.* Philadelphia: Winchell, 1985.

James, William. *The Varieties of Religious Experience.* New York, London, & Bombay: Longmans, Green, 1902.

Jörgensen, Johannes. *St. Francis of Assisi.* Translated by T. O'Conor Sloane. New York: Longmans, Green, 1912, 1913.

Julian of Norwich: Showings. Translated with an Introduction by Edmund Colledge, O.S.A., and James Walsh, S.J., and Preface by Jean Leclercq, O.S.B. New York: Paulist Press, 1978.

Kempis, Thomas à. *The Imitation of Christ.* Edited with an Introduction by Harold C. Gardiner, S.J., Garden City, N.Y.: Image Books, 1955.

The Letters of Saint Teresa. Translated and annotated by the Benedictines of Stanbrook. Introduction by Cardinal Gasquet. 4 vols. London: Thomas Baker, 1919–1924.

The Letters of Saint Teresa of Jesus. Translated and edited by E. Allison Peers. 2 vols. London: Burns, Oates & Washbourne, 1951.

The Life of St. Teresa of Jesus. Written by herself. Translated by David Lewis. London: Thomas Baker, 5th ed., 1932.

Maritain, Jacques. *Art and Scholasticism.* Translated by J. F. Scanlan. London: Sheed & Ward, 1930.

———. *A Christian Looks at the Jewish Question.* New York & Toronto: Longmans, Green, 1939.

———. *Christianity and Democracy.* Translated by Doris C. Anson. New York: Charles Scribner's Sons, 1944.

———. *Freedom in the Modern World.* Translated by Richard O'Sullivan. New York: Scribner's, 1936.

———. *Integral Humanism: Temporal and Spiritual Problems of a New Christendom.* Translated by Joseph W. Evans from the revised French edition [of *Humanisme Intégral*]. New York: Scribner's, 1968.

———. *The Things That Are Not Caesar's.* Translated by J. F. Scanlon. London: Sheed & Ward, 1930.

———. *True Humanism* [1st English edition of *Humanisme Intégral*]. Translated by Margot Adamson. New York: Scribner's, 1938.

Maritain, Jacques–Mounier, Emmanuel. *Correspondance, 1929–1939.* With Introduction and notes by Jacques Petit. Paris: Desclée de Brouwer, 1973.

Maritain, Raïssa. *We Have Been Friends Together.* Translated by Julie Kernan. New York: Longmans, Green, 1942.

———. *Adventures in Grace.* Translated by Julie Kernan. New York: Longmans, Green, 1945.

Maurin, Peter. *Catholic Radicalism.* New York: Catholic Worker Books, 1949.

———. *The Green Revolution.* (Revised, 2nd ed. of *Catholic Radicalism.*) Fresno: Academy Guild Press, 1961.

———. *Easy Essays.* (3rd ed. of *Catholic Radicalism.*) Woodcuts by Fritz Eichenberg. Chicago: Franciscan Herald Press, 1977.

Merton, Thomas. *Contemplative Prayer.* New York: Herder & Herder, 1969).

———. *New Seeds of Contemplation.* New York: New Directions, 1962, 1972.

Michel, Virgil George, O.S.B. *Christian Social Reconstruction.* Milwaukee: Bruce, 1937.

———. *The Liturgy of the Church According to the Roman Rite.* New York: Macmillan, 1937.

————, ed. *The Mystical Body and Social Justice.* Collegeville, Minn.: St. John's Abbey, 1938.

Mooney, Denis, O.F.M. *Blueprint for Holiness: The Christian Mentality.* Kensington, Md.: Xaverian Bookshop, 1953. 3rd printing, 1966.

Mounier, Emmanuel. *Be Not Afraid: A Denunciation of Despair.* Translated by Cynthia Rowland. Foreword by Leslie Paul. New York: Sheed & Ward, [1962].

————. *Oeuvres.* 4 vols. Paris: Editions du Seuil [1961–1963].

————. *A Personalist Manifesto.* translated from the French [*Manifeste au service du personnalisme*] by monks of St. John's Abbey. London, New York & Toronto: Longmans, Green, 1938.

Novissima Verba. Translated by Carmelite Nuns of New York. New York: P. J. Kenedy & Sons, 1951.

Parente, Pascal P. *The Ascetical Life.* St. Louis: B. Herder, 1944; revised, 1955.

Revelations of Divine Love: Shewed to a Devout Ankress by Name Julian of Norwich. Edited with an Introduction by Dom Roger Hudleston, O.S.B. London: Burns, Oates, 1927, 1935 [1st ed.], 1952 [2nd ed.].

Robichaud, Norbert. *Holiness for All.* Translated by a member of the Congregation of the Brothers of Christian Schools. Westminster, Md.: Newman Bookshop, 1945.

The Rule of St. Benedict. Edited by Timothy Fry, O.S.B. Collegeville, Minn.: Liturgical Press, 1981.

St. Francis of Assisi: Writings and Early Biographies. English Omnibus of the Sources for the Life of St. Francis. Edited by Marion A. Habig, 3rd rev. ed. Chicago: Franciscan Herald Press, 1973.

Saint Thérèse of Lisieux, The Little Flower of Jesus. Edited by Rev. Thomas N. Taylor. New York: P. J. Kenedy & Sons, 1926.

Selected Documents of His Holiness, Pope Pius XII, 1939–1958. Washington, D.C.: National Catholic Welfare Conference, [1958].

Soeur Thérèse of Lisieux, The Little Flower of Jesus. Edited by T. N. Taylor. London: Burns, Oates & Washbourne, 1922.

Sorg, Dom Rembert. *Towards a Benedictine Theology of Manual Labor.* Lisle, Ill.: Benedictine Orient, 1949, 1951.

The Spiritual Exercises of St. Ignatius. Translated by Anthony Mottola. Introduction by Robert W. Gleason, S.J. Garden City, N.Y.: Image Books, 1964.

The Story of a Soul. Translated by Michael Day. London: Burns, Oates, 1951.

Tolstoy, Leo. *War and Peace.* Translated by Constance Garnett. New York: Modern Library [1931].

———. *War and Peace.* Translated by Louise & Aylmer Maude. Foreword by Clifton Fadiman. New York: Simon & Schuster, 1942, 1958.

Vishnewski, Stanley. *Wings of the Dawn.* [New York: The Catholic Worker, 1984].

Ward, Maisie. *To and Fro on the Earth: The Sequel to an Autobiography.* London: Sheed & Ward, 1973.

———. *Unfinished Business.* New York: Sheed & Ward, 1964.

The Way of a Pilgrim and *The Pilgrim Continues His Way.* Translated from the Russian by R. M. French. New York: Harper & Brothers, 1952.

The Wisdom of the Desert. Translated by Thomas Merton. New York: New Directions, 1960.

PRIMARY SOURCES: ARTICLES

Connell, Francis J., C.SS.R. Review of *Applied Christianity* by John J. Hugo. *American Ecclesiastical Review* 113 (July 1945): 69–72.

Donovan, Joseph P., C.M. "A Bit of Puritanical Catholicity." *Homiletic and Pastoral Review* 48 (August 1948): 807–814.

Farina, Louis A. "Is Detachment Puritanical?" *Homiletic and Pastoral Review* 49 (February 1949): 356–367.

Fenton, Joseph Clifford. "Nature and the Supernatural Life." *American Ecclesiastical Review* 114 (January 1946): 54–68.

Furfey, Paul Hanly. "From a Catholic Liberal into a Catholic Radical." *America* 127 (11 November 1972): 391–392.

———. "From Catholic Liberalism to Catholic Radicalism." *American Ecclesiastical Review* 166 (1972): 678–686.

Hugo, John J. "Correspondence: Reader Takes Exception to Father Trese's Ten Forty-Five." *Emmanuel* 54 (December 1948): 378–379.

————. "Nature and Grace: To the Editor." *Orate Fratres* 21 (April 1947): 280–283.

Iswolsky, Helene. "Dorothy Day." *The Lamp* 69 (January 1971): 11–12.

Merton, Thomas. "Nuclear War and Christian Responsibility." *Commonweal* 75 (9 February 1962): 509–513.

Michel, Virgil, O.S.B. "The Liturgy and Catholic Women." *Orate Fratres* 3 (July 1929): 270–276.

————. "The Liturgy the Basis of Social Regeneration." *Orate Fratres* 9 (November 1935): 536–545.

————. "The Meaning of the Church's Liturgy." *America* 34 (3 April 1926): 586–587.

————. "The Mystical Body and Economic Justice." In *The Mystical Body and Social Justice,* pp. 53–61. Collegeville, Minn.: St. John's Abbey, 1938.

————. "Mysticism and Normal Christianity: The Place of Liturgy in Mysticism." *Orate Fratres* 13 (October 1939): 545–548.

————. "A Program for a Liturgical Movement." *America* 34 (10 April 1926): 614–615.

————. "The Scope of the Liturgical Movement." *Orate Fratres* 10 (October 1936): 485–490.

Parente, Pascal P. "Nature and Grace in Ascetical Theology." *American Ecclesiastical Review* 108 (June 1943): 430–437.

Tarasevitch, Chrysostom, O.S.B. "Church Unity." *Orate Fratres* 23 (May 1949): 297–302.

————. "A Treasury of Russian Spirituality." *Orate Fratres* 23 (November 1948): 18–21.

Trese, Leo J. "Ten Forty-Five." *Emmanuel* 54 (October 1948): 297–299.

————. "Father Trese Explains." *Emmanuel* 54 (December 1948): 379–381.

Vishnewski, Stanley. "Dorothy Day: A Sign of Contradiction." *Catholic World* 209 (August 1969): 203–206.

————. "Lay Retreats." *The Torch* 27 (July–August 1943): 1–2, 30.

————. "Life in Community." *Catholic World* 185 (August 1957): 346–351.

Vann, Gerald, O.P. "Nature and Grace." *Orate Fratres* 21 (January 1947): 97–105.

————. "Nature and Grace: To the Editor." *Orate Fratres* 21 (April 1947): 283–285.

SELECTED SECONDARY SOURCES:
BOOKS AND UNPUBLISHED DISSERTATIONS

Abell, Aaron Ignatius, ed. *American Catholic Thought on Social Questions.* Indianapolis & New York: Bobbs-Merrill [1968].

————. *American Catholicism and Social Action: A Search for Social Justice, 1865–1950.* Garden City, N.Y.: Doubleday, 1960.

Ahlstrom, Sydney E. *A Religious History of the American People.* New Haven & London: Yale University Press, 1972.

Amato, Joseph. *Mounier and Maritain: A French Catholic Understanding of the Modern World.* University, Ala.: University of Alabama Press, 1975.

Barck, Oscar Theodore, Jr., and Blake, Nelson Manfred. *Since 1900: A History of the United States in Our Times.* New York: Macmillan; London: Collier-Macmillan, 1965.

Barry, Colman, O.S.B. *Worship and Work.* Collegeville, Minn.: St. John's Abbey, 1956.

Beard, Charles A., and Beard, Mary R. *A Basic History of the United States.* New York: Doubleday, Doran, 1944.

Benda, Julien. *The Betrayal of the Intellectuals.* Translated by Richard Aldington. Boston: Beacon Press, 1959.

Bethge, Eberhard. *Bonhoeffer: Exile and Martyr.* Edited by John W. de Gruchy. New York: Seabury Press, 1975.

Brown, Peter. *The Cult of the Saints: Its Rise and Function in Latin Christianity.* Chicago: University of Chicago Press, 1981, 1982.

Chinnici, Joseph P., O.F.M. *Living Stones: The History and Structure of Catholic Spiritual Life in the United States.* New York: Macmillan; London: Collier Macmillan, 1989.

Coles, Robert. *Dorothy Day: A Radical Devotion.* Reading, Mass.: Addison–Wesley, 1987.

Cross, Robert D. *The Emergence of Liberal Catholicism in America.* Cambridge, Mass.: Harvard University Press, 1958.

Dirscherl, Denis, S.J., *Dostoevsky and the Catholic Church.* Chicago: Loyola University Press, 1986.

Dolan, Jay P. *The American Catholic Experience: A History from Colonial Times to the Present.* Garden City, N.Y.: Doubleday 1985; rpt. Notre Dame, Ind.: University of Notre Dame Press, 1992.

Ede, Alfred J. *The Lay Crusade for a Christian America: A Study of the American Federation of Catholic Societies, 1900–1919.* New York & London: Garland, 1988.

Ellis, Marc H. *Peter Maurin: Prophet in the Twentieth Century.* New York & Ramsey, N.J.: Paulist Press, 1981.

Frary, Thomas D. "The Ecclesiology of Dorothy Day." Ph.D. dissertation, Marquette University, 1971.

Le Goff, Jacques. *Time, Work and Culture in the Middle Ages.* Translated by Arthur Goldhammer. Chicago: University of Chicago Press, 1980.

Hall, Sister Jeremy, O.S.B. *The Full Stature of Christ: The Ecclesiology of Virgil Michel, O.S.B.* Collegeville, Minn.: Liturgical Press, 1976.

Halsey, William M. *The Survival of American Innocence: Catholicism in an Era of Disillusionment, 1920–1940.* Notre Dame, Ind., & London: University of Notre Dame Press, 1980.

Hellman, John. *Emmanuel Mounier and the New Catholic Left, 1930–1950.* Toronto, Buffalo, & London: University of Toronto Press, 1981.

Hennesey, James, S.J. *American Catholics: A History of the Roman Catholic Community in the United States.* Foreword by John Tracy Ellis. New York & Oxford: Oxford University Press, 1981.

———, ed. *The Inner Crusade: The Closed Retreat in the United States.* Chicago: Loyola University Press, 1965.

Husslein, Joseph C., ed. *Social Wellsprings,* 2 vols. Milwaukee: Bruce Publishing Co., 1940–1942.

Jedin, Hubert; Repgen, Konrad, and Dolan, John, ed. *History of the Church,* vol. 10: *The Church in the Modern Age.* Translated by Anselm Biggs. New York: Crossroad, 1981.

Kernan, Julie. *Our Friend, Jacques Maritain: A Personal Memoir.* Garden City, N.Y.: Doubleday, 1975.

Lafon, Michel. *Vivre Nazareth aujourd'hui.* Vitry-sur-Seine: Librairie Arthème Fayard, 1985.

Livingstone, Elizabeth A., ed. *The Concise Oxford Dictionary of the Christian Church.* Oxford: Oxford University Press, 1977.

Longpré, Anselme. *Un Mouvement spirituel au Quebec (1931–1962): Un Retour à l'évangile.* Montreal: Fides, 1976.

Louf, André. *The Cistercian Way.* Translated by Nivard Kinsella. Kalamazoo: Cistercian Publications, 1983.

McAvoy, Thomas T., C.S.C., *The Great Crisis in American Catholic History, 1895–1900.* Chicago: H. Regnery Co., 1957.

———. *A History of the Catholic Church in the United States.* Notre Dame & London: University of Notre Dame Press, 1969.

McNeal, Patricia. *The American Catholic Peace Movement, 1928–1972.* New York: Arno Press, 1978.

Marx, Paul B., O.S.B. *Virgil Michel and the Liturgical Movement.* Collegeville: Liturgical Press, 1957.

Miller, William D. *Dorothy Day: A Biography.* San Francisco: Harper & Row, 1982.

———. *A Harsh and Dreadful Love: Dorothy Day and the Catholic Worker Movement.* New York: Liveright, 1973.

———. *All Is Grace.* Garden City, N.Y.: Doubleday, 1987.

Muste, A. J. *Non-Violence in an Aggressive World.* New York & London: Harper & Brothers, 1940.

New Catholic Encyclopedia, 1967 ed. S.v. "Saint," by C. O'Neill; s.v. "Canonization of Saints (History and Procedure)," by P. Molinari.

O'Brien, David J. *American Catholics and Social Reform: The New Deal Years.* New York: Oxford University Press, 1968.

O'Connor, June E. *The Moral Vision of Dorothy Day: A Feminist Perspective.* New York: Crossroad, 1991.

Parmisano, Fabian, O.P. *Catherine of Siena: 600 Years Later.* Mission San Jose, Calif.: Mater Dei Press, 1980.

Parry, David, O.S.B. *Households of God.* Kalamazoo: Cistercian Publications, 1980.

Pells, Richard H. *Radical Visions and American Dreams: Culture and Social Thought in the Depression Years.* New York, Hagerstown, San Francisco, London: Harper & Row, Harper Torchbooks, 1973.

Piat, Stéphane-Joseph, O.F.M., *The Story of a Family.* Translated by a Benedictine of Stanbrook Abbey. New York: P. J. Kenedy & Sons, 1947.

Piehl, Mel. *Breaking Bread: The Catholic Worker and the Origin of Catholic Radicalism in America.* Philadelphia: Temple University Press, 1982.

Roberts, Nancy L. *Dorothy Day and the Catholic Worker.* Albany, New York: State University of New York Press, 1984.

Rogier, Louis J.; Aubert, Roger; Knowles, David; Weiler, A. G., and Ellis, John Tracy, ed. *The Christian Centuries,* vol. 5: *The Church in a Secularised Society.* New York, Ramsey, N. J. & Toronto: Paulist Press; London: Darton, Longman and Todd, 1978.

Sheehan, Arthur. *Peter Maurin: Gay Believer.* Garden City, N.Y.: Hanover Press, 1959.

Shewring, Walter. *Rich and Poor in Christian Tradition.* London: Burns, Oates & Washbourne, 1948.

Statnick, Roger Andrew. "Dorothy Day's Religious Conversion: A Study in Biographical Theology." Ph.D. dissertation, University of Notre Dame, 1983.

Stolz, Anselm, O.S.B. *The Doctrine of Spiritual Perfection.* Translated by Aidan Williams, O.S.B. St. Louis, Mo., & London: B. Herder, 1938.

Ward, Leo R., ed. *The American Apostolate: American Catholics in the Twentieth Century.* Westminster, Md.: Newman Press, 1952.

White, Ronald C., Jr., and Hopkins, C. Howard. *The Social Gospel: Religion and Reform in America.* Philadelphia: Temple University Press, 1976.

Vorgrimler, Herbert, ed. *Commentary on the Documents of Vatican II,* vol. 5: *Pastoral Constitution on the Church in the Modern World.* New York: Herder & Herder, 1969.

Van Zeller, Dom Hubert, O.S.B. *The Benedictine Idea.* London: Burns & Oates, 1959.

SELECTED SECONDARY SOURCES: ARTICLES

Bluett, Joseph P. "Current Theology: The Mystical Body of Christ, 1890–1940." *Theological Studies* 3 (May 1942): 261–289.

Brown, Francis F. "The Retreat: An Encounter with Silence." *The Priest* 38 (April 1982): 38–40.

Cogley, John J. "The Catholic Worker." *Commonweal* 68 (16 May 1958): 180.

Cornell, Tom. "Dorothy Day Recalled: Worker Leader 'didn't want any sugar coating.'" *National Catholic Reporter* 18 (27 November 1981): 1, 16–17.

Cort, John C. "The Catholic Worker and the Workers." *Commonweal* 55 (4 April 1952): 635–637.

———. "Dorothy Day at 75." *Commonweal* 98 (23 February 1973): 475–476.

Coulton, G.G. "The Historical Background of Maritain's Humanism." *Journal of the History of Ideas* 5 (October 1944): 415–433.

Curran, Charles E. "American and Catholic: American Catholic Social Ethics, 1880–1965." *Thought* 52 (March 1977): 50–74.

———. "The Catholic Worker and Paul Hanly Furfey." In *American Catholic Social Ethics,* pp. 130–171. Notre Dame & London: University of Notre Dame Press, 1982.

———. "Paul Hanly Furfey: Theorist of American Catholic Radicalism." *American Ecclesiastical Review* 166 (1972): 651–677.

———. "The Radical Catholic Social Ethics of Paul Hanly Furfey." In *New Perspectives in Moral Theology,* pp. 87–121. Notre Dame & London: University of Notre Dame Press, 1974.

Drolet, Jean-Claude. "Un Mouvement de spiritualité sacerdotale au Québec au XXe siècle (1931–1965): Le Lacouturisme." *Canadian Catholic Historical Association.* Study Sessions, 1973 (Ottawa, 1974): 55–87.

Dru, Alexander. "From the Actione Française to the Second Vatican Council." *Downside Review* 81 (July 1963): 226–245.

Ellis, Marc. "The Legacy of Peter Maurin." *Cross Currents* 34 (Fall 1984): 294–304.

Frary, Thomas D. "'Thy Kingdom Come'—the Theology of Dorothy Day." *America* 127 (11 November 1972): 385–387.

Fry, Barbara. "Retreat Houses, Religious and Lay." *Blackfriars [Supplement]* 47 (March 1946): 44–49.

Gleason, Philip. "In Search of Unity: American Catholic Thought, 1920–1960." *Catholic Historical Review* 65 (April 1979): 185–205.

Haughton, Rosemary. "Signs in the Wind." *New Blackfriars* 52 (May 1961): 200–209.

Hellman, John. "The Opening to the Left in French Catholicism: The Role of the Personalists." *Journal of the History of Ideas* 34 (July–September 1973): 381–390.

La Farge, John, S.J. "The 'Catholic Workers.'" *America* 57 (24 July 1937): 371.

————. "Some Reflections on the 'Catholic Worker.'" *America* 57 (26 June 1937): 275.

Leclercq, Jean, O.S.B. "The Distinctive Characteristics of Roman Catholic American Spirituality." *Louvain Studies* 9 (Spring 1983): 295–306.

————. "The Monastic Tradition of Culture and Studies." *American Benedictine Review* 11 (March–June 1960): 99–131.

Lobue, Wayne. "Public Theology and the Catholic Worker." *Cross Currents* 26 (Fall 1976): 270–285.

Moore, Nina Polcyn. "The Struggle Goes On." *Overview* (July–August 1980): 3.

Piehl, Mel. "The Catholic Worker and American Religious Tradition." *Cross Currents* 34 (Fall 1984): 261–264.

Reinhold, H. A. "The Long Loneliness of Dorothy Day." *Commonweal* 55 (29 February 1952): 521–522.

Schneiders, Sandra M., I.H.M. "Theology and Spirituality: Strangers, Rivals, or Partners?" *Horizons* 13 (Fall 1986): 253–274.

Willock, Ed. "Catholic Radicalism." *Commonweal* 58 (2 October 1953): 630–633.

Wolf, Donald. "Emmanuel Mounier: A Catholic of the Left." *Review of Politics* 22 (July 1960): 324–344.

INDEX